D1570088

*African Americans and Jews
in the Twentieth Century*

African Americans *and* Jews

IN THE TWENTIETH CENTURY

Studies in Convergence and Conflict

EDITED BY V. P. FRANKLIN, NANCY L. GRANT,
HAROLD M. KLETNICK, AND GENNA RAE MCNEIL

University of Missouri Press • *Columbia and London*

Library of Congress Cataloging-in-Publication Data

African Americans and Jews in the twentieth century : studies in
    convergence and conflict / edited by V.P. Franklin . . . [et al.].
        p.   cm.
    Contains revised version of papers presented at the conference
    "Blacks and Jews : an American Historical Perspective" held at
Washington University in St. Louis in Dec. 1993.
    Includes bibliographical references and index.
    ISBN 0-8262-1197-6 (alk. paper)
        1. Afro-Americans—Relations with Jews.   2. Jews—United States—
History—20th century.   3. Afro-Americans—History—20th century.
4. United States—Race relations.   5. United States—Ethnic
relations.   I. Franklin, V. P. (Vincent P.), 1947–   .
E184.36.A34A47   1998
305.8'00973—dc21   98-28555
                                                                CIP

Designer: Mindy Shouse
Typesetter: Crane Composition
Printer and binder: Edwards Brothers, Inc.
Typefaces: Palatino, Tiepolo

*The University of Missouri Press gratefully acknowledges the generous
assistance of Washington University in the publication of this book.*

Contents

Acknowledgments

W E WOULD LIKE to acknowledge the assistance of a number of persons who were instrumental in the presentation of the symposium "Blacks and Jews: An American Historical Perspective," which was held December 2–5, 1993, at Washington University in St. Louis. Our thanks go to Professor Martin H. Israel, then Dean of the Faculty of Arts and Sciences at Washington University, for arranging for generous funding for the symposium. In addition, we would like to thank Professor Gerald Early, Director of African and Afro-American Studies, whose department provided funding and who was also a participant in the symposium. Raye Riggins, Elizabeth Kellerman, and Adele Tuchler provided valued administrative assistance in all of the details of the symposium presentation. We would also like to thank the Department of History and all other departments and programs of Washington University that participated in the symposium. Finally, we would like to acknowledge the valuable contributions from Professors Marc Saperstein, George Washington University; Raymond Hall, Dartmouth College; and John Bracey, the University of Massachusetts, Amherst during the planning for the symposium.

*African Americans and Jews
in the Twentieth Century*

Introduction

V. P. Franklin

T HE NUMEROUS articles, books, and public media events devoted to an examination of Black-Jewish relations in the United States have in many instances generated more heat than light on this very complex and controversial topic. Newspaper and magazine columnists and journalists dominated the discussion in the past, but recently a number of highly visible "public intellectuals" have entered the fray offering their views about what many believe is an important social issue. While the dialogues and debates have been driven by highly publicized incidents involving clashes between Jews and African Americans, the spokespersons and writers who have received the greatest attention often have offered opinions based mainly on their personal experiences and current political agendas. In each of these debates or dialogues certain premises are presented about the nature of Black-Jewish relations in the past, and the participants then offer their assessment of the contemporary relationship in light of the latest well-publicized, unfortunate event.[1]

One of the more important recent works to begin to shine light on the history of Black-Jewish relations is the volume edited by Jack Salzman and Cornel West, *Struggles in the Promised Land: Toward a History of Black-Jewish Relations in the United States* (1997). The twenty-one essays included in this important work range from David Brion Davis's examination of the role of the Jews in the transatlantic slave trade to essays by Jerome Chanes and Theodore Shaw offering Jewish and African

1. See, for example, Henry Louis Gates Jr., "Black Demagogues and Pseudo-Scholars," *New York Times,* July 20, 1992; Michael Lerner and Cornel West, *Jews and Blacks: Let the Healing Begin* (New York: Putnam, 1995); Paul Berman, ed., *Blacks and Jews: Alliances and Arguments* (New York: Delacorte Press, 1994); Michael Lerner and Cornel West, "After O. J. and the Farrakhan-Led Million Man March: Is Healing Possible?" *Tikkun* 10 (November–December 1995): 20–22.

American perspectives on the issue of "affirmative action." In his introduction Jack Salzman emphasizes the need to examine the history of the relations between African Americans and Jews in the United States because it places in bold relief the commitment to social justice and civil rights that to a very great extent defines the nation's most important social and political goals and objectives.[2]

This volume in many ways follows the path of *Struggles in the Promised Land.* The essays included herein are revised versions of papers presented at the conference "Blacks and Jews: An American Historical Perspective," organized by historian Nancy L. Grant and held in December 1993 at Washington University in St. Louis, Missouri. The essays are the result of new historical research conducted on Black-Jewish relations in the United States in the twentieth century. While some of the contributors expand upon and complement the information found in *Struggles in the Promised Land,* others challenge those findings and conclusions. For example, Jack Salzman in his introduction to that work notes that given the checkered nature of the relations between African Americans and Jews "what little can be said with certainty is simply this: the peculiar entanglements of Blacks and Jews have, at times, provided impetus for social justice in the United States and, at other times, have been the cause of great tension." There has been much "dialoguing" and searching for "common ground," but "there is little indication that the liberal coalition occasionally formed by Blacks and Jews has any real chance of being reestablished."[3]

Many of the essays presented in this volume suggest that *in the past* the possibility of forming a Black-Jewish alliance was limited not merely by "great tension" but by significant conflicts of interest between Jewish Americans and African Americans. Indeed, what Salzman describes as Black-Jewish "entanglements" were really examples of historical moments when the social, political, or ideological objectives of Jews and African Americans converged, or when they clashed for specific social,

2. Jack Salzman, "Introduction," in *Struggles in the Promised Land: Toward a History of Black-Jewish Relations in the United States,* ed. Jack Salzman and Cornel West (New York: Oxford University Press, 1997), 17–18. Earlier works that provide historical information on Black-Jewish relations are Robert G. Weisbord and Arthur Stein, *Bittersweet Encounter: The Afro-American and the American Jew* (Westport, Conn: Greenwood Press, 1970); Hasia R. Diner, *In the Almost Promised Land: American Jews and Blacks, 1915–1935* (1977; rpt. Baltimore: Johns Hopkins University Press, 1995); and Jack Salzman, Adina Back, and Gretchen Sullivan Sorin, eds., *Bridges and Boundaries: African Americans and American Jews* (New York: George Braziller and the Jewish Museum, 1992).
3. Salzman, "Introduction," 5.

political, ideological, or, more recently, economic reasons. Many commentators have suggested that during the first half of the twentieth century there was a convergence in the interests of the two minority groups that were "joint sufferers" in American society, culminating in the "grand alliance" of the civil rights coalition of the 1950s and early 1960s. Since the late 1960s, however, with the breakdown of the civil rights coalition and the coming of the Black Power Movement, Black-Jewish relations have been characterized by "great tension" and conflict.[4]

The essays in this volume present significant evidence that throughout the twentieth century in various places and at specific times there have been members of the Jewish community who have united with African Americans to pursue issues and objectives important to both groups. At the same time, however, there is much evidence that before, during, and after the formation of the civil rights coalition in the 1950s and 1960s, there were public disagreements and overt conflicts between Blacks and Jews in various parts of the United States. Thus it would appear more accurate to describe Black-Jewish relations in the United States in the twentieth century as characterized by periods of convergence and points of conflict.

Part I: Convergence in Experience and Ideology

While all of the essays in this volume describe historical moments of both convergence and conflict in Black-Jewish relations, the seven essays in Part I examine primarily instances of experiential and ideological convergence. In "Drawn Together by Self-Interest: Jewish Representation of Race and Race Relations in the Early Twentieth Century," Hasia R. Diner examines several important daily and weekly Jewish publications and finds a widespread preoccupation with racial conditions in the United States and an ongoing critique of the racially motivated violence launched against the African American population. Jewish journalists and editors compared these conditions for Blacks in the United States with the pogroms and other violent attacks on Jews in Eastern Europe. These journalists argued not only that to speak out against these injustices was part of the "Jewish tradition" but also that in doing so they laid

---

4. See, for example, Nat Hentoff, ed., *Black Anti-Semitism and Jewish Racism* (New York: R. W. Baron, 1969); Lenora E. Berson, *The Negroes and the Jews* (New York: Random House, 1971); Joseph R. Washington Jr., ed., *Jews in Black Perspectives: A Dialogue* (Lanham, Md.: University Press of America, 1989); and Jonathan Kaufman, *Broken Alliance: The Turbulent Times between Blacks and Jews in America* (New York: Scribners, 1988).

the basis for an alliance between Blacks and Jews to change the racist, discriminatory practices prevalent in American society.

With the emergence of Marcus Garvey and the Universal Negro Improvement Association in the post–World War I era, many Jewish writers applauded the development and compared the man and the movement to Theodore Herzl and the Zionist movement launched a few years earlier. At the same time, Marcus Garvey was clearly aware of the significance of the Zionist movement for his Pan-African campaigns. In "Black Zionism: Marcus Garvey and the Jewish Question," Robert A. Hill traces the interconnections between Garveyism and Zionism and demonstrates that the two movements represented an ideological convergence with the redemption of Africa considered an objective as significant as the restoration of Palestine. African nationalist Edward Wilmot Blyden preceded Garvey in drawing attention to the relevance of the "Jewish question" to the goal of African redemption. Hill not only examines Blyden's writings on Zionism but also pursues possible connections between Theodore Herzl's activities in London in the late 1890s, the formation of the African Association, and Henry Sylvester Williams's convening of the first Pan-African Congress, held there in 1900. Hill clearly documents the convergence of Zionism and Garveyism at the end of World War I following the promulgation of the Balfour Declaration by the British government, which supported the establishment of a Jewish homeland in Palestine. Garvey wanted the peace negotiators to turn the former German colonies in southwest Africa over to "educated Western and Eastern Negroes." Despite this direct and apparent ideological convergence, Hill concludes that the potential for Black-Jewish conflict in the United States exists when there is a failure to recognize that both Jewish and African American Zionism have deep historical roots in American society.

Jewish anthropologist Franz Boas was one of the most influential social scientists in the first half of the twentieth century. Boas and his students led the campaign to dethrone hereditarian explanations for differences in social and academic achievements for racial and ethnic groups and were politically successful in gaining broad acceptance for environmental arguments in social science circles. Despite his undisputed leadership in the cultural determinist camp, Boas's early training was in the field of physical anthropology, and he often accepted racial determinist explanations for intellectual differences among racial groups. Vernon J. Williams Jr., in "Franz Boas's Paradox and the African American Intelligentsia," presents a detailed analysis of Boas's research and writings on the subject of racial differences and demonstrates that Boas did subscribe to certain racial deterministic views when he described the intellectual capabilities of African Americans, particularly in the early years of his career. However, Williams argues that it was Boas's awareness of the increase in anti-Semitism and racism in the United States in the early decades of the twentieth century that led him to change his earlier views and to emphasize in his public statements and published articles the similarities in the intellectual capabilities of Blacks and Whites. During the first half of the twentieth century, Boas's views were championed and disseminated by W. E. B. Du Bois, Charles S. Johnson, Alain Locke, Abram Harris, Zora Neale Hurston, and other members of the African American intelligentsia in the United States.

Immigrant and second-generation Jewish Americans carved out an economic niche for themselves in the field of entertainment in the early decades of the twentieth century, and in the Hollywood film industry they created "An Empire of Their Own." Popular entertainment in the late nineteenth and early twentieth century was still dominated by black-face minstrelsy in which White (and later Black) musicians and comedians used burnt cork to blacken their faces and performed musical routines and comic sketches based on (and caricaturing) African American musical and cultural traditions. With the coming of the silent films, the leading Black characters were often played by White actors in blackface.

These two trends came together in 1927 in the first "talking movie," *The Jazz Singer,* in which Al Jolson played a blackface singer who was Jewish. Michael Rogin's "Black Sacrifice, Jewish Redemption: From Al Jolson's *Jazz Singer* to John Garfield's *Body and Soul*" presents a detailed cultural and historical analysis of films that depicted certain aspects of Black-Jewish relations in American society. Rogin makes it clear that blackface entertainment became a means for upward mobility and economic advancement for many Jews early in this century. In effect, as was the case with Irish entertainers before them, performing in blackface was how these European immigrants became "Americans." While few Jewish characters appeared in the movies made by Jewish producers in the 1930s and 1940s, *Body and Soul* (1947), starring John Garfield and Canada Lee, portrayed the relationship between a Jewish boxer and his Black trainer. While the film, produced by two Jewish Communists, Abraham Polonsky and Robert Rossen, attempted to dramatize the corrupting influence of capitalism on human relationships, Rogin's analysis reveals a cultural subtext on the nature of Black-Jewish relations, a subtext also found in Jolson's *The Jazz Singer,* in which Jewish redemption was achieved through Black sacrifice.

The attack launched by the House Un-American Activities Committee

(HUAC) against members of the Communist Party not only led to the blacklisting of Abraham Polonsky and other Hollywood producers and actors but also to a large extent explains why communists had so little influence on the emergence of the modern phase of the Civil Rights Movement. When the Montgomery Bus Boycott was launched in December 1955, the leaders of the Communist Party were still reeling from the right-wing attacks led by Sen. Joseph McCarthy earlier in the decade, and thus they failed to recognize the potential significance of the incident. Although FBI Director J. Edgar Hoover and other government officials claimed that the civil rights leaders were communists, or at least communist sympathizers, researchers have unearthed no evidence to support this charge. However, as Murray Friedman makes clear in "The Civil Rights Movement and the Reemergence of the Left," many of the early supporters of Martin Luther King Jr. and the Southern Christian Leadership Conference (SCLC) were communist sympathizers and veterans of left-wing movements and organizations. Friedman focuses on King's closest advisers, including Stanley Levison, Bayard Rustin, Ella Baker, and Harry Wachtel, who solidified the SCLC's financial and ideological relationship with the "New York Afro-American-Jewish radical community." Through Harry Wachtel, King and the SCLC gained access to many wealthy Jewish supporters as well. Friedman demonstrates that the Jewish and other leftists needed the emerging cause of "civil rights" as much as King and the emerging civil rights leadership relied upon the experience, knowledge, and connections of older left-wing activists.

In a recent essay on Blacks and Jews in the twentieth-century South, Deborah Dash Moore touches upon the impact that the emerging Civil Rights Movement had on the southern Jewish community. Following World War II, southern Jews became more politically active, "but not enough to bring them into convergence with African Americans' increasing demands for equal civil rights and for an end to segregation." Moore suggests that southern Jews found themselves caught "between a rock and a hard place . . . between the demands of racist White southerners, who organized the White Citizens Councils beginning in 1954, and the expectations of liberal northern Jews whose defense organizations actively supported equal rights."[5] Cheryl Greenberg's "The Southern Jewish Community and the Struggle for Civil Rights" provides a detailed analysis of this imposing dilemma for southern Jews, based on docu-

5. Deborah Dash Moore, "Separate Paths: Blacks and Jews in the Twentieth Century South," in *Struggles in the Promised Land,* ed. Salzman and West, 282–83.

ments and other archival sources from numerous Jewish organizations, North and South. Greenberg describes how southern Jews responded to the increasingly close relationships that developed between northern-based Jewish organizations and Black civil rights groups beginning in the 1930s. Many southern Jews made it clear not only that they were disturbed by this growing relationship but also that they would prefer a change of direction and wanted these national Jewish groups to assume a lower profile on civil rights. The increasing ideological convergence between Black civil rights groups and national Jewish organizations became the source of some conflict with Jewish groups and branches located in the South, and Greenberg demonstrates that southern Jews were at times successful in slowing down the movement by the national Jewish organizations to support the cause of Black civil rights. While individual southern Jews made notable contributions to civil rights campaigns during these turbulent years, a pattern of resistance to civil rights demands is clearly identifiable, and understandable, in southern Jewish communities, given their vulnerable position before and during the civil rights era.

Jewish intellectuals who believed that demands for Black civil rights would eventually conflict with the political and economic interests of the Jewish community became early recruits to the "neoconservative" ideological camp that emerged in the 1970s and 1980s. Black intellectuals who challenged the federal government's policies on social welfare and affirmative action became highly visible supporters of the "new conservatism" that was a defining characteristic of the Ronald Reagan and George Bush presidencies. The convergence in their beliefs about the need to limit government intervention in the social welfare arena serves as the major link between Jewish neoconservatives and Black conservatives; however, each of these groups has adopted distinctive perspectives on contemporary social and economic issues. While liberal social policies and welfare initiatives are the major bête noire for both Jewish neoconservatives and Black conservatives, there are significant discontinuities in their analyses of the sources of the current social problems and the most appropriate solutions. Nancy Haggard-Gilson, in "Against the Grain: Black Conservatives and Jewish Neoconservatives," examines the writings of Glenn Loury, Stanley Crouch, Shelby Steele, Clarence Thomas, Nathan Glazer, and Irving Kristol on social welfare issues and affirmative action, unearthing a diversity of opinions and viewpoints and exposing significant inconsistencies and weaknesses in their arguments. She concludes that, given the range of the ideological alternatives they represent, Jewish neoconservatives and Black conservatives indeed make strange bedfellows.

Part II. Conflict, Competition, and Matters of Principle

While the essays in Part I provide new information on the broad areas of convergence in the experiences and ideological positions of Jewish Americans and African Americans in the twentieth century, Part II contains discussions of specific instances of conflict in Black-Jewish relations. Throughout the twentieth century both the African American and the Jewish populations were located primarily in large industrial areas and in some instances competed for limited employment opportunities, access to social welfare and educational services, and housing in often crowded urban spaces. Joe W. Trotter Jr.'s "African Americans, Jews, and the City: Perspectives from the Industrial Era, 1900–1950" provides a survey of the literature on Black-Jewish relations in urban areas, North and South. Trotter examines the historical and sociological studies of Black urban life and finds that only a few researchers, such as St. Clair Drake and Horace Cayton in their classic work on African Americans in Chicago, *Black Metropolis* (1945), described Black-Jewish interactions. Even the studies published in the 1960s and early 1970s on the development of the northern Black "ghettos" paid scant attention to the relations between Jews and African Americans. Only more recently have historians, such as Earl Lewis, Mark Naison, and three contributors to this volume, Cheryl Greenberg, Winston C. McDowell, and Marshall F. Stevenson Jr., systematically examined Black-Jewish contacts and reported on areas of conflict and cooperation in urban America.

Trotter finds a similar pattern in the research conducted on Jewish life in the city. Early studies of Jews in New York City, for example, provided little information about their contacts with African Americans, and it is only recently that the topic has been examined. Trotter also discusses the limited information available on Black-Jewish relations in the areas of urban entertainment and culture and concludes that there are many aspects of Black and Jewish urban life in need of exploration by historians and social scientists.

Winston C. McDowell's "Keeping Them `In the Same Boat Together'? Sufi Abdul Hamid, African Americans, Jews, and the Harlem Jobs Boycotts" explores the role of the controversial street orator Sufi Hamid in the first phase of campaigns launched in New York City in the 1930s to gain jobs for depression-ridden Black workers. Nonviolent direct action protests, such as boycotts, became an important weapon for unemployed

Black residents in Chicago, Philadelphia, St. Louis, and other cities in their struggle for survival during the economic collapse. Earlier accounts of Sufi Hamid's role in the jobs campaign point to his targeting of Jewish merchants and businesses. This tactic was viewed as divisive and antagonistic and provided the basis for charges that he was an anti-Semite. McDowell presents a detailed analysis of the economic conditions in Harlem in the early 1930s and the strategies suggested for dealing with the severe Black unemployment. The "quiet negotiations" of African American elites to try to gain jobs for Black workers in the various business enterprises still operating met with little success. McDowell demonstrates that while Sufi Hamid was successful in mobilizing the jobs campaign and forcing the Black elites to recognize the effectiveness of direct action protests, it was almost inevitable that he would be accused of being anti-Semitic since many of the businesses targeted for demonstrations were owned by Jews. In the aftermath of the Harlem Riot in March 1935, Black elites and Jewish merchants blamed the violence on "troublemakers," such as Hamid, and injunctions were issued to halt future jobs protests and demonstrations. By 1935 the first phase of the Harlem jobs campaign had ended, but in movements for jobs launched later in the decade, African American elites, led by Rev. Adam Clayton Powell Jr., recognized the need for nonviolent, direct action protests to obtain economic opportunities for Black workers.

New information on convergence and conflict between African Americans and Jewish Americans in the labor movement is presented in the essays by Marshall F. Stevenson Jr. and Herbert Hill. In "African Americans and Jews in Organized Labor: A Case Study of Detroit, 1920–1950," Stevenson focuses on Black-Jewish relations in the automotive unions in general and the United Auto Workers (UAW) in particular. In the 1920s there were very few African Americans or Jews in Detroit's labor unions; however, in the mid-1930s Congress of Industrial Organizations (CIO) organizers began actively recruiting Black and Jewish workers. Many of these labor organizers were members of the Communist Party and, in keeping with the party's emphasis on building "worker solidarity" across racial and ethnic lines, they targeted Black and Jewish workers for participation in various educational programs and labor councils. During World War II, Jewish communists were particularly active in trying to improve working conditions for the growing number of Black and Jewish workers in the automobile industry, who were often victimized by racism and anti-Semitism. At the end of the war, it was Jewish communists who worked closely with Black union members to gain the election of African Americans to union offices.

Stevenson examines the activities of Black and Jewish communists and their supporters at the UAW's 1943 annual convention to gain the passage of a resolution creating a "Minorities Department" within the UAW international and the appointment of an African American to head the department. The campaign failed for a number of reasons; most important, it failed because of UAW leaders' opposition to giving "preferential treatment" to Blacks, Jews, or other minorities. Although at subsequent conventions the Black-Jewish communist coalition was able to convince the UAW to create a "Fair Practices Committee" to deal with minority discrimination, which eventually became a separate department, the purge of communists from the UAW beginning in 1947 eliminated most of the Jewish leaders who had been part of the earlier Black-Jewish coalition. Those Jewish union members who remained took no leadership role in the antidiscrimination campaigns in Detroit's automotive industry.

Whereas Stevenson's essay describes the convergence of Black and Jewish interests in Detroit's automotive unions in the 1930s and 1940s, Herbert Hill documents interracial conflicts that arose within a number of unions, including those in New York City's garment industry in the 1950s and 1960s. In "Black-Jewish Conflict in the Labor Context: Race, Jobs, and Institutional Power," Hill reviews the activities of the Jewish Labor Committee (JLC) in the 1950s and found that because the JLC leaders consistently defended the racist and discriminatory practices of building trades, industrial, and other unions, they changed what had been a "Black-White conflict into a Black-Jewish conflict." The JLC also on numerous occasions came to the defense of the Jewish leaders of the International Ladies Garment Workers Union (ILGWU) when hearings were held after complaints of racial discrimination were filed by the union's predominantly Black and Latino membership. Hill shows that ILGWU and JLC leaders published reports that distorted the findings of the governmental committees that investigated these complaints and that the Jewish labor leaders then charged the Black and Latino union members who brought these suits with anti-Semitism. When NAACP leaders condemned the racist practices of these same Jewish-led unions, they too were accused of being anti-Semitic. While the Black and Latino workers were merely protesting against discriminatory treatment, just as Jewish immigrant workers had done earlier in the century, by the early 1960s it was "Jewish privilege" that had to be defended. But even though the ILGWU was no longer a "Jewish union," its leaders denounced the Black and Latino members for demanding equal treatment and access to leadership positions.

Hill examines the Ocean Hill–Brownsville incident, which led to the fifty-five-day teachers' strike in New York City in 1968, and points out that Albert Shanker, president of the United Federation of Teachers (UFT), provoked a Black-Jewish conflict by accusing Black parents and teachers of anti-Semitism. In examining recent legal suits brought over the implementation of the government's affirmative action programs, Hill makes it clear that Jewish organizations have generally filed amici briefs opposing these programs. While affirmative action programs were put in place to deal with the lasting effects of racism and discrimination, Hill argues that Jewish opposition to affirmative action is based primarily on self-interest. Hill concludes that whether or not the historical legacy is acknowledged, African Americans' continuing campaigns for social justice and equal economic opportunities will be built upon the cultural traditions found in both the Black and the Jewish communities.

During his lifetime Malcolm X, the outspoken and controversial leader of the Nation of Islam, was accused of preaching anti-Semitism. Since his death in 1965, Malcolm has been linked with other Black nationalist spokespersons who were alleged to have made anti-Semitic remarks and statements. In "The Portrayal of Jews in *The Autobiography of Malcolm X*," I examine the actual statements about Jews and Jewish culture found in this popular and important work, as well as recent research on the issue of "Black anti-Semitism." Contrary to certain widely accepted beliefs, researchers who have conducted surveys in Black communities to determine the existence of anti-Semitic beliefs and attitudes have found that African Americans are no more anti-Semitic in their beliefs than are White Americans; in fact, religious African Americans expressed very positive attitudes toward Jews. In the case of Malcolm X, his public statements have been taken out of context by some historians and other writers, who then labeled him an anti-Semite. However, in the autobiography there are numerous references to Jews and several discussions of the charges of anti-Semitism that were leveled against Malcolm during his public career. While Malcolm made clear his respect for Jewish history and culture, he denounced Jewish Americans when they acted no differently from other "White" Americans and exhibited racist and exploitative attitudes and behavior in their dealings with African Americans and other peoples of color. In the case of some American Jews, it was their "Whiteness" rather than their "Jewishness" that Malcolm found objectionable.

The changes in the U.S. economy in the postindustrial era have decreased the likelihood of further convergence in the socioeconomic status of Jewish Americans and African Americans. In "The Increasing Significance of Class: Black-Jewish Conflict in the Postindustrial Global Era,"

Walda Katz-Fishman and Jerome Scott compare and contrast the economic histories of African Americans and Jewish Americans from the early nineteenth to the late twentieth century, tracing Blacks' movement from field to factory to joblessness in postindustrial cities and Jews' transit from factory to office and their current status as a "privileged minority." Katz-Fishman and Scott argue that the "social safety net" originally put in place with the New Deal social programs and expanded by Lyndon Johnson's Great Society in the 1960s has been unraveling and that both Republican and Democratic politicians in the 1980s and 1990s have participated in this renegotiation of the social contract with the American people. The postindustrial global economy has hurt many low-skilled American workers in general, and African American workers in particular; however, most Jewish Americans have joined the middle and upper classes in the United States and participated in the economic decisions that have overwhelmingly benefited the corporate or "power elite." Katz-Fishman and Scott call for the formation of a new political coalition among racial, religious, and social groups that will challenge the economic decisions of the transnational corporate elite and place the problems of women, children, and the poor at the top of the U.S. social and political agenda in the twenty-first century.

It appears that Black-Jewish relations in the United States in the twentieth century have exhibited more convergences in experiences and ideologies than conflicts. For those who recognize the significance of the history and culture of these two minority groups in defining the nature of the American experience, these essays provide something of a blueprint for lessening tensions and building coalitions for the future. The American experiment is a long way from being completed, and African Americans and Jewish Americans must play their part, together or separately, in making sure that the United States lives up to its reputation as a nation that freely dispenses "liberty and justice for all."

Remembering Nancy Louise Grant (1949–1995)

Genna Rae McNeil

First Fight. Then Fiddle.
. . . having first to civilize a space
Wherein to play your violin with grace.

W HEN GWENDOLYN Brooks wrote "First Fight. Then Fiddle," she did not know of Nancy Louise Grant, who could and did do both with remarkable resolve. What Brooks poetically argued, Nancy Grant understood. Understanding, Nancy used voice and violin, history as truth telling and harmonics as testimony, in the effort "to civilize [this highly racialized] space,"[1] called, ironically, the *United* States of America.

Nancy Grant's lifetime of excellent teaching, her 1990 *TVA and Black Americans: Planning for the Status Quo*, the 1993 conference "Blacks and Jews: An American Historical Perspective," which resulted in this volume, and her work in progress at the time of her death in 1995, "Uncivil Service: The Employment of Blacks in the Federal Government, 1940–1975," were her scholarly responses to injustice, growing out of soul-searching, meticulous researching, and an abiding optimism. Nancy Grant was optimistic about the potential usefulness of history that could "hold, as 'twere, the mirror up to nature; [and] show . . . the very age and body of the time his form and pressure."[2] She could and did, therefore, interpret motifs, harmonies, dissonance, and melodies of a variety of forms of music while acknowledging the unfinished nature of the struggle for justice.

1. Gwendolyn Brooks, "First Fight. Then Fiddle" in *The Poetry of the Negro, 1746–1970*, ed. Langston Hughes and Arna Bontemps, rev. ed. (Garden City, N.Y.: Anchor/Doubleday, 1970), 337.
2. William Shakespeare, excerpt from *Hamlet*, in *The Oxford Dictionary of Quotations*, 3d ed. (Oxford and New York: Oxford University Press, 1979), 434.

Nancy Louise Grant, the daughter of James Earl Grant and Julia Bee Grant, was born on April 16, 1949, in Hartford, Connecticut, the third of three children. Nancy and her two brothers, Robert and James, were deeply loved and constantly encouraged by their parents to pursue a formal education, use their gifts, and excel. This the Grant children strove to do in unique ways (and Nancy would transmit this same message to bright and musically talented nephews to whom she was a close and loving aunt).

Nancy attended the public schools of Hartford. Early exhibiting her ability to integrate music with scholarship, she played the violin in the youth orchestra for her region, but she also was graduated in 1967 from Weaver High School with a distinguished record of scholastic achievement. In 1971, she completed the requirements for the Bachelor of Arts degree and was awarded a B.A. cum laude by Smith College of Northampton, Massachusetts. She received a Master of Arts degree in history from the University of Chicago in 1972. Advised by John Hope Franklin and Barry Karl, she received her Doctor of Philosophy degree (Ph.D.) in history from the same university in 1978.

Nancy Grant by no means enjoyed the customary course of graduate study. A graduate student during what Manning Marable has so well described as the "zenith and decline" of the "Black rebellion,"[3] Nancy was conscious of the need for young African Americans, such as herself, to make themselves useful to the struggle for racial justice. In one sense, she decided *against* music as a career path and *for,* instead, the creation of a body of knowledge that would constitute a usable past for her struggling people. Not dependent on the vagaries of the professional music world to earn a living, she did in another sense choose music to live. It was a choice that freed her from survival concerns as she energetically participated in a variety of ensembles and carefully created a space in which to experience balance and beauty in her life, despite the clear claims on her of the African American liberation struggle.

Having made the choice to become a professional historian and scholar in academe, Nancy Grant might have insisted on a temporary reprieve from the turbulence of the Civil Rights and Black Power Movements. The demands of graduate education loomed large. Due to the assaults by White racists, governments, and law enforcement units on organizations and leaders of the Black Liberation Movement, internal

3. Manning Marable, *Race, Reform, and Rebellion: The Second Reconstruction in Black America, 1945–1990,* 2d rev. ed. (Jackson: University Press of Mississippi, 1990), 114–38.

struggles within the movement, and the increasing attention being paid to partisan politics, some college-educated African American youth had elected to immerse themselves in their formal studies and surface as activists only periodically when egregious wrongs claimed national attention. Others found they best made their contribution through local participation in antiracist organizations.[4] Nancy Grant believed she had the luxury of neither path.

For deeply personal reasons, she had in the late 1960s decided to take her civil rights activism to a new level. She felt the need to be superior in historical studies at the University of Chicago while also being public, passionate, and compelling in her protest against racist oppression. Her brother, Jim Grant, a recent Ph.D. in chemistry, a dynamic civil rights organizer for the Southern Conference Educational Fund, and a reporter for the fund's *Southern Patriot*, had been the victim of a racist frame-up in Charlotte, North Carolina. There confined, he was a political prisoner, one of the "Charlotte 3." (It was alleged that his training as a chemist qualified him especially for being the mastermind of the burning of the Lazy B stables in Charlotte. Then there was also his alleged aiding and abetting of fugitives.) Neither the Charlotte 3's nor the Wilmington 10's racist and political repression by the state of North Carolina would proceed without Nancy's voice being heard. Somewhat awkward as a speaker at political rallies, she never, however, missed any opportunity to defend her brother, resist racist repression, and demand justice for the Charlotte 3 and the Wilmington 10. It was not unusual for her to interrupt her studies and research to travel to North Carolina for just such purposes.[5]

In North Carolina, Nancy Grant was also able to push forward her doctoral work on the racial policies of the Tennessee Valley Authority (TVA). To establish herself among public policy historians, she studied the works of scholars and planners of the New Deal and World War II

4. See Kenneth O'Reilly, *Racial Matters* (New York: Free Press, 1989); Marable, *Race, Reform, and Rebellion*, 114–48; Mary Frances Berry, *Black Resistance/White Law*, 2d rev. ed. (New York: Penguin, 1994), 166–98.

5. Before 1976, it was my privilege to have Nancy stay with me (also an ardent Charlotte 3 and Wilmington 10 supporter within the context of the African American struggle for justice) in my first Durham apartment near Duke University. At such times we talked at length about our commitments to the African American struggle and to the creation of historical scholarship that could make a difference in the lives, conditions, and struggles of African Americans. Although a political prisoner in Charlotte during the 1970s, James Grant was ultimately vindicated and—with a dedication, zeal, and concern for African Americans, particularly the southern poor, that Nancy greatly admired and about which she often boasted—continues his work of community organizing.

era, researched the papers of Howard Odum, and interviewed Guy Johnson. Meticulous research on the federal government's policies and the TVA prompted further travels south to Georgia and Tennessee.[6] TVA planners, Nancy discovered, "severely limited their sights where opportunities for changes in racial relations were concerned,"[7] but she had great plans and a great vision for her career. She steadfastly refused to be bound by limitations usually associated with the systemic racism of the United States.

In 1976, Nancy Grant began her academic career on the history faculty of the University of California at Davis. Two years later, she was awarded the Ph.D. She accepted a position on the faculty of Northwestern University, in Evanston, Illinois, where she held a joint appointment in Afro-American Studies and History from 1979 to 1985. During this time she continued her research and began to publish. "Government Social Planning and Education for Blacks: The TVA Experience, 1933–1945" appeared in Ronald Goodenow and Arthur White's *Education and the Rise of the New South*.[8] Competing successfully for a visiting scholar's position at the Institute for Policy Studies in 1982 and for a Ford Foundation Postdoctoral Fellowship in 1983, Nancy Grant continued her research on the federal government's policies with respect to race. She planned her magnum opus, a history of the employment of African Americans in the federal government, to follow the completion of her TVA study.

Beyond researching, writing, and teaching during the years at Northwestern, Nancy especially enjoyed her relationship with her late colleague, the gifted writer Professor Leon Forrest.[9] They had adjoining offices and regularly "talked, debated and happily agreed about certain

6. In 1975, Nancy Grant spent the summer at the TVA as a researcher in the Office of Equal Employment Opportunity. A published report resulted from her work, "Equal Employment Opportunities in the TVA, 1955–1975" (1975).

7. Nancy L. Grant, *TVA and Black Americans: Planning for the Status Quo* (Philadelphia: Temple University Press, 1990), xxix.

8. See Ronald Goodenow and Arthur White, eds., *Education and the Rise of the New South* (Boston: G. K. Hall, 1981).

9. Leon Forrest passed in 1997, but not without having observed: "When I was creating my last novel, *Divine Days*, I found that it was music and through the soul of the violin, (in the form of Sibelius's Concerto in C) that helped to unleash and inspire the emotions of heart-ache, nostalgia, fire and wonderment, within me, during the composition of certain central passages of my novel. And this in turn, forced me to recall many of my conversations with Nancy" (Leon Forrest, "Eulogy for Nancy Grant," typescript, facsimile courtesy of Harold Kletnick, ca. December 1995, 3). Although he was confident, as was Dylan Thomas, that "death had no dominion," Leon Forrest, too, was stricken with cancer.

issues." Forrest taught, wrote, and praised literature, which he argued "provided . . . the most profound and moving symphonies concerning the human condition." Throughout those years, Nancy Grant taught, wrote, played the violin, and praised classical music: "She believed serious Classical music truly revealed the depths and the zenith of our predicament, better than any of the other arts."[10]

While at Northwestern, Nancy Grant had not only written and published but had also turned her attention as a teacher-scholar to race relations. She served as an adviser for the Ford Foundation's conference on four minorities. Winning a Mellon grant, she developed in 1982 a course on racial minorities of the United States. Her long-held concern for race relations and racial justice assumed a more critical approach as she taught comparatively the histories of African Americans, Native Americans, Hispanic Americans, and Asian Americans in the United States.

Dartmouth College offered Nancy an appointment in its history department, an academic position that allowed her to move closer to her family and provided an opportunity for her to continue to be, as John Hope Franklin would later describe, "the violinist as historian."[11] From 1985 to 1989 she taught, wrote, researched, and played the violin. She participated in numerous professional organizations, including the American Historical Association, the Association for the Study of Afro-American Life and History, the National Conference of Black Studies, the Organization of American Historians, the Organization of Black Women Historians, and the Southern Historical Association. She presented research findings on the federal government and the TVA. The TVA study, to which she had devoted years of research beyond the dissertation, was accepted by Temple University Press. That called for a celebratory violin recital. This work and other research also prompted discussion among scholars in the academy about the work of Nancy Grant. Responding to the interest expressed by historians in St. Louis, she joined the faculty of Washington University in that city.

The move to St. Louis brought Nancy and her husband, Harold Kletnick, to a city with not only a great university but also great classical music. It was very close to ideal. Nancy made a name for herself at Washington University, taking on challenges to African Americans and women and becoming an effective and admired university citizen. Her "work with students was of great importance to her, as was her work

10. Ibid., 1.
11. John Hope Franklin, "The Violinist as Historian," typescript, facsimile courtesy of Harold Kletnick, ca. December 1995.

with women colleagues in and outside of the Department of History."[12] Her friend and colleague Nancy E. Berg, an associate professor of modern Hebrew, early observed that Nancy "didn't let her students, colleagues or friends get away with sloppy thinking or thoughtless speech."[13] Although she taught in the history department, Nancy Grant "exhibited . . . interest in African and Afro-American Studies," "concern and commitment to [the] program."[14] With Gerald Early, chairperson of the African and Afro-American Studies Program, Nancy taught some courses on African American life and culture. She was "of incalculable aid to [Professor Early] in running the African and Afro-American Studies Program."[15] Nancy Grant was respected as "a fine teacher, a committed scholar and a dear and valued colleague. She added much to the life of the University." Always a teacher-scholar, who loved learning as well as teaching, "to the delight of her students, she often wove jazz, rhythm and blues, and gospel into her courses."[16] In 1990 Professor Grant published "Howard Odum: Region and Racism" in the journal *Research and Social Policy*, "Adult Education for Blacks during the New Deal and World War II" in a collection of essays on African American education, and her book, *TVA and Black Americans: Planning for the Status Quo.*[17]

Nancy Grant's *"TVA and Black Americans* . . . was widely and well received."[18] Reviewing the book for the *American Historical Review*, Steven Gelber judged it both a "gracefully written book tell[ing] . . . the sad and seemingly inevitable story of cautious New Deal bureaucrats bowing to local traditions" and a "useful addition to the literature on the New Deal in the South." Gelber placed Nancy Grant's study squarely within the most important historiography of African Americans and the New Deal: "Grant's study of the way in which the Tennessee Valley Authority (TVA) treated blacks reinforces the conclusions of two earlier and more

12. Associate Professor Mary Ann Dzuback quoted in Washington University Communications, "Professor Nancy Louise Grant Dies at 46," typescript news release, ca. October 12, 1995, 3.
13. Berg quoted in ibid., 1.
14. Gerald Early, "Guest Editorial: A Tribute to Nancy Grant," *St. Louis American* (November 9–15, 1995), A6.
15. Early quoted in "Professor Nancy Louis Grant Dies at 46," 2.
16. Carolyn Sanford, "Nancy Louise Grant, Associate Professor of History, Dies at 46," *Washington University Record* 20 (October 19, 1995): 1, 7.
17. See Nancy Grant, "Howard Odum: Region and Racism," *Research and Social Policy* 2 (winter 1990); "Adult Education during the New Deal and World War II: The Federal Programs," in *Education of the African-American Adult: An Historical Overview*, ed. Harvey Neufeldt and Leo McGee (Westport, Conn.: Greenwood Press, 1990); and *TVA and Black Americans.*
18. Franklin, "The Violinist as Historian," 4.

general histories, Harvard Sitkoff's *A New Deal for Blacks* (1978) and Raymond Wolters' *Negroes and the Great Depression* (1970)."[19] Raymond Wolters, reviewing Nancy Grant's study for *Labor History*, praised her presentation of "rock solid evidence" and noted the manner in which she "ably demonstrate[d] that, when it came to race relations, the leaders of the TVA 'shared an ideology of racism and, at best, espoused an "enlightened segregation."' Thus the subtitle of the book. During the years of the Roosevelt administration, TVA was 'planning for the status quo.' "[20] Reviewed, as well, in the *Journal of American History* by Princeton scholar Nancy Weiss, this "comprehensive institutional history" of the TVA by Nancy Grant had achieved scholarly success; "the principal strengths" of her "authoritative study" included, according to Weiss, "its grounding in intensive research in primary and secondary sources, the clarity and accessibility of the narrative, and the persuasiveness of the author's account of the factors militating against progress on the race issue in the TVA."[21]

"Nancy was a flourishing scholar," as John Hope Franklin later recalled.[22] Equally important, her research and scholarly activities mirrored her diverse interests and her concern about the recognition of human equality. Little that might be described as typical of an African American activist-scholar in this era was foregrounded in Nancy Grant's life. Nonetheless, her close friend Christine Ruane, a scholar of Russian history, said best what Nancy Grant's family, friends, and colleagues knew: "Nancy was a person who *spent her whole life* fighting for justice. This commitment shaped everything she did as a scholar, mentor and friend."[23]

With the favorable reception of her TVA study, Nancy Grant, as planned, continued focusing her attention on the racist policies of the federal government and the struggles of African American workers, in particular. She spent additional time in Washington, D.C., not only serving on selection committees and panels for the National Endowment for the Humanities but also mining the rich records of the National Alliance of Postal Workers. (Her father had been an outstanding and dedicated postal worker for decades; in tribute to him she planned a scholarly study of African American employees of the U.S. Postal Service.) She

19. Steven Gelber in *American Historical Review* 96 (April 1991): 632–33.
20. Raymond Wolters in *Labor History* 35 (1994): 145–46.
21. Nancy Weiss in *Journal of American History* 77 (March 1991): 1401–2.
22. Franklin, "The Violinist as Historian," 4.
23. Ruane quoted in Sanford, "Nancy Louise Grant Dies at 46," 1, 7 (italics mine).

continued to conduct her research for the larger study on federal employment of African Americans from 1945 to 1970 at an enviable pace.

A well-respected, tenured associate professor at Washington University, Nancy Grant explored other interests, such as civil rights and slavery. "The Changing Dream: The Speeches of Martin Luther King, 1956–1967" was published by the *New England Journal of Black Studies* in 1991, and later she wrote a substantive introduction to the Bison Books edition of Kate E. R. Pickard's *The Kidnapped and the Ransomed: The Narrative of Peter and Vina Still after Forty Years of Slavery.*[24] All this was consistent with her personal and scholarly interest in the history and the future of race relations in the United States. It is no wonder that Frederick Douglass, the formerly enslaved African American abolitionist, was one of Nancy Grant's heroes. Nancy admired Douglass's uncompromising stands for his beliefs during his lifetime and how true he was to himself in the personal, professional, and political arenas. She concurred in his bold proclamations: "Now, as always, I am for any movement whenever there is a good cause to promote, a right to assert, a chain to be broken, a burden to be removed, or a wrong to be redressed."[25]

Believing it inadequate to teach and research without contributing to the new scholarship on a multicultural, multiracial, and multi-ethnic United States and the struggle for justice, Nancy Grant in 1993 organized the conference "Blacks and Jews: An American Historical Perspective." The proceedings included papers presented by twenty-six historians, sociologists, and political scientists who "examined elements of cooperation and conflict between [B]lacks and Jews."[26] While the speakers revised their papers for publication in a volume Grant planned to edit, she continued her research in African American history.

In 1994, Grant won a coveted fellowship to Harvard University's W. E. B. Du Bois Institute for African American Research in Cambridge. There she wrote and presented research on African Americans and policies concerning their employment. Ill health and a diagnosis of cancer forced her to return to St. Louis before the conclusion of her leave. Despite pain, treatments, hospitalization, and an only slightly encouraging

24. See Nancy Grant, "The Changing Dream: The Speeches of Martin Luther King, 1956–1967," *New England Journal of Black Studies* 9 (fall 1991), and Kate E. R. Pickard, *The Kidnapped and the Ransomed: The Narrative of Peter and Vina Still after Forty Years of Slavery* (Lincoln: University of Nebraska Press, 1995), vii–xv.
25. Frederick Douglass (1884) quoted in the funeral program of Nancy Louise Grant.
26. Carolyn Sanford, "Obituar[y]: Nancy Louise Grant," in *Perspectives* (newsletter of the American Historical Association) 34 (February 1996): 37–38.

prognosis, Nancy Grant continued to serve on community boards such as the Mercantile Library Association and completed the research for her study of St. Louis African Americans in classical music. She took particular pleasure in doing the research for this article, which included hours of conversation with older African Americans of the St. Louis community and occasionally contacting Darwyn Apple, a friend and African American violinist in the St. Louis Symphony. Before her passing, Nancy Grant finished a lengthy study for Washington University's African and Afro-American Studies Program, which became the first in that program's series of occasional papers. In 1996, Gerald Early, the program's chairperson and Nancy Grant's colleague, edited and released "From Showboat to Symphony: Black Classical Musicians in St. Louis, 1920–1980."[27]

Throughout her career, from the 1970s until cancer claimed her physical life in October 1995, Nancy Grant continued her violin performances. During the summer and fall of 1995, she communicated with her talented brother Robert of Portland, Connecticut, about music she desired him to return so that she might consider performance for the sheer delight of it. Music remained until her last days a source of inexpressible joy; from it she gained the energy to continue excelling in the academy and in the struggle for justice.

For studies at Yale University's School of Music, private coaching in Chicago, and, thereafter, performances in a variety of settings, Nancy Grant traveled with her violin as well as with her briefcase. She was a member of the Chicago Musicians Union, and she performed as a member of the Bridgetower Academy String Quartet in Chicago. She could be heard as a studio musician on recordings by the Temptations, in the pit during Broadway musicals staged at Chicago's Shubert Theatre, as part of the local ensemble for performances by Sammy Davis Jr., George Benson, and Smokey Robinson. She delighted in musical expression and always looked forward to annual calls from African American churches that celebrated the Advent season with worship performances of G. F. Handel's *Messiah*.[28]

27. Nancy Grant, "From Showboat to Symphony: Black Classical Musicians in St. Louis, 1920–1980," in *Black Heartland*, ed. Gerald Early (St. Louis: Washington University, 1996), 14–25.
28. See Sanford, "Obituar[y]" and "Nancy Louise Grant Dies at 46." Being one of Nancy's friends who annually sang Handel's *Messiah*, I often compared notes with her on how instrumentalists might count measures and remain together while congregants from time to time expressed their enthusiasm with "shouting," applause, and "Amens" in the midst of a soloist's coloratura passage or the counterpoint of the choir's four sections. Although that was occasionally a daunting task, Nancy

To others, Nancy Grant was remarkable in her ability to combine violin performances with scholarly endeavors and do both with excellence.
For Nancy, it was quite natural to have a briefcase in one hand and a violin case in her other. Following her Ph.D. oral examinations, which John
Hope Franklin remembers Nancy passing "with flying colors," both Professor Franklin and Professor Karl attended her violin recital in downtown Chicago. Franklin later recalled: "It was a thrilling experience, to
hear her and Bill Epstein play the Sonata for piano and violin by César
Franck. The moment I heard her play that day I knew that the historian
would always remain the violinist."[29] Prior to leaving Dartmouth for
Washington University in St. Louis, Nancy Grant again offered her own
musical finale, a summer 1989 recital in which she performed chamber
music and another sonata by one of her favorite composers, Ludwig von
Beethoven. Beethoven's "Spring Sonata" brought enormous pleasure in
rehearsal as well as in performance, and it signaled the beginning of a
new movement for Nancy, to the scholarship and the symphony of St.
Louis, Missouri. Nancy's move to Washington University and St. Louis
at the age of forty-one would prove to be her last.

There was in Nancy a persistence in progress, a strength that grew in
protracted struggles, and a consummate courage in her last days with us,
despite her contempt for the cancer. An unwillingness to be defeated by
disease coupled with an abundance of love from her mother, brothers,
nephews, niece, cousins, husband, friends, and colleagues only fueled
her faith that she—more than body, a being of mind and spirit, as well—
could not be conquered by cancer. As we drove to the airport on September 18, 1995, so that I might return to North Carolina, we talked about
faith, the Lord who was, in truth, her shepherd, and an afternoon presentation on Booker T. Washington for the African and Afro-American
Studies Program. For the event commemorating the 1895 Atlanta Exposition speech, Gerald Early, chair of the program, remembered: "She was
particularly vigorous in her attack against Washington. . . . [S]he came
out for me despite her illness. . . . She had acted in God's eye with . . .
grace and courage and commitment." By her family's, friends', and colleagues' reckoning, Nancy's years were far too short, her time with us as

---

ultimately enjoyed the music, the ecstasy, and testimonies to a living Messiah that
characterized the African American worship experience.

29. Nancy especially loved to perform César Franck's Sonata in A major for violin
and piano. She was also particularly fond of Schubert's "Trout" Quintet and Schubert's chamber music, "Death and the Maiden."

a physical presence far too brief. Yet in a brief span of years, she lived fully and she lived well.

Nancy Louise Grant does not appear among the approximately two hundred women historians included in *American Women Historians, 1700s–1990s*. The editors' criteria resulted in the inclusion of a few of Nancy Grant's friends—such as Mary Frances Berry and Bettye Collier-Thomas—but in the exclusion of many African American historians.[30] Nevertheless, Nancy Louise Grant has a legacy and a lasting voice. The legacy of her teaching and scholarship, as well as of the work that her students have done and will do, will stand the test of time. Her classic study, *TVA and Black Americans* (1990), speaks loudly. Nancy Grant was concerned about her work until the end; in her last days she entrusted the final editing of this volume to V. P. Franklin, her close friend for more than two decades and a fellow historian who participated in the conference on Blacks and Jews. Chiefly because of V. P. Franklin's careful editing and stewardship of Nancy Grant's trust, Nancy Louise Grant—with the scholars she gathered when she conceived of a conference on African Americans and Jews—will continue to speak through this volume. *African Americans and Jews in the Twentieth Century: Studies in Convergence and Conflict* will project her voice and expand the discourse to include her continuing concern about a space in this nation for the practice of justice, the recognition of human equality, and the creation of music, literature, and art.

In remembering Nancy Louise Grant, historian and violinist, no words can introduce this volume, her encore, more beautifully than those of Leon Forrest: "And so with a history text book in one hand, her violin case in the other, I can easily envision the glad grace of Nancy Grant forever instructing us about the meaning of a well-rounded life."[31]

30. Jennifer Scanlon and Shaaron Cosner, eds., *American Women Historians, 1700s–1990s: A Biographical Dictionary* (Westport, Conn.: Greenwood Press, 1996), ix–x, xiii, 19–20, 42–44; see table of contents.
31. Forrest, "Eulogy for Nancy Grant," 3.

I. CONVERGENCE IN EXPERIENCE AND IDEOLOGY

Drawn Together by Self-Interest

Jewish Representation of Race and
Race Relations in the Early Twentieth Century

 *Hasia R. Diner*

B Y AND LARGE, common language usage posits an antithetical relationship between the idea of "self-interest" and that of "friendship."
Scholarly and public rhetoric lauds those individuals who seem to have
displayed behavior that we might label "altruistic," while the possibility
that players in a social or political endeavor had some stake in its
outcome taints their behavior as self-serving. Altruism is good, while
self-interest is inherently bad.

While this is not the place to probe the dichotomization of "self-
interest" and "friendship," the origins of this binary conceptualization,
or the lack of any body of evidence proving the existence of "altruism" as
a real category of behavior, the use of these opposites has surely clouded
our understanding of one phenomenon in the history of race in the
United States, the history of how Jews interacted with and understood
the experiences of African Americans. From the vantage point of the late
twentieth century, it is easy to make statements about altruism and self-
interest. Elements within the Jewish world, although surely not its total-
ity, claim that Jewish contributions to the Civil Rights Movement and to
other forms of advancement for African Americans emanated solely
from the Jewish desire to do good, to act morally in an immoral society.
Elements within the Black world posit past Jewish behavior as utterly
self-serving, calculating, and devoid of moral content. Both sets of voices
tell us more about contemporary politics than about history; both sets of
voices tell the story they want to tell, oblivious to the historical record.

We can understand one part of this misreading of history by examining how Jews in the early decades of the twentieth century viewed
Blacks, how they understood racism against African Americans, and
how their literature interpreted these issues. They quite clearly posited
no distance between advocating for someone else—in this case Black

people—and advancing their own, long-range goals as new Americans. Without saying it directly, they asserted the opposite: self-interest drew these two peoples together.

The media of Jewish public opinion—newspapers and magazines, in both Yiddish and English—and imaginative literature—poems, short stories, novels, dramatic works—as well as sermons, public addresses, and other forms of discourse all acknowledged that the subjugation of Blacks amounted to a "stain of shame on the American flag" (a phrase often repeated in the Yiddish press), that Jews and Blacks shared a field of understanding and a common political agenda, and that the Jew more than any other American could "plead for his stricken brother." Most of the Jews whose words are accessible to us for analysis—newspaper reporters, novelists, rabbis, poets, labor leaders, and philanthropists—recognized, in varying degrees of insight and with varying degrees of clarity, that the advancement of civil rights, the eradication of racial violence, and the creation of a social structure where ancestry would not count in the job market, in the university admissions office, or in other sectors of the supposedly "neutral" sphere of American public life would benefit Jews as much as they did African Americans.

The ways in which Jews acted upon these beliefs corroborates the intensity of the words they used. Obviously, not all Jews participated in the civil rights effort, donated money to philanthropic and other kinds of advancement efforts, signed petitions, or engaged in other demonstrable forms of solidarity. Thus, three points need to be made in order to contextualize the implications of their words. First, a striking number of Jews did in fact "act" in whatever capacity they could to help eradicate racism.[1] Second, just as self-interest and service to others ought not to be considered opposites, so too action and rhetoric function in a manner more complicated than polarities. Writing an editorial against racism, delivering a lecture that lauds the achievements of African American culture and history, and orating in a synagogue on the need for greater equality in the United States all constitute action as well as words. To use language is to act. Finally, the words that the newspapers printed or that the rabbis spoke *were* read and heard. While we have no way of knowing how readers understood the rhetoric or what sense listeners made of the

1. For further discussion see my full-length treatment of this issue in *In the Almost Promised Land: American Jews and Blacks, 1915–1935* (1977; rpt. Baltimore: Johns Hopkins University Press, 1995); the phrase "stricken brother" comes from the response of a rabbi to the NAACP when it was searching for speakers to plead the cause of the association and the plight of African Americans. See "Speakers Bureau Form," March 1919, NAACP Papers, Manuscript Division, Library of Congress.

words, we can with some degree of satisfaction assume from their very repetition, from the frequency with which they were used, that they must have struck a responsive chord.

At the beginning of the twentieth century Jews wrote voluminously about Blacks in America, their history, their present, and even their future. A deep interest in race and racism is evident in the Yiddish press as well as in the English-language Jewish magazines. These publications ran the gamut from the religiously traditional, politically conservative *Yiddishe Tageblatt* to the socialist *Jewish Daily Forward*, through various English periodicals, such as the *American Hebrew*, the *Israelite*, and the *Jewish Messenger*, which clearly catered to an Americanized audience, across the spectrum of political and religious orientations. In each case, the editors and writers kept close tabs on race riots, lynchings, and political and legal decisions touching on the questions of race. They chronicled the achievements of African American men and women in their various endeavors as evidence that the attributions of inferiority that the vast majority of Americans endorsed as true had, indeed, no basis in fact.

Each of the Jewish media of the early twentieth century put its own particular gloss on these issues as befit its audience, reflecting and appealing on the basis of political orientation, level of religious piety, class, linguistic preference (or ability), and other criteria that divided American Jews of these years. For example, the Yiddish papers wrote about race (and about almost everything) in much more florid, emotional, and intense ways than did the English-language publications. Likewise, the socialist *Jewish Daily Forward* saw the problems of race as embedded within the evils of capitalism, while the *Tageblatt* did not. This is not surprising since they espoused different political cultures. But more important, these publications differed little in their condemnation of racism, as behavior and as American ideology.

One of the oldest Yiddish newspapers published in America, founded in 1885, the *Yiddishe Tageblatt* (referred to in English as the "Jewish Daily News") defined itself as an Orthodox newspaper. It constantly editorialized against Reform Judaism on the one hand and socialism—or any other variant of radicalism that flourished in the Jewish enclaves of America and Eastern Europe—on the other. Its stance on American politics leaned decidedly to the conservative side, and it even supported Republican candidates and condemned strikes in the needle trades. Finally, while it did not take a definitive stand on one new, radical movement, Zionism, it tended to publish articles sympathetic to the idea of a return to a Jewish homeland, and it criticized Jewish leaders who themselves criticized Zionist aspirations. The clearly conservative *Tageblatt*, however, minced no words when it came to detailing for its readers the horrors of racism and the violence visited upon Blacks in America.

Hundreds of articles appeared in the *Tageblatt* in the years from 1915 to 1935 dealing with racism and the status of American Blacks. One example of this enormous corpus of commentary may suffice in order to demonstrate the uncharacteristically harsh tone that this newspaper used when dealing with this subject. On the day following the July 2, 1917, race riot in East St. Louis, Illinois, the *Tageblatt* moved its lead editorial to a front page banded in black; in it the editor cried out:

> That which happened in East St. Louis fills every person who has a human heart and soul with horror and shock. In the streets on an American city, over which flies the flag of stars and stripes—the flag of the land of progress and humanity—a slaughter was organized on innocent people. They were murdered in the streets, shot, hanged, beaten and killed. The ground in East St. Louis drank human blood, shed by citizens of the most civilized country in the world.[2]

The *Morgen Journal*, New York's only Yiddish morning newspaper, was founded in 1901 and merged with the *Tageblatt* in 1928. Its editorial policy complemented that of the *Tageblatt*, and its first editor-publisher, Joseph Saphirstein, an immigrant from Bialystok, Poland, claimed that he wanted to prove that "Orthodox Judaism and patriotic Americanism could coexist harmoniously."[3] Yet despite its desire to link traditional Judaism with the American mainstream, the *Morgen Journal* did not hesitate to condemn American policies when they jarred with human rights. In an American history series for its readers—most of whom would have been new Americans—the *Morgen Journal* noted that many of the great heroes of American life had been slaveowners, and George Washington and Thomas Jefferson among them had refused to extend democracy to "millions of human beings who were considered property," while Abraham Lincoln earned the newspaper's praise because he "carried out the ideas of John Brown."[4] The *Morgen Journal*'s tone differed little from that of the *Tageblatt* when it came to detailing the viciousness of racism, and its report on the East St. Louis race riot graphically described how the white mob was "so large, so agitated and so blood thirsty . . . it set on fire the Negro quarter and the poor houses. Women and children were not

2. *Yiddishe Tageblatt*, July 3, 1917, 1.
3. Robert Park, *The Immigrant Press and Its Control* (New York: Harper and Brothers, 1922), 355.
4. *Morgen Journal*, March 29, 1925, 4.

spared by the wild beasts. . . . When Negroes ran out of their burning houses, screaming, they were shot down without mercy."[5] In fact, similar editorials and equally empathetic reportage appeared in the Yiddish press after every race riot and after every lynching. The newspapers seem to have had standard race riot and lynching editorials that they retrieved when needed. The language of the East St. Louis pieces is typical of the rhetoric on race in these newspapers and was often repeated verbatim.

The *Jewish Daily Forward,* the most widely circulating Yiddish news-paper in the United States, which in 1916 boasted a circulation of 198,982, was founded in 1897. For most of its history, it and its editor, Abraham Cahan, functioned as inseparable entities, and its influence rippled through all aspects of Eastern European Jewish immigrant life in the United States. It shaped the Yiddish theater, encouraged the flourishing of Jewish letters, influenced the day-to-day workings of the Jewish labor movement, and articulated a political agenda for the immigrant Jews of New York and the other large cities. Special editions of the *Forward* were published for Philadelphia, Chicago, Baltimore, Boston, and a half-dozen other cities. The *Forward's* socialist politics were evident throughout the newspaper and shaped its policies in every possible way.

In its handling of race and race relations it sounded no more, or no less, passionate than did its more politically conservative and religiously traditional competitors, the *Tageblatt* and the *Morgen Journal.* For exam-ple, on an "ordinary" day in 1921 it reported on a lynching in Georgia. (The Yiddish press used the English word *lynch* and then applied stan-dard Yiddish grammatical patterns to it.) The front-page headline read: "Hair Stands Up When You Read About the Slaughter of Negroes in Georgia." The article went on to sarcastically portray the "civilized whites" who watched with glee as the victim suffered and who cheered as he cried out in pain. "The cries that carried for blocks and blocks were quickly drowned by the cheers of the excited mobs." The *Forward* snidely referred to these lynchings as "folk holidays" of the American people: events of public celebration and markers of a communal culture.[6] The *Forward* used such a phrase to highlight its condemnation not just of lynchings and racism but of the very character of the American people.

Some of the most eloquent and pained discussions of racial violence appeared in the *Forward* and the other newspapers when a riot, lynching, or other act of outrage happened to take place on an American holiday,

5. *Morgen Journal,* May 31, 1917, 2.
6. *Jewish Daily Forward,* August 1, 1915, 1.

the Fourth of July and Memorial Day in particular. In 1927, a few days after Memorial Day, the *Forward* reported on a case involving the mal-treatment of Black convict laborers. "Where," it asked:

> is the spirit of freedom with which our America is always priding it-self? And where is the holiness of the Constitution which is so often mentioned?
>   And Monday, the 30th of May, the American people decorated the graves of those who fell in the great battle to free the slaves in Amer-ica and to free America from the stain of the shame of slavery. The slaves are today not free and on America, the stain of the shame of slavery is still evident.[7]

The only substantive difference between the way the *Forward* pre-sented race relations and the way the other Yiddish newspapers did can be seen in its more Marxist orientation, giving extensive coverage to eco-nomic issues as they involved African Americans and reporting more often—and very positively—on trade union organizing among Black workers. The similarities among the newspapers far outweighed the dif-ferences; they all dwelt on the evils of racism, the connection between racism and American political life, racism's deep and complex connec-tion to American culture, and the efforts by African Americans to ame-liorate their lives through political action. The newspapers treated in great detail the activism of civil rights organizations and the rightness of the fact that "the Negro demands justice; he demands that the law protect him just as it protects the whites; he demands from the government in Washington that it enforce the points written into the Constitution."[8]

If the riots in East St. Louis offered the Yiddish press a context in which to condemn racism, positing the suffering of African Americans as vic-tims, they also offered a graphic example of assertiveness, protest, and solidarity in the Black community. Thus, the politically conservative *Tageblatt* applauded the dignity of the "silent protest" organized by the NAACP in the aftermath of the riots. It described to its readers how the march proceeded down New York's Fifth Avenue:

> Without music, without speeches, without applause, and without resolutions a procession of Negroes marched. . . . It was a quiet protest against Jim Crow, against the injustices done to them, a protest against being locked into separate neighborhoods . . . against constant persecution . . . 10,000 Negroes marched in line in the mourning parade over East St. Louis and 20,000 other Negroes were standing along the streets through which the procession went. The

7. *Jewish Daily Forward*, June 2, 1927, 2.
8. *Morgen Journal*, December 4, 1921, 5.

Negro race silently protested the blood that was spilled. . . . The pro-
cession marched to awaken sympathy, to awaken the American conscience that was asleep.[9]

More important, the *Tageblatt's* analysis of America's racial dilemma recognized that sporadic violence grew out of and was made possible by
other, less dramatic, less gruesome, but constant reminders of racism:
segregation as a fact of everyday life.

Detailing the ways in which the Yiddish press, or other organs of Jewish public opinion, represented the issues of race and racism in the opening decades of the twentieth century would be a worthwhile enterprise in
and of itself. Yet the task at hand involves more than a mere chronicling
of who said what and when. An exploration of the language used and
metaphors invoked deepens our understanding of Jews' perceived self-
interest in representing Blacks.

When the Yiddish press reported on issues involving African Americans it employed the idioms of Jewish history and Jewish life. Race riots
rarely were called "race riots." Rather they were described in the newspapers as "pogroms," and lynchings took place on the "auto-da-fe," the
site of the fifteenth-century Spanish Inquisition where countless Jews and
crypto-Jews—*conversos*—went to their deaths for the fact of their Jewishness. Lynchers might be called "Cossaks" or referred to as the "White
Hundred," the crack troops used by various czarist regimes in Russia in
pogroms against the Jews. African Americans lived in "ghettos," and
accusations against Black men for insulting or raping White women
amounted to "blood libels." Black people in the United States descended
from human beings who had been ripped from their African homes,
thrown into America, and found themselves in their own "golah"
(or "goles"), that is, living in exile and diaspora: these were all loaded
and dense terms in the consciousness of the Yiddish press's readers and
writers.

Let me give two powerful examples of this kind of linguistic linkage in
the Yiddish press. The *Tageblatt, Morgen Journal,* and *Forward* all covered
extensively the activities of Marcus Garvey and the Universal Negro Improvement Association. The movement, which advocated Black economic development, enhanced self-esteem, and, ultimately, a return to
Africa, stirred deep interest in the Yiddish press. The movement, the papers all noted, amounted to a black version of Zionism, a potent movement sweeping the Jewish world on both sides of the Atlantic. Indeed
they referred to it as "Black Zionism." Garvey served as the "Black

9. *Yiddishe Tageblatt,* July 28, 1917, 2.

Herzl," in reference to Theodor Herzl, a leader of the Zionist movement, and on one occasion when a reporter attended a Garveyite rally at Madison Square Garden, he described how all assembled had stood up to sing the "Black Hatikvah," or the Zionist anthem meaning "the hope."

Quite consistently, the *Tageblatt* and the *Morgen Journal*, themselves supportive of Zionism, editorialized that Garvey's organization "with its protests and nationalistic strivings will ring throughout the world and will shake up the conscience of the white population of America," and that perhaps what Blacks needed was "a place of their own under the sun where they could live a free life."[10] The socialist *Forward*, which maintained at most a lukewarm stance toward Zionism, took a more jaundiced view of Garvey, reported less on him than did the other newspapers, and instead offered up A. Philip Randolph, the labor leader and organizer of the Brotherhood of Sleeping Car Porters, as a working-class hero for Americans, Black and White.

For a second example of the entwined imagery of Black life and Jewish life, let me again turn to East St. Louis. The *Forward*, searching for words to describe the horror of the riot, turned to a salient example from the contemporary Jewish experience: the Kishinev pogrom of 1903. "Everywhere the same world," noted the *Forward*,

> Kishinev and St. Louis—the same soil, the same people. It is a distance of four-and-a-half thousand miles between these two cities and yet they are so close and so similar to each other. . . . Actually twin sisters, which could easily be mistaken for each other. Four-and-a-half thousand miles apart, but the same events in both. . . . The same brutality, the same wildness, the same human beasts. There in Kishinev, they ripped open people's bellies and stuffed them with feathers; here in St. Louis, houses were set on fire and women and children were allowed to burn alive. Which is better? It is a matter of taste: some like things stuffed, others like them roasted. . . . The Anglo-Saxon likes an open fire, broiled steak; this is his national food.[11]

Where in all of this can we find the issue of self-interest? How did the Jewish rhetorical stance, as articulated in these Yiddish newspapers, bridge the gap between self-interest and friendship or alliance? How can this rhetoric—and that presented here amounts to a scant fraction of what appeared about Blacks in the Yiddish press, the English-language Jewish press, imaginative fiction, as well as lectures and sermons—be linked to a perceived Jewish self-interest?

10. *Yiddishe Tageblatt*, August 18, 1924, 5; *Morgen Journal*, August 3, 1917, 7.
11. *Jewish Daily Forward*, July 28, 1917, 12.

If we take self-interest to refer not to selfishness or to opportunism but rather to the development of a rhetorical repertoire and a political and cultural agenda, then the gap, so trumpeted in contemporary discourse, appears small indeed. The words through which Jews linked their identities and their fates with those of Blacks amounted to action. Unlike most White Americans of the early twentieth century, they did not seek to distance themselves from African Americans but rather posited a community of interest. Their words, which clearly indicated that they saw Black people through Jewish eyes, may have made the Blacks "objects," but Jews nonetheless included themselves in their vision of the situation of the "other."

The confluence of self-interest and friendship existed on multiple levels. First, those issues that occupied the attention and energy of the Civil Rights Movement in the early decades of the twentieth century and that emerged in the activities and writings of the "race" men and women had a Jewish angle as well. That is, Jews believed that they too suffered from public policies that took into account race. After all, well into the 1930s and 1940s scientific racists considered Jews to be a distinct race with inherent biological and phenotypical characteristics that reflected innate moral and mental deficiencies. This scientific outlook ran through the writings of Madison Grant, E. A. Ross, and many other American biological determinists and served as the scientific justification for Nazi policies. In addition, Jews often found themselves restricted in terms of employment, college and university admissions, housing, and public accommodations. Furthermore, the National Origins Acts of 1921 and 1924, which severely curtailed immigration to the United States on the basis of race, worked to the detriment of perceived Jewish interests, something that would in the 1930s and 1940s become even more painfully clear than it appeared at the time of the acts' passage.

Thus, Jewish representations of Blacks in texts that circulated only in the Jewish world and in those that reached mixed audiences, as well as the Jewish involvement in the Civil Rights Movement and other movements to eradicate distinctions among Americans based on ancestry—of whatever kind—coincided with the Black political agenda just as they did with the Jewish agenda, and that shared participation can be attributed to a shared self-interest. Jews ultimately believed that a society that did not make distinctions between people in matters of public policy—broadly defined—was a better place for both Jews and African Americans.

The confluence of self-interest and alliance can be viewed on a deeper and more cultural level. Jews came to America as permanent immigrants and sought almost immediately to integrate themselves into their new home and carve out for themselves a special niche in that place. Forging a Jewish-Black alliance provided them with several handy tools for accomplishing that mission. Taking up the cause of Blacks provided them, first, with a special mission, a mission for which they believed they were perfectly suited by their history and their present situation. After all, through the medium of race and race relations, they could prove how much they had internalized the "true" principles of American culture—those principles encoded in the Constitution and in the Declaration of Independence—and how much more American they should be considered than the "real" Americans, who by their actions and their words denied the basic principles of American life.

As such, on a cultural level, Jews assumed their familiar and comfortable role as middlemen. They stood between White Americans, privileged and insensitive, and African Americans, bearers of a unique culture and victimized by the society in which they had to live. Jews argued that they understood Black people as no other Americans did and that they had an important role to play in cleaning off that "stain of shame" from the American flag. As the *Tageblatt* understood it, again in the context of East St. Louis:

> A Jewish heart is more moved by reading the banners which were carried in the East St. Louis Silent Protest, thinking about the injustices being done to the whole race. Who but a Jew can taste oppression? Who but a Jew knows so well what it means to be dealt out segregation laws and pogroms? Jews who have lived through all of these things in the Old World can well empathize with those who walked in the procession, can feel the oppression which the march protested.[12]

This empathy, picked up by all of the newspapers—and again by the whole panoply of other literary sources beyond the scope of this essay—obliged Jews to do something for Blacks and with Blacks. The *Forward,* writing in 1920 about an upsurge in union activity among Black workers, reported that Blacks were "placing much hope in the Jewish unions, the Jewish Workmen's Circles, the Jewish socialist organizations." Black Americans, the newspaper asserted with great certainty,

> are turning to us with more hope than to any other workers organizations because the Jews can sympathize and empathize more with them. That which the Negroes suffer in America, the Jews in many parts of Europe are now suffering in a more massive degree. Many of

12. *Yiddishe Tageblatt,* July 30, 1917, 3.

us ourselves were oppressed in Old Russia as the Negroes are now in the free America. We can understand them better and therefore we sound their appeal wide and quickly.[13]

The key phrase, one repeated constantly by the Yiddish press, is "in the free America." The Yiddish press (and again this would be true for almost any other Jewish source of the early twentieth century) emphasized that American society had not lived up to its creed and that it was the role of the Jews to bring the nation to task and to place the needs of Blacks onto the American political agenda. In doing this, they believed, they not only helped Blacks but also served the larger society, contributing to the welfare of all. And this service might possibly bring in its wake benefits for American Jews. It would win them thanks and recognition for doing a crucial job that no one had heretofore taken up, and that in turn would be of immense help in solidifying the social and political lot of the Jews.

The issues of Black exclusion and oppression provided a stalking-horse for American Jewish writers who constantly fretted over the power of anti-Semitism in America and in Europe. While out of fear they often tried to downplay the extent of anti-Jewish action and sentiment in the United States, they held up the indisputably worse position of Blacks as an apt illustration of the negative forces at work in the country, forces that had the power to crush the dreams of an immigrant generation and that could make the United States less than they had hoped for, and more like all of their previous diaspora homes. Analyzing the rhetoric Jews employed when inveighing against racism helps probe the subtle roots of their involvement and the degree to which the words and deeds grew out of a self-interest that made alliance possible.

Being "good" to Blacks, championing their cause, was depicted as a natural outgrowth of the Jewish tradition, and as ethnic group leaders the writers, editors, rabbis, and orators had a real stake in the preservation of the Jewish tradition, however they defined that. They believed that their efforts and concerns for African Americans set Jews apart from other Americans, and apart from most Christians. This became in effect part of the American version of the concept of the Chosen People, the American adaptation of the message of Sinai. Indeed, in a 1942 work, "What Is Torah: A Cantata for Unison Chorus and Piano," written by Ira Eisenstein and Judith Kaplan Eisenstein for the Reconstruction movement's celebration of Shavuot, the springtime holiday celebrating the giving of the Torah, the first chorus asks repeatedly, "What is Torah?" The other choruses offer hundreds of sung and spoken answers: "it is the

13. *Jewish Daily Forward*, January 5, 1920, 3

anguish of a people enslaved," "it is the land the soil, mother earth . . . Eretz Yisrael," "it is a dim bet hamidrash [study house], . . . a lone kabbalist in mystic contemplation," "it is a mother crooning over her babe." And, among these dense Jewish references, the chorus continues:

> The Torah is Israel's gift to humanity . . . the impress of Israel upon the civilizations of mankind . . . the cornerstone of the great western religions . . . the inspiration of modern ideals of freedom, equality, justice. Torah is the hope of the Negro people, plunged into poverty and despair. . . . In all their tragic years upon this continent, the memory of Israel's struggle has kept their faith alive.[14]

Thus, the rhetoric of Jewishness and the imagery of Black people and their condition in the United States conjoined to help prove that Jews had a special mission in America and that Jewishness truly deserved, like the faith of "the Negro people," to be "kept . . . alive."

While Jewish leaders and writers wanted to retain the integrity of their group and the core of their culture, they also felt compelled to prove to Americans that Jews did not constitute an unassimilable group, selfish (clearly worse than self-interested) and miserly, two of the most repeated stereotypes of Jews since Medieval times. Rather Jews could orate in the press—and from the pulpit and the podium as well—on how American they had become, how fundamentally they had internalized the principles of the Constitution and the Declaration of Independence, and how well versed they had become with the "true" meaning of American history.

In fact, they assumed the posture that they, only one generation out of the ghetto—and indeed in some places in Eastern Europe they still inhabited it—had internalized those principles and had learned that history better than had the "real" Americans. By doing this, they claimed the right to call themselves American. In articles galore, in novels, poems, and short stories, they placed Jews in the position of helpers of American Blacks and thus countered the arguments so often hurled against them. One example of this process, drawn from an English-language Jewish publication, the *American Hebrew*, could just as likely have appeared in any of the dozens of such publications. The 1924 news item described a substantial investment by philanthropist Julius Rosenwald in a Black-owned insurance company that had stood on the brink of bankruptcy. The firm's owner, Herman E. Perry, opposed by a group of White bankers, had turned to Rosenwald for help, and Rosenwald had assisted

14. Ira Eisenstein and Judith Kaplan Eisenstein, "What Is Torah: A Cantata for Unison Chorus and Piano" (New York: Jewish Reconstructionist Foundation, 1942).

him with keeping his business afloat. More important than the details of the story is the nature of the Jewish reporting of it. The *American Hebrew*, after presenting the bare-bones details of the story, remarked, "Here's an item for Ford's Folly. A group of Nordics in the South—white 100 percent, American money lenders—were about to stop Herman E. Perry, Negro financier of Atlanta . . . when a JEW by the name of Julius Rosenwald stepped in."[15] The story resonated with Jewish concerns. It appeared at the height of the Jewish alarm and confrontation with Henry Ford over his publication of "The Protocols of the Elders of Zion" in the *Dearborn Independent.* Some at the time were positing the existence of a "Nordic" race as a superior group, and nativists in the United States had successfully pushed through immigration restrictions aimed at those who could never qualify for "one hundred percent Americanism," as the popular phrase of the day was cast. Thus, the *American Hebrew* story portrayed the Jew as the generous benefactor, not the usurious moneylender. The moneylenders had become White southerners.

A Jewish preoccupation with security and an overwhelming need for recognition were felt most acutely in the early decades of the twentieth century when the Jewish population of America was stabilizing and at the same time groping for a comfortable niche in American life. The various rhetorical devices they created allowed them to locate their behavior and words in the soil both of Judaism and of "real" Americanism. The use of Black issues as a vehicle to bring American Jewry through the confusing and tortuous path toward accommodation emerged most keenly in this period. In these years the Jewish fascination with Black America, concern with race, and abhorrence of racism highlighted the ways in which the interests of Jews and of Blacks at that time came together, with self-interest and friendship part and parcel of the same phenomenon. Rather than standing in opposition to each other, Jewish needs and African American needs reached a confluence that made them one and the same in both words and deeds.

15. *American Hebrew* 105 (July 3, 1925), 262.

Black Zionism

Marcus Garvey and the Jewish Question

—————————— *Robert A. Hill* ——————————

> One of the first successes of our movement, one that is even now perceived in its larger outlines, is the transformation of the Jewish Question into a Zion Question.
>
> THEODOR HERZL

> Africa remains the heritage of Black people, as Palestine is of the Jews.
>
> MARCUS GARVEY

> From beyond the rivers of Ethiopia my suppliants, even the daughter of my dispersed, shall bring mine offering.
>
> ZEPHANIAH 3:10

A FRICA WAS the great desideratum of Marcus Garvey and the Garvey movement. Calling for "Africa for the Africans, those at home and abroad," Garvey preached a doctrine that he also called "African Redemption," one that looked to the restoration of Africa. "Like the other heretofore oppressed peoples of the world," Garvey declared in November 1918, in the immediate aftermath of the signing of the Armistice, the New Negro had now taken to the political stage "determined to get restored to him his ancestral rights" in Africa.[1] In a circular issued around the same time proclaiming his movement "THE GREATEST MOVEMENT IN THE HISTORY OF THE NEGROES OF THE WORLD," Garvey called attention to the wider political context of the times. "The Irish, the Jews, the East Indians and all other oppressed peoples are getting together to demand from their oppressors Liberty, Justice, Equality," he declared, "and we

---

1. *Negro World* (hereafter *NW*), editorial, November 30, 1918, cited in *The Marcus Garvey and Universal Negro Improvement Association Papers* (Los Angeles and Berkeley: University of California Press, 1983–), 1:303, cited hereafter as *MGP*.

now call upon the four hundred millions of Negro People of the world to do likewise."[2] Of the three movements singled out by Garvey for special mention, however, that of redeeming "bleeding Ethiopia and scattered Ethiopia" bore the greatest political resemblance to Jewish Zionism.[3]

By no means the least aspect of this affinity was Garvey's attainment of the mythic status of a modern-day redeemer, or Black Moses, as he was called, of his people. The affinity between Garveyism and Zionism was striking and became increasingly pronounced over time. Speaking before the fourth international convention of the Universal Negro Improvement Association (UNIA) in August 1924, the Dahoman Kojo Tovalou-Houenou went so far as to declare the Garvey movement to be "the Zionism of the Black Race."[4] The redemption of Africa, which Garvey took to mean that Africa must be for the Africans, and them exclusively, was thus on a par, ideologically, with the Zionist goal of restoring Palestine for the Jews.[5] The goal of Jewish restoration also served as the key political paradigm for the sense of unity that the leaders and supporters of the scattered Garvey movement sought to communicate. "Old Glory, when you come back, won't you cry aloud and recognize Palestine for the Jews officially, Ireland for the Irish officially, and Africa for the African officially?" implored Rev. J. W. H. Eason, speaking before the opening of the first UNIA convention in Madison Square Garden in August 1920.[6] From Johannesburg, South Africa, the same sentiment was expressed. "The first object of the Association," wrote a UNIA supporter in *Abantu-Batho*, "is to unite all the various classes of Negroes in America and to infuse amongst them a spirit of race consciousness so as to claim themselves a Nation within the principle of self-determination, like the Jews who are returning to Palestine as a small nation under the protection of the League of Nations . . . there to establish a Jewish Kingdom as of old." "After all is said and done," a Garvey supporter in South Africa, Enock Mazilinko, wrote the *Negro World* to say, "Africans have the same confidence in Marcus Garvey which the Israelites had in Moses."[7]

The sympathetic quality of this ideological identification with Jewish Zionism infusing the rhetoric of Garvey and his movement was in contrast, however, with the political pressure that Garvey and other Blacks

2. *MGP*, facsimile, 1:315.
3. *NW*, February 1, 1919 (cited in *MGP*, 1:356). Garvey was speaking in New York City on January 26, 1919.
4. *Les Continents*, August 1924.
5. *NW*, April 5, 1919 (cited in *MGP*, 1:396).
6. *MGP*, 2:506.
7. *Abantu-Batho*, November 11, 1920; *NW*, February 9, 1929.

felt they were subjected to by Jews and Jewish interests. Thus, while Jewish Zionism served as a kind of political paradigm in the articulation of Black nationalist consciousness, Jews as a social force were also experienced by Garvey and other Black nationalist spokesmen as a source of political pressure hindering the fullest expression and attainment of Black self-determination.

The dialectical nature of this opposing movement of paradigm and countervailing pressure, and the various forms it has assumed, is what makes Garvey such a pivotal figure in the unfolding of the relationship between Blacks and Jews in the United States. "The fact is," Roi Ottley asserted, "Marcus Garvey was the first Negro leader to raise the 'Jewish question' in Negro life."[8] The Garvey movement is also crucial in the examination of Black-Jewish relations for an important reason having to do with the nature of Jewish identity. It was the architect of political Zionism, Theodor Herzl, who emphasized, addressing the First Zionist Congress in August 1897, that one of the movement's seminal achievements was "the transformation of the Jewish Question into a Zion Question."[9]

Historically, it was, in reality, not Garvey but the venerable African sage Edward Wilmot Blyden who first recognized the special significance of the Jewish question in the advancement of Black consciousness. Like so much else that he contributed in pioneering the ideology of African nationalism, Blyden welcomed the birth of political Zionism and its charter promulgated at the First Zionist Congress. In 1866 Blyden visited the Holy Land—"to see Jerusalem and Mount Zion, the joy of the whole earth," as he would refer to the trip in his pamphlet *The Jewish Question.* The full record of Blyden's visit to Jerusalem and his impressions are reported in his booklet *From West Africa to Palestine.*[10]

"I have taken, and do take," Blyden declares in *The Jewish Question,* which is dedicated to the Jewish merchant Louis Solomon of Liverpool and West Africa, "the deepest possible interest in the current history of the Jews—especially in that marvellous movement called Zionism." He then argues that what Zionism signifies is the promise of regeneration of humanity as a whole. Referring to the central role played by Theodor Herzl in the unfolding, Blyden goes on:

8. Roi Ottley, *New World A-Comin': Inside Black America* (1943; rpt. New York: Arno Press, 1968), 122.
9. "Opening Address at the First Zionist Congress," Basel, Switzerland, August 29, 1897, in *Zionist Writings: Essays and Addresses of Theodor Herzl,* trans. Harry Zohn (New York: Herzl Press, 1973), 1:134.
10. Edward Wilmot Blyden, *The Jewish Question* (Liverpool: Lionel Hart and Co., 1898) and *From West Africa to Palestine* (Freetown, 1873).

> Theodor Herzl has put forth ideas in his "Jewish State" which have
> given such an impetus to the real work of the Jews as must tell with
> enormous effect upon their future history. It has created an agitation
> which is stirring thinking minds all over the civilized world. It is
> making many a leader of thought in philosophy, science, and religion
> revise his position.[11]

Blyden welcomed the salutary effect that he claimed had resulted from
"that 'tidal wave' from Vienna—that inspiration almost Mosaic in its
originality and in its tendency, which drew crowds of Israelites to Basle
in August, 1897, and has drawn them thither again in 1898" (8). He took
special note of the regenerative effect of Zionism upon the Jews themselves. "It is gratifying," he declared, "to notice that the Zionist movement is having its effect upon the whole Jewish community, or rather,
upon all the Jewish communities—both Zionists and Anti-Zionists—raising them out of an indifferent materialism into spiritual contemplation,
and to a more active sense of racial privileges and responsibilities" (8).

Blyden cautioned Jews, however, that they had "a far higher and no-
bler work to accomplish for humanity than establishing a political power
in one corner of the earth" (8). As part of the larger impulse of spiritual
reform that he saw animating humanity, Blyden urged upon Jews a role
that would help reverse the deleterious effects upon Africans and other
non-White peoples that were the "concomitants of [Christian] civilization." "These perishing peoples," he declared, "are looking anxiously for
some influence to save them from what by many of their Christian teachers is supposed to be their inevitable and melancholy destiny" (12).

Africa had special claim upon the Jews in this undertaking. "Have the
Jews no witness to bear in inter-tropical Africa?" he asks and then answers the question thus: "If the world owes an immense debt to the Jews,
the Jews as well as the rest of mankind owe an immense debt to Africa."
It was in Africa that the Jews found "the house of preservation," out of
which they "grew to be a nation." Moreover, Blyden asserts, "there are
thousands of Jacob's descendants hidden there under Ethiopian garb . . .
remnants of Jews there to-day, who have never left it since Jacob, with
seventy souls, entered it from Canaan" (16).

Blyden combines his extraordinary eulogy of the Jews with a harsh critique of the shortcomings of "the purely secular agencies of Japhetic rule"
arising out of the vicissitudes of European colonial rule in Africa. He then
ends his evaluation with an entreaty that the Jews assist in the regeneration of Africa:

11. Blyden, *The Jewish Question*, 7; hereafter cited in the text by page number.

Now Africa appeals to the Jew ... to come with his scientific and
other culture, gathered by his exile in many lands, and with his
special spiritual endowments, to the assistance of Ishmael in the
higher work for Africa which Japheth, through a few struggling representatives, is laboring heroically under great disadvantages to
carry out. ... They would find there religious and spiritual aspirations kindred to their own, and they would recognize the existence in
the people of large possibilities for the higher work of humanity—
possibilities of which now, as the African is a complete stranger to
them they can have no conception whatever. (23-24)

The significance that Blyden attached to Jewish Zionism as a program
of racial, political, and spiritual regeneration, coming at a time when
Africa was reeling from the effects of European partition and coloniza-
tion, was undoubted. It seems probable that the same would have been
true for other Blacks, whether or not they arrived at the view indepen-
dently or came to it through the influence that Blyden's writings exerted
throughout fin-de-siècle Africa and among Africans of the dispersion.

Ironically, students of the Pan-African movement seem to have overlooked the possibility of this connection. In particular, there does not appear to be any awareness of the connection in the various accounts of the
historic Pan-African Conference of 1900 in England, out of which was be-
queathed to the political vocabulary of the twentieth century the important concept of organizational Pan-Africanism. This silence is curious,
especially when it is recalled that Herzl's original "Solution of the Jewish
Question" first appeared in England in January 1896, causing the editor
of the *Jewish Chronicle* to assert that "this is one of the most astounding
pronouncements which have ever been put forward on the Jewish question."[12] Herzl's *Der Judenstaat* was translated and published in England
later in 1896, the same year the young Trinidadian Henry Sylvester
Williams, who would originate the idea and become the architect of the
Pan-African Conference, arrived in England. Herzl also spoke in England
in July 1896. His visit caused a stir regarding the Jewish cause that was reflected in the English newspapers; a major interview with him appeared
in the *Sunday Times* of London on July 5, 1986.

In his formal address before a dinner of the Maccabean Club in London, Herzl renewed his call "for a Jewish State."[13] But whereas this audience was made up of upper-middle-class and wealthy Jews who were
"lukewarm and hesitant" about his plan for a Jewish state, the effect was
exactly the opposite when he addressed an enthusiastic rally of Jewish

12. Cited in David Vital, *The Origins of Zionism* (Oxford: Clarendon Press, 1975),
257–58.
13. *Zionist Writings*, trans. Zohn, 34–43.

workingmen in the East End of London. The latter meeting was both a personal triumph and a huge political success; Herzl recorded that during it he "saw and heard my legend being born."[14]

The program of Herzl's Jewish State consisted of two parts. The first called for the establishment of a Society of Jews that would be the political body responsible for Jewish national affairs ("the organ of the national movement") and that, most important, would have "the political authority to negotiate with governments on behalf of the Jewish people."[15] It was also the substance of the proposal made by Herzl at the Maccabean Club dinner. The second part of the Zionist program as enunciated by Herzl called for setting up a chartered Jewish Company that would be the technical body for managing the exodus and resettlement of the Jews in Palestine. The longest chapter in *Der Judenstaat* is devoted to the details of this second body, which Herzl proposed should be situated in London and established under British law.

Was Herzl's 1896 proposal for a Society of Jews a factor in Henry Sylvester Williams's thinking when he issued the call, in 1897, for the creation of an African Association? In the absence of concrete evidence, it is impossible to know with any degree of certainty. What is known is that Williams sustained himself in England, while studying for the bar at Gray's Inn in London, by lecturing for the Church of England Temperance Society, which, according to one of his biographers, "took him to all parts of the British Isles speaking under the auspices of parish churches."[16] Williams also supported himself by lecturing for the National Thrift Society.

The African Association was formally organized in London on September 24, 1897, a month after the launching of the historic First Zionist Congress in Switzerland on August 29, 1897. While the timing of the two events could have been nothing more than coincidence, it is interesting to note the similarity of aims between Williams's African Association and Herzl's proposed Society of Jews. The constitution of the African Association states that its goals were to secure

14. *The Complete Diaries of Theodor Herzl*, ed. Raphael Patai, trans. Harry Zohn (New York: Herzl Press and Thomas Yoseloff, 1960), 1:421–22.

15. Vital, *Origins of Zionism*, 264.

16. Owen Charles Mathurin, *Henry Sylvester Williams and the Origins of the Pan-African Movement, 1869–1911* (Westport, Conn.: Greenwood Press, 1976); see also J. R. Hooker, *Henry Sylvester Williams: Imperial Pan-Africanist* (London: Rex Collings, 1975); Clarence G. Contee, *Henry Sylvester Williams and Origins of Organizational Pan-Africanism: 1897–1902* (Washington, D.C.: Howard University, Department of History, 1973); and Imanuel Geiss, *The Pan-African Movement: A History of Pan-Africanism in America, Europe and Africa*, trans. Ann Keep (New York: Africana Publishing Co., 1974), 176–98.

to Africans and their descendants throughout the world their true civil and political rights, to ameliorate the condition of our oppressed brethren in the continents of Africa, America, and other parts of the world, by promoting efforts to secure effective legislation, to encourage our people in education, industrial and commercial enterprises, to foster friendly relations between the Caucasian and African races, to organize a bureau, a depository, for collections of authorized writings and statistics relating to our people everywhere, and to raise a fund to be used solely for forwarding these purposes.[17]

Like Herzl's Society of Jews, the African Association was organized to negotiate on behalf of African interests with the imperial British government. The pamphlet containing the rules and objectives of the African Association states that the association had been organized because there was no "body of Africans" in Britain to represent "native opinion in national matters affecting the destiny of the African race." It planned therefore to promote and protect the interests of persons claiming African descent, wholly or in part, "in British colonies and other places . . . by appealing to British and colonial governments to redress their wrongs."[18]

The Society of Jews as proposed by Herzl, however, was designed, in the words of David Vital, to "do much more than negotiate. It would promote scientific study of the demography, economic resources, and public opinion of the Jews."[19] In relation to the internal affairs of the Jewish people, the society would attempt to create in the form of public institutions the indispensable nucleus of the future Jewish state.

The year that the African Association was formed, Williams spent a good deal of time, we are told, in the company of his visiting Trinidadian compatriot Emmanuel M. Lazare, who was a lieutenant with the Trinidadian contingent of artillery that had come to England to participate in the celebration of Queen Victoria's Diamond Jubilee, held in June 1897, and a well-known solicitor in Port of Spain. From the name *Lazare,* one might surmise that his father was Jewish. According to Owen Charles Mathurin, one of the biographers of Williams, Lazare's father was from Guadeloupe and was a member of the French regiment Chasseurs d'Afrique who had settled in Trinidad in the nineteenth century.[20]

Beyond what he might have learned from reading English newspapers and through his own network of contacts in the East End of London,

17. *Mirror* (Port-of-Spain, Trinidad), June 1, 1901; *Report of the Pan-African Conference* (London, 1901), 1.
18. *Report of the Pan-African Conference,* 1, cited in Mathurin, *Henry Sylvester Williams,* 47.
19. Vital, *Origins of Zionism,* 265.
20. Mathurin, *Henry Sylvester Williams,* 33–34.

where the major Jewish community in England resided, Williams might also have picked up from discussions with Lazare information and ideas regarding the effect that the agitation unleashed by the Zionist crusade was having among Jews. An echo of Zionist sentiment can be heard in the item for discussion on the agenda of the 1900 Pan-African Conference organized by the African Association that referred to "Europe's Atonement for her Blood-Guiltiness to Africa."[21]

Whatever the precise nature of the ideological influences that inspired Williams to form the African Association in 1897 and thereafter to organize the Pan-African Conference in 1900, it is noteworthy that none of his biographers or commentators explores in any detail the issue of Herzl and the contemporary Zionist agitation. "The name 'African Association' may perhaps be linked with the stillborn project of Thomas Hodgkin more than a generation earlier," notes Imanuel Geiss, "but until further material becomes available one must beware of making such hasty conjectures." Mathurin asserts (with no actual evidence) that "in naming the [Pan-African] conference, Williams and his group must have been aware of the pan-Slav movement," and goes on to mention the existence of the pan-German movement. Clarence G. Contee is just as nonspecific, although he does mention the existence of Zionism as a possible influence, in listing contemporary "pan-movements at the end of the nineteenth-century—Pan-Slavism, Pan-Germanism, Zionism, Pan-Anglo-Saxonism."[22]

Notwithstanding the seeming reluctance of scholars to explore the connection with Zionism with greater rigor, the fact is that all subsequent movements of Black emigration or Black autonomy in the twentieth century have necessarily been compared with the parallel attempts spearheaded by Jewish Zionism. Thus, in October 1915, following the return to America of a party of dispirited survivors of Chief Alfred Charles Sam's "African movement," the *New York Age* made the comparison explicit: "The Jews, with all their racial and religious solidarity, with all their tremendous wealth, which enables them to bring pressure on the governing powers, have failed in their plan to re-establish themselves as a nation in Palestine: much less then is the possibility that the American Negro can accomplish a similar task in Africa."[23]

World War I and the diplomacy associated with the wartime crisis

21. Alexander Walters, *My Life and Work* (New York: Fleming H. Revell, 1917), 253, cited in Hooker, *Henry Sylvester Williams*, 31.
22. Geiss, *Pan-African Movement*, 177; Mathurin, *Henry Sylvester Williams*, 52–53; Contee, *Williams and the Origins of Organizational Pan-Africanism*, 17.
23. "Chief Sam's Expedition," editorial, *New York Age*, October 14, 1915.

changed the entire picture of the attempt to establish a Jewish state in Palestine. Out of the exigencies of war came the singular event that transformed the movement to establish a Jewish homeland in Palestine, placing it on an entirely new political footing. This event was the British government's issuance on November 2, 1917, of the famous Balfour Declaration, which stated, "His Majesty's Government views with favour the establishment in Palestine of a national home for the Jewish people, and will use its best endeavours to facilitate the achievement of this object, it being clearly understood that nothing shall be done which may prejudice the civil and religious rights of existing non-Jewish communities in Palestine, or the rights and political status enjoyed by Jews in any other country."[24]

The declaration was taken by Zionists and their supporters to imply official British endorsement of the concept of an independent Jewish Palestine. The start of Jewish restoration was now a political fact, based upon the unprecedented legitimacy and consequent international diplomatic backing that the Balfour Declaration made possible. The impact upon Zionism of this singular political event was enormous. Zionism, after being trapped in a sort of political limbo, was now infused with new life, as it gained rapid ascendancy in Western Europe, the United States, and among world Jewry.

The impact of this Zionist ascendancy was also felt among African Americans. W. E. B. Du Bois responded with his essay "The Negro's Fatherland," published in *Survey* on November 10, 1917. It called for the establishment of a "great free central African state" that would compensate Blacks for the Atlantic slave trade. "The African movement means to us what the Zionist movement means to the Jews," Du Bois declared, "the centralization of the race effort and the recognition of a racial fount."[25]

Following the signing of the Armistice, Garvey would make a statement that showed how carefully he had been watching these events, particularly the official endorsement of Jewish claims. "This war has brought about a change," Garvey declared, speaking in Bethel AME Church in Baltimore, Maryland, on December 18, 1918:

> It has driven the men of all races to be more selfish, and Negroes, I think Negroes of the world, have been observing, have been watch-

24. David Vital, *Zionism: The Crucial Phase* (Oxford: Clarendon Press, 1987), 293.
25. Robert A. Hill, "Jews and the Enigma of the Pan-African Congress of 1919," in *Jews in Black Perspectives: A Dialogue*, ed. Joseph R. Washington Jr. (Lanham, Md.: University Press of America, 1989); also quoted in David Levering Lewis, *W. E. B. Du Bois: Biography of a Race, 1868–1919* (New York: Henry Holt and Co., 1993), 565.

ing carefully, and have been scrutinizing all these statesmen I have named; the statesmen of America and the statesmen of England, and in four and a half years of war, whilst observing them, whilst listening to every word that fell from their lips, we never heard one syllable from the lips of Woodrow Wilson, from the lips of Theodore Roosevelt in America, from the lips of Bonar Law or Balfour in England, as touching anything relative to the destinies of the Negroes of America or England or the world.[26]

Just the month before, on November 11, 1918, Garvey had cabled to British foreign secretary Arthur Balfour the UNIA's peace aims, which had been announced at a meeting of the UNIA held the previous evening. Although the statement declared that the aims were to be submitted to "the Allied Democracies of Europe and America, and to the people of democratic tendencies of the world," a search of official archives has turned up only a single copy, namely, the one sent to Balfour. Among the UNIA's peace aims was the demand that "the captured German colonies in Africa be turned over to the natives with educated Western and Eastern Negroes as their leaders."[27] The agitation for the turning over of these ex-German colonies in Africa to the autonomous control of "educated Western and Eastern Negroes" was, ideologically, the specific demand that allows Garveyism to be equated with Zionism.

The equation was further reaffirmed in June 1919, when Henrietta Vinton Davis, one of the UNIA's leading lights, speaking at a public meeting in New York, "recit[ed] the valor of first the native Jamaican Negro troops, who volunteered for the war, and who through their charges over the hot Palestinian deserts and up the Mesopotamian Mountains made it possible for the Jewish dream of a restored Jerusalem to become a reality."[28] Her statement is important not only for its conjunction of Jewish aims with the sacrifices of Black Jamaican soldiers but also because it alerts us to the possibility that the model of the UNIA's own Universal African Legion might have come from the Jewish Legion, the military formation of Jewish volunteers in World War I that was the brainchild of militant Zionist Vladimir Jabotinsky, to whom Garvey bears more than a passing ideological resemblance. The members of the Jewish Legion fought as part of the British army to drive the Turks out of Palestine, or Eretz Israel.[29] To elucidate the character of his

26. *MGP*, 1:332.
27. *MGP*, 1:288.
28. *NW*, June 28, 1919, cited in *MGP*, 1:448.
29. Vital, *Zionism: The Crucial Phase*, 228–33; see also Eleanor F. Horvitz, "Philip Paige and the Jewish Legion," *Rhode Island Jewish Historical Notes* 10, no. 1 (1987): 17–25; Matityahu Pinchas, "Pinchas Rutenberg and the Establishment of the Jewish

African Legion, Garvey would himself refer to the example of the Zionists.[30]

The same equation with Zionism was heard when Garvey rose to address the opening of the historic first UNIA convention in Madison Square Garden in August 1920 and read from a telegram "received from Louis Michael [Michel], a Jew from Los Angeles, California." The telegram, which was addressed to the UNIA, stated:

> Los Angeles, Cal., August 1, 1920. Delegates of the Universal Negro Improvement Association: As a Jew, a Zionist and a Socialist I join heartily and unflinchingly in your historical movement for the reclamation of Africa. There is no justice and no peace in this world until the Jew and the Negro both control side by side Palestine and Africa. Louis Michael.

The telegram supplied concrete evidence justifying Garvey's declaration that the UNIA was "in sympathy with the Zionist movement," a sympathy that was also extended to the nationalist causes of Ireland, Egypt, and India.[31]

Who was Louis Michel? Unfortunately, very little is known about him. According to U.S. Bureau of Investigation reports monitoring radical activities in southern California in 1921, Michel was a Russian Jew and socialist who had become a naturalized American citizen. It was reported that during the campaign to deny Asians the legal right to own land in California, he addressed Black audiences in opposition to the proposed legislation. In September 1919 Michel was reported to have spoken before a large Black audience in Los Angeles on the topic, "Why I Am a Friend of the Negro." Later, in 1921, he spoke in Los Angeles on "The Second Emancipation of the Negro." A Bureau of Investigation agent reported that in his speech Michel "advocated Socialism, glorified [Eugene] Debs, and advocated the return of the Negro to Africa and the Jew to Palestine to escape the present American system of Government and prejudice and persecution encountered here."[32]

According to a report that appeared in the *California Eagle*, Michel was

---

Legion of 1914," *Studies in Zionism* (Israel) 6, no. 1 (1985): 15–26; and Morton H. Narrowe, "Jabotinsky and the Zionists in Stockholm (1915)," *Jewish Social Studies* 46, no. 1 (1984): 9–20.

30. Edmund David Cronon, *Black Moses: The Story of Marcus Garvey and the Universal Negro Improvement Association* (Madison: University of Wisconsin Press, 1955), 199; also *Marcus Garvey: Life and Lessons*, ed. Robert A. Hill and Barbara Bair (Los Angeles and Berkeley: University of California Press, 1987), liv.

31. *MGP*, 2:499.

32. *MGP*, 2:509, n. 2.

the author of an epic poem, consisting of sixty stanzas, titled "The Tortured Negro, or The Cry for Justice." Composed and published by the author in 1919, the poem was said to have garnered plaudits from a number of eminent Black men, including Morgan State College Dean William Pickens.[33] It was at the time in circulation "among all classes of people in California."[34] Described as "Mr. Michel's masterpiece," the poem represented "an honorable plea for justice for the 15,000,000 Negroes in the United States who are as nearly American as it is possible to be."

The same issue of the *California Eagle* contained an essay by Michel titled "The Black Man" and written at the explicit request of the publisher. The headline stated that it was authored "by a Jew" and that its purpose was to ask the question, "If I were a colored Man what would I do?" At the end of the lengthy article, Michel gave a brief autobiographical description. "I am a free lance Jew," he stated, "who is not expressing the sentiments of my race, but only my own, personal ideas, that neither Jewish Rabbi nor Jewish layman can control." He continued:

> Some of my Jewish racemen are contemptible snobs and hypocrites, who, forgetting their own plights of former days of their lives in this and other countries, would not lift a finger to help the tortured Negro of America to regain his compromised rights. The majority of the Jews, however, feel for the suffering Negro, though many of them fear to speak out. The writer has no fear and he deems it his duty to speak out regardless of results.

In December 1919 Michel once more contributed to the pages of the *California Eagle,* this time a poem "dedicated to Marcus Garvey, the Moses of the Negroes."[35] The final piece of writing that I have been able to find by Michel is a poem published in *Negro World* on November 18, 1922, titled "The Four Greatest Negro Movements."

By comparison with the gains made by Jewish Zionists, the struggle for Black self-determination was at an impasse. Speaking in Washington, D.C., on September 24, 1920, Garvey criticized past Black leadership, specifically mentioning Booker T. Washington and his successor as head of Tuskegee, Robert Russa Moton, for failure to prepare Blacks for the opportunities presented by the outbreak of the European war. "Because Washington did not prepare us, because Moton did not prepare us," Garvey declared, "there is no Africa for the Negro as there is a Palestine for the Jew, a Poland for the Poles, but what they did not do in the years past

33. "Reaching the High Tide," *California Eagle,* September 13, 1919.
34. "The Tortured Negro or the Cry for Justice," *California Eagle,* September 13, 1919.
35. "Garvey's Ships Float Negro Nation," *California Eagle,* December 13, 1919.

we are going to do now."[36] Garvey was alluding to the official approval bestowed by the supreme council of the League of Nations in April 1920 upon the Balfour Declaration. The British government established a civil administration in Palestine on July 1, 1920, and in August slightly more than 10,000 immigrants arrived in Palestine, all but 315 of them Jewish. The majority of the Jewish group arrived under the auspices of the Zionist World Organization. The British mandate for Palestine was officially approved in July 1922 by the Treaty of Sèvres.

It is clear that Zionism is central not only to the Jewish sense of identity but also to the formation and content of the Pan-African political identity. What we are faced with, in the case of Garvey's relationship with Jewry, however, is the reality of competing Zionisms, one Jewish and the other Black. This is a situation fraught with the possibility of conflict between the two groups. Are Jews able and willing to accept coexistence with an equally valid Black Zionism, or is it their view that there can be only a singularly valid Jewish Zionism? Are Blacks usurpers of and trespassers upon Jewish traditions when they look to Africa as their Zion? If this is not allowed, how can we explain the depth of attachment that African Americans and other descendants of Africa feel and have felt for centuries toward the biblical injunction that "Princes shall come out of Egypt; Ethiopia shall soon stretch out her hands unto God" (Ps. 68:31).

This might be a matter of theological disputation, though the implications for social and political behavior are readily apparent. However, the decisive factor in defining the nature of the relationship subsisting between African Americans and American Jews is not ideological but has to do with the foundation of a national entity. If the foundation of Jewish Zionism was, historically, the Jewish communities of Russia, Poland, and Rumania, conversely the foundation of Black Zionism is America and the African American community. Jewish emigrants from Russia and Eastern Europe represent a displacement to America of Paleo-Zion. From the African American point of view, this represents an encroachment upon the turf of the Black community. It was in Harlem that the program for Africa's redemption was nurtured under the banner of the Garvey movement. It was in Odessa and Vienna that the program for the reclamation of the Jewish homeland was nurtured and given organizational reality. Are African Americans able and willing to recognize that America is, ideologically and historically, not just a nation of Black and White but rather a land comprising multiple nationalisms? Can they recognize that Jewish

36. *MGP*, 3:16.

nationalism has put down strong historical roots in America and had a role in informing the pursuit of the African American Zion?

Once again, the issues that such recognition raises go beyond the purely ideological to the fundamental difference separating the experience of the Jewish and the African American national communities within the United States. African Americans, to put it bluntly, are not going anywhere. Jewish Americans have had the option to leave, and have had it since the founding of the state of Israel, even if they do not choose to exercise it. Ironically, it seems that having the Jewish state of Israel has greatly facilitated the extraordinary assimilation of Jews into post–World War II American society and the consequent relaxation of self-imposed constraints aimed at preserving traditional Jewish identity. Conversely, however, if the African American quest for equal treatment is to be realized in this land, it will, ultimately, be achieved only through the basic transformation of its community, a transformation that will be the most profound that America has ever yet experienced.

Franz Boas's Paradox and the African American Intelligentsia

Vernon J. Williams Jr.

D URING THE past five decades several scholars have celebrated the monumental role that Franz "Uri" Boas played in initiating a social scientific revolution on the issue of race. In earlier publications, I sought to demonstrate that he slowly emerged as an enlightened apostle of antiracism—only after he had virtually nullified the significance of anthropometric measurements of cranial capacities in his assessments of the capabilities of Blacks and had experienced prolonged contacts with members of the African American intelligentsia.

This essay, which treats Boas's changing thought on African Americans, is marked on one end by Boas's first extended conceptualization of the "Negro Problem" in his "Human Faculty as Determined by Race," published in 1894, and on the other end by his last extended discussion of African Americans in the last edition of *The Mind of Primitive Man,* published in 1938. It seeks to substantiate three arguments. First, I will show that Boas emerged as an enlightened apostle of antiracism for our times only after he had virtually nullified the significance of anthropometric measurements in his assessment of the capabilities of African Americans. Nevertheless, as late as 1915, Boas's racial vision was restricted by severe limitations. His attempts to make inferences concerning the capabilities of African Americans led him to conclude that there might be slight differences in the hereditary aptitudes of Blacks and Whites—for example, in music. Second, I will demonstrate that Boas's analysis of prejudice and his particularistic, rational scientific approach to Africans led him to conclude that discrimination was the salient variable in American race relations. Indeed, Boas was forward-looking when he attacked the problems of prejudice and argued that individual merit, not race, should determine the class position of individual Blacks in American society. Third, I will argue that despite the schisms in Boas's writing on race up until 1938, his

54

position changed and evolved; his positions on race were dynamic. He was always conscious of the growing impact that African Americans were having upon the nation's economic, social, and cultural life and conscious also of the increase in anti-Semitism in this environment. Thus, one of the most obvious results of my research is a demonstration of the conflict between science and ideology in the thought of Boas. Boas was an adherent of a naturalistic worldview, and as new empirically verifiable data were uncovered by other scholars, his points of view on the condition and destiny of African Americans changed and evolved on some issues, but remained intact on others. This is not to say the issues were strictly scientific and not political, but rather to suggest that Boas's political awakening affected his beliefs as much as did his empirical research. Put another way, "political beliefs" were as salient as "scientific commitments" in countering the claims of overt racists.

After 1915 Boas not only used the liberal environmentalist argument to dispel the myth of "racial hereditary characteristics" but also acted as adviser to Melville Herskovits, Otto Klineberg, Ruth Benedict, Zora Neale Hurston, Margaret Mead, and Ashley Montagu. These scholars and researchers built on and disseminated the Boasian perspectives on the capabilities of African Americans, the problem of race prejudice, and the achievements of Africans, not only in the fields of physical anthropology, cultural anthropology, and literature but also in the broad public arena from the 1910s to the 1960s. Furthermore, Boas transformed the thought of members of the African American intelligentsia, including Booker T. Washington, W. E. B. Du Bois, Monroe N. Work, George W. Ellis, Carter G. Woodson, George E. Haynes, Alain LeRoy Locke, Charles S. Johnson, Charles H. Thompson, Abram Harris, and Zora Neale Hurston. Indeed, "it was in the area of race," as Marshall Hyatt has concluded, "that Boas had his greatest impact on American and on future intellectual thought."[1]

Put simply, Boas—albeit grudgingly—attempted to extricate race relations theory from *most* of the racist assumptions of late-nineteenth-century social science. Once Boas had established that White prejudice, not the assumed innate racial traits, was the major obstacle to Black progress, it became exceedingly difficult after 1930 in anthropology and sociology to rationalize the castelike system in the United States, which was based on the assumed congenital inferiority of people of West and Central African descent. In sum, flowing from what I call the "Boasian paradox"—the contradiction between philosophically egalitarian sentiments

1. Marshall Hyatt, *Franz Boas—Social Activist: The Dynamics of Ethnicity* (New York: Greenwood Press, 1990), 4.

and his recontextualization of traditional European physical anthropology—was a prescriptive statement—that in a just society African Americans should *approximate,* not assume, a distribution in each socioeconomic class in the United States proportional to their size in the overall population. Thus, despite his imprisonment in the racist paradigm of late-nineteenth-century physical anthropology, which stated that Blacks were physically different from and somewhat inferior to Whites, Boas at times succeeded in qualifying the inferences drawn from the empirical data to suggest that racism had shaky foundations; he thereby first adumbrated the position of modern-day liberals on the issue of the destiny of African Americans in the social order of the United States. Indeed, Boas felt that once they resolved their problem of group identity, African Americans *could* be assimilated.

I

The father of modern American anthropology was born into a liberal Jewish household in Minden, Westphalia, Germany, on July 9, 1858, a decade following the republican revolutions that swept Europe. By the time of Boas's birth it was clear that the revolutions, which had been characterized by an emphasis on liberalism and the creation of democratic republican nations, had failed. Nevertheless, Boas's parents—his father, Meier, a successful merchant, and his mother, Sophie, the founder of the first Froebel Kindergarten in Minden—were the close associates of many prominent "forty-eighters," such as Carl Schurz and Abraham Jacobi, who married Sophie's younger sister. In such a setting, Boas was inculcated with the liberal ideals of the revolution of 1848—ideals to which he held firmly throughout his life. So intense was the fervor for the ideals of the revolution of 1848 in the Boas household that their Jewish background had few direct intellectual consequences for the young Franz. Although Boas, as Marshall Hyatt has pointed out, "was raised an orthodox Jew," he later recalled that his religious education "was purely sop for his grandparents, who were orthodox." According to Boas, his "parents had broken through the shackles of dogma." "My father," he continued, "had retained an emotional affection for the ceremonial in his parental home, without allowing it to influence his intellectual freedom. Thus I was spared the struggle against religious dogma that besets the lives of so many young people." Nevertheless, Boas's ethnicity had a decisive impact on his later anthropology and politics.[2]

2. Ibid.

As was customary in Germany during this period, Boas attended several universities: Heidelberg, Bonn, and Kiel. He was awarded the doctorate in physics with a minor in geography at Kiel in 1881. His dissertation, "Contributions to the Understanding of the Color of Water," sought to determine the intensities of light striking different types of water. Confronting the problem of subjectivism when he tried to distinguish between two lights that produced slight differences in the color of two different types of water, Boas recalled in 1939 that the experiments suggested to him that "there are domains of our experience in which the concepts of quantity . . . with which I was accustomed to operate are not applicable."[3] The relativity of experience and the relationship between the physiological and the physical were two major philosophical problems he would confront in his later anthropological work.

After an uneventful year at Berlin University and another year in the German army, Boas studied and waited for a teaching position in the increasingly conservative and anti-Semitic academic community in Bismarck's Germany. The disappointed Boas went to Baffin Island, formerly Baffinland, in northeast Canada in 1883 to write a book. Although the transition from physics to ethnology, as George W. Stocking Jr. has demonstrated, "was not abrupt," his experience among the Eskimo sowed the seeds for his attempt to understand the laws of human nature some two years later. His field experience among the Eskimo was important, compelling Boas to change disciplines. After his return to Germany, while working at the Ethnological Museum in Berlin, Boas wrote: "After a long intercourse with the Eskimo, it was with feelings of sorrow and regret that I parted from my Arctic friends. I had seen that they enjoy life, and a hard life, as we do; that nature is also beautiful to them; that feelings of friendship also root in the Eskimo heart; that, although the character of their life is so rude as compared to civilized life, the Eskimo is a man as we are; that his feelings, his virtues and his shortcomings are based in human nature, like ours."[4] Boas's ambivalence toward the Eskimo—the tension between his "philosophical egalitarianism" and his cultural chauvinism that is obvious in the above passage—would later be reflected in his statements on African Americans.

Seeking better career opportunities in which to pursue ethnology, and hoping to marry Marie Krackowizer, whom he had met during her visit

3. George W. Stocking Jr., *Race, Culture, and Evolution: Essays in the History of Anthropology* (New York: Free Press, 1968), 143.
4. Quoted in Melville J. Herskovits, *Franz Boas: The Science of Man in the Making* (New York: Scribner, 1953), 1.

in Germany in 1881, Boas emigrated to the United States in 1887. Boas married Marie that year, but he suffered tremendous setbacks in his attempts to secure employment in Anglo-American-dominated institutions. Virulent anti-Semitism pervaded the nation when Boas entered the country. Jews of German descent, who had begun to be affected by anti-Semitism as early as the 1880s, witnessed a decline in their status. Later, during the 1890s, their opportunities in Anglo-American-dominated institutions and housing were narrowed, as a direct result of the influx of large numbers of Eastern European Jews since the 1880s. His post as geographical editor of *Science* was not funded in 1888; he was forced to resign a position as a docent in physical anthropology at Clark University in 1892; and he was dismissed from a temporary position as chief assistant of anthropology at the World's Columbia Exposition in Chicago in 1894. William Rainey Harper, the president of the University of Chicago, refused to offer him a professorship in 1894, citing Boas's inability to "take direction" as one of the reasons behind his decision. In 1894, Boas was unemployed and mourning the death of his young daughter.

In sum, when Boas delivered his outgoing address as vice president of Section H of the American Association for the Advancement of Science in Brooklyn, New York, in August 1894, he was expressing liberal convictions that flowed from a worldview that was unique in the United States—convictions that were a direct product of the remnants of liberal ideals in Germany, his scientific training, and his marginal status in the anthropological community. Furthermore, this attack on the racist orthodoxy permeating both European and American social scientific communities was bound inextricably to the so-called Negro problem in both the North and the South and the virulent anti-Semitism that pervaded the nation.

In the turn-of-the-century United States, extreme and irrational Negrophobia pervaded every aspect of the nation's life and was a formidable obstacle to a rational discussion of the condition of African Americans. The reconciliation between the North and the South that had taken place in 1877 had resulted in the subordination of Blacks in the South by the early 1880s. As a consequence, the period from roughly 1890 until 1920, despite the economic gains that some Blacks made, was one of the lowest points in the history of White-Black relations in the United States. Indeed, through disfranchisement, Jim Crow laws, extralegal violence, and the removal of Blacks from skilled labor, Whites had consolidated their higher castelike position by 1900. In the North these forms of blatant racism had been less extreme, yet prejudice and discrimination had exacerbated the social problems of Blacks and stymied their progress. Suffice it to say, the period saw some of the most shameful episodes in the area of "race relations" in American history. The level of the discussion of the intellectual capabilities of African Americans was an obstacle that Boas, because of his adherence to physical anthropological assumptions, had the most difficulty surmounting. For the most significant myths espoused in the dominant discourse stated that African Americans were a homogeneous race whose low status in American society was due to their defective ancestry and/or an instinctive White prejudice, which prevented them from contributing to society, or was due to certain "mores" that excluded them from communal life with Euro-Americans.[5]

Under the title "Human Faculty as Determined by Race," Boas presented views that George W. Stocking Jr. and Marshall Hyatt claimed were the genesis of themes that he pursued throughout the rest of his career. Although I concur in Hyatt's argument that Boas's ethnic status was the primary motivating force behind his attacks on anti-Negro prejudice, it should be noted that "Human Faculty as Determined by Race" contains sections that reveal Boas's own bigotry toward African Americans as well. Rationalizing Boas's bigotry, Stocking wrote in 1968: "Given the atmospheric pervasiveness of the idea of European racial superiority, it is hardly surprising that Boas wrote as a skeptic of received belief rather than a staunch advocate of racial equipotentiality. Despite his basic liberal humanitarian outlook, he was a white-skinned European writing for other white-skinned Europeans at the turn of century, and he was a physical anthropologist to boot." In 1974, Stocking pointed out that "one is struck by the limits of Boas' critique in 1894." Although Stocking is aware of Boas's limitations, he has suggested that those limitations in no way detract from the fundamental Boasian stance in reference to race.[6] It is curious that Boas's analysis of the physical characteristics of Blacks and his "men of high genius" hypothesis, which he propounded as late as 1938 and which is discussed below, contain biases that detract from his stature as a philosophical egalitarian.

Boas's assessments of racial determinist arguments in the various branches of the social sciences were contradictory in 1894. On the one hand, he demonstrated the primacy of cultural determinants in accounting for historical achievements and the psychological makeup of

5. Vernon J. Williams Jr., *From a Caste to a Minority: Changing Attitudes of American Sociologists toward Afro-Americans, 1896–1945* (Westport, Conn.: Greenwood Press, 1989), 34–57.

6. Stocking, *Race, Culture, and Evolution*, 189; George W. Stocking Jr., ed., *A Franz Boas Reader: The Shaping of American Anthropology, 1883–1911* (Chicago: University of Chicago Press, 1974), 220.

different races. On the other hand, he acquiesced to racists by insisting that physical anthropological assumptions of the direct relation between intelligence and brain weight or cranial capacity were relevant. Boas even thought bodily form might have certain influences on the psychological makeup of races. The schism between the values of cultural determinism and racial determinism was the major weakness in his philosophical position on race and was a direct product of his methodological rigor. Although Boas's sentiments resonated with his penchant for emphasizing cultural determinism, he still could not reconcile those sentiments with physical anthropological assumptions about racial differences. The tension is evident in his analysis of racial determinism from the historical and physical anthropological perspectives.

From the historical perspective, the young Boas attacked the paradigm of the proponents of the comparative method. By assuming that there was a direct relationship between a race's achievements and the intellectual capacities of its members, the evolutionary anthropologists had essentially confounded "achievement" with "an aptitude for achievement." Similarly they judged any deviation from the White type as "a characteristic feature of a lower type." Boas insisted that the superiority of Western civilization could be accounted for on grounds other than those that suggest the superiority of the White race's mental faculty. He argued that other races, such as the Indians of Peru and Central America, had evolved civilizations that were similar to that from which European civilization had its origins. However, European civilization, favored by the "common physical appearance, contiguity of habitat and modern differences in modes of manufacture" of its inhabitants, spread rapidly. When European civilization came into contact with races outside its domain, assimilation of non-Whites was difficult because of the "striking differences of racial types, the preceding and the greater advance in civilization." The advocates of Northern and Western European superiority, he stressed, had ignored the fact that their civilization, which arose under favorable circumstances and spread rapidly, had "cut short" the advancement of non-European civilization "without regard to the people whom it was developing." The evolutionists' historical explanation of the low status of non-Whites was wrong, because "historical events rather than race appear to have been much more potent in leading races to civilization than their faculty, and it follows the achievements of races do not warrant us to assume that one race is more highly gifted than the others."[7]

7. Franz Boas, "Human Faculty as Determined by Race," in Stocking, ed., *Franz Boas Reader*, 223–27.

Boas's criticisms of the evolutionists exposed the ethnocentric fallacy of ranking non-White societies according to the characteristics they shared with European and American civilizations and revealed his cosmopolitan and liberal sentiments. But his evaluation of racial intellectual differences from the physical anthropological framework was infused with concessions to staunch racists. In the 1880s and early 1890s, Boas had been influenced significantly by the works of prominent Continental physical anthropologists, such as Paul Broca and Paul Topinard, and directly by Rudolph Virchow, with whom he had contact at the meetings of the Berlin Anthropological Society in 1882. Furthermore, throughout his career Boas was certain that physical anthropological data could clarify important ethnological questions.[8] Boas worked within the essentialist framework developed by Broca, the father of modern physical anthropology, who wrote in 1873 in reference to a statistical table he had illustrated: "The table shows that West Africans have a cranial capacity about 100 c.c. less than the European races. To this figure we may add the following: Caffirs, Nubians, Tasmanians, Hottentots, Australians. These examples are sufficient to prove that if the volume of the cranium does not play a decisive role in the ranking of the races, it nevertheless has a very real importance."[9] Thus, Boas speculated, in the early jargon of the discipline, that "it would seem that the greater the central nervous system, the higher the faculty of the race and the greater its aptitude to mental achievement." According to Boas, there were two methods useful in determining the size of the central nervous system: one could measure either the weight of the brain (which provided the most "accurate results") or the size of the cranial cavity. He conceded that both the brain weight and the cranial cavities of Whites, on the average, were "larger than those of most other races, particularly larger than that of the Negroes."[10] Boas's conclusions were not new. As early as the 1840s, the "American School" of anthropology, of which Samuel George Morton, Josiah C. Nott, and George R. Gliddon were prominent members, had based a major part of its defense of the southern practice of slavery on the comparative measurements of the cranial cavities of Blacks and Whites.[11]

Despite Boas's physical anthropological assumptions, he exercised considerable restraint in interpreting data that were based solely on the

8. Stocking, *Race, Culture and Evolution*, 163–64.

9. Quoted in Stephen Jay Gould, *The Mismeasure of Man* (New York: W. W. Norton, 1981), 87.

10. Boas, "Human Faculty as Determined by Race," 232.

11. William R. Stanton, *The Leopard's Spots: Scientific Attitudes toward Race in America, 1815–1859* (Chicago: University of Chicago Press, 1960).

relatively simple mathematical techniques of means, medians, and per-
centiles. On a visit in England in 1889, he had become acquainted with Sir
Francis Galton. He appropriated the eugenicist's science of biometrics
and used it to demonstrate that the "frequency distribution" of the cranial cavities of Blacks and Whites overlapped. He pointed out that Topinard's measurements revealed that 55 percent of Europeans, compared
to 58 percent of "African Negroes," had cavities in the range of 1,450 to
1,650 cubic centimeters; however, those with cavities greater than 1,550
cubic centimeters included 50 percent of Whites and 27 percent of Blacks.
He inferred: "We might, therefore, anticipate a lack of men of high genius
[among the Negroes] but should not anticipate any lack of faculty among
the great mass of [N]egroes living among whites and enjoying the leadership of the best men of the race."[12]

The statement reflects obvious tension between liberal humanitarian
sentiments and the ideas of racism. On the one hand, he implied strongly
that Blacks would produce proportionately fewer men capable of shaping either the nation's or the world's affairs; on the other hand, he was
arguing for the significance of individual differences regardless of a person's race. *All* Blacks, in other words, were not intellectually inferior to *all*
Whites, yet disproportionately fewer Blacks had the mental faculty req-
uisite to shape the course of history.

Indeed, in 1894 the distinction between the position of Boas and that of
ethnocentrists in institutions dominated by persons of British ancestry
was slight. Illustrative of this argument are statements regarding the apelike physical characteristics of the "Negro" by the leading "scientific" authorities on race at the turn of the century. A Kentucky-born professor of
paleontology at Harvard, Nathaniel S. Shaler, in 1890 stated unequivocally that the Negro was "nearer to the anthropoid or pre-human ancestry of man." In 1896 Edward D. Cope, a Pennsylvania-born Quaker and
professor of geology and mineralogy at the University of Pennsylvania,
argued that the Negro was apelike because of his flat nose, his jaws that
projected beyond the upper part of the face, his facial angle, "the defi-
ciency of the calf of the leg, and the obliquity of the pelvis." Daniel G.
Brinton, a former medical doctor who was appointed professor of lin-
guistics and folklore at the University of Pennsylvania, was typical of the
northern White supremacists in anthropology who thought the Negro
had apelike characteristics. "The adult who retains the more numerous
fetal, infantile or simian," he wrote in 1890, "is unquestionably inferior to

12. Boas, "Human Faculty as Determined by Race," 316.

him whose development has progressed beyond them. . . . Measured by these criteria, the European or white race stands at [the] head of the list, the African or [N]egro at its foot."[13] In sum, most European and American physical anthropologists believed the Negro was an apelike barbarian in their midst whose physique prevented him from attaining civilization.

When speaking of the physical characteristics of Blacks in "Human Faculty as Determined by Race," Boas clearly manifested the arrogance of his contemporaries when he wrote: "We found that the face of the [N]egro as compared to the skull is larger than that of the American [Indian], whose face is in turn larger than that of the white. The lower portion of the face assumes larger dimensions. The alveolar arch is pushed forward and thus gains an appearance which reminds us of the higher apes. There is no denying that this feature is a most constant character of the black races representing a type slightly nearer the animal than the European type." Nevertheless, using the tools of science as the basis for all the anthropometric measurements he obtained on the various races, Boas concluded, "We have no right to consider one [race] more ape-like than the other."[14] The question of course remains whether Boas, despite the qualifications that he made, successfully convinced a male, white-skinned European and American audience of his skepticism after making such graphic statements about the simian characteristics of Negroes.

Boas's "men of high genius" hypothesis was a pitfall from which he was never fully able to extricate himself, and the tenacity with which Boas held to this conviction demonstrates that one aspect of his views was severely limited by his belief that some racial differences were real. However, even in his own day this hypothesis was demonstrated as suspect. Both the anatomist E. A. Spitzka and the sociologist William I. Thomas pointed out that the brain sizes of eminent Whites varied enormously. Furthermore, Thomas pointed out in 1895 in "The Scope and Method of Folk-Psychology" that "functionally . . . the importance of the brain has been unduly emphasized by certain anthropologists. There is far less direct connection between intelligence and brain mass and form than was at the time presumed." While Thomas believed there was sufficient evidence to conclude "that the cerebral lobes are the seat of consciousness," it was nonetheless true that "the brain is no more essential to

13. Quoted in John S. Haller Jr., *Outcasts from Evolution: Scientific Attitudes of Racial Inferiority, 1859–1900* (Urbana: University of Illinois Press, 1971), 178, 191; quoted in Gould, *Mismeasure of Man*, 116.
14. Boas, "Human Faculty as Determined by Race," 230, 232.

intelligence than is the circulation, or digestion, or the liver." According to Thomas, "intelligence is the mediation of action, and all organs and tissues cooperate in forming an association, are equally important with the brain."[15] Although Spitzka and Thomas clearly cast grave doubts on Boas's "men of high genius hypothesis" and subsequent scientific research has confirmed their arguments, both men at this juncture were unable to rid themselves of their racial biases and deemed Blacks to be intellectually inferior to or temperamentally different from Whites, despite their own evidence to the contrary.

Boas's 1900 address before the American Folklore Society reflected the tension between his liberal humanitarian sentiments and the evidence from physical anthropology. He was willing to pursue the cultural determinist position to some extent. Boas argued that the mind of primitive man differed from that of civilized man not in its organization, as the advocates of the comparative method had proposed, but rather in the experiences to which it was exposed. The mental functions—abstraction, inhibition, and choice—were all found among primitive peoples; thus, there was no justification for the argument of Herbert Spencer that primitive peoples occupied a lower evolutionary stage. In the same address, however, Boas retreated to the argument of Black inferiority when he confessed: "A number of anatomical facts [such as cranial sizes] point to the conclusion that the races of Africa, Australia, and Melanesia are to a certain extent inferior to Asia, America, and Europe." Nonetheless, Boas argued that there was "no satisfactory evidence" available on whether differences in the size of the brain were "accompanied by difference in structure" of the brain.[16]

Boas's ambivalence concerning Black capabilities also extended to his discussion of their psychology. He admitted that the descriptive psychological evidence on which Edward B. Tylor and Spencer based their generalizations about primitive peoples had suggested that non-Whites were more fickle and passionate and less original than Whites. To him, such arguments were not convincing "because causes and effects were so closely interwoven that it is impossible to separate them in a satisfactory manner, and we are always liable to interpret as racial characteristics what is only an effect of social surroundings." Even on that issue, however, Boas infused physical anthropological assumptions into psychology and immediately genuflected to reactionary beliefs:

15. William I. Thomas, "The Scope and Method of Folk-Psychology," *American Journal of Sociology* 1 (November 1895): 436–37.

16. Boas, "The Mind of Primitive Man," *Journal of American Folk-Lore* 14 (January–March 1901): 1–11.

Based on these considerations, we believe that in the more complicated psychological phenomena no specific differences between the
higher and lower races can be found. By this, however, we do not
mean to say no differences exist or can be found, only that the
method of investigation must be different. It does not seem probable
that the minds of races which show variations in their anatomical
structure should act in exactly the same manner. Differences of structure [of the brain] must be accompanied by differences of function,
physiological as well as psychological, and as we found clear evidence of differences in mental structure [of the brains] between the
races, so we must anticipate that differences in mental characteristics
will be found.

Then, in a feeble attempt to qualify those statements, Boas once again
argued that there were variations in all races: "As all structural differences are quantitative, we must expect to find mental differences to be
of the same description, and we found the variation in structure to overlap, so that many forms are common to individuals of all races, so
we may expect that many individuals will not differ to their faculty,
while a statistical inquiry embracing the whole race would reveal certain
differences."[17]

Between 1894 and 1915, the increasing migration of Blacks from the
rural areas in the southeastern states to New York City stimulated Boas
to take part in reformist activities centering around the condition of the
Black migrants and compelled him to modify his views concerning the
capabilities of Blacks. Between 1890 and 1910, the Black population of
New York City almost tripled. In 1910 there were 91,709 Blacks in Manhattan, the Bronx, Queens, Richmond, and Brooklyn. Of that population,
60,534 lived in Manhattan, while 22,708 lived in Brooklyn. "The average
Negro migrant," Gilbert Osofsky wrote, "obviously found life harsh and
difficult. For those who came, however, conditions in the North did offer
a measure of self-respect and the possibility for future advancement that
was generally denied the Negro in the South." Nonetheless, the net effect
of the Black migration was to initiate racial violence and antagonism and
exacerbate the "social problems" brought about by urbanization. Although recent studies of African American migrations have attempted to
demonstrate that the realities of life in the North for most southern
African Americans were disappointing, I nevertheless concur in the argument made by many historians that conditions in the North at the turn
of the century were more amenable to progress because Blacks in the
urban-industrial North had greater educational opportunities, were

17. Boas, "Human Faculty as Determined by Race," 239.

subject to less blatant forms of discrimination, and were able to exercise their voting rights.[18]

Fortunately, Boas was aware of the need to provide a "scientific" opinion on the "Negro problem." In 1896 he had obtained a position as lecturer at Columbia University, due to an initial appointment as assistant curator at the American Museum of Natural History by his friend Frederic Ward Putnam, and he was tenured in 1899. He joined with Progressive urban reformers, such as Mary White Ovington, Victoria Earle Matthews, Frances A. Kellor, and William Lewis Bulkley, who were concerned with the welfare of African Americans, and searched for order in a city characterized by disorganization and pathological conditions. Boas and Ovington, one of the founders of the NAACP, were also members of the Greenwich House Committee on Social Investigation, a moral reform organization to which other members of the Columbia University faculty belonged, including Edwin R. A. Seligman, Vladimir Simkhovich, Edward T. Devine, Livingston Farrand, Franklin H. Giddings, and Henry R. Seager. Furthermore, Boas published his point of view in the social service magazine *Charities* in 1905, when that magazine devoted an entire issue to the migration of Blacks and the social problems that had arisen as a result of that movement. In addition, Boas penned an article for the first issue of *Crisis*, the organ of the NAACP, in 1910.[19]

In the *Charities* article, "The Negro and the Demands of Modern Life," Boas apparently tried to resolve the issues he had raised in 1894 when he argued that Blacks would produce proportionately fewer "men of high genius" than Whites. Although he once again pointed out that the "average" Negro brain was "smaller than that of other races," and that it was "plausible that certain differences of form of brain exist," he nevertheless cautioned that the data did not conclusively demonstrate differences in intellectual ability. Modifying his 1894 position, which had suggested a direct relationship between brain weight and mental ability, Boas argued, "The inference in regard to ability is . . . based on analogy and we must remember that individually the correlation between brain weight

18. Gilbert Osofsky, *Harlem: The Making of a Ghetto, Negro New York, 1890–1930* (New York: Harper and Row, 1963), chap. 2; Carole Marks, *Farewell—We're Good and Gone: The Great Black Migration* (Bloomington: Indiana University Press, 1989); James R. Grossman, *Land of Hope: Chicago, Black Southerners, and the Great Migration* (Chicago: University of Chicago Press, 1989); George M. Fredrickson, *The Arrogance of Race: Historical Perspectives on Slavery, Racism, and Social Inequality* (Middletown, Conn.: Wesleyan University Press, 1988), 265.

19. Mary White Ovington, *Half a Man: The Status of the Negro in New York* (New York: Longmans, 1915), ix. Boas, "The Negro and the Demands of Modern Life," *Charities* 15 (October 7, 1905) and "The Real Race Problem," *Crisis* 1 (December 1910).

and ability is often overshadowed by other causes, and that we find a considerable number of great men with slight brain weight." Although Boas admitted that factors other than brain weight "often" determined mental ability, he was still too committed to physical anthropological assumptions to dismiss them completely. Immediately contradicting his statement, he penned a non sequitur: "We may, therefore, expect less average ability and also, on account of probable anatomical differences, somewhat different mental tendencies." Then, in an attempt to minimize the purported differences between the races, Boas brought forth the same argument that he had used in 1894: "We may, with the same degree of certainty, expect these differences to be small as compared to the total range of variations found in the human species."[20]

Boas attempted to give a favorable impression of African Americans, despite the measurements indicating that their average cranial cavities were smaller than those of Whites. In a passage that directly attacked segregation in the public schools, he wrote: "There is every reason to believe that the Negro when given the facility and opportunity will be perfectly able to fill the duties of citizenship as well as his white neighbor. It may be that he will not produce as many great men as the white race, and his average achievement will not quite reach the level of the average achievement of the white race, but there will be endless numbers who will do better than the defectives whom we permit to drag down and retard the healthy children of our public schools."[21] Rhetoric aside, Boas was confronted by an irreconcilable dilemma. As a physical anthropologist, he adhered to the assumptions of his field. The above passage reflects the paradox that had been part and parcel of his thought since 1894. Insofar as Boas thought Blacks would be "able to fill the duties of citizenship as well as his white neighbor," he was making the case for the full participation of Blacks in American life. Yet his formulation of the "approximate" intellectual equality of Blacks and Whites reflected both his progressive and his reactionary values. To the extent that Boas was arguing for the necessity of taking into account individual differences in assessing a person's capabilities—and therefore his or her intrinsic worth in the marketplace—he was making the case for differentiation in the Black class structure. But by suggesting Blacks were only approximately equal to Whites, Boas was either consciously or unconsciously providing the rationalization for some discrimination in the economic sector.

Nevertheless, as early as 1905, Boas revealed in his correspondence a

20. Boas, "The Negro and the Demands of Modern Life," 86.
21. Ibid., 87.

healthy skepticism concerning the inferences drawn from the assessments of anthropometric data, basing his objections on the insufficiency
of that data. As the quotes I will present in this section demonstrate, Boas
always indicated he was an empiricist who had to account for the data he
had. Furthermore, he stated constantly that the empirical data were inadequate to support racist conclusions and that they pointed to a lack of
support for the argument of Black inferiority based on racial difference.
Writing to Edward T. Devine, a colleague at Columbia and the general
secretary of the Charity Organization, on October 21, 1905, Boas emphasized "the desirability of collecting more definite information in relation
to certain traits of the Negro race that seem of fundamental importance in
determining the policy to be pursued towards that race." The problem
that Boas found to be paramount concerned "the determination of the
period of development of the Negro race as compared to the white race."
Proponents of Negro inferiority claimed that there was an "early" intellectual "arrest of development of the Negro child." Boas, who had "gone
over available material with some care," found the evidence to be
"wholly insufficient, and that really the problem must be taken up
more." He thought that he could "definitely solve our problem" if he
could "get a trained observer to collect data on stature, weight, size of
head, development of nose, time of eruption of teeth (milk teeth and permanent teeth), puberty and senility." "At the same time," he continued,
"I should try to make a test of preliminary cases showing the rapidity of
development of practice in [N]egroes and in whites on some psychological experiment, selecting a test in which influence of school-teaching
could count for but little."[22] During this period, as I will show, Boas
thought psychological testing could provide a definitive statement on the
capabilities of Blacks as compared to Whites.

Boas was even more precise about the problems confronting students
of race when he contacted Vladimir G. Simkhovich, a colleague at Columbia University and a member of the Cooperative Social Settlement
Society of the City of New York, on March 15, 1906, in an attempt to gain
monies for anthropometric studies of the Negro.

> Among the questions that can readily be taken up are particularly the
> following:
>   (1) Is there an earlier arrest of mental and physical development
> in the Negro child, as compared with the white child? And, if so, is
> this arrest due to social causes or to anatomical and physiological
> conditions?

22. Boas to Edward T. Devine, October 21, 1905, Boas Papers, American Philosophical Society, Philadelphia.

(2) What is the position of the mulatto child and of the adult mulatto in relation to the two races? Is he an intermediate type, or is there a tendency of reversion towards either race? So that particularly gifted mulattoes have to be considered as reversals of the white race. The question of the physical vigor of the mulatto could be taken up at the same time.[23]

Simkhovich did not fund the project; instead, he referred Boas to other possibly sympathetic philanthropists. On October 10, 1906, Boas turned to Felix Adler, a close associate, proposing a museum whose investigation "would have the most important bearing upon the question of a general policy to be pursued in regard to the Negro." "The questions that are obscure," he stated unequivocally, "in reference to this point are innumerable. We do not know the significance of the slightly different type of organization of the brain. We do not know the laws of growth and of development of the [N]egro race; and all these, taken together, should be investigated, and the result of an unbiased, patient investigation of these problems should be of the very greatest help in all practical problems."[24] Boas seemed to be suggesting at this point that physical anthropology had the potential for providing data on the Negro on which public policy should be based.

Although Boas assumed a skeptical posture before Whites who were possible sources of funding for his proposed projects on the anthropometry of the Negro and mulatto, it should be stressed that he held a conviction that most Negroes were inferior to most Whites. Expressing this conviction to Rev. James Boddy of Troy, New York, in May 1906, Boas asserted, "You may be aware that in my opinion the assumption seems justifiable that on the average the mental capacity of the [N]egro may be a little less than that of the white, but that the capacities of the bulk of both races are on the same level." Boas admitted that he could "find neither any history nor any anatomical considerations in proof of any considerable inferiority of the [N]egro race." Always guided by the assumptions of physical anthropology, he conjectured that "it seems of course likely that owing to the differences of anatomical traits, mental differences also exist." But he nonetheless concluded that "the differences are slight as compared to the variability found in each race."[25]

It should also be noted that Boas's methodological puritanism often prevented him from espousing the belief that the equipotentiality of Blacks was a scientific fact to Blacks who sought his expertise. For

23. Boas to Vladimir G. Simkhovich, March 15, 1906, Boas Papers.
24. Boas to Felix Adler, October 10, 1906, Boas Papers.
25. Boas to Rev. James Boddy, May 7, 1906, Boas Papers.

example, in response to a paper by R. R. Wright Sr., the African American president of Georgia State Industrial College, in which Wright asked Boas to cite "some authorities" that he could "consult upon the ancient history of the African Race, or the Negro in particular," Boas wrote in 1907:

> I think you understand my view in regard to the ability of the Negro quite agrees with what you say in your paper. I wish, however, that it were possible to take up a careful study of this subject, and to present the results to our fellow-citizens in a convincing manner. Unfortunately it does not help us that we ourselves have clear convictions in regard to this subject. The reasons for our convictions should be represented in an answerable form, and I believe the only thing that will serve this purpose will be a very painstaking and detailed presentation of the results of studies of African ethnology on the one hand, and of the anatomical features of the central nervous system of the white race and of the [N]egro race on the other.[26]

In other words, Boas exercised extreme caution in expressing his convictions; he thought the need for further research was a prerequisite for making the case against rigid racial determinism.

Despite his penchant for refusing to express his convictions, before reform-minded persons Boas had begun by 1909 to minimize the significance of racial intellectual differences between Blacks and Whites. After reviewing the data on the size of the Negro brain in a short article that appeared in *Crisis,* Boas stated unequivocally: "The existing differences are differences in kind, not in value. This implies that the biological evidence also does not sustain the view, which is so often proposed, that the mental power of the one race is higher than that of the other, although their mental qualities show presumably differences analogous to the existing anatomical and physiological differences." Boas's thought at this juncture was uneven, however. That same year he published an article, "Race Problems in America," in *Science* in which he stated unequivocally that he believed there were fundamental differences between Whites and Blacks:

> I do not believe that the [N]egro is, in his physical and mental make-up, the same as the European. The anatomical differences are so great that corresponding mental differences are plausible. There may exist differences in character and in the direction of specific aptitudes. There is, however, no proof whatever that these differences signify any appreciable degree of inferiority of the [N]egro, notwithstanding the slightly inferior size, and perhaps lesser complexity of structure,

26. R. R. Wright Sr. to Boas, January 2, 1907, Boas to R. R. Wright Sr., February 27, 1907, Boas Papers.

of his brain; for these racial differences are much less than the range of variation found in either race considered by itself.

Nevertheless, aware of the scientific doubts about physical anthropological explanations of differences in the mental makeup of Blacks and Whites, Boas continued:

> I think we have reason to be ashamed to confess that the scientific study of these questions has never received the support either of our government or of any of our great scientific institutions; and it is hard to understand why we are so indifferent towards a question which is of paramount importance to the welfare of our nation. The anatomy of the American Negro is not well known; and, notwithstanding the oft-repeated assertions regarding the hereditary inferiority of the mulatto, we know hardly anything on this subject. If his vitality is lower than that of the full-blooded [N]egro, this may be as much due to social causes as to hereditary causes. Owing to very large numbers of mulattoes in our country, it would not be a difficult matter to investigate the biological aspects of this question thoroughly; and the importance of the problem demands that this should be done.[27]

In 1911, Boas published *The Mind of Primitive Man*, which included excerpts from his previously published essays on race but also contained up-to-date data supporting most of the conclusions he had been developing since 1894. It was complete in its refutation of crude racial determinist thinking, complete in its indictment of crude racial prejudice, and cogent in its presentation of the assimilationist arguments.

In 1912, Robert H. Lowie, one of Boas's former students, writing in the *American Journal of Sociology*, lucidly explicated his mentor's position in reference to the inferences that could be drawn from a critical assessment of the data on "the Negro" emanating from physical anthropology. "The Negro race may not produce as many minds of exceptional ability as the white race; but so far as its average performance is concerned Boas arrives at the conclusion that there is no evidence for believing in a racial inferiority that would unfit an individual Negro to take his part in modern civilizations."[28]

The Mind of Primitive Man, however, did not mark the culmination of Boas's thought on Blacks during the Progressive Era. In his foreword to Mary White Ovington's *Half a Man* in 1915, he made his final summation of Boasian anthropology when he stated: "Many students of anthropology recognize that no proof can be given of any material inferiority of

---

27. Boas, "Race Problems in America," in Stocking, ed., *Franz Boas Reader*, 23.
28. Robert H. Lowie, review of Boas's *The Mind of Primitive Man*, *American Journal of Sociology* 17 (May 1912): 830–31.

the Negro race; that without doubt the bulk of the individuals composing the race are equal in mental aptitude of the bulk of our own people; that, although their hereditary aptitude may lie in slightly different directions, it is very improbable that the majority of individuals composing the white race should possess greater ability than the Negro race."[29] Boas had, in essence, minimized the significance of purported intellectual differences between Blacks and Whites insofar as he stressed the fact that the masses of both races were virtually equal. Nonetheless, he raised a key issue that was far from resolved at his death in 1942. Were the slight differences in "hereditary aptitude" that he detected socially significant? In other words, what were the implications of slight differences in racial aptitudes for the professions and highly skilled trades? Boas could not answer these questions; and they continue to be debated even to this day.

Despite Boas's admission that it was practically impossible to separate the social and the hereditary features of the mental makeup of Whites and Blacks, he had argued in 1894 that "investigations based on physiological psychology and experimental psychology will allow us to treat the problem in a satisfactory manner." "In these and in detailed studies of the anatomy of the central nervous system," Boas suggested strongly, "we must look for a final solution of our problem." In reference to addressing the "psychological problem while excluding such factors," Boas argued that it could be accomplished by investigating "the psychical processes of great numbers of individuals of different races who live under similar conditions." Although that feat had not been accomplished so as "to draw far-reaching conclusions," Boas mentioned "that two psychologists found differences of favorite colors between children of different races and different ages; that attempts have been made to show that the minds of [N]egro children cease to develop sooner than those of white children, although the results are not conclusive. Modest investigation of the senses of simpler mental activities of children will give the first satisfactory answer to the important question of the *extent of racial differences* of faculty. The schools of our country, particularly those of larger cities, open a vast field for researches of this character."[30]

By 1920 the efforts of psychologists to investigate "psychical processes" had proliferated. Boas, however, always the methodological puritan, would reject their findings because they lacked methodological rigor. He and his students, including Herskovits, Mead, Montagu, and

29. Boas, foreword to Ovington, *Half a Man*, vii–viii.
30. Boas, "Human Faculty as Determined by Race," 240 (italics mine).

Klineberg, would become the leading adversaries in the fight against the attempt of psychologists to prove Black inferiority on the basis of aptitude tests. It is clear from Lowie's explication of Boas's position that Boas thought—as Frank H. Hankins astutely pointed out in his criticism of the former—that "racial differences though real are less extensive and important than popular opinion has heretofore supposed."[31]

Although Boas worked within the same essentialist framework as the racists, that should not detract from the subversiveness of his position on the capabilities of African Americans in the context of the discussion of turn-of-the-twentieth-century race relations. The initial response to Boas in the field of anthropology was hysterical. In his presidential address to the American Association for the Advancement of Science in 1895, Daniel G. Brinton asserted: "The black, the brown and red races differ anatomically so much from the white, especially in their splanchnic [visceral] organs, that even with equal cerebral capacity, they could never rival the results by equal efforts."[32] Yet, by the early 1900s Boas, due to his security at Columbia, and his ties to the Smithsonian Institute, the American Association for the Advancement of Science, and the American Ethnological Society, had become a powerful figure in American anthropology. His political domination of the discipline resulted in the triumph of his position within that discipline after 1920.[33]

In the closely allied discipline of sociology, the initial responses to the Boasian position on the capabilities of Blacks were determined by the ethnic and sectional backgrounds of the partisans, the extent to which they accepted "scientific naturalism" as a worldview, and their perception of the social structural changes that were affecting Blacks in the nation.[34] By 1918, however, the Boasian position had triumphed. His disciple Robert E. Park, the leading student of race relations, summed up the position of the most prominent sociologists that year when he wrote: "[T]he question remains where Boaz [sic] left it when he said that the black was little, if any, inferior to the white man in intellectual capacity and in any case, racial as compared with individual differences were small and relatively unimportant."[35] During the next few decades,

31. Frank H. Hankins, *The Racial Basis of Civilization* (New York: Knopf, 1926), 323–24.
32. Daniel G. Brinton, "The Aims of Anthropology," *Proceedings of the American Association for the Advancement of Science* 44 (December 1895): 12.
33. Hyatt, *Franz Boas—Social Activist*, 79.
34. Williams, *From a Caste to a Minority*, 69–73, 84–98.
35. Robert E. Park, "Education and Its Relation to the Conflict and Fusion of Cultures: With Special Reference to the Problems of the Immigrant, the Negro and Missions," *Publications of the American Sociological Society* 13 (December 1918): 40–41.

sociologists would become some of the staunchest supporters of the Boasian position on the capabilities of Blacks.

For Du Bois, as well as for Kelly Miller and Monroe N. Work, physical anthropology held the key to the nature of racial differences. All three scholars felt compelled to recontextualize the discourse on race in physical anthropology, which had been dominated by the pronouncements of Frederick L. Hoffman in his *Race Traits and Tendencies of the American Negro*, published by the American Economic Association in 1896.

Hoffman, a German-born employee of the Prudential Insurance Company, made the claim that he was "free from personal bias which might have made an impartial treatment of the subject difficult." Nevertheless, the conclusion of the work was an expression of the rampant Darwinism that predicted the impending extinction of African Americans. It was Hoffman's argument that African Americans after the antebellum period were deteriorating physically and morally because of their "race traits and tendencies" rather than because of the adverse conditions to which they had been subjected. For Hoffman, it was "not in the conditions of life but in race and heredity that we find the explanation." Even persons of mixed ancestry were, according to Hoffman, subject to physical and moral deterioration—primarily because "the mixture of the African with the white race has been shown to have seriously affected the longevity of the former and left as a heritage to future generations the poison of scrofula, tuberculosis and most of all, of syphilis."[36]

In a thirty-three-page review of Hoffman's work that was the first publication of the American Negro Academy, Kelly Miller, who had been a professor of mathematics at Howard University since 1890, demonstrated that Hoffman reached his conclusion "from *a priori* considerations" and his "facts have been collected in order to justify it." Miller concluded, "It is a condition and not a theory that confronts" the African American.[37]

During the same period, W. E. B. Du Bois was attempting to discredit the myth that suggested that African Americans formed a homogeneous group whose members (except the mulattoes) should be treated alike. While Boas, on the basis of his anthropometric measurements and his analysis of the African background of African Americans, was issuing a prescriptive statement—that is, that individual merit, not race, should determine a person's position in the American social order, Du Bois was

36. Frederick L. Hoffman, *Race Traits and Tendencies of the American Negro* (Philadelphia: American Economic Association, 1896), preface, 312, 188.

37. Kelly Miller, "A Review of Hoffman's *Race Traits and Tendencies of the American Negro*" (Washington, D.C.: American Negro Academy, 1897), 36.

uncovering empirical evidence and offering explanations for the stratification that existed among African Americans in the 1890s. Indeed, the
idea of an African American class structure had its origins in American
sociology at the turn of the century in Du Bois's scholarship. The idea,
which was a product of the clash between left-liberal and mainstream
progressives and Darwinians, has persisted for almost a century as a key
analytical concept in social science discussions of race relations in the
United States. At present, it raises important questions about the relative
significance of "race" and "class" as determinants of the status of African
Americans, and it is central to the arguments of such distinguished contemporary scholars as Alphonso Pinkney, Thomas Sowell, and William J.
Wilson.

Du Bois's idea of an African American class structure had its origins in
his attempt to rebut the Darwinian prediction of the impending extinction of African Americans as developed in Hoffman's *Race Traits*. To Du
Bois, it was apparent that Hoffman did not have the insight to offer a
"proper interpretation of apparently contradictory social facts." Du Bois
noted, "If, for instance, we find among American Negroes today, at the
very same time, increasing intelligence and increasing crime, increasing
wealth and disproportionate poverty, increasing religious and moral activity and high rates of illegitimacy in births, we can no more fasten upon
the bad as typifying the general tendency than we can upon the good."[38]
Du Bois argued emphatically that Hoffman was incorrect in assuming
that such contradictory facts pertained to "the race" rather than to the
class structure that had developed since emancipation. Du Bois, in other
words, believed that the extent of Black progress or retrogression was determined by the individual's rank within the Black class structure. At the
same time, he was certain that White prejudice was an obvious obstacle
to Black progress.

Du Bois, whose orientation was a product of both his inferior status as
an African American in an Anglo-American-dominated society and his
academic training in the United States and Germany, anticipated the
work of Robert E. Park and W. Lloyd Warner in the first three decades of
the twentieth century. In his 1899 book, *The Philadelphia Negro*, Du Bois
gathered empirical data that suggested that class differentiation already
existed in Black America. He wrote that "wide variations in antecedents,
wealth, intelligence and general efficiency have already been differ-
entiated with this [African American] group." Despite his emphasis on

---

38. W. E. B. Du Bois, review of *Race Traits and Tendencies of the American Negro* by
Frederick L. Hoffman, *Annals* 9 (January 1897): 127–33.

differentiation in Philadelphia's major black community, Du Bois brought forth ample evidence suggesting that the attitudes and behavior of the White population "limited and circumscribed" the opportunities of even "the better classes" of African Americans.[39] Thus, for Du Bois, despite the differentiation of the African American class structure, "race" was the most salient variable in American race relations.

For the African American educated elite, the implications of Boas's assessments of the cranial cavities of Blacks and Whites were revolutionary. For the Harvard-educated Du Bois, Boas's analysis of anthropometric measurements of cranial cavities was truly subversive. Furthermore, at an early date Du Bois was cognizant of the centrality of physical anthropology as a buttress to the dominant discourse in science on "race." As early as 1898, Du Bois, in his "Study of the Negro Problems," stated that "anthropological measurement" was one of the four "practical divisions" for "the study of the Negro as a social group." For Du Bois the division included a scientific study of the Negro body:

> The most obvious peculiarity of the Negro—a peculiarity that is a large element in many problems affecting him—is his physical unlikeness to the people with whom he has been brought into contact. This difference is so striking that it has become the basis of a mass of theory, assumption, and suggestion which is deep-rooted and yet rests on the flimsiest basis of scientific fact. That there are differences between the white and black races is certain, but just what those differences are is known to none with an approach to accuracy.[40]

Du Bois initiated a relationship with Franz Boas in 1905, a friendship that lasted for more than three decades. On October 11 of that year, Du Bois sent Boas a letter informing him that Atlanta University was planning to conduct a study of the Negro physique for a conference and soliciting Boas's expertise in identifying the best and latest works bearing on the anthropology of the Blacks—particularly their physical measurements, health, and so on. In offering Boas the opportunity, Du Bois indicated that the Atlanta study would be a "great opportunity . . . for physical measurement of the Negro," provided Columbia University would fund the project. In his October 14 reply, Boas indicated that he could not refer Du Bois "to anything that is particularly good on the physical anthropology of the Negro." He went on to suggest that he would query Columbia University officials concerning the possibility of

39. W. E. B. Du Bois, *The Philadelphia Negro: A Social Study* (1899; rpt. New York: Schocken Books, 1967), 5–9.
40. W. E. B. Du Bois, "The Study of the Negro Problems," *Annals* 11 (January 1898): 19.

gaining funding for the study.[41] Although Boas did not accept Du Bois's invitation to Atlanta University for the May 29, 1906, conference, he did go to Atlanta two days later and spoke to an audience of Black working people, preachers, and professionals on the African background of African Americans rather than on their anthropometric measurement.

In *The Health and Physique of the Negro American,* which was based on the anthropometric measurements of more than a thousand students at Atlanta University, Du Bois in 1906 quoted a memorandum by Monroe N. Work, who was teaching at Savannah State that year, in which he took to task scholars, such as Robert B. Bean, who held that the brain of the African American was smaller than that of the Euro-American. Although Work made no reference to Boas (who had refuted Bean's argument that same year), Work concluded:

> The best evidence seems to indicate that the organization and, there-fore, the details of the structure of the central nervous system are con-tinually being modified through life. That is, changes are constantly occurring. These changes, which are many and varied, are caused by age, occupation, nutrition, disease, etc. This fact of constant change makes it very doubtful whether any uniformity in the finer details of structure will be found in white brains, particularly if they are brains of different sizes from persons of different ages, statures, etc., and the cause of death not being the same. These facts, in connection with the well established fact that those characters which are said to be dis-tinctive of particular races are found with more or less frequency in other races, seem to indicate that what has been described as being peculiar in the size, shape, and anatomy of the Negro brain is not true of all Negro brains. These same peculiarities can no doubt be found in many white brains and probably have no special connection with the mental capacity of either race.[42]

Du Bois indeed understood the implications of Work's and Boas's as-sessments of anthropometric measurement for the myth of the homo-geneity of African Americans as a group. When speaking to the National Negro Conference, which preceded the initial organization of the NAACP in 1909, Du Bois asserted that the address of Boas's disciple Liv-ingston Ferrand before the conference "left no doubt in the minds of lis-teners that the whole argument by which Negroes were pronounced

41. W. E. B. Du Bois to Boas, October 11, 1905, Boas to W. E. B. Du Bois, October 14, 1905, Boas Papers.

42. W. E. B. Du Bois, *The Health and Physique of the Negro American: Report of a Social Study Made under the Direction of Atlanta University, Together with the Proceedings of the Eleventh Conference for the Study of the Negro Problems, Held at Atlanta University on May the 29, 1906* (Atlanta: Atlanta University Press, 1908), 27.

absolutely and inevitably inferior to Whites was utterly without scientific basis."[43] Du Bois, nevertheless, was uncritical of Boas's reservations about black equality.

Boas's position even influenced the thought of Black conservatives, such as Booker T. Washington, who were also victimized by the forces of racism and reaction in the South. This argument is perhaps best illustrated by the correspondence between T. E. Taylor, a representative of the sixty-seventh district in the Iowa state legislature, and Booker T. Washington. Taylor wrote Washington on September 5, 1915, concerning a lecture by James K. Vardaman (Mississippi's governor from 1904 to 1908) in Independence, Iowa, in which Vardaman "asserted that the Negro's skull hardens at the age of puberty and from that age on there is no mental development." Taylor did not accept the theory. And he asked Washington: "What facts can you give me on this point?" In a long response signed in Emmett J. Scott's handwriting, the Tuskegeean wrote:

> For discussion of what the best scientists have to say concerning this question I refer you to the recent volume of the Macmillan Company entitled "The Mind of Primitive Man" by Professor Franz Boas of Columbia University, who is, I understand, the leading authority on the question of the mental ability of races. Another interesting discussion of this same subject is by Professor W. I. Thomas of the University of Chicago, in his book on "Sex and Society" in the chapter on "Mind of Woman and the Lower Races." If your public library has the back numbers of the American Journal of Sociology, you will find this same article by Professor Thomas published therein sometime during the period 1906–1908.[44]

Like Du Bois, the Tuskegee researchers interpreted Boas's position as an attack on crude racism that did not draw distinctions between the relative abilities of different Blacks and stated that all Whites were superior to all Blacks.

For the Harvard and Oxford University–educated philosopher Alain LeRoy Locke, Boas's ideas served as a point of departure for his own work. Locke was an assistant professor of English and instructor in philosophy and education at the Teachers College at Howard University. Paraphrasing Boas, Locke wrote in 1916: "Because of differences [in] anthropological [factors], anthropological points of comparison have now been reduced to such a narrow margin in each instance that the

43. Quoted in Elliott M. Rudwick, *W. E. B. Du Bois: A Study in Minority Leadership* (Philadelphia: University of Pennsylvania Press, 1961), 123.
44. T. E. Taylor to Booker T. Washington, September 5, 1915, and Booker T. Washington to T. E. Taylor, September 14, 1915, Booker T. Washington Papers, Library of Congress, Washington, D.C.

variations between individuals of the same race, and even the same nation, more than outspan the maximum variability between what are regarded as cognate races of mankind." The net effect of Boas's ideas, Locke noted, was to argue that "a really pure science of race is . . . undesirable, not so much because it is impossible, but because even though it were realized, it would be impracticable, particularly as contrasted with whatever current practical theories of race are prevailing in society. It could never successfully hope to compete with what men really believe human society to be." Locke concluded, "To the extent, therefore, that any man has race, he has inherited either a favorable or an unfavorable social heredity, which unfortunately is [typically] ascribed to factors which have not produced [it], factors which will in no way determine either the period of those inequalities or their eradication."[45]

Boas influenced members of the African American elite beyond those who belonged to the American Negro Academy. George Washington Ellis, the Chicago-based attorney and former secretary of the Liberian Legation, in the *Journal of Race Development* (to which he was a frequent contributor) concluded in 1915 that "the ethnological science has been such an influential factor in creating, diffusing and crystallizing race prejudice in the social minds of Whites." Nevertheless, the "new ethnology" written by Franz Boas and Alexander Chamberlain (a former student of Boas's and the editor of the *Journal of Race Development*), in which Ellis believed the truth was being told concerning Blacks and Whites, asserted that "physical features, the cephalic angle, the texture of hair, the shape of the head, the color of the skin, the size or shape, or the size and weight of the brain, have *little or nothing* to do with the capacity of mind or the moral quality of the soul; that like other race varieties, the Negro is a product of the complex and subtle forces of his milieu . . . acting upon him for centuries past; that there is no naturally superior and inferior race, and that no race has a monopoly on either beauty, intellect or culture."[46]

In short, like the White participants in the dominant discourse, members of the African American intelligentsia had conceived of "race" as a

45. Alain LeRoy Locke, "The Theoretical Scientific Conceptions of Race," in *Race Contacts and Interracial Relations*, ed. Jeffrey C. Stewart (Washington, D.C.: Howard University Press, 1992), 5–12.

46. George W. Ellis, "Psychology of American Race Prejudice," *Journal of Race Development* 6 (January 1915): 312 (italics mine); see also Ellis's "The Negro in Democracy," *Journal of Race Development* 7 (July 1916), 78, and "Factors in the New American Race Situation," *Journal of Race Development* 8 (April 1917): 486. Ellis was aware of Boas's innovative thinking as early as 1907. See George W. Ellis to Boas, May 28, 1907, Boas Papers.

supraindividual organic identity, using such terms as racial *essence,* racial *genius,* and racial *soul.* They were cognizant that Boas offered them by far the best deal they were going to get from the dominant White academy, and they accepted it. The African American elite, which was more biologically assimilated and acculturated than the Black masses, accepted Boas's ideas uncritically—primarily because his argument seemed to suggest that caste barriers did not recognize color and class distinctions. The African American elite now had an argument for acceptance on an individual basis. Thus, although Boas's philosophy suggested that few of them could shape history, it also suggested that there was no basis for the argument that they should be excluded from participating in society on a basis of equality.

II

Despite Boas's adherence to the assumptions of physical anthropology and experimental psychology, he nonetheless knew that Whites determined the status of Blacks in the American social order and that White attitudes and behavior confined Blacks to a low position. Thus, during the years from 1894 until 1915, Boas time and again identified the racial prejudice of White Americans as the primary determinant of the status of African Americans. He wrote in 1894:

> When, finally, we consider the inferior position held by the Negro race of the United States, who are in the closest contact with modern civilization, we must not forget that the old race-feeling of the inferiority of the colored is as potent as ever and is a formidable obstacle to its advance and progress, not withstanding that schools and universities are open to them. We might rather wonder how much has been accomplished in a short period against heavy odds. It is hardly possible to say what would become of the Negro if he were able to live with the Whites on absolutely equal terms.[47]

In 1909, Boas suggested that anthropology had demonstrated "that the impression which we gain from the failure of the American Negro to manifest himself in any of these directions [industry and art] is due, not to native inability, but to the degrading conditions under which he has been placed for generations."[48] In 1911 Boas argued that the purported "traits of the American Negro are adequately explained on the basis of his history and social status." "The tearing-away from the African soil and the consequent complete loss of the old standards of life," Boas

47. Boas, "Human Faculty as Determined by Race," 226.
48. Boas, "Industries of the African Negroes," *Southern Workman* 38 (April 1909): 225.

argued unequivocally, "which were replaced by the dependency of slavery and by all it entailed, followed by a period of disorganization and by a severe economic struggle against heavy odds, are sufficient to explain the inferiority of the status of the race, without falling back upon the theory of hereditary inferiority." Finally, in 1915, Boas argued that White racism was far more insidious than anti-Semitism in the United States. "The Negro of our times carries even more heavily the burden of his racial descent than did the Jew of an earlier period; and the intellectual and moral qualities required to insure success to the Negro are infinitely greater than those demanded from the white, and will be greater, the stricter the segregation of the Negro community."[49]

Boas believed White prejudice served an important practical function. He drew an analogy between prejudice and "the old instinct and fear of the connubium of patricians and plebeians, of the European nobility and common people, or of the castes of India." These "emotions and reasoning," Boas suggested, related "particularly to the necessity of maintaining a distinct social status in order to avoid race-mixture." Sociologists, who were the leading authorities on the issue of prejudice, assumed that it was either "instinctive" or in "the mores" and that Whites especially opposed racial intermixture because they identified racial solidarity with the ideal of racial purity. Although Boas argued that White prejudice was "not a physiological dislike," as proved by the existence of a large "mulatto population," it was nevertheless, as the sociologists had argued, "an expression of social conditions that are so deeply ingrained . . . that they assume a strong emotional value." Boas concluded that although laws might "retard the influx of white blood considerably, they cannot hinder the gradual progress of intermixture."[50]

In his "Problem of the American Negro," published in the *Yale Quarterly Review* in 1921, Boas attacked racists by criticizing their interpretations of anthropometric data. After reviewing the findings of physical anthropologists on the Negro, he did not draw invidious distinctions between Blacks and Whites. Moreover, his "men of high genius" hypothesis was conspicuously absent. He willingly admitted "that, on the average, the brain of the [N]egro is slightly smaller than the brain of the European." Yet his inferences suggested the possibility of functional similarities. "The response on the part of brains," Boas surmised, "of different structure and size to the demands of life may be very much the

49. Boas, *The Mind of Primitive Man* (New York: Macmillan, 1911), 272; Boas, foreword to Ovington, *Half a Man*, vii–viii.
50. Boas, *The Mind of Primitive Man*, 272.

same." Furthermore, Boas was critical of some of the psychological experiments. Early in his career Boas had believed that experimental psychology would provide definitive insights on the issue of racial mental differences. After twenty-seven years he had discovered, however, that the investigations into the mental abilities of Black and White children were biased. Boas wrote: "I am not convinced that the results that have been obtained are significant in regard to racial ability as a whole. The variability of the results is also very marked and there is an overlapping of racial traits." He was intent on pushing the liberal environmentalist argument as far as possible. Responding to a study by M. R. Trabue that was based on the culturally biased Army Alpha and Beta tests, Boas argued that northern Blacks were not inherently superior to southern Blacks. He asserted that it was not true that only "the gifted Southern Negroes emigrated." In argued lucidly that prejudice adversely affected test results:

> [I]n the absence of sound proof this [inherent intellectual] superiority may just as well be explained by the assumption that Northern [N]egroes are exposed to a wider range of experience than Southern [N]egroes. Anyone who knows the abject fear of the Southern [N]egroes who are put under the control of an unknown white officer in foreign surroundings, anyone who knows the limitations of early childhood and general upbringing of [N]egroes in the South, will accept these findings, but will decline to accept them as a convincing proof of the hereditary inferiority of the [N]egro race.

To prove that cultural factors were more significant for an understanding of the plight of African Americans than the study of heredity, Boas, as he had since 1906, turned to a discussion of African achievements to demonstrate that the traits of African Americans were not racial traits. Africans had made achievements essential to world civilization.[51]

Another article that demonstrated the maturation of Boas's thought on race, "What Is Race," appeared in the *Nation* in 1925. In that piece he sought to delimit the boundaries of the "Nature versus Nurture" controversy. He mentioned Blacks only once; yet the implications for the discussion of the so-called Negro problem were clear. In a change from his pre-1920 writings, Boas argued it was wrongheaded to try to "judge" an individual "by the size of his brain" or by his physiological or mental functions, because those forms and functions "vary enormously in each race, and many features that are found in one race are also found belonging to other races." Indeed, it was "impossible to speak of hereditary

51. Boas, "The Problem of the American Negro," *Yale Quarterly Review* 10 (January 1921): 386–87, 388–89, 390.

racial characteristics because the traits characterizing any individual occur in a number of human races." Although Boas believed there are obvious differences in the appearance and behavior of certain "social groups," this did not "imply that these characteristics are hereditarily determined." It was obvious to him that "racial strains, when subject to the same social environment, develop the same functional tendencies." When addressing the controversial issue of racial mental differences, Boas pointed out correctly that the "occurrence of hereditary mental traits that belong to a particular race has never been proved." For him, it was safe to infer that the "behavior of an individual is therefore not determined by his racial affiliations, but by the character of his ancestry and his cultural environment." One could "judge the mental characteristics of families and individuals, but not of races."[52]

It would be an overstatement to assert that Boas completely rid himself of racist anthropological assumptions. When *Anthropology and Modern Life* was published, Boas was appalled at the literature that had been written "based on the assumption that each race has its own mental character determining its cultural or social behavior." Boas stated unequivocally that the concept of racial types was "based on subjective experience." There were "no pure races." Nevertheless, Boas still argued that

> the distribution of individuals and of family lines in the various races differs. When we select among the Europeans a group with large brains, their frequency will be relatively high, while among the Negroes the frequency of occurrence of the corresponding group will be low. If, for instance, there are 50 percent of a European population who have a brain weight of more than, let us say 1,500 grams, there may be only 20 percent of Negroes of the same class. Therefore, 30 percent of the large-brained Europeans cannot be matched by any corresponding group of Negroes.

Defending this practice of comparing the brain sizes of races, Boas thought it was justifiable as long as "we avoid an application of our results to individuals." The results could not be applied to individuals because "the brain in each race is very variable in size and the overlapping of individuals in the races is marked." "It is not possible," he asserted firmly, "to identify an individual as a Negro or White according to the size and form of the brain, but serially the Negro brain is less extremely human than that of the White."[53] This "men of high genius" hypothesis still appeared in the highly revised 1938 edition of *The Mind of Primitive*

52. Boas, "What Is Race?" *Nation*, January 28, 1925, 90–91.
53. Boas, *Anthropology and Modern Life* (New York: Norton, 1928), 18, 38, 40.

Man. A captive of nineteenth-century physical anthropology, Boas never quite escaped.

The thought of Franz Boas on Blacks, in essence, was paradoxical as late as 1938. He was torn between his commitment to physical anthropological assumptions, which suggested that the races were not equal, and his commitment to cultural anthropology, which suggested that White prejudice was an obvious obstacle to Black progress. Furthermore, his study of the material culture and history of the West African ancestors of African Americans raised serious questions about his assumption of Black physical inferiority. Boas's egalitarian instincts would, however, eventually prevail; for the relentless social structural changes that brought the "social problems" of Blacks into visibility after 1900 were exacerbated as more Blacks moved to New York City during World War I. Although the social structural changes would have emancipatory implications for Blacks after World War II, racism triumphed in anthropology and sociology for another decade and a half. The persistence of racism in disciplines dedicated to determining the laws of human nature gives credence to historian George Fredrickson's statement that "history in general does not . . . provide much basis for the notion that passionately held fallacies are destined to collapse because they are in conflict with empirical reality."[54]

III

As several historians have noted, during the 1920s and 1930s, Boas and his students—most notably Margaret Mead, Melville J. Herskovits, and Otto Klineberg—were critical of the methodologies of psychologists such as George Oscar Ferguson, Carl C. Brigham, Joseph Peterson, and Lewis M. Peterson—formulators of the Army Alpha and Beta tests. The latter group used these "intelligence" tests to prove "scientifically" that the vast majority of African Americans were inferior to persons of Northern and Western European descent. Furthermore, the historian V. P. Franklin has demonstrated that African American psychologists, such as Howard Hale Long, Horace Mann Bond, Herman Canady, Martin D. Jenkins, Joseph St. Clair Price, and Doxey Wilkerson were skeptical of the claims of EuroAmerican intelligence testers and published refutations of White psychologists' suspect conclusions during the years between 1923 and 1940.[55]

It is interesting to note that some African American social scientists, in

54. Fredrickson, *Arrogance of Race*, 179.

55. V. P. Franklin, "Black Social Scientists and the Mental Testing Movement, 1920–1940," in *Black Psychology*, 2d ed., ed. Reginald L. Jones (New York: Harper and Row, 1980), 201–15.

their effort to recontextualize the findings of scientific racists, sought the expertise and support of Franz Boas. On April 13, 1925, Charles S. Johnson, who was the editor of the National Urban League's journal, *Opportunity: Journal of Negro Life,* and who would go on to establish himself as one of the country's leading authorities in the field of race relations, wrote Boas concerning an article by Howard Hale Long of the Department of Research of the Washington, D.C., Public Schools. Johnson wrote that Long's article, which seemed "to be extraordinarily well supported, questions seriously the validity of psychological comparisons of races based upon the current mental tests." Johnson pointed out that Long had "measured and studied thousands of children of different races" and that "his results seem to show that the mental age[s] of white and colored children are not commensurable; that a mental age on the Binet scale for a colored child means more than the same mental age on the same scale for a white child; and that although a colored child might actually have a mental ability, equal to that of a white child, he would nevertheless have a lower mental age." Boas indicated to Johnson on April 25, 1925, that he was "interested" in reading the paper and asked Johnson to forward him a copy of it.[56]

By 1928, Boas was working on a study of intelligence tests. Abram Harris, one of his former students who went on to establish himself as a leading economist, wrote Boas concerning a meeting that he had had with Charles H. Thompson, a professor of education at Howard University who had received his doctorate in psychology at the University of Chicago. Thompson was interested, Harris wrote on June 22, 1928, "in making an analysis of cultural factors as they affect the results of mental testing upon Negroes." "I told him," Harris continued, "you are interested in the same thing or something similar to it." On June 23, Thompson wrote Boas indicating that he had spoken with Harris and that Harris had suggested that he write "with the possible idea of effecting some sort of cooperation." Thompson wanted some specific information from Boas. He asked: "Granting the fact that the results of intelligence and educational tests are conditioned by environment, and I think recent investigations show that we must grant this fact—a. How may this influence be measured, and b. What are the results of such measurements?" Despite Thompson's query, Boas on July 5 indicated only that he would "be very glad to hear . . . about the work" Thompson was doing.[57]

56. Charles S. Johnson to Boas, April 13, 1925, and Boas to Charles S. Johnson, April 25, 1925, Boas Papers.
57. Abram Harris to Boas, June 22, 1928; Charles H. Thompson to Boas, June 23, 1928; and Boas to Charles H. Thompson, July 5, 1928, Boas Papers.

Boas was willing, however, to reveal some aspects of his project when Howard Hale Long contacted him on March 13, 1929. Long had been informed by Abram Harris that Boas was "preparing some mental tests for pupils with varying cultural backgrounds." "I am quite sure," he added, "that I do not wholly understand what your program is, but for some time the conclusion has been forcing itself upon me that the current mental tests are not suitable in some respects, for a large number of Negro children." In his reply on March 18, Boas indicated that he was "trying to get in detail the social background of individual children and during the year . . . intending to work out a psychological test on the basis of this information." Boas did not expect that he could "give any kind of definite information until about the end of the present calendar year."[58]

Whatever happened to Boas's unbiased mental test is a mystery. There are no indications either that it was widely administered to persons of varying social backgrounds or that it demonstrated significantly different results for African Americans. In short, despite his sometimes curt replies to African Americans, Boas throughout his career was a source of support for African Americans who wanted to recontextualize the conclusions of the dominant discourse of scientific racism.

In sum, Boas was no racist. He never asserted or advocated that Euro-Americans should maintain a privileged and protected status vis-à-vis African Americans, but on the issue of significant physiological differences his statements were ambiguous. Although harboring doubts about the eventual achievement of a biracial egalitarian society, Boas did not view the purported defective ancestry of African Americans as sufficiently significant to justify their exclusion from the community of scholars or from citizenship in the nation-state. Compared to most White scholars at the beginning of the twentieth century, on the issue of "race and human development" Franz Boas certainly was far ahead of his times.

58. Howard Hale Long to Boas, March 13, 1929, and Boas to Howard Hale Long, March 18, 1929, Boas Papers.

Black Sacrifice, Jewish Redemption

From Al Jolson's *Jazz Singer* to
John Garfield's *Body and Soul*

 *Michael Rogin*

ALMOST FROM the moment of its inception in the late nineteenth century, the immigrant Yiddish press began to protest against the denial of equality to African Americans. "Pogrom in Pennsylvania" is the headline Alfred Kazin remembers above the 1920s *Jewish Daily Forward* report of a lynching. Driven by race prejudice from their European homes, and facing anti-Semitism in the United States, Jews were the White ethnic group most identified with Blacks and most supportive of civil rights for racial minorities. The tensions between Jews and African Americans so widely advertised today were not absent in the first half of the twentieth century, to be sure, in urban neighborhoods and the entertainment business for example. But from the founding of the NAACP through the 1960s Civil Rights Movement, Jews were heavily overrepresented among the White activist opponents of racial inequality. Lynchings and race riots, pogroms in the promised land, were, in the phrase Hasia R. Diner quotes from the Yiddish press, "a stain of shame on the American flag."[1]

Many Jews who were entering the melting pot had their own stain of shame, however: burnt cork. For by the turn of the twentieth century Jewish entertainers were the major blackface performers. Although Jewish blackface has been viewed as a form of Jewish sympathy for Blacks— "one woe speaking through the voice of another," in Irving Howe's

---

1. Alfred Kazin, "Jews," *New Yorker,* March 7, 1994, 72; Hasia R. Diner, *In the Almost Promised Land: American Jews and Blacks, 1915–1935* (1977; rpt. Baltimore: Johns Hopkins University Press, 1995). I owe "the stain of shame" to Hasia Diner, "Drawn Together by Self-Interest: Jewish Representation of Race and Race Relations in the Early Twentieth Century," above. The present essay is adapted and revised from my *Blackface, White Noise: Jewish Immigrants in the Hollywood Melting Pot* (Berkeley and Los Angeles: University of California Press, 1996), where the claims made in these opening paragraphs are documented and much fuller bibliographic support is provided.

words—even the least offensive burnt-cork stereotypes caricatured and demeaned African Americans. Minstrelsy appropriated Black performance practices and reproduced them in distorted versions. Blackface was a form of what James Snead calls " 'exclusionary emulation,' the principle whereby the power and trappings of Black culture are imitated while at the same time their Black originators are segregated and kept at a distance." At the forefront of the struggle for equal political rights for all citizens of the United States, immigrant Jews also played a central role in the creation of a racialized twentieth-century mass culture.[2]

Immigrant Jews and their children, for whom race prejudice violated the American creed, were invoking the promise of the Declaration of Independence that all men are created equal. Blackface emerged out of the doctrine of White supremacy that supported the slave-owning author of the Declaration and the independence for which he spoke. The Declaration of Independence founded the new nation politically in natural rights. Blackface minstrelsy, the first form of American mass culture, founded the new nation culturally on racial wrongs. Along with the frontier myth, blackface emerged in the Age of Jackson to give the United States its second declaration of independence, its distinctive national culture. Both the original Declaration and burnt cork presided over the melting pot, making new identities out of the diverse peoples of the Old World. Playing with the racial domination and desire hidden beneath claims to formal equality, blackface was a rite of passage from the Old World to the New. Blacking up as members of particular, often stigmatized ethnic and regional groups, performers (and through them their audiences) wiped off the burnt cork as White Americans. A ritual of conversion in which Black bodies saved White souls, blackface gave access to states of experience imagined as Black without imprisoning Whites in a fixed Black identity. Putting on and taking off burnt cork, "White Negro" Irish, "Oriental" Jews, and other immigrants subject to invidious racial distinctions took control of their blackness by showing it was only skin deep. Blackface was a form of racial masquerade. It passed ethnics into White Americans by distinguishing them from the African Americans for whom they spoke and who were not permitted to speak for themselves.[3]

2. Irving Howe, *World of Our Fathers: The Journey of the East European Jews to America and the Life They Found and Made* (New York: Harcourt Brace Jovanovich, 1976), 563; James Snead, *White Screens/Black Images* (New York: Routledge, 1994), 60.

3. See Alexander Saxton, *The Rise and Fall of the White Republic: Class Politics and Mass Culture in Nineteenth-Century America* (New York: Verso, 1990); David R. Roediger, *The Wages of Whiteness: Race and the Making of the American Working Class* (New

Blackface was the most popular form of mass entertainment in the United States in the half century surrounding the Civil War. When vaudeville, Tin Pan Alley, and Hollywood supplanted the minstrel show, they did not so much displace as incorporate minstrelsy. And they did so under Jewish auspices. Jews—Al Jolson, Eddie Cantor, George Jessel, George Burns, Sophie Tucker—had pretty well taken over vaudeville blackface by the early twentieth century. Jewish moguls invented Hollywood, in Neal Gabler's phrase; they dominated the Big Eight studios from the mid-1920s until the end of classic Hollywood, and the major, transformative, Hollywood movies—*Birth of a Nation, The Jazz Singer,* and *Gone with the Wind*—grounded themselves in the values of White over Black. Jewish songwriters—Irving Berlin, Jerome Kern, and George Gershwin, to name only the most famous—created some of their most popular melting-pot American music from African American sources; among their contributions were Berlin's "Alexander's Ragtime Band," Kern's *Show Boat,* and the Gershwin song sung by Al Jolson in blackface that launched the Jazz Age, "Swanee."[4]

"The musical amalgamation of the American Negro and the American Jew" gave birth to melting-pot music, in the phrase of Gershwin's first biographer, Isaac Goldberg.[5] *Amalgamation* was the word for forbidden interracial sexual congress; "musical miscegenation" filled the public and private spaces prohibited to actual African Americans. Popular culture productions that, like *Show Boat,* commented critically on that process even as they exemplified it (Magnolia, who has learned to sing from Julie's "colored folks" music, gets her starring chance when the one drop rule that labels Julie "Black" drives her from the stage) were rare; to see anatomized unselfconsciously the typical workings of musical amalgamation, we must watch the show that premiered in Hollywood the same year that *Showboat* opened on Broadway.

The Jazz Singer (1927), the first talking picture, brought together

York: Verso, 1991); Eric Lott, *Love and Theft: Blackface and the American Working Class* (New York: Oxford University Press, 1993).

4. For the preeminent Jewish role in blackface, Hollywood, and Tin Pan Alley see Neal Gabler: *An Empire of Their Own: How the Jews Invented Hollywood* (New York: Crown, 1988); Howe, *World of Our Fathers,* 562; Lester D. Friedman, *Hollywood's Image of the Jew* (New York: Ungar, 1982), 19; Marc Slobin, "Some Intersections of Jews, Music, and Theater," in *From Hester Street to Hollywood: The Jewish-American Stage and Screen,* ed. Sarah Blacher Cohen (Bloomington: Indiana University Press, 1983), 31; Gary Giddins, *Riding on a Blue Note: Jazz and American Pop* (New York: Oxford University Press, 1981), 5–17.

5. Isaac Goldberg, "Aaron Copland and His Jazz," *American Mercury* 12 (September 1927): 63–64, and *George Gershwin* (New York: Simon and Schuster, 1931).

blackface and vaudeville, Tin Pan Alley and Hollywood. It starred Jolson, the blackface performer who was the most popular entertainer of his day. Burnt cork in *The Jazz Singer* transforms the cantor's son, Jakie Rabinowitz, into the American mass idol, Jack Robin. Replacing Jakie's inherited cantor robes, burnt cork kills the jazz singer's father. At the film's climax Jolson first sings Kol Nidre on the Day of Atonement over his father's dead body, then sings "My Mammy" in blackface to his Christian girlfriend and his Jewish mother. "Spiritual miscegenation" between Black and Jew—this term comes from the afterword to Israel Zangwill's 1908 play, *The Melting Pot*—will preside over the earthly intermarriage between the Jewish son and the object of desire forbidden to African Americans, the White American girl.[6]

Resistance to Americanization in *The Jazz Singer* comes only from the Jewish family, not from American nativism. But the racism and anti-Semitism repressed from the film's narrative return in the blackface identification between African Americans and immigrant Jews. Blackface raises the Jewish son above the people he is leaving behind, the immigrant Jewish community of his parents and the African Americans he ventriloquizes. Their sacrifice is carried by the film's final shot, which lingers on the blackface singer with his arms stretched out as on a cross. Crucified as the son of the Old World Jewish father and as the New World Black, Rabinowitz is reborn as the American success story, Jack Robin. In signifying Jewish generational conflict, burnt cork blocks out and stands in for the African Americans who undergird ethnic upward mobility by remaining fixed in place.[7]

Two decades after *The Jazz Singer*, in the brief period when Jewish radicals were making Hollywood films, they tried to take back *The Jazz Singer*. Jewish social activists, especially those in the Communist Party and other leftists groups, were distinctively allied with African Americans in the struggle for equal rights, whereas Jews who donned burnt cork performed White supremacist stereotypes as the American badge of belonging. The contrast was not so black and white, however, since both minstrelsy and civil rights were invested in crossing the racial line. On the one hand, while elite and powerful Jews spoke for the more

6. I first discussed *The Jazz Singer* in "Blackface, White Noise: The Jewish Jazz Singer Finds His Voice," *Critical Inquiry* 18 (spring 1992): 417–53, now revised and incorporated into *Blackface, White Noise*. Israel Zangwill, *The Melting Pot* (New York: Macmillan, 1914), 207.

7. Cf. David Levering Lewis, "Parallels and Divergences: Assimilationist Strategies of Afro-American and Jewish Elites from 1910 to the Early 1930s," *Journal of American History* 71 (December 1984): 543–64.

powerless Blacks in the civil rights arena, few Blacks spoke for the Jews. On the other hand, Jewish blackface represented a form of identification with the pariah group, not just racial aversion. The Hollywood race liberals who finally, in the wake of the Nazi defeat, made films about racism and anti-Semitism, were helping to bring blackface as national culture to an end. But their films bore an unacknowledged indebtedness to the tradition they were trying to leave behind.

Fascinated with racial masquerade, giving Jews the role of helping Blacks, forcing from out of the Black body the abject emotionality that embarrassed assimilating Jews, such popular postwar films as *Gentleman's Agreement*, *Pinky*, and *Home of the Brave*—I have argued elsewhere—project the political unconscious of blackface culture from within the program for equality. Gregory Peck pretends to be a Jew in *Gentleman's Agreement*; in *Pinky*, the White actress Jeanne Crain plays an African American passing as White. Like blackface, Jewface and whiteface imagine what it would be like to belong to another racial group. But just as the Jewish jazz singer rises through the mask of the people themselves forbidden to cross the racial line, so *Gentleman's Agreement* advocates integration for Jews, whereas *Pinky* endorses segregated institutions for Blacks. A Jewish soldier crippled by racism was the protagonist of the Broadway play *Home of the Brave*. The movie replaced the Jewish victim with a Black and moved the Jew to the position of the doctor who effects the cure. This substitution, signaling sympathetic identification between Jew and African American, was intended to transfer the fight against Nazi anti-Semitism to the attack on American Jim Crow. The result, however, was to invade and humiliate the Black soldier in the name of his rescue, to reduce him to the feminized emotionality familiar from blackface performance.[8]

Here I examine one of the first in the postwar cycle of race relations films, and the first Hollywood film to place at its center the relations between an African American and a Jew, the Abraham Polonsky/Robert Rossen collaboration *Body and Soul*. Now a film noir classic, *Body and Soul* was made in 1947, at the apogee of Communist influence in the motion picture business. If any film gives credence to the hallucinatory charge that a Communist conspiracy was seizing control of Hollywood— the charge that revived the House Un-American Activities Committee (HUAC) and propelled Ronald Reagan of the Screen Actors Guild onto

8. These films are discussed in my *Blackface, White Noise*, chap. 7. See also Thomas R. Cripps, *Making Movies Black: The Hollywood Message Movie from World War II to the Civil Rights Era* (New York: Oxford University Press, 1993).

the national political stage—this is the one. With its mixture of urban poetry and left-wing propaganda, *Body and Soul* was a creature of the Popular Front, the Communist/liberal alliance that joined reform politics to popular culture in the name of recovering a usable American past. HUAC targeted both *Body and Soul* and *Crossfire,* the other antiprejudice film noir made the same year. *Body and Soul's* director, Robert Rossen, and screenwriter, Abraham Polonsky, along with *Crossfire's* producer, Adrian Scott, and director, Edward Dmytryk, had been members of the Communist Party. Like the stars of *Body and Soul,* Canada Lee, John Garfield, and Anne Revere, they were all about to fall victim to HUAC. The political persecution of Garfield and Lee contributed to their early deaths during the Hollywood inquisition.[9]

But if the shared fate of the two male stars, martyrs to HUAC, ironically consummated the bond the film wanted to forge between African Americans and Jews, the problem within the movie itself lay less in the obviousness of the conscious message than in the buried unconscious one. Although *Body and Soul* may seem to sacrifice art to politics, its political unconscious actually resurrects the cultural myth from which Rossen and Polonsky were trying to escape.

Body and Soul revived the genre of the Jewish generational conflict film that had reached its apogee with *The Jazz Singer.* Just as *The Jazz Singer* was the first film to make Jewish blackface its subject and not just its method, so *Body and Soul* was the first Hollywood film to place at its center the relationship between an African American and a Jew. Investigating the meaning of blackface for the immigrant Jewish son, *The Jazz Singer* locates the immigrant Jew inside the African American, whereas *Body and Soul* establishes a bond between two separate men. Although Black serves as an intergenerational transitional object in both films, *Body and Soul* repudiated the Jewish exploitation of Black embedded in the

9. On Hollywood and HUAC see Larry Ceplair and Steven Englund, *The Inquisition in Hollywood: Politics in the Film Community, 1930–1960* (Berkeley and Los Angeles: University of California Press, 1983), 421, *passim;* Victor Navasky, *Naming Names* (New York: Viking, 1980); Michael Rogin, *"Ronald Reagan," the Movie, and Other Episodes in Political Demonology* (Berkeley and Los Angeles: University of California Press, 1987), 27–30. Unlike Lee, Revere, and Polonsky, Rossen and Garfield were not blacklisted. Garfield's struggle to appear as a cooperative witness before HUAC while refusing to name names ended with his death in 1952. The next year Rossen testified before the committee and was allowed to continue making movies. See Robert Sklar, *City Boys: Cagney, Bogart, Garfield* (Princeton: Princeton University Press, 1992); Samuel J. Rosenthal, "Golden Boychik: Star-Audience Relations between John Garfield and the Contemporary American Jewish Community" (Master's thesis, Annenberg School of Communication, University of Pennsylvania, 1993), 90, 131–32.

first talking picture. Despite trying to take back *The Jazz Singer*, however, *Body and Soul* ends by falling under its sway.

On both the Black and the Jewish fronts, *Body and Soul* marked a new departure for the motion picture business. Hitler's rise to power and the Americanizing moguls' wish for invisibility had driven Jews from in front of the camera. "You can't have a Jew play a Jew," Samuel Goldwyn was quoted as saying. "It wouldn't work on the screen." Rossen's own first screenplay, *They Won't Forget* (1937), converted the lynched Atlanta Jewish factory manager Leo Frank into a Yankee professor. After the cycle of generational conflict films had come to an end in the mid-1930s, Gentile actors starred as Jews in the rare movie on a Jewish theme. John Garfield was the first Jew allowed to play a Jewish leading man in more than a decade.[10]

Even more revolutionary was the African American presence in the film. Although Jolson's blackface mask intended sympathy for African Americans, it confined them to emotional primitivism. A single Black menial appeared briefly in the Jolson film, and when African Americans got roles in talking pictures—as mammies, buffoons, and entertainers— they were forced to work within the constraints of racial stereotype. The first postwar films to center on racial prejudice, *Crossfire* and *Gentleman's Agreement*, had confronted anti-Semitism rather than anti-Black racism. *Body and Soul*, whose bond between Jew and African American prepared the ground for subsequent treatments of discrimination against Blacks, created one of the first substantial, ungrotesque African American film roles. Canada Lee, who played the part, felt liberated from Hollywood racism; he rejoiced that the word *Negro* was never used in the film. But just as blackface in *The Jazz Singer* grounds White freedom in Black servitude by standing in for actual Blacks, so omitting the racial word in *Body and Soul* fails to free the African American actor from inheriting the sacrificial role. It is now time to look at the movie.[11]

10. Patricia Erens, *The Jew in American Cinema* (Bloomington: Indiana University Press, 1984), 125–85. Goldwyn is quoted on p. 140, and in Otto Friedrich, *City of Nets* (New York: Harper, 1986), 354–55, who assigns the remark to the exclusion of a different actor (Sam Levene instead of Paul Muni) from a movie of the 1940s instead of the 1930s. See also "They Won't Forget," *Variety Film Reviews*, June 30, 1937. Rossen was working from a novel that had already converted Frank from Jew to Gentile. As for Garfield, just before making *Body and Soul* he starred in a remake of the 1920 Jewish generational conflict film, *Humoresque* (1946). However, the remake ignored the issue of assimilation so prominent in the original and virtually eliminated its protagonist's ethnicity.

11. Cripps, *Making Movies Black*, 214. On the depiction of African Americans in motion pictures generally see Donald Bogle, *Toms, Coons, Mulattoes, Mammies, and Blacks:*

John Garfield (a.k.a. Julie Garfinkle) wakes from a nightmare in the first scene of the film. Close-ups of a sweating face and the screaming sound of "Ben! Ben!" introduce the agitated, claustrophobic aura of the former Group Theater and Warner Bros. star. Who is Ben? All the audience knows from the overheated first few minutes of the film is that Ben's death has sent the Garfield character back to his mother. Garfield gets a diegetic name, Charley, and an occupation, boxer, but we learn nothing more about Ben. Although he "couldn't find a place to lie down . . . after they took Ben away," and although he is defending his title that night, Charley's mother tells him to leave her house.

"You thinking about Ben, Charley? Everybody dies. Ben. Shorty. Even you." The scene has shifted to the prebout dressing room. Charley is in his trunks, but the speaker and the meaning of his menacing words are a mystery. The rest of the film—until it returns to the championship fight—is the flashback that motivates this opening.

Ben, we will learn, is a Black boxer (Canada Lee), for whose death Charley feels responsible. Desperate for money and with a blood clot in his brain, Ben had thrown his own championship match to Charley, receiving the promise that his head would be spared. Because "the crowd likes a killer," however, the gangster who fixed the fight did not tell Charley that Ben had been paid to lose. Charley thinks he knocked Ben out fairly; shocked when he hears the truth, he takes on the damaged ex-champ as his trainer.

Ben replaces Shorty, the boyhood friend who has been Charley's caretaker and conscience up to now but who was killed by the mob. Gangsters, we already know, had also killed Charley's father when they bombed a speakeasy next to his candy store. Charley's desire not to end up poor like Pop had propelled him into the fight game over his mother's objections. To her wish that her son could have grown up in a better neighborhood, "so he wouldn't make a living hitting people," Pop had answered, "You think I picked the East Side like Columbus picked America?" The rhetorical question locates immigrants on the side not of Columbus and pioneer freedom but of Indians and slaves. Underscoring the limited choices faced by the immigrant poor, Mom is forced to ask for charity after Pop is killed. Her responses to the visiting social worker's questionnaire name for the first time what we already know: "Race: white. Religion: Jewish."

An Interpretive History of Blacks in American Films, 2d ed. (New York: Continuum, 1989). The five race relations films that followed *Body and Soul* are *Pinky, Lost Boundaries, Home of the Brave, Intruder in the Dust* (all 1949), and *No Way Out* (1950).

Standing with the immigrant Jewish working class, *Body and Soul* attacks the parvenu who rises, like the jazz singer, by leaving his community behind. Boxing is a "business." Charley is "not just a kid who can fight. He's money." (In an inside joke at the expense of the studio system, Roberts, the gangster to whom Charley sold his body and soul, shares his name with Bob Roberts, the producer of this [also named with tongue in cheek] Enterprise Studio film.)[12] Once Charley is champ, his agreement to throw his title defense and bet against himself is an "investment." This way of making money is opposed by both his mother (Anne Revere) and Peg (Lili Palmer), the artist he wants to marry. Jewish girl and Jewish mother join in repudiating Charley for choosing the path of gangster-capitalism.

"I can't marry you. It'd just mean marrying [Roberts]," explains Peg. *Body and Soul* opposes that intermarriage, which also entails Charley's liaison with a torch singer. The showgirl with whom the jazz singer falls in love, rewarding his move from cantor's son to mass culture, becomes the temptress in *Body and Soul*. The Garfield film chooses against intermarriage and for interracial solidarity between Black man and Jew.

"The neighborhood," which does not know that Charley has chosen capitalism against it, has put its money on the champ. "Everybody's betting on you," a local named Shimin tells Charley. The only character marked by name and accent as distinctively Jewish, Shimin appears in this scene (and no other) to remind Charley, "Over in Europe the Nazis are killing people like us. Just because of their religion. But here Charley Davis is champeen."[13] Ben echoes the message: "It always felt so good after the fight. Walk down Lenox Avenue. Kids all crazy for you. And proud." Not only is Charley following Ben in selling out his own people; he has also risen on Ben's back, as the graphic shots of the Jewish fighter knocking down the African American make all too literal. Peg cringes during the pummeling; the torch singer shouts, "Kill him, Charley! Kill him!" *Body and Soul* insists on what *The Jazz Singer* shows in spite of itself,

12. Enterprise Studios was an independent production company set up by Garfield; it made two films before the blacklist, *Body and Soul* and the Polonsky/Garfield production *Force of Evil*. According to Polonsky, film studios worried about lawsuits from people with the same name as movie villains. Bob Roberts was Garfield's agent. Saying, "I won't sue you," he suggested the use of his own name. Abraham Polonsky, telephone interview, April 18, 1995. See also Michael Shepler, "*Body and Soul*," in *McGill's Survey of Cinema, First Series*, ed. Frank V. McGill (Englewood Cliffs, N.J.: Prentice Hall, 1980), 1:195–97. When Tim Robbins named his 1992 political satire *Bob Roberts*, he was surely referencing *Body and Soul*.

13. Augmenting the documentary effect, Shimin Rishkin was played by a Jewish comedian of the same name. See Rosenthal, "Golden Boychick," 99.

that the Black face represents the sacrificed immigrant Jewish community. The left-wing film takes the side of the pariah against the upwardly
mobile Jewish son.

"You fixed the fight, didn't you?" Ben demands of the champ after his
invocation of Harlem. The thought agitates the trainer, who punches
Charley's exercise bag to show him how to win. Roberts enters and or-
ders Ben out of the training camp. "You don't tell me how to live." "No,
but I'll tell you how to die." The distraught Black man collapses back-
ward, gets up, starts swinging wildly ("I can take it; I'm the champ") and
falls facedown. The scene replays the end of Ben's fight with Charley,
only this time the ex-champ is dead. He has left behind Charley's nightmare. The next night the Jewish fighter rises four times from the canvas,
finally knocking out his Irish challenger in the last round.

Polonsky had resisted an early effort to eliminate the Black fighter
from his film. As he put it half a century later, "There is an obvious deep
relationship between people held not so much in contempt but in a deep
antipathy by society. Garfield [was Polonsky referring to the actor standing up for the script or the character who stood up for Ben?] refused to be
part of the betrayal."[14]

The Garfield/Polonsky Jewish-Black identification gave *Body and Soul*
its innovative power; still, the movie could not escape its past. In finish-
ing off Ben and elevating Charley, *Body and Soul* tells the truth (embedded in *The Jazz Singer*) about the contrasting prospects in the United
States for African Americans and Jews. Faithfully mirroring the greater
obstacles to Black than to Jewish success, *Body and Soul* conditions Jewish-
Black solidarity on Jew knocking out Black. But although it insists on the
contaminated character of Charley's victory, the result is to turn boxing
history inside out. The first version of the *Body and Soul* screenplay based
Charley on Barney Ross, a Jewish boxer from the ghetto whose father
owned a candy store, who had won the lightweight and welterweight
world boxing championships and a silver star at the Battle of Guadal-
canal during World War II. When Polonsky added the Black prizefighter
to the plot, he reversed the actual relations between Jewish and Black
boxers in the period. During the 1930s and 1940s, African Americans
were taking over boxing from Jews and other White ethnics: Joe Louis
knocked out Maxie Baer, Henry Armstrong knocked out Barney Ross.
Baer disparaged Louis before their fight; Louis punished him in the ring.
Film censorship had originated to stop audiences from seeing documentary footage of Jack Johnson defeating Jim Jeffries. Charley may not be a

---

14. Polonsky interview.

great White hope (Jack London's term for Jeffries); even so, no Black man knocks him down. Unlike Jeffries, Baer, and Ross, Charley Davis beats his Black opponent.[15]

Black boxers did throw fights in this mob-controlled sport, but it was Jake La Motta who lay down for Billy Fox (the African American) in the year *Body and Soul* was made. Although *Body and Soul* exposed the fix that undergirds White ethnic success, it participated in spite of itself in the cultural ritual that forged White manhood in racial conflict in the ring. When the White fighter became Jewish, he inherited the culture's wish for a victory of White over Black. *Body and Soul* wanted to repudiate that wish, but it could not film Black victory.[16]

Body and Soul remade Clifford Odets's generational-conflict boxing drama, *Golden Boy*. (Denied the starring role in the Group Theater production of the play, Garfield had accepted a Warner Bros. offer and left New York for Hollywood. He was too ethnic for the 1939 movie, however, which starred William Holden, and so produced *Body and Soul* himself to have another shot at the part.) Odets's golden boy, Joe Bonaparte, gives up the ring and returns to his Italian father after he kills a Black boxer. As will Charley, so a worried Joe visits the Black boxer's dressing room following the knockout. The refusal of forgiveness by the boxer's brothers—the first time in Hollywood that Blacks did not give Whites what they wanted (and the last time for another quarter century)—is overcome by their father. To an orchestral, Negro spiritual background (in the movie), the father tells Joe that we all carry burdens, and his son's death is Joe's. Like the shot of "The Chocolate Drop" face down in the ring—which is repeated when Charley knocks out Ben—the message of ethnic reparation moves from one boxing film to the other. Just as it ends *Golden Boy*, so aggression against the Black boxer introduces Charley's bond with Ben.[17]

Knowing his victory was contaminated, Charley promises to "look

15. Ibid; Gerald Early, *The Culture of Bruising: Essays on Prizefighting, Literature, and Modern American Culture* (Hopewell: Ecco Press, 1994); Shepler, "*Body and Soul*," 195–96. For instruction in boxing history, I am indebted to conversations with Early and with Norman Jacobson.

16. Early, *Culture of Bruising,* 10–38, 91; Harry Carpenter, *Masters of Boxing* (New York: A. S. Barnes, 1964), 55.

17. In his last role on stage, in the 1951 Broadway revival of *Golden Boy*, Garfield finally got to play Joe Bonaparte. On Garfield and *Golden Boy* see Sklar, *City Boys*, 82, and Rosenthal, "Golden Boychik," 31, 131. The Jewish boxer Benny Leonard had beaten the Black fighter Kid Chocolate (I learned from Norman Jacobson) for the lightweight crown in the 1920s. I have also benefited from conversations with Isabelle Rogin about the play and the film of *Golden Boy*.

after Ben." Charley may have something to atone for, but also, as he puts it, "I need someone I can trust." It is Ben who looks after Charley. He and the torch singer enter Charley's life together as replacements for the Jewish mother and Peg. The Black man not only takes care of the fighter after (since the movie is in flashback) his mother turns him out; he also replaces her as Charley's conscience. But whereas his Jewish mother is judgmental and unforgiving (she resembles Cantor Rabinowitz; as part of the larger change in representations of family dynamics in the twenty years between *The Jazz Singer* and *Body and Soul,* the parents have switched roles), Ben offers basic trust. Supporting Charley as his mother does not, saving him from destructive self-interest, Ben succeeds where Mom fails. Leslie Fiedler's American *Liebestod,* in which White men escape the demands of women into doomed interracial male solidarity, was moving from the Protestant frontier to the urban ghetto. A year before Fiedler published his "Come Back to the Raft Ag'in, Huck Honey!" Ben played Nigger Jim. Both the jazz singer and the champ look forward to marriage. But the transformative bond for both (here Canada Lee succeeds Jolson himself in blackface) is with a Black man.[18]

"What're ya gonna do, kill me?" Charley challenges Roberts once he has won the fight he was paid to throw. "Everybody dies." The speech inverts Roberts's death sentence on Ben, for the words Charley hears before entering the ring and now throws back at the gangster were first spoken by Roberts to Charley's manager when they set up the Black champion. "Everybody dies" establishes Ben's legacy to Charley, the bond between Black and Jew. Only one body is resurrected, however; in this film's spiritual miscegenation, Ben has died to save Charley's soul.

In the barely lit, arresting opening shot of *Body and Soul*—set at night and undecipherable until the end of the film—Charley's exercise bag swings slowly above an empty canvas. We will come to learn that punching the bag had set off Ben's fatal attack just a few hours before, and as the camera pans from the swaying object to Charley's nightmare, the exercise bag evokes the body of a lynched Black man. That opening shot has two sources. When Robert Rossen was forced to change the lynched Leo Frank from Jew to Yankee in *They Won't Forget,* he preserved Frank's lynching as the final scene of the film. As a mob drags the convicted innocent from the train transporting him to state prison, the last shot shows another passing train hitting a mail sack and dropping it into a boxcar.

18. Leslie Fiedler, "Come Back to the Raft Ag'in, Huck Honey!" *Partisan Review* (June 1948), reprinted in *An End to Innocence* (Boston: Beacon Press, 1952). Cf. Fiedler *Love and Death in the American Novel* (New York: Continuum, 1960), and Lott, *Love and Theft.*

Rossen did not forget the last frame of *They Won't Forget;* ten years later he turned it into the opening shot of *Body and Soul.* Since the lynched Frank was the exception, the mail bag stands in as well for the mass of lynched southern Black bodies. It thereby reunites the Black and Jewish protagonists of the Leo Frank case, whose opposition had set against each other Black and Jewish groups involved in the trial. For it was a Black handyman, himself probably guilty of the crime, who was coerced into testifying against Frank.[19]

If Leo Frank was one memory behind the swinging exercise bag that opens *Body and Soul,* the other—"Black body swinging in the southern breeze, Strange fruit hanging from the poplar trees"—was Billie Holiday's signature song, "Strange Fruit." The Jewish Communist songwriter Lewis Allan had written "Strange Fruit" for Holiday a few years before. (Allan's real name was Meeropol, and he and his wife would later adopt the children of the executed Ethel and Julius Rosenberg.) "Strange Fruit" was originally recorded at Café Society, Barney Josephson's integrated Greenwich Village nightclub frequented by such artists as Canada Lee, Paul Robeson, Benny Goodman, and Polonsky himself. If the filmmakers had attended Billie Holiday's 1946 Los Angeles concert at the Embassy Theater, they would have heard her sing "Strange Fruit" when they were beginning work on the picture.[20]

"It is the tragic heroic fate of the Black American to bring humbly forth grand humanity from a social oppression that thoroughly contradicts the possibility of humanity itself," notes Gerald Early in *The Culture of Bruising.* "It is the same urge, the same spirit, that motivates Uncle Tom." When Harriet Beecher Stowe was taking communion in a small New England church, she received a vision of a Black slave being beaten to death. Rushing home, she began *Uncle Tom's Cabin,* the most popular novel of the nineteenth century. "The first part of the book committed to writing was the death of Uncle Tom," Stowe later wrote. *Uncle Tom's Cabin,* with Tom played in blackface, was the most popular touring

19. *They Won't Forget,* dir. Mervyn Le Roy (Warner Bros., 1937). On Black-Jewish divisions over the Leo Frank case see Jeffrey Melnick, *Ancestors and Relatives: The Uncanny Relationship of African Americans and Jews* (Cambridge: Harvard University Press, forthcoming). Thanks to Jonathan Buchsbaum for first alerting me to *Body and Soul's* opening shot.

20. Lewis Erenberg, "Impressions of Broadway Night Life," in William R. Taylor, ed., *Inventing Times Square: Commerce and Culture at the Crossroads of the World* (New York: Russell Sage, 1991), 176; Billie Holiday, "Strange Fruit" and liner notes, *Billie Holiday,* Commodore Records CCK 7001; Billie Holiday, "Strange Fruit" and liner notes, *Lady in Autumn: The Best of the Verve Years,* Polygram 849 43614; Polonsky interview (Polonsky did not attend the Los Angeles concert, however).

theatrical in the years following the Civil War. Although the word *Negro* is never uttered in *Body and Soul*, Canada Lee plays the Black Christ. The spirit that presides over this left-wing motion picture conjoins Karl Marx to Harriet Beecher Stowe.[21]

Jolson had performed Uncle Tom's suffering—ending "My Mammy" with his arms outstretched in *The Jazz Singer*, playing mammy (the father who loses his "Sonny Boy") in *The Singing Fool*. Crucified in burnt cork, as a Black man, the jazz singer rose as his regenerated White self. Black sacrifice also restores Charley (on *The Jazz Singer* model) to his championship, his mother, and his love. The Jewish boxer has succeeded the African American as mob-sponsored champion paid to throw away his crown. Peg warned Charley that he would end up like Ben; thanks to Ben, he does not. Taking up the blackface jazz singer's cross, Ben dies for Charley's sins.

If *The Jazz Singer* was one doubles movie behind the Garfield/Lee collaboration, Oscar Micheaux's 1924 *Body and Soul* was another. Paul Robeson played in that all-Black film both a rapist masquerading as a minister and his virtuous brother—"two souls . . . warring . . . in one Black body" in W. E. B. Du Bois's famous words. When Rossen and Polonsky redistributed the parts into Black soul and White body, they enabled the one to save the other.[22]

Was a different relation imaginable in 1947 between African American and Jew? Taken from an earlier movie, the title *Body and Soul* in turn suggested as sound track for the film the jazz standard "Body and Soul." Originally written by the Jewish songwriter Johnny Green, the 1939 Coleman Hawkins version of the tune was an artistic and popular success, still heard on jukeboxes when *Body and Soul* was released. If Hawkins's interpretation was insufficiently thematic and melodic for the film, Rossen and Polonsky could have turned to the 1935 Benny Goodman/Teddy Wilson/Gene Krupa performance. Goodman, one of the original investors in Café Society, had broken the Jim Crow barrier in musical ensembles when he hired Teddy Wilson for the tour on which they recorded "Body and Soul." Both the Goodman/Wilson and the Hawkins

21. Early, *Culture of Bruising*, 37.
22. Although *Body and Soul* was Robeson's first film, and although he traveled in the same circles as the makers of the Garfield movie, the source of that film's title may rather have been an obscure 1931 Cagney motion picture, also *Body and Soul*. Polonsky could not remember in 1995 from which earlier film the title of his was taken. See Polonsky interview; Sklar, *City Boys*, 279; Martin B. Duberman, *Paul Robeson* (New York: Knopf, 1988), 77. Thanks to Jane Gaines and Stephen Best for the Micheaux connection.

recordings were instances of "musical amalgamation" in which African Americans had leading, independent roles. Closer to home, Rossen and Polonsky could have used Billie Holiday's own version, with which she had followed "Strange Fruit" at the 1946 Los Angeles concert. They knew this music; Polonsky remembers dancing with his wife to Benny Goodman's "Body and Soul" at the Hotel Pennsylvania in New York. In the end, though, whether forced by the Musicians Union or by their own sense of Hollywood requirements, they incorporated Green's tune into a brooding, melodramatic, orchestral background noise credited to composer Hugo Friedhofer and conductor Emil Newman. The European high-culture choice, repeated in making Charley's girlfriend an artist, came at Black expense. Jazz Age White popular music replaces the sound of Black jazz in *The Jazz Singer*. But whether Euro- or American-centric, the result is the same. Like the absence of jazz in *The Jazz Singer*, the missing jazz in *Body and Soul* points to the African American sacrifice that both movies register—mammy singer on the cross, Ben on the canvas—even as they enact it.[23]

23. Billie Holiday also recorded with the Teddy Wilson orchestra in the late 1930s. On "Body and Soul," the music, see *The Smithsonian Collection of Classic Jazz*, selected and annotated by Martin Williams, Columbia P6 11891 (Washington, D.C., 1973), side 4 and p. 24; and Billie Holiday, "Body and Soul," *Lady in Autumn*; Polonsky interview. Polonsky does not remember the music as an important issue in the film.

The Civil Rights Movement and the Reemergence of the Left

Murray Friedman

IN 1955 THE civil rights battleground shifted dramatically from the courts to the streets. Before, the struggle against racism had been waged largely by White liberal lawyers and social scientists, most of them northerners, many of them Jews. In courts and classrooms they had led the intellectual assault against discrimination, seeking to establish the principle of equality before the law. In spite of their many achievements, however, the pace of change was slow. Southern Blacks continued to encounter racism in schools, in public accommodations, and in their daily lives.

Starting with Rosa Parks's historic refusal to move to the back of the bus in Montgomery, Alabama, in December 1955, local Blacks took matters into their own hands. Under the leadership of a little-known Black minister, Rev. Martin Luther King Jr., a bus boycott was begun in that city. Black churches and their members became the focal point of protest activities.

The Montgomery campaign was not the first Black-only attempt to develop a southern boycott. In June 1953, even before the Supreme Court handed down its momentous decision in *Brown v. Board of Education*, a mass bus boycott had been undertaken in Baton Rouge, Louisiana, by Blacks impatient with the slow-moving legal actions of the NAACP. The White establishment in Baton Rouge ultimately worked out a compromise in which two front seats were reserved for Whites, the rear seats for Blacks, and every seat in between would be occupied on a first-come, first-served basis. This was accepted by the local Black leadership as a

This essay was originally published in Murray Friedman's *What Went Wrong? The Creation and Collapse of the Black-Jewish Alliance* (1995). It is here reprinted in a slightly modified form by permission of the Free Press.

temporary measure. King and Ralph Abernathy, another Montgomery minister, were well aware of the partly successful Baton Rouge model and consulted with the leadership there. Where Montgomery differed was that there, for the first time, large numbers of Blacks directly confronted and effectively disrupted the system felt to be responsible for their oppression—and won.[1]

Before Montgomery, King had had very little experience as a civil rights leader, and the movement he led only gradually gained national attention.[2] Historian J. Mills Thornton has pointed out that the protest, like that in Baton Rouge, attracted surprisingly little notice. Not until it became linked with what Clayborne Carson has termed the "Afro-American-Jewish radical community" and the remnants of the organized left did the southern protest movement gain broader attention.[3]

As it happened, the American left was greatly in need of a cause at this time. Whether liberals or labor leaders, pacifists or socialists, Communists or fellow travelers, members of the left had played an important role in helping to shape the welfare state under Presidents Roosevelt and Truman. But by the 1950s, with its influence diminished and its numbers reduced by congressional witch-hunts and internal antagonisms, the left was in almost total disarray. Liberals and leftists who testified before the House Un-American Activities Committee (HUAC) and other investigative bodies often found themselves ostracized by their friends and neighbors. Former *Washington Post* reporter Carl Bernstein has written poignantly about his father, an official of the United Public Workers of

---

1. Aldon D. Morris, *The Origins of the Civil Rights Movement: Black Communities Organizing for Change* (New York: Free Press, 1984), xi, 25, 132.

2. Coretta Scott King, *My Life with Martin Luther King, Jr.* (New York, Rinehart and Winston, 1969), 41–42. Both he and his wife, however, had broader backgrounds than many of their colleagues. Following undergraduate work at Morehouse College in Atlanta, he studied at Crozer Theological Seminar outside Philadelphia and later earned his doctorate at Boston University. Among those who greatly influenced him were the pacifist A. J. Muste, who introduced him to the concept of civil disobedience, and Reinhold Niebuhr, from whom he learned an awareness of Christian pragmatism. Coretta in the 1940s studied music at Antioch College in Ohio, where a sizable portion of the student body was Jewish. For a year she dated a Jewish student. Martin Luther King Jr., *Stride toward Freedom: The Montgomery Story* (New York: Ballantine, 1958); David I. Lewis, *King: A Critical Biography* (Baltimore: Penguin, 1970), 37. See also David J. Garrow, *Bearing the Cross: Martin Luther King, Jr., and the Southern Christian Leadership Conference* (New York: William Morrow, 1986); and Taylor Branch, *Parting the Waters: America in the King Years 1954–63* (New York: Simon and Schuster, 1998).

3. Clayborne Carson Jr., "Blacks and Jews in the Civil Rights Movement," in *Jews in Black Perspectives: A Dialogue,* ed. Joseph R. Washington Jr. (Lanham, Md.: University Press of America, 1989), 117.

America and a Communist, who along with his wife was called to testify before the HUAC in the summer of 1954.[4] Many accused of Communist affiliations or sympathies were driven from jobs in government, universities, and public schools. More than one hundred Communist Party leaders were convicted under the Smith Act, which made it a crime to teach or advocate the forceful overthrow of the government. Others were indicted under state sedition laws. Meanwhile, Democratic socialists Walter Reuther and Philip Murray spearheaded a campaign against a number of Communist-controlled unions, including the United Public Workers of America.[5]

Many disillusioned Jewish leftists became depoliticized. Some responded as if they had been cast adrift. David Horowitz, a principal figure in the New Left and an active supporter of the Black Panthers in the 1960s, wrote that his own parents never spoke out publicly. Like thousands of other former Communists, they had left the party but could not leave the faith.[6]

The Montgomery bus boycott also coincided with Nikita Khrushchev's widely publicized 1956 denunciation of the crimes of Stalin and Khrushchev's own deployment of Soviet tanks and troops to crush the Hungarian democratic revolution. These events depleted the ranks of the American Communist Party even further. So great was its loss of membership, Taylor Branch suggests, that J. Edgar Hoover entertained the idea of using informers to gain control of the party at its convention in February 1957. Debates raged among the shrinking core of party regulars as to how to face these devastating developments.[7]

The badly discredited Stalinist left, led by William Z. Foster, ordered party leaders and other stalwarts underground to escape prosecution. Another faction, while retaining its Marxist perspective, sought to "Americanize" the party. Early in 1956 leaders of the latter faction, many of them Jewish, such as John Gates, editor of the *Daily Worker,* and Joseph Starobin, the former foreign editor, as well as Eugene Dennis, suggested taking a new look at the causes of the party's failures. In the ensuing struggle the Foster faction won out.

According to Irving Howe, the Americanizers stayed in touch with one

4. Carl Bernstein, "My Parents Belonged to the Communist Party," *Moment,* August 1989, 407. See also Bernstein, *Loyalties: A Son's Memoir* (New York: Touchstone, 1989).
5. Maurice Isserman, *If I Had a Hammer: The Death of the Old Left and the Birth of the New Left* (New York: Basic Books, 1987), 4.
6. David Horowitz, "Still Taking the Fifth," *Commentary* 88 (July 1989): 53.
7. Branch, *Parting the Waters,* 211; Isserman, *If I Had a Hammer,* 9.

another, forming a kind of reserve apparatus ready to go into action at the first hint of social ferment. They were present in the Civil Rights Movement and the peace groups as a powerful though informal organizational presence. Maurice Isserman has written that the most influential adult radical group in the 1960s was probably this party of ex-Communists— "a party that could do almost everything that a more formally organized radical group could do in the same situation: everything, that is, except recruit new members."[8]

What was vaguely envisioned at the time of the Montgomery bus boycott was a new left, though not necessarily the New Left that would emerge so forcefully in the sixties. Thus, the socialist (and bitter anti-Communist) Michael Harrington has written that he and his colleagues set out in search of the Black masses. While they did not know much about average Blacks and were sometimes guilty of condescending and manipulative impulses, Harrington insists that he and his colleagues were ultimately good for the movement and for Black people.[9] This African American–Jewish radical community in New York and elsewhere became the "seed-bed for civil rights activism" in the 1960s.[10]

The figure who now emerged as the critical link between the embattled left and the newly emerging southern Black protest movement was Bayard Rustin. A West Indian, Rustin had been raised by his grandparents in West Chester, Pennsylvania, where, as he later recalled, Blacks could not walk safely through the streets.[11] When the Great Depression forced him out of college, Rustin, a Quaker, moved in with relatives in Harlem, joining his Quaker background with the nonviolent strain in the Civil Rights Movement. The model was Mohandas Gandhi, the martyred Indian leader who preached a form of pacifist defense against the evil in society. Rustin attended the tuition-free City College of New York at night while earning a living as a backup vocalist for folksingers Leadbelly and Josh White. During this time he joined the Young Communist League.

In 1939 Rustin met A. Philip Randolph and established a lifelong friendship with him. Rustin was impressed, he later said, by "this man

8. Howe, "New Styles in Leftism," *Dissent* 12 (summer 1965): 300–301; Isserman, *If I Had a Hammer*, 33.

9. Michael Harrington, *Fragments of the Century* (New York: Saturday Review Press Dutton, 1973), 95. In varying ways Harrington's memoirs, William Barrett's *The Truants: Adventures among the Intellectuals,* and Paul Hollander's *Political Pilgrims,* all dealing with this period, have commented on the need of intellectuals for some form of meaning in a society that has lost its sense of religion.

10. Carson, "Blacks and Jews in the Civil Rights Movement," 117.

11. Harrington, *Fragments of the Century,* 99.

of great dignity and inner beauty." Randolph became Rustin's mentor, perhaps representing the father he had never had. Arnold Aronson, who knew both men, remarked on the tenderness of their relationship, recalling that when Randolph became physically helpless late in life, Rustin would patiently spoon-feed him.[12]

When the Communist Party ordered Rustin to toe the party line following Germany's June 1941 invasion of the Soviet Union, he quit the party and helped Randolph organize the March on Washington, which forced President Roosevelt to ban discrimination in defense industries.[13] Under Randolph's tutelage Rustin learned important lessons in the theory and practice of building mass movements by combining the themes of racial and economic justice. Randolph arranged for him to meet A. J. Muste, the head of the Fellowship of Reconciliation (FOR), which had been organized in England in 1914 to seek social change through the "confrontation of ideas." The organization came to the United States one year later and quickly grew into the nation's leading exponent of pacifism. Rustin so impressed the British activist that Muste appointed him FOR's youth secretary, and Rustin traveled widely as the organization's "itinerant Gandhian." In that capacity he helped James Farmer organize the Congress of Racial Equality (CORE) in New York in 1942.[14]

Tall, angular, animated, and full of ideas, Rustin was a popular figure on the left in the forties and fifties. Harrington recalled how he, Muste, David Dellinger, and others seeking the "beloved community" often gathered at parties in Rustin's Greenwich Village apartment, where their host would play the harpsichord and sing Elizabethan songs and old spirituals.[15]

Howell Raines tells that, shortly after the start of the Montgomery bus boycott, Rustin received a telegram from the writer Lillian Smith, a member of FOR, urging him to meet with Martin Luther King Jr., who had agreed to help organize the effort. Rustin discussed the idea with Randolph, Farmer, and John Morsell of the NAACP; they agreed that he should go. Randolph raised the money for the trip. On his first visit to

12. Jervis Anderson, "Randolph, Martin, and the March on Washington Movement," *American Educator* (winter 1988): 16; interview with Arnold Aronson, January 11, 1989, American Jewish Committee Oral History Library, New York Public Library, Jewish Division.

13. Branch, *Parting the Waters*, 170; Harrington, *Fragments of the Century*, 99.

14. James Farmer, *Lay Bare the Heart: An Autobiography of the Civil Rights Movement* (New York: Arbor House, 1985), 162; Morris, *Origins of the Civil Rights Movement*, 159; Harrington, *Fragments of the Century*, 99.

15. Branch, *Parting the Waters*, 168; Harrington, *Fragments of the Century*, 101.

King's house, Rustin was stunned to find armed guards stationed outside and a gun on a chair inside. King explained that the firearms were to be used only in self-defense, but Rustin was struck by the presence of such weaponry, which ran totally counter to the concepts of nonviolence that FOR espoused. Glenn Smiley, an alumnus of the organization, had already started instructing the boycott leaders in the tactics of nonviolence. Soon the message got through; within six weeks Rustin was able to report that there were no more armed guards and that King had dissociated himself from all forms of violence.[16]

Rustin found in King an odd and appealing mixture of determination and vulnerability. "I need your help," King told entertainer Harry Belafonte, who had also joined King's entourage. "I have no idea where this movement is going." After several lengthy conferences, King and Rustin reached agreement on how supporters in the North could assist the Montgomery Improvement Association, the central vehicle of the bus boycott. King knew that Communists and other radicals, in seeking to alleviate working conditions in the South, had worked alongside Blacks in textile mills and union shops. But he himself opposed communism and recognized the perils that lay ahead if his actions appeared to be influenced or controlled by leftists. The Improvement Association, which was in fact a grassroots organization, must give the appearance of having developed all the ideas and strategies used in the struggle, King told Rustin.[17]

With this remark King unknowingly laid out the future agenda of the Black-Jewish alliance. Until Montgomery, Jews had dominated the alliance; after Montgomery, Blacks would do so. It would remain a symbiotic relationship from which both sides would draw strength, but no longer would Jewish leaders and other outsiders call the shots. They would work behind the scenes, providing money and advice to King and his lieutenants, who would head the movement, win the headlines, and endure the arrests and jail sentences. Later, large numbers of Jews would join in protest activities in the South and expose themselves to some of these dangers, but only as a part of the new Black thrust and subordinate to its direction. The Black masses now became the central force in the civil rights revolution.

Following King's instructions, Rustin worked quietly in the background as an all-purpose aide. He helped set up mass meetings; he did

16. Howell Raines, *My Soul Is Rested* (New York: Putnam, 1977), 53, 56; Garrow, *Bearing the Cross*, 73; Morris, *Origins of the Civil Rights Movement*, 157.
17. Branch, *Parting the Waters*, 56, 208; Garrow, *Bearing the Cross*, 72.

chores; he helped King answer the mail, write speeches, and plan for meetings. He telephoned key people all over the country to drum up support. When things got tough and people needed to be fed, Rustin and King cosigned letters asking for money.

Taylor Branch, one of King's biographers, saw Rustin as filling a far more significant role than that of a mere factotum. Rustin opened up the movement to the outside world by virtue of a range of experience and influences that reached far beyond the Black church spirit that had thus far sustained the yearlong boycott. Another early supporter, Harris Wofford (later President Kennedy's special assistant for civil rights and a U.S. senator from Pennsylvania), viewed the relationship less charitably. He considered Rustin a sinister, manipulative influence on King, who was treated like a puppet performing symbolic actions planned by a "Gandhian high command."[18] Rustin prepared the way for Stanley David Levison, who now entered the scene.

In the summer of 1956, with the boycott gaining momentum, Rustin introduced King to Levison, who would become King's closest White friend and most reliable colleague for the remainder of his life, according to Coretta King.[19] Levison would epitomize the Black-Jewish alliance's new look, just as Louis Marshall had typified the relationship in the 1920s. Although both men were lawyers active in civil rights organizations—Marshall as head of the American Jewish Committee and Levison as an unsalaried official of the American Jewish Congress—they exhibited far more differences than similarities, differences that reflected the changes that had swept the Civil Rights Movement (and the Black-Jewish relationship) in the intervening years. Marshall was an establishment figure, one of the nation's most honored Jews. Apart from his association with the congress, the most radical of the Jewish agencies, Levison had little interest in Jewish affairs. He was the prototypical "non-Jewish Jew" described by Isaac Deutcher; that is, a man with no strong Jewish attachments, who sought a world free of all forms of group identity that he felt interfered with class solidarity. Levison was a political radical who had worked on behalf of Ethel and Julius Rosenberg and in efforts to abolish the McCarran Act and other limitations on political expression. He was also a financial pillar of the Communist Party and other radical

18. Harris Wofford, *Of Kennedys and King* (New York: Farrar Straus Giroux, 1980), 115.
19. David J. Garrow, *The FBI and Martin Luther King, Jr.: From Solo to Memphis* (New York: Norton, 1981), 15; *New York Times*, September 14, 1979; Branch, *Parting the Waters*, 208.

groups. Although Levison won no honors in his lifetime, he was enormously influential behind the scenes and throughout King's career.

Born in New York in 1912, Stanley Levison grew up in modest circumstances on Long Island. The son of an accountant, he was radicalized by the poverty he saw during the Great Depression. He attended the University of Michigan—his identical twin, Roy, studied at Ohio State—and earned a law degree as a night student from St. John's University in 1938 and a Master of Laws the following year. Instead of practicing law, however, he invested in real estate and other business ventures and quickly made a great deal of money. His success in the business world did not at all dampen his radicalism.

While Roosevelt was in the White House, both Levison and his brother, a journalist (who later changed his name to Bennett), were active in Democratic politics. When Congress hounded American Communists after World War II and passed laws to restrict their activities, Levison sprang to their defense. According to his brother, he raised money for party leaders who had gone underground to elude Smith Act prosecution. Roy described Stanley and himself at this time as fellow travelers, violently opposed to McCarthyite tactics. He recalled that Stanley had a talent for raising funds from left-wing contributors who would rather give money to him personally than give it directly to the Communist Party.[20] He lived frugally; causes rather than people mattered most to him, according to his close friend and business associate Joseph Filner.[21]

Levison's opposition to the McCarran Act, which required the registration of officers of the Communist Party, and his support of the Rosenbergs brought him under the surveillance of the Federal Bureau of Investigation. In June 1953, FBI files listed Levison as a Communist, and throughout his involvement with King and even after King's death, the bureau watched him closely—so closely, indeed, that one early report passed along the intelligence that Levison "allegedly had a hemorrhoid condition."[22] In this period the FBI also suspected Communist

20. Interview with Roy Bennett, October 26, 1989, and telephone interview, October 28, 1989. Levison's first wife, however, describes him at this time as a Stalinist who followed every twist and turn in Soviet policy. When she criticized the Hitler-Stalin pact of 1939, she claims, he reacted sharply. "It was like criticizing the pope," she says. Telephone interview with Janet Kennedy, January 27, 1991.

21. Levison, Filner says, never let him take him out to expensive restaurants. "Travel economy and give the first-class difference to social and political charities," he said; interview, January 27, 1991.

22. Levison Headquarters FBI file, sec. 2, June 9 and 19, 1953; also, undated, probably 1953, p. 20.

infiltration of the American Jewish Congress and other left-liberal organizations. Levison was a leader of the congress's West Side Manhattan
branch.[23] (Communists did in fact seek to take over the congress after
World War II, according to longtime official Will Maslow. They were
rebuffed, however.)[24]

Numerous American liberals and leftists were attracted to communism in the thirties and forties, before the crimes of Stalin were fully un-
veiled and the failures of the Soviet system became widely known. Many
joined cells or lent their names to party causes. However, Levison's involvement went much deeper, according to historian and King biographer David J. Garrow, who bases his account in part on information
obtained from former FBI agents, who in turn relied on FBI informants
high up in the party. Garrow believes Levison's role as a financial angel
for the Communist party began in 1945 or 1946. The bureau was informed that Levison, in 1953 or early 1954, began assisting in the management of Communist Party finances. When the party's national
treasurer, William Weiner, died in 1954, Levison became the interim chief
administrator of its highly secret funds. In this connection, according to
Garrow, he is said to have created business fronts to earn or launder
money for the party.[25]

Was Levison acting under Communist discipline when he entered the
King movement? The FBI, and especially J. Edgar Hoover, believed he
was. For years the bureau listened in on Levison's phone conversations.
It did the same with King after he emerged as the most powerful Black
leader in the United States. This surveillance remained in place throughout the sixties. A result of this spying was the FBI's subsequent circulation of rumors about King's extramarital affairs in an effort to undermine
him. But Levison, it would appear, was the initial target of this shocking
investigation.

Although he would remain a man of the left throughout his life, Levison (according to Branch) was a fiercely independent thinker, and as the
fifties wore on, he did not automatically accede to every twist and wrinkle
in the party line. The party, for example, initially derided the Supreme

23. Levison Headquarters FBI file, sec. 7, p. 17. See also Paul Lyons, "Philadelphia
Jews and Radicalism: The American Jewish Congress Cleans House," ed., *Philadelphia
Jewish Life, 1940–1985*, ed. Murray Friedman (Philadelphia: Seth Press, 1986), 107–23;
telephone interview with Will Maslow, May 20, 1988. Levison would retain his links
with the congress even as his ties to King deepened and began to absorb most of his
energies.
24. Garrow, *The FBI and Martin Luther King*, 32.
25. Ibid., 34–40, 43. See also his note, p. 239.

Court's 1954 school desegregation decision as running counter to Moscow's stated goal of "separate national development" for American Blacks. But Levison worked with Rustin, Randolph, and others to help implement the historic ruling. For the same reason, U.S. Communists opposed the Montgomery bus boycott, which Levison strongly supported.[26]

Possibly because of these differences, late in 1955 Levison began to cut back on his party work, and the FBI's interest in his activities subsequently slackened for a time. The break was not abrupt, however, suggesting that, as with so many on the left, his radical friendships and associations were not so easily cast aside. Even after beginning his association with King in 1956, Levison continued to make pro forma contributions to the party. He continued, also, to keep in touch with Communist leaders, or as his brother put it, they kept in touch with him.[27]

26. When the question of Levison's party associations arose in subsequent years, Rustin dismissed them. He made the point that Levison took positions that the party could not be happy about. In an interview with the author on October 3, 1985, Rustin said that Levison was not a Communist during the time Rustin worked closely with him. Rustin's close associate Norman Hill makes the same point. Interview, May 16, 1990, p. 5, Oral History Library, American Jewish Committee. See also Branch, *Parting the Waters*, 209. Joshua Muravchik, in a review of *Parting the Waters*, challenges Branch's benign treatment of Levison. He argues that Levison was hardly an independent thinker and the *Brown* decision resulted in "a quick change in the party line" on school desegregation (*Commentary* 87 [April 1989]: 63).

27. Lillian Gates—an upper-echelon leader of the New York State Communist Party in the 1950s, whose husband, John, was editor of the *Daily Worker*, the party organ—claims Levison attended one or more meetings of the party convened late in 1956 or early in 1957, when it was split into three warring factions and faced extinction. The meetings, she reports, were convened to hear the views of Levison and one other person, neither of whom was a formal party member. Lillian Gates believes Levison was a "submarine" in the King movement, that is, a secret party agent whose mission was to infiltrate the civil rights organization to promote party purposes. Janet Kennedy, Levison's first wife, believes this, too. But neither woman can produce hard evidence, and Levison's subsequent behavior suggests this is hardly likely. Telephone interviews with Janet Kennedy, June 8, 1990; Lillian and John Gates, February 22, 1990; and Lillian Gates, June 7, 1990. Branch, *Parting the Waters*, 211–14, 945, has an account of a party meeting. It was Lillian Gates, not John, who was present. The latter claims not to have been involved at this "truce" meeting or meetings. According to Branch and my own interviews with Lillian, there is no indication that Levison expressed any view on the party's future. Branch reports that at one point Levison took a call from King, causing those present to become worried. They feared, he claims, the FBI was listening in and might use such a conversation to destroy King as they did Paul Robeson. Garrow doubts that Levison attended the truce meetings or that King would call him in such a setting (interview, October 19, 1991). Interview with Bennett, October 26, 1989, and by phone October 28, 1989; interview with Navasky, November 14, 1989. Navasky was the first, or among the first, to break the story of the FBI wiretaps on the telephones of King and Levison; "The Government and Martin Luther King," *Atlantic Monthly*, November 1970, 43–52.

In February 1956, before joining King's inner circle, Levison, working with Rustin and Ella Baker, a former field secretary of the NAACP, formed an organization called In Friendship to help victims of segregationist vigilantism. Randolph was persuaded to serve as chairman. The group drew heavily from broad elements of the Black-Jewish-labor alliance and the left generally. Levison served as the American Jewish Congress liaison with the group, which operated from a building that he partly owned on Fifty-seventh Street in New York. The new organization collected money for, among other causes, the Alabama bus boycotters in a May 1956 Madison Square Garden rally.[28]

Ella Baker, at that time not as well known as Levison or Rustin, had come of age during the depression. She was raised in North Carolina and moved to New York in 1927, working with the Young Negro Cooperative and the Works Progress Administration. Just before World War II she joined the staff of the NAACP and as director of branches worked especially to strengthen the organization in the South. During these years she became friendly with members of the Communist Party and other leftists bent on provoking mass action. While president of an NAACP branch, Baker had also been associated with Levison in fighting the McCarran Act. Together with Rustin, they had talked about the need for developing a mass force in the South that could counterbalance the NAACP, whose leadership, for them, was too tame. The three were, in short, authentic products of the New York African American–Jewish radical community; working together they became a strong triumvirate supporting King when he most needed that support.[29]

One of the Jewish leftists who worked on behalf of In Friendship was Arthur Kinoy. In his autobiography Kinoy told of being shaped by the drive, latent in those who have experienced discrimination and exclusion, to seize the tools of knowledge and learning normally reserved for a society's elite. At Harvard he joined the leftist John Reed Society and in his subsequent law practice spent much of his time backing Communists, real or suspected. He defended leaders of the United Electrical, Radio,

28. Levison FBI Headquarters File, sec. 7, pp. 82, 84. Adam Fairclough, *To Redeem the Soul of America: The Southern Christian Leadership Conference and Martin Luther King, Jr.* (Athens: University of Georgia Press, 1987), 31. Interview with Taylor Branch, June 23, 1989. In an interview in 1970, Levison said In Friendship was formed early in 1955. This would be when he was still actively involved in party activities. February 14, 1970, Civil Rights Documentation Project, pp. 1–2, Moorland-Spingarn Research Project, Howard University, Washington, D.C.

29. John Britton interview with Ella Baker, June 19, 1968, Civil Rights Documentation Project, Moorland-Spingarn Research Project; *New York Times*, December 18, 1986.

and Machine Workers of America when their union was thrown out of the organized labor federation for alleged Communist front activities, and he assisted in the defense of the Rosenbergs and of Communist Party members tried under the Smith Act. Later he would gain notoriety with William Kunstler in representing the Chicago Seven at their trial for violently opposing the Vietnam War.[30]

When Ella Baker, soon to be In Friendship's executive director, returned from Montgomery and recruited Kinoy to support the boycott, he jumped at the chance to get back into the fray. He felt instinctively that this new struggle would lead him again down friendly and familiar paths. In Friendship, he wrote, "brought those of us who had been so immersed in the Cold War tensions into a close relationship with an exploding new social force."[31]

The NAACP and other civil rights groups committed to more conventional tactics were not entirely comfortable at first with the kind of mass action that had occurred in Montgomery. Not long after the boycott ended, Levison recalled a meeting at Randolph's office with John Morsell, the second in command under Roy Wilkins at the NAACP, at which the veteran socialist leader Norman Thomas was also present. Morsell recounted a discussion with Wilkins in which the latter claimed that mass action had been discredited by Hitler. Hitler had brought hundreds of thousands into public squares, and as a consequence the average person looked with suspicion on such gatherings. Thomas exploded. The day of mass action had just begun, he said. Wilkins also believed that the NAACP's paramount position had been usurped, and he was worried as well about the possibility of Communist infiltration.[32]

What helped unite the movement's various strands—King's demonstrators, In Friendship's leaders, the NAACP, the Black-Jewish labor alliance—was the Prayer Pilgrimage for Freedom, held in Washington on May 17, 1957, the third anniversary of the *Brown* decision. The Prayer Pilgrimage helped bring together the older northern Black leadership and the new breed of more militant southern Blacks spurred on by the success of the boycott led by King. Medgar Evers, the NAACP's Mississippi representative, was elected secretary of the pilgrimage, and Bayard Rustin became chief of staff. While the event was consciously planned by an

30. Arthur Kinoy, *Rights on Trial: The Odyssey of a People's Lawyer* (Cambridge: Harvard University Press, 1983), 2, 41–51, 82, 116.
31. Ibid., 151–53.
32. Morris, *Origins of the Civil Rights Movement*, 120; Garrow, *Bearing the Cross*, 490; Mosby interview with Levison, p. 20, in Civil Rights Documentation Project, Moorland-Spingarn Research Project.

all-Black organizing committee, according to Coretta King, its leaders relied heavily on In Friendship's racially integrated members. Levison
worried about funding; Rustin drafted strategy memos; the NAACP's
Wilkins took care of details in Washington through his man there,
Clarence Mitchell; and two of Rustin's young aides, Rachelle Horowitz
and Tom Kahn, helped organize busloads of students from Brooklyn College and other nearby schools to join the Black ministers coming up from
the South.[33]

As the Prayer Pilgrimage drew near, Wilkins grew increasingly anxious. Fearing that the White House might interpret the event as a militant
power play, he issued a statement disclaiming any intent of exerting
pressure on the executive branch. In King's view, however, that is exactly
what the pilgrimage was designed to do. He saw it as the first large-scale
attempt to secure positive social action in Washington since the advent of
McCarthyism. In this he was undoubtedly correct.[34]

The event in front of the Lincoln Memorial was a forerunner of the
more famous August 28, 1963, March on Washington. It gave King his
first major audience outside the South, and he made the most of it. The
theme of his speech was the crucial importance of the franchise for all
Americans, regardless of creed, color, or social class. Both Levison and
Rustin had prepared working papers for him, but the speech was basically his own. "I'm better at words than you are," he had told them. A
crowd estimated at from fifteen to thirty thousand heard King speak that
day. His remarks, though brief, were delivered in the soaring cadences
that years later would electrify huge throngs and galvanize an entire
nation. "Give us the ballot," he said, "and we will no longer plead—we
will write the proper laws on the books." Harrington, who was there,
wrote later that people were stirred because King touched a level deeper
than speech.[35]

As its New York backers had hoped, that one event helped the protest
movement break out of its small-town southern setting and into the national spotlight. The press started covering King's activities in greater
depth. President Eisenhower sent word that he wanted to meet with him.
Vice President Richard Nixon did, in fact, meet with him. (King asked

33. Harrington, *Fragments of the Century*, 104; interview with Rachelle Horowitz,
January 11, 1988, p. 13, Oral History Library, American Jewish Committee; Branch,
Parting the Waters, 216.
34. Kinoy, *Rights on Trial*, 155–57. King, *My Life*, 159; Branch, *Parting the Waters*, 217.
35. Branch, *Parting the Waters*, 216–17; Garrow, *Bearing the Cross*, 93; Harrington,
Fragments of the Century, 104. The ideas in a Levison letter to King and Rustin's working paper, "The Next Step for Mass Action in the Struggle for Equality," served as the
basis for King's speech.

Levison and Rustin to draw up a list of requests to submit to the vice president; they coached him in minute detail.)

In the months that followed, a series of Youth Marches for Integrated Schools, initiated by Randolph, were organized. They set the pattern for later demonstrations. A number of young activists—Bob Moses, Eleanor Holmes Norton, Norman Hill, Tom Kahn, and Rachelle Horowitz— gained their earliest experiences in protest demonstrations here, as did Wyatt Tee Walker, a northern-born preacher occupying a Virginia pulpit.[36] Walker would later become the executive director of the Southern Christian Leadership Conference (SCLC).

More than ten thousand young people took part in the first youth march, and thirty thousand in the second. Suddenly the left was out of the lofts and on the streets in the thousands, as Harrington enthusiastically recalled. Beyond the struggle against Jim Crow statutes, he saw a bitter battle against the entrenched economic and social elements underlying the society's racism.[37]

The normally reserved Levison was elated too. The demonstrations reminded him of thirties student activism in support of trade unions. He wrote King that if America's young were stirred from their lethargy, the results would be felt throughout society. The demonstrations were in fact precursors of the later and larger demonstrations of the 1960s and provided experience to many who would later take on leadership roles in the New Left.[38]

Learning that Randolph had thanked Levison for his help in the second march, J. Edgar Hoover stepped up surveillance on him.[39] Hoover believed that Levison was orchestrating the Washington marches and King himself, but that was certainly not the case. Although Levison was not calling the signals, he became increasingly influential as he and King became better friends. At first King was guarded, but over time he grew fond of Levison and his family and came to trust him completely. The two men would talk for hours on the phone, usually late at night, discussing fund-raising, speech making, and civil rights strategy. Andrew Young, later one of King's key aides and President Carter's ambassador to the United Nations, said that Levison was one of the few with whom King could let his hair down and also one of the few who felt free to criticize King to his face. According to Garrow, the secret of their

36. Isserman, *If I Had a Hammer*, 186.
37. Harrington, *Fragments of the Century*, 106–7.
38. Paula Pfeffer, *A. Philip Randolph, Pioneer of the Civil Rights Movement* (Baton Rouge: Louisiana State University Press, 1990), 169; Branch, *Parting the Waters*, 245.
39. Garrow, *Bearing the Cross*, 235.

relationship was very simple: Levison wanted nothing for himself, and King knew it.

Rachelle Horowitz, Rustin's aide, saw Levison as a good organizer, fund-raiser, and writer but also as more of a plodder than the charismatic Rustin. She saw Rustin as the idea man, Levison as the man who put the ideas into words.[40]

In subsequent years, although King would travel widely with his "road buddies"—Ralph Abernathy, Wyatt T. Walker, Clarence Jones, Bernard Lee, and Andrew Young—it was only with Levison that he formed a separate inner circle. On the big questions agreement was assumed and largely unspoken. However, King, the Baptist minister, refused to accept Levison's agnosticism. "You don't know it, Stan," King told Levison, "but you believe in God."[41]

When King was stabbed and nearly killed by a deranged woman in a Harlem department store in September 1958, Levison, Rustin, and Ella Baker met Coretta King at the airport. While King slowly recovered from his wounds, Levison watched over the cash contributions flooding in in response to King's successes. Several times King offered to pay him, but Levison refused. In a letter to King, he self-depreciatingly referred to the "abhorrent" skills he had acquired in the commercial jungle and declared that using them in the liberation struggle was as positive a reward as anyone could ask.[42]

King's great strength was oratory, and his New York adviser sought to exploit this talent, even going so far as to seek a sponsor for a weekly half hour on the radio. Although King never got a radio program, Levison negotiated and obtained for him a book contract with Harper Brothers. The book that resulted was *Stride toward Freedom* (1958), an autobiographical account of the Montgomery action. Levison supervised the project, contributed sections (as did Rustin and Wofford), and did not hesitate to criticize King's writing. He told King that his account of the Montgomery protest sounded egotistical. There were also serious omissions and misinterpretations, Levison told him, concerning voting and registration, Black self-improvement, and pursuit of social goals. With the final chapter unfinished and the deadline approaching, Levison, Rustin, and Wofford each drafted passages that were integrated into the published text. Although hurriedly put together, *Stride toward Freedom* was nevertheless well received. It was critical of Black Montgomery prior to the boycott,

40. Horowitz interview, January 11, 1989.
41. Branch, *Parting the Waters*, 227, 860.
42. Garrow, *The FBI and Martin Luther King*, 28.

noting especially the crippling factionalism and lack of unity. Its central message, however, came through loud and clear: in effecting social change, street protests by ordinary Black folks were as important as NAACP lawsuits, perhaps more so.[43]

Although King welcomed the assistance of Levison, Rustin, and other advisers, he was far from a puppet in their hands. The still inexperienced civil rights leader needed their help; but they needed him, too, as an instrument of their social vision. King skillfully integrated their ideas and the ideas of others into often brilliant plans of action. He displayed an extraordinary instinct for knowing where to strike next and how to move. In a conversation after King's murder (transcribed by the ubiquitous FBI), Rustin and Levison spoke freely of themselves as having guided not so much King's direction as his mode of pursuing that end. They saw themselves as vehicles for the expression of ideals he either held or would accept.[44]

The Levison-Rustin-Baker team was a remarkable alliance that bore little resemblance to the Black-Jewish linkages of the past. Rustin was not accepted in the Black middle-class establishment; nor was Levison, despite his American Jewish Congress connections, a part of the organized Jewish community. His Communist associations were known among civil rights insiders, and a number of Jewish civil rights activists, no doubt spurred by FBI warnings, kept their distance from him. Baker, a woman in King's heavily masculine world, felt even more strongly than her two partners that the leadership of the movement must come from below. (In time this conviction would bring her into conflict with King, who, she came to feel, like Moses, seemed unaware that it was the movement that made him rather than the reverse.)[45]

In casting about for a means to extend the Montgomery protest movement throughout the South, King considered many options. Like Rustin, Levison, and Baker, King understood that Whites could not dominate the new thrust in civil rights. Blacks had to run their own independent church-based organization. With this in mind, Rustin and Levison drafted a memorandum that led to the genesis of the SCLC. King agreed with their suggestions, and while Rustin drew up an agenda, King contacted other southern ministers and arranged for a meeting. The SCLC was to be an umbrella organization that affiliates—mostly ministers and their churches—could join in loose confederation. It did not have

43. Garrow, *Bearing the Cross*, 111–12.
44. Ibid., 649.
45. Britton interview with Baker, 34–37.

individuals as members and therefore would not invade the turf of the NAACP or other groups.[46]

Ella Baker later suggested that the idea was conceived in the North, not in Montgomery. After the boycott victory there was a complete let-down and not much was happening. Levison also noted that the talent for organization came from New York (which is where Rustin, Baker, and he came from), but he added that the impetus for the SCLC came from Blacks and the genius of King. He found it very difficult to single out one individual as the originator of the SCLC idea but named many other contributors besides King: Fred Shuttlesworth, C. K. Steele, Ralph Abernathy, Mrs. King, Randolph, Rustin, Baker, and himself. In brief, the SCLC was the result of much collective discussion, though unquestionably the one who clarified and organized the discussion was King.[47]

With King's approval, Rustin, Levison, and Baker drew up a list of prominent southern Black ministers and activists who could serve as a nucleus for a coordinating group and sent them a letter. King called them all together for the SCLC's founding meeting early in 1957. The SCLC was structured to capitalize on King's growing prestige. To finance a central office in Atlanta with a full-time executive director and a paid staff of field workers, the group would need an annual budget of $200,000. The operating methods of the organization were quickly established: Whites would be encouraged to support it in various ways, but it would be led by Blacks. Indeed, many of King's southern supporters were barely aware of the role of Levison in the development of the organization.[48]

Once the SCLC was launched—In Friendship was now dissolved—Rustin and Levison labored behind the scenes in New York to assist King with fund-raising and coalition building. They connected him not merely with the pacifist fringe but also with such major figures of labor and the left as Randolph, Norman Thomas, and Ralph Helstein, the Jewish head of the Packinghouse Workers, who brought in the SCLC's first big

46. Fairclough, *To Redeem the Soul*, 29; Ralph David Abernathy, *And the Walls Came Tumbling Down* (New York: Harper and Row, 1989), 311.

47. Britton interview with Baker, 34–37; Mosby interview with Levison, February 14, 1970, p. 16, in Civil Rights Documentation Project, Moorland-Spingarn Research Project; Morris, *Origins of the Civil Rights Movement*, 83, 302.

48. Fairclough, *To Redeem the Soul*, 33, 38, 44; Eugene P. Walker, "A History of the Southern Christian Leadership Conference, 1955–1963: The Evolution of a Southern Strategy of Social Change" (Ph.D. diss., Duke University, 1978), 45. According to Walker, SCLC recording secretary Fred Shuttlesworth and first vice president C. K. Steele did not know about Levison's counsel to King "nor his suggestions for the organization."

contribution of $27,000.[49] They helped him draw on Walter Reuther for funds and Chester Bowles for political influence. They were also able to guide him in distinguishing between the rhetoric appropriate to an audience of Black trade unionists and the etiquette of an immediate thank-you note for a generous contribution from Corliss and Margaret Lamont.

Early in 1957 Levison and Rustin persuaded King to launch a voter-registration campaign. They sent Baker to Atlanta to set up an SCLC office for the effort and to organize Crusade for Citizenship rallies. Levison drafted a letter that went out over King's signature seeking to enlist the support of Blacks and sympathetic Whites in the registration drive. The campaign would not conflict with NAACP efforts, the letter made clear, but would instead implement the legal advances of that organization. The registration of Black voters quickly gained momentum. The Kennedy administration later joined numerous liberal groups in rallying to the cause, and the Council of Federated Organizations (COFO) coordinated the drive in the South. But at the outset, the idea was Levison and Rustin's.

King had originally planned to name Rustin the SCLC's first executive director. He chose not to, however. Rev. John L. Tilley was appointed to the position; Baker was to replace him a year later, and she in turn was succeeded by Rev. Wyatt T. Walker. As the protest movement intensified, King came under increasing pressure from Congressman Adam Clayton Powell of Harlem and from AFL-CIO officials to remove Rustin from his inner circle. King's followers in the South also feared that Rustin's early Communist associations, coupled with his well-known homosexuality, would hurt the SCLC. Earlier, Levison himself had advised King against sending Rustin south to work on the Crusade for Citizenship. Now, at a critical moment, Levison did not speak up for his friend. Horowitz describes him as joining the pack of those opposed to broadening Rustin's role.[50]

Ironically it had been Rustin who brought Levison into King's entourage in the first place. Moreover, Levison's own earlier Communist ties would ultimately damage King far more seriously than Rustin's undergraduate link to the Young Communist League. Perhaps Rustin, with his flamboyant personality and background, seemed more threatening to King's southern supporters than Levison, who shunned the spotlight. In any case, Rustin was deeply hurt by Levison's lack of support. From 1960 until the March on Washington in 1963, he had little to do with

---

49. Fairclough, *To Redeem the Soul,* 38–39; Mosby interview with Levison, 18.
50. Horowitz interview, January 11, 1988.

King. Levison, however, remained King's key northern adviser. In spite of mounting pressure from the FBI, King resisted severing his ties with the radical New Yorker until President Kennedy himself intervened in 1963 and persuaded him to do so for the sake of pending civil rights legislation.

In mapping strategy and weighing major decisions, King looked time and again to Levison for guidance or for evaluations of individuals such as Andrew Young, who wished to join King's campaign. (Levison found the young clergyman unfocused but competent and recommended that King accept him, which King did.)[51]

Levison also recruited Jack O'Dell, a young Black radical he had met while working with Rustin on the youth marches. O'Dell proved particularly helpful in fund-raising, but his appointment set off alarm bells at the FBI, which knew of O'Dell's suspected Communist associations. Levison had been aware of those ties yet chose to put King at risk, possibly out of high regard for O'Dell as an administrator but more likely out of hostility to red-baiting tactics. King kept O'Dell on the SCLC's payroll and asked him to run its two-person office in New York, where O'Dell spent 90 percent of his time raising money. By intensive direct-mail efforts O'Dell and Levison developed a list of nine thousand people who would contribute twice a year to SCLC. Thus did these two men from radical backgrounds, in another illustration of the Black-Jewish alliance in microcosm, muster much of the financial backing for King's efforts in the South. "There is no way to calculate what Stanley Levison and Jack O'Dell have meant to SCLC in this regard," Wyatt T. Walker told the group's 1960 convention.[52]

In this period, another Jewish figure, Harry Wachtel, joined King's movement. Wachtel's credentials were similar to Levison's: he was a successful left-wing New York lawyer and businessman seeking to use his skills (as Levison had said of himself) for socially constructive ends. Wachtel, who was counsel and executive vice president of the McCrory Corporation, was troubled by his company's segregated workforce. He obtained an introduction to King and asked his advice: should he stay with McCrory or resign? King advised him to stay and fight segregation from within the company. Wachtel did so, but he began giving much of his personal time to King, setting up a tax-exempt foundation for

51. Branch, *Parting the Waters*, 575.
52. Ibid, 285, 575; Garrow, *Bearing the Cross*, 168. Garrow does not agree with Branch as to O'Dell's importance to King.

him and enlarging his connections among New York's wealthiest Jews. Although Levison later told Young that only some 10 percent of the SCLC's money came from Jews because Jews understandably found it difficult to contribute to Christian organizations, Jewish support was important enough that King's advisers considered dropping the word *Christian* from the organization's title. Rustin never failed to remind King to mention the *Judeo*-Christian tradition in his speeches.

Whereas Levison's friends were generally limited to leftists and labor union leaders, Wachtel had contacts in many fields and cities. In Washington, for example, he knew Abe Fortas, one of the capital's top lawyers (later named by Lyndon Johnson to the Supreme Court). Wachtel and his wife traveled with the Kings to Oslo in 1964 when King received the Nobel Peace Prize. After King's assassination, Wachtel handled his estate and negotiated the book contract for Coretta King's reminiscences.[53]

In 1962 Wachtel set up the Gandhi Society with the help of Levison, Theodore Kheel, Clarence Jones, and William Kunstler. Kunstler envisaged the organization as a provider of emergency legal assistance, analogous to the NAACP's Legal Defense Fund; but Levison, Wachtel, and Jones saw it as a fund-raising vehicle, and eventually this is what it became. Within the SCLC itself, rivalries over control and for King's favor would soon develop between his New York and southern supporters. There was a certain amount of resentment against Levison among some of the latter, possibly because he was Jewish. Others who knew of Levison's role chose to ignore it.

As the organization began to take shape, King asked Wyatt Walker to head up the Atlanta operation. Walker, a man of abrasive personality, demanded to have complete authority inside the organization even as he agreed to promote the charismatic King. This brought him into direct collision with the New York group. King asked him to meet privately with Levison and Rustin in New York before assuming the post. Walker balked. He saw no reason to do so since the two men were not even on the SCLC's board. Nevertheless, they met and reached a compromise. Walker felt he had established his primacy; Levison and Rustin believed they had blocked Walker's attempt to seize power—he wanted to abolish all of King's support organizations in New York and control all fundraising out of Atlanta. There would, in effect, be two operations backing King.[54] Despite these power plays, King kept the team alive and effective.

53. Interview with Harry Wachtel, October 24, 1985.
54. Branch, *Parting the Waters,* 300.

In 1960 the SCLC was still a blueprint; by 1962 it had acquired professional fund-raisers, recruited full-time organizers, and absorbed a healthy dose of administrative talent.

The historian must be careful not to claim too much for the role of the left in the emerging Civil Rights Movement. By 1954, the movement was well underway and American consciences had been pricked by Black activism at every level in the border and upper South. There is reason to believe, in fact, that the left—weakened by McCarthyism and the cold war—seized upon King and the Civil Rights Movement to regain some of its vitality and popular support.

This said, it would be a mistake to fail to recognize the importance of Rustin, Baker, Levison, and others on the left to King and his subsequent activities. Sociologist Doug McAdam has noted that activism requires not only idealism but also formal organization and informal social networks to structure and sustain collective action. It was the Black-Jewish-labor network in New York that helped the collective action in the South. The network provided the organizational skills, funding, media connections, and broader political contacts in Washington and elsewhere needed to sustain the movement. Thanks in part to that remarkable alliance, what began as a protest by local Blacks against intolerable conditions in one Alabama city evolved under the leadership of King into a massive civil rights effort that would change America forever.[55]

55. Doug McAdam, *Freedom Summer* (New York: Oxford University Press, 1988), 237.

The Southern Jewish Community
and the Struggle for Civil Rights

Cheryl Greenberg

W HEN WE SPEAK of Jews involved in Black-Jewish political partner-
ships during the civil rights era, northern Jews generally come to
mind: leaders of the Anti-Defamation League (ADL) or American Jewish
Congress (AJCongress), or young people joining the Student Nonviolent
Coordinating Committee and the Congress of Racial Equality (CORE),
participating in marches or teaching in Freedom Schools. The evidence
clearly documents a striking level of involvement by both Jewish elites
and the broader Jewish community in litigation, legislation, fund-raising,
and political organizing on behalf of civil rights and equality. Much of
that activity benefited Jews as well, of course, because discrimination on
the basis of religion was outlawed along with that based on race (although some efforts, such as the challenge to segregated public schools,
had no impact on Jewish life at all). Regardless of one's explanation for
their motivation, Jewish organizations and individuals did affiliate themselves with the Civil Rights Movement, or at least its liberal side, far more
routinely than did any other religious or ethnic group.

But there is another Jewish community as well, that of the South,
which played a far more ambivalent role in the struggle for Black civil
rights. By and large Jewish activists were northern, and their southern
coreligionists often frustrated them by their reluctance to pursue civil
rights efforts as avidly as northern Jews would have them do. This essay
explores the wary relationship of southern Jews to the Civil Rights Movement and the impact that wariness had on the northern-based Jewish
agencies that embraced the struggle more forthrightly. During the period
under scrutiny, 1930 through 1960, there was little change in the position
of southern Jews, whose fear of anti-Semitism and desire to fit into their
surroundings militated against any public action that flew so directly in
the face of local public opinion. Yet in those same years national Jewish

organizations and much of the northern Jewish community that constituted the bulk of their membership underwent a transformation of attitude toward civil rights that led them to greater, and more public,
involvement in that struggle. The Civil Rights Movement thus complicated relations among Jews at the same time that it complicated relations
between Blacks and Jews—indeed, between Blacks and Whites—more
broadly.

I. The Southern Jewish Community: Anti-Semitism and Racism

The Jewish community in the South was relatively small and perceived
itself as exceedingly vulnerable. Although a bastion of fundamentalist
Christianity and political conservatism, the South tended as a whole not
to be as anti-Semitic as one might expect. Most Jews assumed that was
because the southern way of life was so embedded in race as the great divide that Jews were included within the framework of whiteness. Nevertheless, a strong evangelical and fundamentalist tradition, the periodic
resurgence of anti-Semitic organizations, and the widely held canard that
all Jews were communists insured that anti-Semitism was never far from
the surface. Jews had seen evidence of that close up with the lynching of
Leo Frank, accused of molesting and killing a young White woman in
1913. Only he and an African American janitor were suspects, and the
fact that racist southerners chose to accept the word of the Black man in
this case reminded Jews that while racism might be the stronger, suspicion of Jews did not lag far behind. As Daniel Elazar put it, "In sum, the
Jews were accepted but were not really at home. Southern Jews . . . remained far more conscious of being Jews despite conditions that otherwise would have promoted assimilation . . . because they were so clearly
aware of not being part of white Protestant society."[1]

Such concerns were well founded. A 1938 "Memorandum on Proposed
Study of Southern Anti-Semitism" by Frank McCallister of the Workers'
Defense League (WDL) for the American Jewish Committee (AJC) and
the Jewish Labor Committee (JLC) cited the "existence of numerous
vigilante 'shirt' movements"; "phenomenal revival and growth of the
Knights of the Ku Klux Klan" and their organization of "a systematic

---

1. Daniel Elazar, *Community and Polity: The Organizational Dynamics of American
Jewry* (Philadelphia: Jewish Publication Society of America, 1976), 59. Frank was
lynched in 1915. For a closer analysis of Black-Jewish relations and the Leo Frank case
see Jeffrey Melnick, *A Right to Sing the Blues: African Americans, Jews, and Cultural
Power* (forthcoming).

boycott campaign against Jewish business men and job discrimination against Jewish workers"; growth of "anti-Semitic sentiment among workers employed by Jewish operators . . . [and] distribution by the tens of thousands of anti-Semitic leaflets, pamphlets, stickers, and various publications." His final report of the following year concluded, "Despite the small Jewish population in the area . . . there is a great deal of substantial evidence indicating a growing anti-Semitism. This is expressed . . . in the increasing social discrimination and tightening of quota systems in schools as well as loss of job opportunities." That same year the NAACP contacted the AJC with concerns about the rising virulence of Klan anti-Semitism in Atlanta, Miami, and elsewhere in the South and proposed a conference to "determine the possibility of working out a program of cooperation."[2]

Nazi-inspired anti-Semitism did ease after the war. But the cold war and the emergence of a more visible civil rights struggle offered new opportunities for the expression of anti-Jewish sentiment, since anti-Semites blamed Jews for both. The push by the CIO and to some extent the AFL to unionize southern industries also furthered anti-Semitic rhetoric "as a device to scare workers away from labor organizations" (according to the generally pro-labor ADL) by linking unions to communism and in turn to Jews. Some southern governors and congressmen continued to employ anti-Semitic speech and, in the words of the ADL, "showed marked hostility to Jews." In September 1950, to take just one example, the ADL reported that "there are nineteen individuals [running for office] who are of concern, fifteen of whom have clear anti-Semitic records. . . . In addition there were four [other] candidates who introduced racism into their campaigns." All but three resided in the South. As ADL Director Benjamin Epstein noted in 1957,

> Almost without exception, violence in the South over school desegregation has been accompanied by anti-Semitic tirades of the rankest type. John Kasper and Asa Carter, two of the most prominent leaders of the White Citizens' Councils, use anti-Semitism as a stock in trade, claiming that the Negroes were docile enough until whipped up by

2. Frank McCallister, "Memorandum of Proposed Study of Southern Anti-Semitism," August 8, 1938, p. 1, and "Report on Survey of Anti-Semitism in the South," 1939, p. 53. Also see McCallister, "General Observations," report [1938]. His final report surveyed ten southern states and interviewed approximately seven hundred individuals. NAACP to AJC: Brendan Sexton to Morris Waldman, June 10, 1938. All in NAACP Papers, box I H 11, Manuscript Division, Library of Congress, Washington, D.C.

Jewish agitators as part of a devious Jewish conspiracy for world domination.[3]

The Stoner Anti-Jewish Party provides an illustration of the links drawn between Jews and Blacks in the minds of anti-Semitic White racists.

> The Stoner Anti-Jewish Party is a political Party whose main and primary object is to serve CHRISTIANITY and AMERICA by . . . making it unlawful and impossible for Jews to live in North America. . . .
> The Stoner Anti-Jewish Party believes in ANTI-JEWISM. . . . The Stoner Anti-Jewish Party believes that North America is for White Gentiles only. It believes in White Supremacy. It definitely proposes that all niggers in North America be lawfully re-settled in Africa. . . . It believes that all Orientals should be re-settled in the Orient.[4]

Organized expressions of anti-Semitism were pervasive throughout the South and posed a real threat to the Jewish community there. Thus Jews generally feared to diverge in any way from the behaviors of their White Christian neighbors. In fact Jews in the South acted so much like other Whites that McCallister noted even "Gentile leaders, who were prone to be anti-Semitic, in many cases explained that 'we have only the high-type Jew here, not like the kikes in New York.' " Jewish assimilation to southern White norms, he argued, limited anti-Semitism substantially.

Jews from both North and South acknowledged this pattern of Jewish adherence to southern White attitudes. Harry Golden, a writer and longtime southern resident, himself a racial liberal, noted the southern Jew's

> relentless struggle to become *one* with the population mass which surrounds him. . . . The studied attempt to avoid all debate . . . has been in force so long that it would be hard to find six Jews below the Mason-Dixon line who hold sufficiently strong convictions to be "accused" of anything. . . . Primarily the Jews of the South reflect to a

3. Benjamin Epstein, *Anti-Semitism in the United States: A Current Appraisal,* ADL pamphlet, 1957, p. 9, AJC Vertical Files (hereafter AJC VF): "Anti-Semitism," AJC library, New York, N.Y.; "hostility": ADL press release, April 18, 1949, p. 4, NAACP Papers, II A 363; 1950: ADL, *The Facts* 5 (September 1950). *The Facts* was a monthly newsletter issued by the ADL's Civil Rights Division. See also Atlanta Jewish Community Council, Committee on Community Relations, "Review of Minutes, Decisions and Policies, 1946–1953," pp. 7–11, AJC VF: "Communities: GA." Unions: see, for example, Charles Sherman, ADL, to Richard Gutstadt, Benjamin Epstein, William Sachs, members of the Committee on Labor Relations, memorandum on "Conditions in the South," April 23, 1946, p. 3, ADL microfilm "Yellows 1946 Negro Race Problems" (hereafter ADL "Y 1946 NRP"), ADL archive and library, New York, N.Y.
4. Pamphlet, n.d., in NUL Papers, series 6, box 22, Manuscript Division, Library of Congress.

large extent the mores, the hopes, the politics, and even the prejudices of the society around them.[5]

Such behavioral assimilation was nowhere more marked than in matters of race relations. A 1951 survey by the ADL revealed that unlike the
practice in the North, no Jewish Community Center in the South accepted Black members, and most limited them from any participation at
all. "The youth of Jews [at a synagogue] had an interracial week," noted
the Chattanooga, Tennessee, Urban League in disgust, "—no Negroes
present."[6]

Many southern Jews in fact held more liberal views on race than did
their White Gentile neighbors but hesitated to speak out for fear of inten-
sifying anti-Semitism or stirring up charges of communism. In July 1946
when a Jewish man in South Carolina, Mr. Rosenfeld, wrote a letter to the
editor of the *Florence Morning News* urging African Americans not to
vote, local Jews scrambled to make it clear to Black readers that he did
not represent their community's views. The president of the local B'nai
B'rith lodge persuaded Rosenfeld to stop writing such letters. Nevertheless, a "Jewish source" the newspaper interviewed who "deplored" the
remarks and insisted that "[t]here is absolutely no bitterness towards the
colored people among the Jewish people" and "[a]s minority groups,
the two should maintain mutual empathy for each other's plight" refused to be quoted by name.

Other Jews embraced the mores of the region and acted indistinguish-
ably from their racist fellow Whites. Frank McCallister lamented in 1938
that although the best hope for fighting southern anti-Semitism was to develop propaganda stressing that "essentially the problem of the Jew is tied
up with all other racial minorities," he was forced to conclude the tactic
would fail "due to the prejudice against the Negroes, even among Jews."

Time did not seem to alter such attitudes. Almost a decade later, when
Alexander Miller, director of the ADL's Southern Regional Office, informed the national office about Rosenfeld's letter and the local Jewish
reaction, he noted that he could issue "a general statement to the Negro
press indicating that Rosenfeld's attitude is not indicative of the general
attitude of the Jewish group." Yet he hesitated: "There, of course, are
many dangers attendant upon . . . such a statement . . . including . . . the
fact that many of our own group here in the South might not go along

5. McCallister, "Report on Survey," 54; Harry Golden, "The Jews of the South," [AJ]
Congress Weekly 18 (December 31, 1951): 9, 10, 11.
6. Arnold Forster to CRC and ADL Regional Offices, memorandum, January 26,
1951, ADL "Y 1949–52 NRP." TN: in reference to a Reform synagogue. Handwritten
notes, n.d., NUL Papers, series 6, box 22.

with us."[7] In 1951 S. Andhil Fineberg of the AJC noted in reference to anti-racist efforts in Miami that local Jews generally "share the feelings of other Southern whites. . . . It would be impossible to say to what extent the Jews of Miami will support programs on behalf of Negroes which Jews in Northern cities heartily endorse." Although "in some highly admirable but limited instances" individual Jews acted forthrightly on matters of racial justice, they preferred not to do so publicly. Therefore, Fineberg concluded, "whatever programs are undertaken on behalf of the Negroes in the Miami district *will have to be done in cooperation with non-Jewish people likewise favorably disposed toward Negro advances.*"[8]

Long-standing and marked class distinctions helped to maintain the gap between southern African Americans and Jews and kept the latter more closely allied with the White community. In business as in social behavior, most southern Jews strove to model their racial practices as closely as possible on those of other Whites. And because many southern Jews, like their northern counterparts, established small retail enterprises and proved more willing than other southern Whites to serve a Black clientele, a great deal of Black-Jewish interaction occurred in such hierarchical venues. Charles Sherman's 1946 memorandum to the ADL Committee on Labor Relations minced no words: "It must be stated bluntly that with respect to them [African Americans] Jews are vulnerable in the South. The only Jew a Negro meets in the city is a pawn broker, grocer, insurance agent or landlord. The only Jew a sharecropper meets is a storekeeper or tradesman. As far as the Negro is concerned, Jews represent exploitation."[9]

Certainly Black southerners throughout this period noted the tendency of local Jews to emulate the racist attitudes and behaviors of the surrounding community. In 1935 the secretary of the Indianapolis YMCA acknowledged "some feeling of antagonism [in the Negro community] against the Jews, not as a group, but directed at a class who conduct business in a Negro community and make their entire living there but turn nothing back to the group in the matter of employment of Negroes."[10] In his typically pointed style, George Schuyler of the *Pittsburgh Courier*

7. McCallister, "General Observations," 2–3. Miller to Abel Berland, July 12, 1946, and attached letter to *Lighthouse and Informer* (which quotes the unattributable source), July 12, 1946, both ADL "Y 1946 NRP." It is possible Miller was that source. Miller is identified in ADL documents variously as director of the Southern, Southeastern, and Southwestern Regional Office.

8. S. Andhil Fineberg to John Slawson, memorandum re "The Situation in Miami," January 21, 1952, p. 3, AJC VF: "Communities: Miami FL" (italics in original).

9. Sherman to Gutstadt et al., memorandum re "Conditions in the South," p. 4.

10. F. E. De Frantz to Walter White, December 26, 1935, NAACP Papers, II L 7.

reported much the same based on his travels through the South that same year.

> Negroes of all classes . . . are quite unconcerned about . . . the fate of the Jews. Indeed, I am not at all exaggerating when I state that a surprising number of articulate Negroes seem to derive a sort of grim satisfaction from the Nazi persecution of the Jews. They contend that their local Jews have been indistinguishable from the "crackers" in their attitude toward Negroes; that as employers they work them harder and pay them less than other whites, and that never have they raised their voices against the rigid bars confronting Negro athletes everywhere in the South.
>
> I am seldom shocked by human conduct . . . but I confess that the callous indifference of our brethren toward this question which bordered on passive anti-Semitism surprised me no end.[11]

Some African Americans understood the dilemma Jews faced, particularly as the civil rights struggle heated up following the *Brown v. Board of Education* decision. As Kenneth Clark wrote in 1957, "The more sensitive and articulate southern Negroes are aware of this delicate predicament of Jews in the South today." Yet, as he hastened to add, "there has been only one case of a Southern Jew openly and actively identified with the struggle for desegregation." He concluded:

> The Southern Negro . . . looks upon the position of the Southern Jew as being difficult and delicate. He believes that it reflects, among other things, the tenuousness of the Jews' position in the community, the coercive pressures of the more rabid segregationists, the general and inclusive significance of whiteness in a Southern community, and the understandable reluctance of the Southern Jew to expose himself in a situation where he can be harmed without contributing positively to the resolution of a complex social problem.[12]

Nevertheless, the reality of southern Jewish emulation of racist mores continued to stir resentment and anger among African Americans throughout the 1940s and 1950s. A domestic worker writing to the *Chicago Defender* in 1956 complained that her northern Jewish employer had changed when the family moved South. In New York, "I couldn't ask for a better situation. I was treated almost as if I were a member of the family." After they moved to Florida,

> The madame told me things would have to be a little different for a while so as not to offend their gentile neighbors. I didn't see what difference it made since the gentiles were snubbing all the Jews anyhow. . . .

11. George Schuyler to Walter White, December 22, 1935, NAACP Papers, II L 7.
12. Kenneth Clark, "A Positive Transition," *ADL Bulletin* (December 1957): 5.

I stopped eating with the family.... And we stopped being friendly like one big family because they treated me more like a servant than they had before.

I'm not forgetting that I was a servant, but we had not acted that way before we went South....

Finally I left them. I could not get used to the southern way of life. I can't understand why people who are discriminated against discriminate against others.[13]

Black anger at Jewish racism was rooted at least in part in this sense of expectations betrayed. Because African Americans and Jews were fellow victims of bigotry, both Blacks and northern Jews expected more from Jews than from other Whites. In 1945 Alex Miller noted

the growing clamor of some Negro leaders for active participation by Jews in helping them. They feel that the Jews, as fellow objects of persecution, should be the first to rush to the aid of the Negroes and at the same time should be the last themselves to act in a prejudiced manner.

This is, of course, completely in variance with the behavior pattern of the Southern Jewish community, which has clothed itself quite completely in the mores of this area.[14]

As a result, even if Jews acted no worse than southern White Gentiles, their racism was often targeted specifically for criticism by Black leaders and the Black press. Walter White of the NAACP lamented the situation in Baltimore, where the nine largest department stores, seven owned by Jews, refused African American customers. The owners, he reported after meeting with them, "justify it on the ground that they might lose some white trade if they stopped discriminating against Negroes. One of the leading Jewish department store heads even became offended because I very mildly pointed out the parallel between what Hitler was doing to Jews in Germany and what Jewish and Gentile merchants were doing to another minority group right here in the United States." The AJC commented, defensively but accurately, "Objectively, there are Jewish owned stores that accept Negro customers and Christian owned stores that do not. However, there can be no doubt that most of the blame for the situation is placed on the Jews."[15]

13. Quoted in "Southern Exposure," *Chicago Defender*, December 15, 1956. The writer was not named.

14. Alexander Miller to Lou Novins, memorandum re "Negro-Jewish Relations," August 16, 1945, ADL "Y 1945 NRP."

15. Walter White to Victor Ridder, November 29, 1938, NAACP Papers, I C 208; also see White to Claude McKay, December 23, 1938. AJC, "The Truth about Baltimore," report, January 1939, p. 37, AJC Library.

Although virtually all White-owned stores in Durham, North Carolina, both Jewish and Gentile, served Black customers in the rear, the *Carolina Times* ran a story in 1945 insisting, "Jews in the South Must Stop Practices of Discriminating [Against] Negroes in Stores." It argued that Jews did so "to impress that they are one in intent and spirit with the southern white in denying Negroes the chance to spend their money on a basis of equality," and observed,

> The Negroes who are acquainted with this peculiar situation . . . are not sure of the Jewish position toward the Negro at all, despite all the talk that is heard in the North from Jewish leaders. . . . With these Negroes, the excuse that the Jew who discriminates is "not representative" of the "forward thinking" element among the Jews does not hold water.
>
> They contend that the Jews are a minority people as are Negroes and, if kinship is mutual in problems arising out of this minority status, then common cause should unite both people in stamping out unfair practices in all ranks of the racial lineups. . . .
>
> As minorities, Jews and Negroes must get together and those of the Jews that violate the racial bonds . . . must be publicly denounced and descried.[16]

Thus the same racist behaviors other Whites routinely practiced became more of an issue when the practitioner was a Jew.

Singling out Jews' religion did offer African American protesters an effective vehicle for their antidiscrimination arguments, especially during World War II. Jesse Thomas, the director of industrial relations for the National Urban League (NUL), described his efforts to integrate a Louisville factory. One

> situation that gave me a hearty laugh occurred during the war when Austin Scott and I called on the owner of a textile plant in Louisville to discuss the employment of Negro power machine operators. The owner sent for his plant superintendent who happened to be Jewish. He asked the superintendent whether or not he thought Negroes could be integrated in the plant. The superintendent . . . immediately replied that it could never be done—that white girls would not work with Negroes. I reminded him of the fact that he was Jewish and there were white people who objected to working under Jews. He promptly replied that they couldn't be good Americans and object

16. Dan Gardner, "Plain Talk," *Carolina Times,* May 28, 1945, 4. The first page carried the news article, "Manager of Butler's Shoe Store Says Negroes to Be Waited On in Rear Only." Also see J. Harold Saks to Nissen Gross, memorandum, September 5, 1945, ADL "Y 1945 NRP"; Miller to Novins, "Negro-Jewish Relations," states the manager was in fact not Jewish.

to working under him. I promptly asked him how they could be good Americans and object to working with Negroes. He said, "The difference is my face is white"—at which time I reminded him again that his white face made no difference to Hitler who was kicking the Jews' pants all over Europe. The end of the story is that we convinced the owner of the plant that it could be done, and in a few weeks there were 150 or more Negro girls working for him.[17]

Jewish organizations, with their national headquarters based in the North, felt of two minds about this singling out of southern Jews for criticism. On the one hand, they believed racist business practices inappropriate and sought to persuade Jews to cease such behaviors. After a complainant brought the situation to its attention in 1951, for example, the ADL worked with Leo Levi Memorial Hospital in Arkansas, a B'nai B'rith institution, to end its policies against admitting and serving Black patients.[18] On the other hand, they also argued that such singling out of Jews for widespread practices itself smacked of anti-Semitism.

In response to a complaint in the *Pittsburgh Courier* against Garfinkel's and Kaplowitz's department stores in Washington, D.C., for example, the ADL insisted:

Washington is essentially a Southern community, and practices the same discrimination as in the South, but it is definitely due to the pressure of non-Jews. This Jewish store apparently followed along in the trend, but all of the leading non-Jewish stores maintain the same policy. The fact that other people are guilty of similar things does not excuse the Jewish store, but it does throw a different light upon the assertions.

Similarly, another memorandum admitted that "the policy of these two stores is definitely one of discrimination against the colored people" but complained that since it "represents the unwritten policy of all the major

17. Jesse Thomas to Alfred Smith, *Chicago Defender*, November 7, 1947, NUL Papers, series 4, box 10. Smith published the story virtually verbatim in his column "Adventures in Race Relations," November 29, 1947.
18. B'nai B'rith, through the ADL, insisted on a change of policy, although not without internal prodding. The documentation suggests an AJCongress member was instrumental in bringing the issue to the ADL's attention. J. A. Robinson, president, Leo Levi Memorial Hospital, to Mrs. Abraham Azulay, September 14, 1951; Azulay to Maurice Bisgyer, ADL, October 3, 1951; draft letter, unsigned [Fannie McLaughlin, administrator, Leo Levy Hospital?] to Azulay [December 13, 1951?]; John Horwitz [ADL?] to Bisgyer, telegram, December 18, 1951; Harold Braverman to McLaughlin, December 26, 1951; Horwitz to Bisgyer, January 3, 1952; Bisgyer to Philip Houtz, executive director, National Jewish Hospital at Denver, January 2, 1952, all ADL "Y 1949–52 NRP."

department stores in Washington . . . the singling out of Jews . . . because of their policy is not altogether fair." The AJC report on Baltimore department stores made the same point.[19]

Despite such social and economic pressures to comply with discrimination, some southern Jews acted openly on behalf of Black civil rights. Mayme Osby Brown of New Orleans, editor of the *Louisiana Weekly*, wrote to Walter White in 1935, "we count the Jewish element as being among our best friends. The several Jewish rabbis are always allied with us in any progressive movement, and their aid is usually among the first to be sought by us in any undertaking. They speak for us and to us whenever requested, and their meetings are always open to us, with no segregation."[20]

Obviously, no single position describes all southern Jews. As one example of the divergent behaviors within the community, in 1952 White contrasted a Fort Lauderdale Jewish choir that sang in a Black church despite being threatened with violence by the local police and a Jewish-owned hotel twenty-six miles away in Miami that refused to accept African American guests. Historians Ray Mohl and Henry Green have uncovered notable examples of individual Jews prominent in the civil rights struggle in Florida. Several Jewish lawyers and activists joined the fight against police brutality against Blacks and helped write and pass state anti-Klan legislation. A Black and Jewish–led CORE chapter in Miami desegregated local lunch counters in the late 1950s. In several cities Jews were prominent in Civil Rights Congress chapters. Other studies have documented Jewish individuals and groups, particularly those on the left, working for racial justice elsewhere in the South. Nevertheless, as Mohl notes, "[G]iven the power and persistence of bigotry and racism . . . these Jewish efforts on behalf of civil rights seem rather

19. Garfinkel, it turned out, had converted to Unitarianism, and thus got the Jewish community off the hook. Max Kroloff to Leonard Finder, December 6 [8?], 1941. The complaint appeared in Roy Wilkins's syndicated *Watchtower* column in 1941. Similar, in response to the same column: Abel Berland to Finder, September 12, 1941. Also see *In Fact*, November 3, 1941; Irving Maxon to ADL, November 1, 1941; Finder to Maxon, November 7, 1941, all ADL "Y 1941 NRP"; criticism of Hutsler's Department Store in the *Baltimore Afro-American*, October 13, 1942; and the Jewish response: Finder to Nathan Kaufman, October 30, 1942, ADL "Y 1942 NRP." The ADL did intervene, successfully in several cases, to try and convince Jewish store owners to end their racist practices. See for example Finder to Louis Fabricant, September 9, 1941, ADL "Y 1941 NRP."

20. Mayme Brown to Walter White, December 16, 1935. Similar from the president of the New Orleans NAACP: Jas Gayle to White, December 20, 1935. Both NAACP Papers, II L 7.

minimal in retrospect."[21] The vast majority of southern Jews, regardless of their personal political beliefs, avoided any involvement in civil rights despite the emergence and intensification of the struggle in the South.

*II. National Jewish Organizations and the Emerging Southern
Civil Rights Movement*

Meanwhile, national Jewish organizations, based in the North, were undergoing a transformation in their commitment to civil rights. During the 1930s they, like southern Jews, did not publicly embrace the cause of racial justice. Unlike southern Jews, however, whose position remained fairly constant for the next two decades, by the mid to late 1940s the national organizations came to identify increasingly energetically with the civil rights struggle. Their change of heart came about for complex reasons, including the recognition of shared interests in antidiscrimination protections such as the Fair Employment Practices Committee (FEPC) and the unenforceability of restrictive housing covenants; the rise of civil rights as an increasingly visible scandal in light of Soviet cold war propaganda; a post-Holocaust realization that when any group was threatened, others would soon suffer as well, which helped to broaden the definition of self-interest to embrace the cause of all minorities; and the increased staffing and political clout that the postwar boom in membership and funding brought, which permitted them to expand their agenda beyond immediate and parochial concerns. While especially in the 1940s and 1950s the majority of these activist Jews came from the ranks of the elites—leaders of national Jewish organizations, lawyers, government officials—the northern Jewish community itself became increasingly concerned with civil rights as well, a concern evidenced, for example, by the increased rates of Jewish giving to Black organizations from the NAACP to the Southern Christian Leadership Conference to (later) the Student Nonviolent Coordinating Committee and by the substantial amount of material on civil rights taught in Jewish religious education programs and preached from pulpits in numerous northern synagogues. (The other core of Jewish civil rights activists, from the Communist Party and other

21. White: Milton Ellerin to Gilbert Balkin, ADL, December 12, 1952; Balkin to Ellerin, December 15, 1952, ADL "Y 1949–52 NRP." Similarly: Leonard Greenberg, memorandum "Re: Milton Kramer," [1946], ADL "Y 1946 NRP." Henry Green, *Gesher Va'Kesher: Bridges and Bonds* (Atlanta: Scholars Press, 1995); Ray Mohl, "South of the South? Jews, Blacks, and the Civil Rights Movement in Miami, 1945–1960" (unpublished paper based on presentation at Southern Historical Association, 1992), esp. 13–14, 31–37 (quotation on 14).

leftist groups, played a pivotal role in the movement as well, one beyond the scope of this chapter.)

This commitment sprang from a broad understanding of self-interest rooted in a universalist vision of justice that the broader Jewish community embraced (at least rhetorically) especially after the war. Immigrant Jews came by and large from more liberal and less religious segments of European Jewry; the second and third generations came to stress the universalist nature of Jewish ethics and to enshrine it, even more than tradition or ritual, as the heart of Judaism. This fit well with the emerging liberalism of postwar America and offered socially insecure Jews a way of feeling fully American. It also allowed them to hold onto that portion of their religious heritage least likely to conflict with the demands of integrating into a generally Christian culture. If ritual proved too restrictive, one could remain a Jew by one's ethical commitments. Finally, the holocaust brought into sharp focus the importance of shoring up every person's civil rights and civil liberties. Constrained, of course, by anticommunism and other countervailing conservative pressures, and generally more limited to words than to actions, the sense that to be a Jew demanded ethical universalism nonetheless flourished, particularly in the North, and helped shape many Jews' self-identities as social liberals. Certainly in the mainstream Jewish community elites clearly led the charge for civil rights, but they could not move dramatically beyond the positions held by the members of the organizations for which they worked and on whom they relied financially. Indeed, it was precisely this dependency that southern Jews would exploit to slow their national organization's civil rights activities.

The changing political style of Jewish agencies also helped propel them into more extensive civil rights activity by the mid-1940s. Not until after the war did Jewish groups become willing to speak out publicly on any controversial issue. A 1937 discussion by the AJCongress Governing Council, for example, decided in response to information about the growing strength of the KKK to appoint a committee "to see whether the problem is one with which the Congress should deal," although it had been aware of the Klan's anti-Semitic activities (not to mention its anti-Black actions) since the AJCongress's founding. A decade later, Jewish organizations had become visible partners in civil rights efforts. The ADL began sustained civil rights work by 1943. The AJCongress created its Commission for Law and Social Action (CLSA) in 1946; this group addressed itself to civil rights issues and was headed by Will Maslow, the former director of field operations for the FEPC. The AJC and National

Council of Jewish Women (NCJW) stepped up their previous efforts. While there was always ambivalence in Jewish agencies about how far to push on the question of Black rights, certainly organizational commitment to civil rights solidified over time. Beginning with small and hesitant steps during the war, Jewish organizations gradually expanded their role. As Hubert Delany noted (with a bit of exaggeration) at the 1956 AJCongress convention, fifteen years earlier:

> We were told that the American Jewish Committee would not concede that their problems coincided here and there with ours. . . . That was our problem.
> It was when the [AJ]Congress came into being with real influence, that the leaders of the NAACP and the leaders of the Jewish Community got together, and from then on, we have worked side by side.[22]

By the end of the war Jewish agencies were monitoring racial, class, and religious tensions in the South and pointed explicitly to the centrality of racial justice to the achievement of peaceful intergroup relations. At the September 1946 ADL National Commission meeting, Alex Miller

> indicated that in the current nationwide struggle between liberal and reactionary forces, the lines have become most sharply drawn in the South. . . . He suggested that the Anti-Defamation League, by working with other progressive forces in the South, can help to turn the scales toward a more liberal and progressive Southern region. Mr. Miller suggested that the League assist liberal Southern groups through subvention, guidance and manpower.

Although a WDL report had expressed disappointment that so few Jews attended a November 1938 meeting of the Southern Conference for Human Welfare in Birmingham, in 1949 the ADL approvingly reported as evidence of a " 'more enlightened' attitude in the South" the fact that a southern meeting for equal rights was "prominently attended." Indeed, by the late 1940s the ADL routinely joined the NAACP, NUL, National Council of Negro Women (NCNW), and several other African American and religious groups in southern meetings on "human relations" that issued joint policy statements calling for action to end discrimination and racial violence and committing themselves to join in such actions.[23]

22. AJCong Governing Council meeting, minutes, April 6, 1937, p. 4, AJCong box "Governing Board 1935–38," AJCong library, New York, N.Y.; Delany at AJCong 1956 National Convention, panel: "Integration: The Position of the Jewish Community in the South," transcript, p. 61, AJCong box "National conventions 54–58."
23. 1949: ADL press release, April 18, 1949, p. 4. 1938: McCallister, "Southern

By the end of the decade Jewish groups, and the ADL in particular, were not only monitoring racial tension and violence throughout the South but were also advocating specific actions in response. After several instances of police brutality and Klan activity in Birmingham directed at African Americans in the late 1940s, for example, Alex Miller urged public exposure: "If ever there was a community that needed a thorough-going exposé on its race relations, either by a national radio commentator or by an expert reporter from some newspaper, it is Birmingham Ala. A good reporter will find here, I believe, a fear-stricken community resembling one in a totalitarian state rather than in a democratic, freedom-loving country."[24]

Over time, and particularly as northern Jews became more willing to support civil rights (or at least to challenge southern segregation), the ADL became increasingly willing to seek congressional, Justice Department, and FBI investigations of racial violence and to lobby the federal government to change discriminatory policies in government offices located in the South. Initially reluctant to challenge legal segregation, the ADL reconsidered well before the *Brown* decision. In 1947 it was still counseling caution. Frank Trager's proposal to make a film on school desegregation brought this warning from the ADL's Southeastern Regional Office:

> [T]here should be taken into consideration the fact that segregation exists in Southern schools by law and that the film would, therefore, not be acceptable on that basis in the South. Even the liberal organizations of the South have not yet gone so far as to advocate abrogation of educational segregation laws. . . . Alex [Miller,] too, says, "one rule of thumb is to avoid any type of picture which might show social contact."[25]

By 1952 the ADL had reversed itself. When informed of a recent Navy Department order "permitting segregation of civilian personnel in Navy facilities in states having a policy of racial segregation," Sol Rabkin of the

Conference for Human Welfare, Birmingham, Alabama, November 20–23, 1938," 1, 3, NAACP Papers, I H 11; "Report on Survey," 17–18. Miller: ADL National Commission meeting, minutes, September 21–26, 1946, pp. 6–7, ADL warehouse, box 176. ADL, NAACP et al.: see for example the description of a May 15, 1952, meeting in Birmingham and the statement issued there, reported in NAACP, Roy Wilkins, "Report of the Secretary," June 9, 1952, pp. 8–11, NAACP Papers, II A 145.

24. Alex Miller to Arnold Forster, memorandum, December 27, 1950, p. 2, ADL "Y 1949–52 NRP."

25. Fred Grossman to Frank Trager, memorandum, May 5, 1947, ADL "Y 1947 NRP."

ADL's Civil Rights Division declared his ignorance of the ruling but added:

> I think it is safe to say that the ADL's general policy is one of opposi-
> tion to segregation based on race, religion, ancestry or national origin
> in any facilities open to the public, as well as in all facilities operated
> by State or Federal governments. The ADL also believes that it is the
> duty of the Federal government to do whatever it can to insure ab-
> solute equality of treatment to all its citizens, regardless of race or
> creed and, therefore, to refuse to sanction racial segregation in any of
> its facilities. From this it would follow that we would be opposed to
> an order such as you describe.

To give a sense of its emerging priorities, in October 1955 the ADL National Executive Committee passed five resolutions: one on UNESCO,
one on civil liberties, and three on civil rights (on public school desegregation, Emmett Till's murder, and segregation in federal programs).[26]

The ADL and other Jewish groups acted not only on the national but
also on the state and local levels. When two Black prisoners were killed
by a sheriff in Florida in 1951, the NAACP telegraphed the ADL requesting that it ask the governor to respond. As Arnold Forster explained by
return mail, "The ADL has already taken action by sending a wire, together with other major Jewish organizations [AJC, AJCongress, JLC,
Jewish War Veterans, National Jewish Community Relations Advisory
Council (NCRAC), and Union of American Hebrew Congregations
(UAHC)], to [the] Attorney General. . . . If there is anything further you
think we can do, please let us know." The telegram expressed shock at
the "shameful occurrence" which "lead[s] us strongly to suspect a per-
version of the American tradition of justice and equal treatment before
the law" and requested that an "investigation be conducted as vigorously and speedily a possible and that every action warranted by the
facts be undertaken with firmness."[27]

26. Congressional investigation: see for example Alex Miller to Arnold Forster,
memorandum, January 7, 1952, ADL "Y 1949–52 NRP," re "anti-Negro rampage" in
a small Georgia town. FBI and Justice: see for example Miller to Herman Edelsberg,
December 2, 1948; Edelsberg to Miller, December 6, 1948, memorandum re "Mallard
case," all ADL "Y 1948 NRP," regarding the lynching of Roy Mallard near Vidalia,
Ga. Navy: Sol Rabkin to Nathan Perlmutter, December 17, 1952, ADL "Y 1949–52
NRP." The ADL often cooperated in matters of this kind. See for example NAACP
press release, "Will Defend Columbia Riot Victims to Utmost Limit; 19 Organizations
Pledge to NAACP," March 14, 1946, ADL "Y 1946 NRP." ADL National Executive
Committee: ADL press release to the Anglo-Jewish Press, October 24, 1955, ADL mi-
crofilm "chisub," reel 12.

27. Walter White to ADL, telegram, November 9, 1951; Arnold Forster to White,
November 14, 1951; AJC, AJCong, ADL, JLC, JWV, UAHC, NCRAC, to Attorney
General J. Howard McGrath, telegram, n.d., ADL "Y 1949–52, NRP."

Nor were these efforts necessarily led by northern Jews; many of the activists came from the local community. Burnett Roth, for example, a Miami resident who began his political life fighting restrictions against Jews, moved to embrace racial justice not long after. By 1947 he and the ADL office he represented succeeded in locating White donors for a Black woman with a rare blood type, passing anti-Klan legislation, and sponsoring (and carefully orchestrating) several integrated political events that occurred without incident. These included a local memorial service for President Franklin Roosevelt, a train trip out of Miami to an American Veterans Committee convention in Milwaukee, banquets in Miami for the AVC and for the Negro Service Council, and a meeting of the Dade County Fair Rent Council with the Miami Beach City Council in which "so far as it is known, for the first time at this meeting Negroes and whites sat together on an unsegregated basis at the Miami Beach City Hall." As Gilbert Balkin, also of the local ADL office, noted, "This . . . gives the lie to the oft-contended positions of the NCCJ [National Conference of Christians and Jews] and other groups that Negroes cannot be invited to participate in Brotherhood Week and similar celebrations in this area 'because of the local situation.' " In another letter to the national body he concluded, "There is really nothing particularly remarkable in the above cases. They simply illustrate that 'it can be done,' given the will to put into action the democratic principles easily agreed upon in theory. . . . Each successfully completed program . . . constitutes an advancing step forward in the march of democratic progress in the South."[28]

By the early 1950s the ADL was so active in the antisegregation effort in the South that the UAW turned to it for advice concerning Memphis. The local union hall there had designated separate toilets for Blacks and Whites, and the codirector of the UAW's Fair Practices and Anti-Discrimination Department contacted Rabkin for advice in drafting a policy on the subject. Rabkin described the segregation ordinances in place and possible legal challenges to them. He noted that litigation

28. Gilbert Balkin to J. Harold Saks, memorandum re "Negro-White Relations—Miami Area," July 16, 1947 (includes "gives the lie" quotation); and memorandum, July 18, 1947 (blood); Saks to Balkin, memorandum in reply, July 24, 1947; Balkin to Frank Trager, memorandum re "Negro-White Relations—Miami Area," August 26, 1947 (includes "nothing remarkable" and "first time" quotations). All ADL "Y 1947 NRP." Establishing the ADL Miami office: see ADL Executive Committee meeting, minutes, December 2, 1940, p. 2; ADL Executive Finance Committee meeting, minutes, March 3, 1941, p. 1, both ADL warehouse, box 178. Similarly, Balkin to Evelyn Gresser, memorandum re "Dade County Civil Rights Council," October 26, 1947, ADL "Y 1947 NRP"; AJCong and NAACP, *Civil Rights in the United States in 1952: A Balance Sheet of Group Relations* (New York, 1952), 9.

based on private use "might well succeed. On the other hand, if you lose in the lower courts you may be denied the use of the hall for a substantial period of time. Those are the dangers to be balanced. . . . I know what choice I would make, and I hope that you and your people make the same choice."[29]

The ADL's advocacy of antisegregation litigation paralleled that of the NAACP. After noting that he was "in complete agreement" with a speech Thurgood Marshall delivered at the Fisk University Institute on Race Relations in 1950, Rabkin continued, "In fact, if you read the analysis we sent out on the decisions you will note that we said much the same things." He saw the recent court decisions as "almost certainly serv[ing] to make southern gradualism a good bit less gradual" and concluded, "Finally, I agree with Mr. Marshall that segregation in public . . . schools is on the way out, and that we now have the tools with which to destroy all governmentally-imposed racial segregation. I, too, feel that it will take time as well as courage and determination, but that it will be done."[30]

At the same time, the ADL recognized that its greatest contribution to the struggle might be public education. Although it stressed the need for the kind of litigation work done by the NAACP and contributed research, supporting briefs, and even financial contributions on occasion, it understood as well the importance of rallying the White community behind integration. Thus it produced and distributed pamphlets and films, conducted discussion groups with local civic and religious bodies, and publicized peacefully integrated events as evidence that desegregation harmed no one. It reported, for example, the "most heartening" news that the Fulton County Medical Society voted in 1952 to admit African American doctors to "scientific" membership (hospital and local AMA participation but no voting rights). The ADL called it a "forward step" and noted that this was the fourth such action in Georgia. The agency even monitored the 1949 exhibition baseball game between the Cleveland Indians and the New York Giants in Houston when Satchel Paige and Larry Doby played, "the first Negroes to ever play in organized ball at Buff Stadium." The crowd, the observer reported, was good humored and well behaved. As an internal memorandum from 1952 put

29. William Oliver to Sol Rabkin, March 11, 1952; Rabkin to Oliver, April 14 and 15 (latter includes quotation), 1952, ADL "Y 1949–52 NRP." For more on ADL work with the CIO see, for example, Fred Grossman to Frank Trager, memorandum; Benjamin Epstein to Arthur Goldberg, CIO, June 1, 1950; Alex Miller to Dorothy Nathan, AJC, March 11, 1949; all ADL "Y 1949–52 NRP."

30. Sol Rabkin to Alex Miller, memorandum, August 29, 1950, ADL Y "1949–52 NRP."

it, although " 'White Supremacy' still prevails throughout the South" the advances that had been made to date in "reducing discrimination against Negroes in the South . . . to a considerable extent . . . were brought about by a small but active group of white citizens in the South who in ever increasing measure cooperated with their colored fellow citizens in breaking down some of the barriers between whites and Negroes."[31]

Nor, of course, was the ADL the only Jewish organization active in the South. By the late 1940s the AJCongress, under the leadership of progressive activist Rabbi Stephen Wise, a signer of the original call to found the NAACP, was working closely with African American groups to further civil rights causes, although it had little local organization in the South. Where it did, in Miami for example, it actively fought the Klan and engaged in joint efforts with the ADL, NAACP, NCCJ, and other organizations to promote integration. Nationally it joined with the Brotherhood of Sleeping Car Porters in 1955 to establish a committee for the "rescue, relief, and rehabilitation of victims of race terror" in the South. Its leaders testified before Congress on civil rights legislation and committed its CLSA to litigation against segregation North and South. Its Women's Division embraced the cause equally avidly. The AJC joined in legal briefs and desegregation efforts and helped to raise money for civil rights causes. Along with the Rosenwald Fund it funded Kenneth and Mamie Clark's research into Black self-perception, the famous "doll studies" that proved so persuasive in the *Brown* decision. The JLC worked with unions and labor organizations to further the cause of civil rights.[32]

31. "Reducing discrimination": ADL, "Memorandum," n.d. [cover letter Paul Hartman to Blanche Eisenstein, August 6, 1952], p. 1, ADL "Y 1949–52 NRP." Fulton county: Arthur Levin to Louis Krapin [illegible], memorandum, October 30, 1952. Baseball: Tom Freedman, memorandum re "Observations Observing a Segregated Audience Observing a Non-Segregated Athletic Contest," April 7, 1949. Five days later, Alex Miller reported the same positive response in Atlanta when the Dodgers came, despite KKK threats that they could not play in the South. Miller to "JHS," April 12, 1949. Other examples: ADL press release, December 3, 1950; Brant Coopersmith, ADL, to Oscar Cohen, February 28, 1951. All ADL "Y 1949–52 NRP."

32. AJCong and BSCP: "In Friendship" Coordinating Committee (the Executive Board included the AJCong, American Veterans Committee, BSCP, JLC, NAACP, United Hebrew Trades, WDL, and several unions), "Memo on 'In Friendship,' " [February 20, 1956]; A Philip Randolph to "Dear Friend," February 17, 1956; Reverend James Robinson, Ashley Totten, Rabbi Edward Klein to Lester Granger, NUL, December 19, 1955; Granger to Executive Staff, memorandum, December 29, 1955 (which reported some hesitation by the NAACP); Nelson Jackson to Granger, memorandum re "Your scheduled meeting on January 5, 1956," December 30, 1955 (expressing reservations of the NUL), all NUL Papers, series 1, box 49. For a full catalog of CLSA activities see AJCong, "CLSA Monthly Reports" and "Report of Activities," in AJCong library. For the AJCong in Miami also see Mohl, "South of the South?" The

Some of the most active Jews in civil rights were women. Jewish women organized Miami's CORE chapter, for example. And one of the most active organizations involved in civil rights was the NCJW. That group testified before Congress on behalf of numerous bills including extension of the FEPC, making lynching a federal crime, and amending Senate cloture rules to limit southern filibusters and against the poll tax and racially based immigration restrictions. The NCJW routinely met with other progressive organizations, particularly the NCNW, and worked with them to plan southern women's conferences and organize education programs, letter-writing campaigns, and consumer action against discrimination, segregation, and racial violence. In 1943 its San Antonio chapter lobbied Congress to abolish the poll tax. In Charleston, it was the only Jewish group to join the effort to integrate the police force. Indeed, the NCJW had begun interracial programs and civil rights efforts at least a decade earlier than the male-dominated Jewish organizations had. For example, the NCJW added a plank to its platform condemning lynching years before the other Jewish agencies did, and in Baltimore while the AJC and ADL defended the racist practices of Jewish store owners, Jewish women organized petition drives as shoppers to urge a change of policy.

In a rather provocative aside in her report on the 1952 Women's Leadership Conference held at Bethune-Cookman College, NCJW's Katharine Engel observed with a certain maternalistic pride:

> As a representative of a Jewish group I was extremely interested in a point that was made to me by four different Negro women—none of them realizing the point had been made by the others. Each one said, "Mrs. Engel, we have watched Jews, not only take care of their own, but others. We, Negroes cannot keep up with the needs of our people. Whenever and wherever possible, we are trying to do something for others to emulate the example of Jews."[33]

JLC Papers, including its "Civil Rights Newsletters," are in Tamiment Library, New York, N.Y. For a critical look at the JLC's activities and its failure to challenge racism within the trade union movement see Herbert Hill, "Black-Jewish Conflict in the Labor Context," in this volume. AJC: see, for example, John Slawson, AJC Oral History Library, New York Public Library, Jewish Division, and the AJC VF: Negro Jewish Relations (hereafter NJR): "AJC." The AJCong, AJC, ADL, NCJW, JLC, Central Conference of American Rabbis, and several other Jewish organizations filed supporting briefs in *Brown* and other civil rights cases.

33. See the papers of the NCJW and its Washington branch for more detail, in the Manuscript Division, Library of Congress. For Miami see Mohl, "South of the South?" Testimony before Congress: NCJW Papers, box 117 and *passim*. The NCJW was also active in other progressive struggles including public housing, federal aid to

Despite the unconscious paternalism of much of Jewish involvement in the Black civil rights struggle, and never disputing that working for Black civil rights often proved of direct benefit to Jews, these women and men continued to understand their commitment in terms of Judaism's universalist ethics. And their organizations consistently sought strategies as broad as their vision to guide them in their policy making. "I am most interested in . . . the election of [African American] Dr. Hampton to the city council of Greensboro," Oscar Cohen of the ADL wrote to staffer Ted Freedman in 1951.

> This is a most wonderful development. . . .
> It seems to me that this is indicative of the revolution which is occurring in the South. Why is it that this has happened in Greensboro? Could it have happened last year—five years ago—ten years ago? If not, what has happened in the interim? What are the causes of the changes . . . ?
> Perhaps we have an opportunity here of putting our finger on the precise causes of the phenomenon of radical change in Southern mores.[34]

III. Southern Jewry's Challenge to National Organizations

Most members of the southern Jewish community by no means saw things eye to eye with their national organizations. They consistently pressed their national representatives to keep out, to be silent, to avoid confrontation. In one particularly egregious example, a NCRAC delegate from Norfolk, Virginia, claimed at a 1958 plenary session that Roy Wilkins of the NAACP had told him "not only does the activity of the Jewish community not help the Negro in the south, but it is actually harmful in the fight against segregation." Isaac Toubin, the executive director of the AJCongress, vehemently denied this and asked Wilkins for confirmation. Wilkins, "astonished (and disturbed)," flatly denied both the statement and the sentiments behind it, adding:

---

education, fair labor laws, and immigration. Katharine Engel, NCJW, "Report of Mrs. Irving M. Engel on the 1952 Women's Leadership Conference," April 29, 1952. On the same conference see Olya Margolin to Elsie Elfenbein, January 25, 1952; NCJW [Olya Margolin], "Report on Strengthening the Forces of Freedom," n.d., all NCJW Papers, box 72. Charleston: John Harris, "Progress Report to members of the [NUL] Interracial Committee," [1950?], p. 2, NUL Papers, series 6, box 21. San Antonio: NCJW National Committee on Social Legislation meeting, minutes, May 28, 1943, NCJW Papers, box 141. Baltimore: see comments of Mrs. Rogers at the AJCong 1956 convention, "Integration," 79–82.

34. Oscar Cohen to Ted Freedman, August 13, 1951, memorandum, ADL "Y 1949–52 NRP."

I fully understand the feelings of some members of Southern Jewish communities on the integration struggle. They would prefer not being identified with it in any way. They regret the pronouncements and activities of their national Jewish agencies on the topic. . . . Southern Jewish leaders have been vigorous in advancing the position that national Jewish agencies should not "embarrass" them by stating forthright views in support of desegregation. I think I can understand their position even if I cannot agree with it.

But for them to go to the extreme of attributing to me a statement [such as this] . . . is carrying matters pretty far.

We have rejoiced in the aid and understanding we have received . . . from courageous members of the American Jewish community, North and South. It is discouraging, indeed, that in their anxiety to remain above the conflict the dissidents should resort to hearing what was never said and disseminating what was never even a thought, much less a word.[35]

The urging of southern Jews that Jewish national agencies keep their distance from civil rights put intense pressure on northern Jewish organizations, reliant as they were on their membership for financial support as well as policy decisions. On the one hand, by the late 1940s it had become evident to Jewish agencies that they had to move forward regardless of the feelings of their southern constituency. On the other, many Jews in the South continued to believe their national organizations were placing them in danger by taking such overtly antisegregation positions, and some northern Jews concurred. S. Andhil Fineberg of the AJC explained:

The American Jewish Committee . . . took the position that all racial segregation and discrimination should cease. This meant that some of the American Jewish Committee leadership, especially in Alabama and Georgia, resented the Committee's position. . . . Southern members came [to our annual meetings] . . . to protest . . . holding that the Jewish agencies by being so liberal and pro-Negro openly were creating great difficulty for Southern Jews. And let me say here that most of the Southern Jews took a remarkably good stand. . . . But they did not want to show their hands too clearly. There will never be adequate credit given to the Jews of the South, who were wise enough not to take the public leadership of the desegregation movement in the South. They did not want to add anti-Semitism to anti-Negroism and realized that they were subject to certain retaliations that the Christian Southerner did not face.

The AJC resolved the dilemma by deciding "never to undertake activity in a local community against the opposition of the local community

35. Toubin, AJCong, to Roy Wilkins, executive secretary, NAACP, June 18, 1958; Wilkins to Toubin, June 26, 1958. Both AJC VF NJR: "AJCong."

organization," as George Hexter explained at a 1949 NCRAC meeting. "Local communities in the South can not be expected to implement fully the national policy of all-out opposition to anti-Negro discrimination; but this . . . does not mean that any Southern chapter of the American Jewish Committee has ever said that it opposed the policy nationally." The ADL hedged similarly. Rhetorically it stood firm on the question of civil rights. "The ADL must have one set of unequivocal principles upon which its operations are based," Ben Epstein insisted. "ADL stands for FEPC in Atlanta, Georgia, as well as in New York City."[36]

Yet in practice the ADL bowed to the reality of southern Jewish resistance. During his testimonial at Rabbi Stephen Wise's memorial service in 1949, Walter White criticized the ADL for publishing tolerance literature in two versions, one depicting a Black boy among a sea of children, and one without him. "It seems to me that if members of the ADL living in the South cannot stand up for brotherhood of all human beings, including Negroes, there is very little point in spending money to print 'brotherhood' literature at all," he wrote the ADL in a follow-up letter. Ben Epstein responded that while his organization was "vigorously opposed to" the decision to print two versions (it had been done by a quasi-independent agency, the Institute for American Democracy), "This does not at all detract from the fact that some materials will be more acceptable in the South than others. . . . We have found that those designs depicting Negroes in positions of equality are not generally used."[37] Indeed, some southern ADL offices had long refused to use any national ADL materials highlighting racial equality. "They suggest that sectional material and literature be created for the South that would leave out reference to race and base their appeal on an inter-faith foundation," Charles Sherman reported in 1946. Taking up the line Epstein would follow, he equivocated, "While this method will have to be employed in some cases, it is no solution at all as far as the problem itself is concerned." Even the Reform movement's Central Conference of American Rabbis, among the most liberal of Jewish groups, struggled over the question of how forthrightly to act in southern communities. A 1960 proposal to prohibit northern rabbis from entering a "troubled" southern community (as part of a civil

36. NCRAC meeting, minutes, September 9–11, 1949, New York, p. 5, ADL "Y 1949–52: pro-org—CRC." The minutes paraphrase Hexter rather than quote him directly. Benjamin Epstein to Walter White, June 9, 1949, NAACP Papers, II A 363. Fineberg: S. Andhil Fineberg, oral history, January 30, 1974, pp. 132–34, AJC Oral History Library.

37. White testimonial: May 25, 1949, p. 11, NAACP Papers, II A 362. White to Ben Epstein, June 2, 1949; Epstein to White, June 9, 1949. Both NAACP Papers, II A 363.

rights demonstration) without the local rabbi's consent was defeated only after a great deal of debate; the final resolution required northern rabbis to inform local rabbis in advance of their coming.[38]

Southern Jews enjoyed some success in slowing or disengaging their national groups partly because their doubts reinforced and exacerbated hesitations among the national leadership. Strong public pronouncements on civil rights masked internal divisions reflecting the hesitations not only of Jewish elites but of the American Jewish population more broadly. While these doubts did lessen over time, they were never fully resolved, and as initial concerns eased, new issues arose to replace them. Southern Jews exploited the fact that virtually no policy decision came without some internal struggle.

Agency hesitations centered primarily around tactics, not goals. While liberal Jewish organizations recognized the importance for the Jewish community of ending all forms of discrimination, particularly after African American victories such as the fair employment practices law redounded to the advantage of Jews as well as Blacks, they had doubts about the more public and confrontational methods of African American agencies. Jewish groups remained reluctant to embrace any sort of mass action tactics, since they smacked of the demagogic rabble-rousing that had proved so ruinous to Jews in Europe. Second, not only Jews but most liberals remained committed to moderation throughout this period. Even the NAACP hesitated at first over such confrontational tactics as massive nonviolent civil disobedience.[39] These organizations, like their constituents, had generally not thought through the gradualism of liberalism

38. Sherman to Gutstadt et al., p. 4. CCAR: Fineberg, oral history, p. 138.
39. Both of these arguments are true not only for Jewish groups but for White liberals generally, argues Walter Jackson, "White Liberal Intellectuals, Civil Rights and Gradualism, 1954–1960," in *The Making of Martin Luther King and the Civil Rights Movement,* ed. Brian Ward and A. J. Badger (New York: New York University Press, 1996); and Steven Gillon, *Politics and Vision* (New York: Oxford University Press, 1987). Jewish fears of demagoguery in mass action: see for example AEB [Abel Berland, ADL] to BG, memorandum re "Meeting of the Civic Service Committees," August 6, 1947 regarding a CORE boycott in Chicago; Samuel Markle to William Sachs, December 28, 1946, regarding the Fellowship of Reconciliation's call for a bus boycott. Both ADL "Y 1947 NRP." Similar doubts by Black liberal agencies: see for example NUL Executive Board meeting, minutes, November 9, 1943, pp. 3–4, NUL Papers, series 11, box 5, and note 41. Every organization grappled with the question of whether to demand full racial equality, knowing it would fail given the strength of the prosegregation forces, or seek compromises in order to achieve partial goals. See for example Arnold Forster to National Civil Rights Committee, memorandum re "Anti-Segregation Amendments to the Federal Aid to Education Bill," June 28, 1955, ADL "chisub," reel 12.

that came across as racism to many in the Black community and on the left. This was particularly true in the 1940s, when most Jewish organizations had just begun formal civil rights efforts and had not yet fully embraced the cause. It can be illustrated by a "Negro-Jewish incident" in Washington, D.C., that came to the attention of the ADL in 1943. Morris Milgram, the national secretary of the WDL (which, it must be noted, the ADL and other Jewish agencies supported) and a Jew, was evicted from his apartment by his (Jewish) landlord, Mr. Reiskin. It seems Milgram and his wife "invite[d] a number of Negroes into their apartment creating a great animosity, particularly among Southern army officers." As a result of complaints, brought even by the Black janitor, and because "on one occasion Mr. Reiskin found a Negro woman in a bath robe present only with Mr. Milgram in the morning hours," the landlord "was forced to file a notice of eviction."

It was at this point that the ADL stepped in. Paul Richman met with Mrs. Milgram (her husband was out of town) and Reiskin, and both were "adamant with regard to their rights." Mrs. Milgram consulted with "Negro lawyers" and insisted that Office of Price Administration guidelines protected her from eviction for violating local segregation customs. She threatened to take the case to the Supreme Court if necessary. It was of great concern to the ADL that "apparently . . . the Negro press . . . are watching this incident." Richman tried to impress upon Mrs. Milgram "that it was not a matter between the Reiskins and the Milgrams but rather a matter involving whites and Negroes in which the Jews would be in the middle and no matter what happened the Jews would get the blame either from the Negroes or from the whites. Inasmuch as the whites would necessarily have their way either by law or by force, it was silly to knock their heads against a stone wall." Mrs. Milgram, however, "knows all the answers and does not believe in the effectiveness of our methods. I tried to be as sympathetic and understanding as I possibly could but she would not relent."

Richard Gutstadt, to whom Richman wrote for advice, seemed particularly uneasy that "implications of miscegenation may prove very disastrous if publicity breaks about this case." He understood the dilemma clearly that "opposed to the [N]egro interest is the social composition [illegible] in Washington." It was evident where the balance lay for him; since Mrs. Milgram refused "to listen to any arguments of expediency," weightier voices of persuasion had to be brought in. He offered to contact the leaders of the JLC and through them of the Socialist Party (of which the Milgrams were members) and "obtain some opinions on the

Milgrams."[40] It is remarkable that only a few years later, the same ADL would be testifying publicly on behalf of desegregation and against bigotry and racial violence and filing briefs in lawsuits against exactly such situations as this.

The Journey of Reconciliation, sponsored in 1947 by CORE and the Fellowship of Reconciliation (FOR) in an effort to desegregate interstate transportation in the South, provides a fascinating example of the conflict for liberals between fear of confrontational tactics and desire for racial justice. Thurgood Marshall of the NAACP warned African Americans that any "disobedience movement on the part of Negroes and their white allies ... would result in wholesale slaughter with no good achieved." Dr. Trigg, an African American member of the Southern Regional Council, told George Harrison of the ADL "that he did not wholly approve of this type of action. He felt that this 'planned' direct action only tends to antagonize people." As Harrison observed, "The Southern Regional Council as a whole, believe[s] in going very slowly." Jewish leaders likewise debated the wisdom of the effort. Harrison reported that a meeting of organizational heads in Chapel Hill "questioned whether anything new could be gained by such a trip. . . . Alex [Miller] feels that the significance of this projected plan is that there is a group willing to act instead of just talking. I personally question the wisdom of this type of action. . . . On the other hand, George Houser [of the FOR] . . . states that he received encouragement from Mary McLeod Bethune, A. Philip Randolph and several others." Frank Trager responded, "Whereas I would not recommend that they carry on such a project, since I am myself not prepared to do it, nonetheless I would in no way attempt to argue them out of it. . . . If in their conscience they find this to be a desirable thing to try, I say, more power to them."

Although no Journey participants came from the major Black or Jewish organizations, both groups came around afterward. The NAACP provided legal defense for those charged with violating segregation laws. The ADL monitored the Journey and the ensuing court cases closely, and Sol Rabkin wrote to Houser in November to congratulate him.

> We here at the Anti-Defamation League have read your report on the Journey of Reconciliation through the South, and found it one of the most exciting social documents we have ever come across. . . .
> We are . . . very much interested in developments in connection

40. Paul Richman to Richard Gutstadt, memorandum, July 6, 1943; Gutstadt to Richman, memorandum in reply, July 15, 1943, ADL "Y 1943 NRP." There was no resolution in the files.

> with the arrests. . . . If any . . . result in convictions, and you appeal
> [them] . . . we would seriously consider joining in the appeals as am-
> icus curiae.
>   We wish to commend you in the good fight you are carrying on to
> end Jim Crow.

Inspired to apply the technique to matters of direct Jewish interest, William Sachs of the ADL sent "a token contribution to the work of the Fellowship of Reconciliation. It occurs to me that if teams of Jews and Christians could take similar bold action in their approach to resorts and hotels, we might ultimately be able to break down the discriminatory barrier that exists in that field."[41] Thus did self-interest, liberalism, and civil rights activity combine and recombine to constantly reshape the ac-tivist landscape.

   Although they did ease in time, some Jewish hesitations about a full embrace of the civil rights agenda, or at least its more confrontational tac-tics, remained among the national leadership. The chairman of the ADL explicitly committed the agency in 1947 to the protection of the rights of all minorities, and in every case the national policy remained staunchly proactive on desegregation and racial discrimination. Nevertheless, the ADL's National Executive Committee sharply debated until the mid-1950s how centrally the ADL should involve itself in such issues of indi-rect relationship to anti-Semitism. These internal divisions, like the external pressures of the southern constituency, slowed action. A year after *Brown*, well after the ADL had formally committed itself to active support of integration, Henry Epstein protested that the organization's program division still did "not consider desegregation a priority prob-lem" in terms of preparing materials for school and community use. (The result of this debate, as of the others, was a reaffirmation of the ADL's commitment to both the principles of desegregation and a plan of action to spur its implementation.)[42]

41. Bayard Rustin, "Beyond the Courts," AP column for syndication, December 28, 1946. See also CORE, *CORELATOR* (March 1947): 1–2; George Houser and Rustin, "Journey of Reconciliation," report, [1947]; Houser to George Harrison, June 23, 1947; FOR press release, "Judge Tries to Give Six Times Maximum Term in Jim Crow Bus Case," June 27, 1947. ADL doubts (primarily over its advocacy of a boycott): Markle to Sachs. Quotations: Harrison to J. Harold Saks, memorandum, March 20, 1947, p. 2; Frank Trager to Harrison, Miller, Saks, memorandum, April 2, 1947; Sol Rabkin to Houser, November 13, 1947; William Sachs to Trager [re contribution], June 16, 1947, all ADL "Y 1947 NRP." Marshall: "Negroes Cautioned on Resistance Idea," *New York Times*, November 23, 1946, 17.
42. See, for example, ADL National Commission meeting, minutes, May 14–15, 1949, pp. 17–18, ADL warehouse, box 176; ADL NEC meeting, minutes, January 1955, pp. 17–19, ADL warehouse, box 178. The claim that the ADL was not committed to

Southern Jews tried to exploit this faith in gradualism and reluctance to take what appeared to be precipitous action. Despite decades of involvement by the NCJW against restrictive housing covenants, for example, a southern delegate to the group's 1943 conference used the excuse of the need for further study to block passage of a resolution opposing such covenants. Mrs. Levy was

> a Southerner by adoption, but I live in a part of the country where segregation has become a matter of great concern. This prevents the purchasing of property in white areas by colored people. We all realize that there is something to the fact that we are going to have to break down old customs, but it seems to me that we need to be well prepared before we present this [resolution] to the group. . . . It is a very serious thing and has led to rioting in many of the southern cities.[43]

The 1951–1952 spree of dynamiting and bombing in the Miami area that killed the state NAACP head and his wife, and damaged Jewish synagogues, a Catholic church, and a Black housing project, brought both mutual cooperation between Black and Jewish groups and a certain hesitation on the part of Jewish groups to push that cooperation too far and thereby alienate local Whites. Along with the NUL, the NAACP, and other Black groups, the NCJW, the ADL, and virtually every other major Jewish organization issued strong denunciations of the violence and demanded immediate and effective measures to apprehend the criminals and to prevent further violence. The ADL, AJC, and NAACP launched their own investigations of the incidents. Nevertheless, the AJC report clearly reflected the ambivalence of the organized Jewish community and the agency's reluctance to jeopardize what it perceived as precarious acceptance by White Gentiles.

> Since the apprehension of vandals and criminals is basic to an orderly society wherein Jews and others may live securely, one cannot safely ignore tension and reprisal taking place in connection with the improvement of the state of the Negro members of a community.
> At the same time, there is a relationship of Jews to white Christians that needs to be maintained on friendly terms.[44]

---

intergroup programming on race issues is exaggerated. See for example Arthur Levin to J. Harold Saks, memorandum re "Crossville, Tenn," ADL "Y 1948 NRP."

43. NCJW, 17th Triennial Convention, November 1943, minutes, vol. 2, pp. 393–94, NCJW Papers, box 43. Actually, it was an amendment to a resolution against discrimination. For a variety of reasons, including complaints of vagueness, the amendment failed; the resolution passed.

44. Fineberg to Slawson, memorandum re "The Situation in Miami," quoted material p. 3. Responses to violence: NCJW: Mrs. Irving [Katharine] Engel to J. Howard

This fear of going public with views different from those of White Christians was, of course, the central issue for most southern Jews, and this argument proved quite effective for slowing the implementation of national policy. Because the ADL could undertake new actions only by a vote of its chapters, southern groups managed to postpone the ADL's filing of an amicus brief in the *Briggs v. Elliott* and *Brown v. Board of Education* cases for months. In *Briggs*, for example, the ADL's Southern Regional Board passed a resolution urging the national organization not to file an amicus brief. Although "after much discussion" the ADL decided to file, the Southern Regional Board then urged it to reconsider "with such vehemence and genuine sincerity" that the ADL postponed its decision until the next National Commission meeting, although others, including the AJCongress, had already acted. The southern representative of that group, Alfred Smith, insisted that "All men of good will—and we are certainly in that category—want with utmost sincerity to see an extension of the democratic principle of equal civil rights in all fields" but denied that this was the way to attain it. With southern opposition so strong, a public identification with desegregation would mark Jews as a "disloyal minority" and reduce ADL workers "to a position of inertness." Other southern speakers made similar arguments, reminding listeners of the danger of anti-Semitism. While acknowledging that the AJCongress and AJC had taken pro-desegregation positions, they insisted those organizations had little southern presence and so their stands were of less consequence. While some northern members expressed support for the southern position, the ADL ultimately voted to proceed with the filing. After the *Brown* decision B'nai B'rith groups in Louisiana, Mississippi, and Virginia passed resolutions requesting the ADL to reconsider its stand on school desegregation; two southern lodges passed resolutions in approval of the ADL's position.[45]

McGrath, February 8, 1952, NCJW Papers, box 73. ADL: ADL press release, [1952], ADL "Y 49–52 NRP." Similarly: NUL Board of Trustees, resolution, January 17, 1952, NUL Papers, series 11, box 4; NUL press release, January 23, 1952, NUL Papers, series 5, box 35.

45. Desegregation cases and southern resistance: see for example Arnold Forster to National Civil Rights Committee, memorandum re "ADL Brief Amicus in public elementary school segregation cases," July 21, 1952; memorandum, August 20, 1952; memorandum re "Briefs Amicus in Racial Segregation Cases," October 13, 1952, all ADL "chisub," reel 12. ADL National Commission meeting, minutes, October 20, 1951, addendum page regarding the Southern Regional Board resolution, ADL warehouse, box 176. Reconsider: David Rose, ADL Commission meeting, 1952, pp. 94–96; Smith: pp. 97–104; vote to proceed: p. 126. Also see AJC Domestic Affairs Committee

Jewish organizations also hesitated to act publicly on behalf of southern civil rights out of a fear of being accused of communism. Because Jews were routinely cast as communists by anti-Semites, and because any civil rights activity was also automatically so labeled, Jews tried whenever possible to take a backseat in any public integration or antidiscrimination effort. This fear was not unfounded, as the repeated references to Jewish communist agitators by those who practiced or advocated racial violence made clear. In 1958 Edwin Lukas of the AJC noted with concern that "Huge quantities of primitive anti-Semitic literature have been poured by organized . . . hate mongers . . . . blaming Jews for nearly everything that has happened in the South—from Lee's surrender and Sherman's march, to the Supreme Court decision [in *Brown*] itself." NUL's Lester Granger found that the escalation of attacks and accusations leveled against civil rights agencies as communist fronts was "increasingly better organized" after the *Brown* decision "and plays directly into the hands of racist groups." In other words, cooperation among progressive groups was more necessary than ever to combat the increased threat of violence, and yet it was more dangerous than ever for groups to enter into such coalitions. As Ray Mohl noted in reference to the Miami bombings, "these attacks linked white racism, anti-Semitism, and anti-Communism—a powerful brew in the South and in the United States in the 1950s."

Whether well founded or not, fear that civil rights activity would spur anti-Semitic violence had an impact on Jewish civil rights efforts in the South. As Lukas lamented, as a result of the rhetorical allegations that civil rights equaled communism, and the increasingly aggressive and violent efforts to defend segregation as the Civil Rights Movement got underway, "communication between Negro and white groups, around a variety of urgent intergroup problems, has been almost entirely suspended in about eight . . . southern states, and is carried on desultorily in the others." Certainly southern Jews used the fear of spurring anti-Semitism to defend their desire to remain aloof from the civil rights struggle. In 1956 at a board meeting of the ADL's southern region, the regional director "reported that the Jewish communities of Alabama, Georgia, South Carolina and Tennessee generally do not at this time wish to be publicly identified with the desegregation fight; that there has been a tremendous growth of citizens groups fomenting opposition to desegre-

---

meeting, minutes, October 8, 1952, p. 5. B'nai B'rith: ADL NEC meeting, minutes, January 15–16, 1955, p. 18, ADL warehouse, box 178.

gation; . . . while there is some anti-Semitic involvement it is not generally overt but can easily become so in tension situations."[46] The fear of communism was directly implicated, as the ADL Southern Regional Board's claim that supporting desegregation would make Jews appear a "disloyal minority" reveals.

The accusations of Communism slowed civil rights action for both African American and Jewish organizations in less direct ways as well. Both struggled to distance themselves from any hint of militancy for fear it would discredit them with the larger society and therefore compromise their effectiveness; this sharply limited the choices of strategy available. Judge Jane Bolin resigned from the board of the NAACP in 1950 because, she argued, it was so fearful of the communist label that it abandoned virtually all of its effective tactics. The NAACP's "program has become sterile and barren. . . . Nor can the NAACP continue to blind the public to its lack of a positive and alive program by continuing to yell 'Communist' and 'fellow traveler' about every Board member and branch" that demanded less talk and more action. "Our organization has blown the Communists up to such fantastic proportions that we give them more of our attention and time than we do the American Negro." The NAACP rejected all help it received from the Communist Party or its front organizations, as did virtually every other liberal Black or Jewish group; most also routinely rejected for membership or as a speaker anyone suspected of communist sympathies. The NUL, under attack for its allegedly subversive activity, took great pains to separate itself from other more confrontational civil rights agencies, and several of its leaders volunteered to testify before the House Un-American Activities Committee to defend themselves against accusations they might be communists or communist sympathizers. Recent evidence has revealed cooperation with the FBI's anticommunist efforts by no less than Thurgood Marshall.[47]

46. Mohl, "South of the South?" 12. Lester Granger to Officers and Directors of the National Newspaper Publishers Association, October 13, 1955, NUL Papers, series 1, box 49; ADL NEC meeting, minutes, January 7–8, 1956, p. 9, ADL warehouse, box 178; Edwin Lukas, "New Threats to Freedom of Voluntary Association," to Detroit Public Schools Human Relations Institute, March 1, 1958, pp. 19–20, NUL Papers, series 1, box 4.
47. Jane Bolin to Arthur Spingarn, March 9, 1950, Jane Bolin Papers, box 3, Schomburg Center for Research in Black Culture, New York, N.Y. Allegations of communism: see for example Georgia Commission on Education, *Communism and the NAACP*, pamphlet, 1958, AJC VF "names: NAACP." NUL: see Theodore Leskes, AJC, to Manheim Shapiro, memorandum re "Attack on the Urban League," September 28, 1956; M. Leo Bohanon, St. Louis UL, to Furman Templeton, Baltimore UL, October 7, 1955, both NUL Papers, series 1, box 49; "GWR" [NUL] to "REB," memorandum re "Meeting May 21, 1956 . . . ," June 2, 1956, NUL Papers, series 1,

When Jews came under similar attack Jewish organizations also responded by distancing themselves from the most visible representatives
of the Civil Rights Movement. For example, when Murray Friedman reported that southern Jews repeatedly complained that "Jews are behind
the NAACP," Alex Miller offered suggestions to counter these "unjust
and un-American accusations." After making the reasonable argument
that the Jews did not control the NAACP or any other non-Jewish organization, he went a step further. "As far as Jewish organizations are concerned," he wrote, "they do not support or subvent the NAACP." While
some Jewish "and many more Christian" agencies "work in harmony"
with the NAACP and other groups on mutual objectives, "we probably
have more projects going with chambers of commerce than we do with
the NAACP." Although some Jews did serve on the NAACP board, "the
idea of holding Jews collectively responsible . . . is . . . ridiculous." When
such accusations are levied, Miller suggested, "Tell your constituents to
get as mean and angry and offensive as possible."[48] While clearly not intending to do so, the vehemence of Miller's comments reflected a deep
fear of identifying fully with the positions espoused by the confrontational civil rights agency.

Although fear of being labeled communist constrained Black and

---

box 50; and "subversion and the UL" folders in box 49. HUAC: for example Ira de Au-
gustine Reid testified March 11, 1956 "at his own request," as did Lester Granger on
July 14, 1949, NUL Papers, series 1, box 155. NAACP: see for example Roy Wilkins,
NAACP press release, "The Patterson-Wilkins Correspondence," November 23, 1949,
and related materials, NAACP Papers, II A 369, and NAACP files on the Civil Rights
Congress; NAACP press release, "NAACP Says Public Being Misled on Groveland
Florida Case," August 20, 1952; Philip Lerman to Oscar Cohen, memorandum re
"Committee to Free Walter Irvin," July 17, 1952; Milton Ellerin to Gilbert Balkin, July
31, 1952, all ADL "Y 1949–52 NRP." Barring communists: see for example NUL to Mr.
Clagett, May 9, 1956, NUL Papers, series 1, box 49; Walter White to NAACP Branches,
memorandum "re communist infiltration," August 29, 1950; Roy Wilkins to NAACP
Branches, October 18, 1949, both NAACP Papers, II A 369; ADL National Commis-
sion meeting, May 16, 1947, p. 4; National Commission meeting, "Reports on the
Communist Party," October 21–22, 1950, pp. 19–25, both ADL warehouse, box 176;
ADL National Administration Committee, memorandum re "Advising BB Lodges
concerning . . . Booking [Communist Party] Speakers," November 18, 1946, ADL
warehouse, box 42; AJC "Statement of Policy Toward Communist Affiliated and
Communist Led Organizations," June 27, 1950, JLC Papers, box 21–5.
48. Alex Miller to Murray Friedman, December 31, 1958, ADL "Y 1953–58: Orgs:
NAACP." Also see "Hitler's Communism Unmasked," ADL Fireside Discussion
Group, Chicago, 1938. "Jewish Communism Is a Lie!" insisted one of dozens of articles put out by Jewish groups seeking to refute the accusation in public forums. *The
Modern View*, February 15, 1940. Both in AJC inactive VF: "Communists and Jews."

Jewish organizations, at times they were able to turn fear of communism to their advantage. "Lynching and Oppression of Negroes Best Communist Propaganda Says White," read one NAACP press release regarding the 1930 testimony of Walter White before the Fish Committee, which was investigating communist activity in the United States. "The thing that can best stop the spread of Communist propaganda among Negroes in this country, in my opinion, is drastic action by the United States Government and its citizens, to put an end to lynching, segregation, disenfranchisement, and other forms of brutal bigotry," White had testified.

Twenty years later, the NUL urged President Truman to abolish Jim Crow in Washington, D.C., to integrate Blacks into policy-making bodies of government and into all new agencies, and to establish a permanent FEPC by executive order, thus strengthening American democracy "unhampered and unfettered by those forces which make our democracy a mockery in the eyes of the world and which all too frequently give our enemies justifiable reasons to spread propaganda against us." "Our fundamental program of action, designed to assure an equal opportunity to all to enjoy the benefits of a democratic society, is in the long run the most effective answer to communism," the ADL's Subcommittee on Communism insisted in 1950. "In attacking discrimination against all minority groups we are attempting to remove the strongest arguments which the Communists make in their effort to discredit the United States in the eyes of other nations."

Because they recognized the danger in allowing their goals to be dismissed as simply a communist plot, liberal Black and Jewish agencies also waged a stalwart battle for civil liberties, insisting on free speech and the legitimacy of their liberal values and opposing most forms of surveillance and what they viewed as the excesses of government loyalty investigations. For example, the ADL's subcommittee's report continued, "For us to abandon any part of that program [against discrimination] in the vain hope of removing a weapon from the hands of our adversaries [who accuse us of communism] would be to abandon our self-respect as well as the rest of our compatriots with whom we are properly associated. It is unthinkable that we should do this." A joint statement by the NCJW, AJC, AJCongress, ADL, JLC, Jewish War Veterans, ADA, ACLU, American Friends Committee on National Legislation, NCRAC, and several other social agencies and unions opposing the anticommunist Mundt-Ferguson-Johnson and Nixon bills insisted that "the only important fear which we need have of Communists in this country today is that they will provoke us into suicide, by piecemeal destruction of our own free institutions."[49] With communism as with liberalism, organizations found themselves walking a fine and often shifting line between embracing and avoiding controversy.

Not every hesitation among Jewish leaders to become involved in civil rights boiled down to racism or fear of confrontation, demagoguery, or communism. Sometimes they simply differed in their visions of how to achieve equality, a problem that became increasingly acute as the Civil Rights Movement took to the streets. A 1963 ADL report, "The Negro Revolt," while critical of much of the new militancy of the Civil Rights Movement as it was emerging under groups like the Student Nonviolent Coordinating Committee and CORE, opposed the tactics of those groups because it believed

> [t]he increasing militancy, the threat to replace the NAACP as the leading Negro organization and more activity, do not necessarily result in better overall strategy. For example, in the estimation of many, the real breakthrough in the South will come as the result of the power of the Negro vote. It is true that the sit-ins and the freedom rides have made some inroads into established institutions, but these are small advances compared to the massive barriers against Negro equality. One wonders whether the tremendous effort put into the Albany movement, which has achieved little so far, could better have been spent in trying to register Negroes.

It also argued that northern racial problems were too complex and intractable for simple solutions like busing.[50] Thus throughout the civil rights era Jewish agencies found ample reason to withhold full support from the civil rights struggle.

Despite such severe and ongoing internal doubts about specific civil rights strategies, however, Jewish groups came increasingly to recognize that they must finally act. Their hesitations played into the hands of reluctant southern Jews and discredited the national organizations in the eyes of the rest of the civil rights community. And act they did. But

49. Fish: NAACP press release, September 27, 1930, NAACP Papers, I C 229. NUL: "Tentative Statement to Be Presented to the President at White House Conference," [1951?], pp. 1–2, NUL Papers, series 1, box 155. ADL: ADL National Commission meeting, minutes, October 22, 1950, p. 20. The subcommittee was part of the Chicago Executive Committee. Civil liberties statement: n.d., p. 2, NCJW Papers, box 74.
50. ADL, "Fact Sheet II: The Negro Revolt," January 1, 1963, pp. 1–2, ADL "chisub," reel 12. Recognizing Black resentment and frustration, it nonetheless committed itself to continued support of civil rights. The AJCong and AJC both issued similar reports: Nathan Edelstein, "Jewish Relationship with the Emerging Negro Community in the North," address to NCRAC, June 23, 1960, AJC VF NJR: "AJCong"; Isaiah Terman, "With Respect to Jews and Race Relations," August 20, 1963, AJC VF NJR: "AJC 1938–69."

Jewish agencies also recognized that the only way to get around their southern constituents, as well as to bolster northern Jewish support, was to develop materials designed to persuade southern Jews to promote rather than resist racial integration. They began with a direct appeal to self-interest, contending that equal rights for Blacks directly protected Jewish interests. A 1941 ADL handbill, "That the Klan Is a Threat Today," urged Jews to oppose the Klan wherever they saw it, regardless of its immediate target: "Though some leaders declare the Klan, in its resurrected form, will not be anti-Semitic, the inescapable fact is that the nightshirt organization represents an extra-legal movement to take the law into its own hands so far as Negroes and Catholics are concerned. And when any minority race or faith is attacked, other minorities inevitably become the targets of hate." As Arnold Forster observed in reference to violence in Columbia, Tennessee, in 1946, "anti-Semitic and anti-Negro activity frequently go hand in hand and the latter should be of as much interest to us as the former."[51]

Jewish agencies frequently pointed out that anti-Semites used prosegregation organizations to disseminate their propaganda. A 1954 ADL report on the emergence of groups such as the National Association for Advancement of White People (NAAWP) noted not only their dangerous commitment to racism but also the anti-Semitic articles in their publications, including one in both the *American Nationalist* and the NAAWP president's first newsletter with the headline, "South Indignant as Jew-Led NAACP Wins School Segregation Case." As Abel Berland put it, "While the Anti-Defamation League was organized to combat anti-Semitism, its program is based on the thesis that the strengthening of the democratic principle as it applies to all groups will help secure the equal rights of Jews as well."[52]

51. Handbill in ADL, "Confidential Memo: Anti-Semitic Propaganda," [1941], in AJC VF "Anti-Semitism: ADL." Tennessee: Arnold Forster to J. Harold Saks, April 30, 1946, ADL "Y 1946 NRP." Similarly: Leonard Finder, ADL, to Jacob Petefsky [illegible], Amalgamated Clothing Workers of America, August 14, 1942, ADL "Y 1942: discrimination." ADL office files and meeting minutes in the 1940s and 1950s, particularly those of its Civil Rights Division, are filled with anti-Klan efforts. As a result, anti-mask and anti–cross burning statutes were passed in dozens of southern communities and five southern states. See Sol Rabkin and Morris Abram, "Federal Anti-Klan Legislation," report, May 5, 1949 (which details ADL reasoning and strategy on the subject); Arnold Forster to Civil Rights Committee, memorandum re "Anti-Mask Legislation, Free Speech, Group Libel . . . ," May 20, 1949, both ADL "chisub," reel 12 ; ADL National Commission meeting, minutes, May 14–15, 1949, pp. 8–9; ADL, "Memorandum" [on progress in the South, 1952], pp. 2–3.
52. Citizens Councils: ADL NEC meeting, minutes, January 7–8, 1956, pp. 9–11. See also *The Facts* (September 1954): 21; AJCong 1956 convention, "Integration," 59–60.

In addition to equating fighting racists with fighting anti-Semites, Jewish agencies also noted that civil rights victories redounded to Jews' direct benefit. A fund-raising letter for the NAACP sent by the chairman of the ADL, Meier Steinbrink, to ADL leaders in 1949 laid out this self-interest argument explicitly:

> I want to cite three of the many achievements of the NAACP which make all Americans and particularly members of the Anti-Defamation League indebted to the NAACP.
> It was the NAACP which started the fight . . . against restrictive covenants which culminated in the Supreme Court victory in 1948. Our Anti-Defamation League filed a brief amicus curiae. . . .
> And it was the NAACP which caused the United States Supreme Court to reverse its unfortunate decision in the Leo Frank case . . . in Moore vs. Dempsey. . . .
> It was the Association which called the meeting on August 6, 1946 of 41 organizations of which the ADL was one out of which came the President's Committee on Civil Rights.[53]

Similarly, Will Maslow, writing for the NCRAC in 1954, evaluated the potential of legal strategies in achieving the agendas of Jewish agencies. He painstakingly traced the proceedings of numerous court cases, most of which were prosecuted by the NAACP on behalf of African Americans, and noted their direct or indirect usefulness for Jews. The 1948 Supreme Court decision declaring restrictive covenants unenforceable "did not of course smash all the fences enclosing Negro ghettoes," although it did speed "the process of integration in housing. The decision was also applicable to covenants aimed at Jews, illustrating the principle that one minority's legal victories inure to the benefit of other groups." School desegregation cases were not "as speedy or as certain," but "can there be any doubt that . . . the long and arduous effort was worth it?"

Furthermore, he pointed out, legislation on behalf of African Americans such as that creating the FEPC helped Jews as well, both because religious discrimination was outlawed along with racial and because any effort to decrease discriminatory behaviors also benefited Jews as a vulnerable minority group.

> Even the campaign to enact civil rights legislation is beneficial, not only in educating the community about the evils of job bias but also

---

Jewish control: *The Facts* (September 1954): 22–23. Berland: Berland to Albert Kennedy, National Federation of Settlements, July 9, 1945, ADL "Y 1945 NRP."

53. Steinbrink, fund-raising letter for ADL members, n.d. It appears Walter White actually wrote the letter and Judge Steinbrink signed it. Cover memorandum, White to Mr. Wilkins and Mr. Moon, May 18, 1949, NAACP Papers, II A 363.

> in causing those who have uncritically accepted stereotypes about the capabilities of minority groups to re-examine their practices. . . . Even if the legislation does nothing but drive discriminatory practice underground, it still serves a useful function [for Jews]. It is much more difficult for a personnel manager to discriminate against Jews when he has no ready means of determining whether an applicant is a Jew.[54]

Passing, of course, was a far less available option for African Americans, suggesting that such legislation sometimes proved more useful for Jews than for African Americans.

Jewish agencies also employed more subtle self-interest arguments to persuade southern Jews of the need to support civil rights. As Alex Miller presciently pointed out in 1945:

> What I am concerned with, if I am correct in analyzing the forthcoming struggle in the south, is that if the Jewish community as a whole adopts a reactionary and prejudiced attitude toward the Negro, they may lose their liberal allies while not gaining any help from the other group. This point I have begun to hammer home in B'nai B'rith meetings and before other Jewish groups, in addition to which I make the point that I feel that it is immoral for us who have known persecution through the ages to submit another group to similar treatment.[55]

A quadruple lynching in Monroe, Georgia, in 1946 offered Miller a chance to try this approach. The NAACP requested a meeting of representatives from several liberal organizations, including the ADL, AJC, and AJCongress, to discuss possible action. The ADL not only issued a press release condemning the violence but also involved itself in the ensuing local struggles between liberal and conservative Jews. At a joint meeting of the Atlanta Jewish Community Council and the local ADL, Miller read the press statement and "a long discussion ensued as to whether or not the Atlanta Committee should take a similar action." As Miller noted, the "usual hesitant ones" opposed action "for the usual reasons. (1) Fear of identifying the Jewish groups with the Negro group. (2) Fear of sticking our necks out. (3) Fear of consequences to be visited on the Jewish group by Klan members and their adherents." The interventionists finally won the day, arguing "(1) That it is time for the Jewish group to ally itself openly with the liberal and progressive groups in the

54. Maslow, "The Advance of Community Relations Objectives Through Law and Legislation," October 25, 1954, for NCRAC Conference of Committee on Reassessment, December 1954, pp. 4–7 (quotations on 4, 6), NAACP Papers, II A 387.

55. Miller to Novins, "Negro-Jewish Relations," p. 2. Similar argument following the *Brown* decision: ADL, NEC meeting, minutes, October 22–23, 1955, p. 11, ADL warehouse, box 178.

South. (2) That instead of thinking of the consequences of our action upon those who are our potential enemies, rather should we think of the consequences . . . upon our potential allies and friends. (3) That passing this resolution will have definite educational value on the Jewish group itself."

The resolution placed the JCC "on record as decrying and condemning the recent unprovoked attack upon the lives of four Negro citizens" and declared, "We believe the time has come for all good citizens of Georgia to recognize any violation of the sacredness of human life by mob action as a real threat and danger to rights and privileges of every citizen." Miller noted that this "was the first time that an important Jewish community of the South took positive action of this type" and hoped it would inspire similar actions in the future. "You will note also how my own thinking has changed from my original point of view when this office was first opened some eighteen months ago. Perhaps, it is because we have been able to educate to some extent our own people so that we are no longer as far in advance of them as we used to be."

This optimistic assessment received some support two weeks later. Rabbi Youngerman of Congregation Mickve Israel in Savannah had written a letter to the local newspaper urging the passage of antilynching legislation, which "had put him in considerable difficulty with his Congregation and . . . there was a possibility of his being ousted." The congregation, Miller noted, "is dominated by a Jewish group which is almost completely assimilated . . . and has adopted the coloration of the Savannah, white community." Miller "telephoned Youngerman immediately and gave him my thinking. Among other things, I thought that it was time the Jews of the South began to take their place shoulder to shoulder with other progressive and liberal groups; that while there is a certain value to the strategy of not being out alone in the front—there is also a certain value to not being caught standing in the rear with the worst elements." The strategy succeeded, and after hearing the rabbi's defense, the congregation tabled a motion condemning his action, instead offering him "an overwhelming vote of confidence." Nevertheless, Youngerman noted, "my opponents are not taking this lying down. They refused to join the vote of confidence and are now taking steps to prevent Mickve Israel from being 'taken over by the "kikes." ' "[56]

56. NAACP meeting: Walter White to ADL [et al.], telegram, July 31, 1946; Harold Cowin, ADL, to Arnold Forster, memorandum re "NAACP Meeting, Re: Lynchings in Monroe, GA," August 6, 1946 (which reported the presence of forty-three organizations including the CIO, AFL, NCCJ, American Veterans Committee, Negro Elks, YMCA, YMHA, AJCong, AJC, Freedom House, and ADL). ADL condemnation: press

Similarly, in 1947 under their umbrella organization, the NCRAC, the AJC, AJCongress, ADL, Jewish War Veterans, UAHC, and twenty-four Jewish Community Councils publicly supported opening the National Theater in Washington, D.C., to Black patrons, despite the opposition of local Jews, including the theater owner. The NCRAC defended its stand on the ground that its constituent groups were "dedicated to the struggle against prejudice, bigotry, intolerance, and discrimination on grounds of race, religion, and national origin, wherever and in whatever forums they may manifest themselves." Northern Jewish organizations similarly supported southern desegregation efforts even when no Jews were involved. They argued that Jews had everything to lose, and little to gain, by staying out of the struggle. It was clear the civil rights revolution would come with or without the support of southern Whites; Jews would do far better to embrace it than to fight a rearguard action that was doomed to failure.[57]

Ultimately, Jewish agencies broadened the self-interest argument to embrace the equality of all as central to Jewish security. In perhaps the most neatly packaged argument of this type, Shad Polier of the AJCongress proclaimed, "The CLSA view[s] the fight for equality as indivisible and as part of the general struggle to protect democracy against racism. Hence any manifestation of racism, whether against Jews,

---

release, August 1, 1946. Atlanta JCC and ADL: Miller to Forster, memorandum, August 5, 1946 (includes Miller's quotations on the meeting); Atlanta JCC, "Review of Minutes . . ." (contains resolution text). Youngerman: Miller to J. Harold Saks, Abel Berland, Irving Rosenbaum, memorandum, August 26, 1946 (includes quotations by Miller on Youngerman's situation); Louis Youngerman to Miller, August 22, 1946 (includes vote and "opponents" quotation). All but Atlanta JCC in ADL "Y 1946 NRP." The "kikes" reference, distinguishing "pushy" and left-leaning "New York Jews" from the more genteel and racially conformist southern Jews, paralleled that used by the southern anti-Semites quoted by McCallister. A certain amount of self-hatred, or the acceptance of negative stereotypes of one's own group, was not uncommon among either Blacks or Jews.

57. National Theater: Paul Richman to J. Harold Saks, memorandum re "National Theater, Washington, D.C.," May 7, 1947; NCRAC, "Letter to Actors Equity re: National Theater, Washington," n.d., both ADL "Y 1947 NRP." Efforts with non-Jewish owners: for example, in 1951 filing amicus briefs in support of desegregating Washington, D.C., restaurants by reaffirming the validity of its 1873 antidiscrimination law (Isaac Franck to Arnold Forster et al., memorandum re "Municipal Court of Appeals' Decision on 1872–1873 Anti-Discrimination Laws," May 28, 1951; Frances Levenson and Sol Rabkin to CRC offices, AJC Area Offices, ADL Regional Offices, memorandum re "Washington, D.C. Civil Rights Statute," June 13, 1951); or testifying before the Washington, D.C., Recreation Board during hearings on desegregating city playgrounds (Sol Rabkin, ADL, to Herman Edlesberg, April 28, 1952). All ADL "Y 1949–52 NRP."

Negroes, Japanese, Puerto Ricans, or others, affect[s] all Americans. . . . Any victory achieved *by* the Jewish community or any other group *for* the Jewish community or any other group is a victory for all."[58]

Jewish organizations were aided in their efforts to expand the notion of self-interest by the broader trend in the northern Jewish community to redefine Judaism as synonymous with liberalism. Thus in making their point about the importance of civil rights, Jewish leaders from synagogues to political agencies stressed their interpretation of Judaism as a universalist rather than a particularist religion, rooted in a historical national identity. Because Jews had experienced centuries of persecution, they argued, they were therefore obliged to aid other such victims. As justification they cited not only Jews' own recent history but the biblical call for social justice, "because you were slaves in the land of Egypt." Equality, they insisted, was the only acceptable moral position for a religion claiming to be ethical. As Philadelphia delegate Max Klinger argued hyperbolically in a 1956 AJCongress convention debate about the position of southern Jews vis-à-vis integration efforts, the resolution under discussion "should read that we are certain as Jews, the Southerners must agree that they are for integration. . . . I don't believe that we can recognize a Jew as one who doesn't believe in the difference between good and wrong, and we certainly all of us believe in fighting for good rather than standing for evil." Frank Goldman, president of B'nai B'rith, ADL's parent organization, urged members to support desegregation because "the ADL was created to implement certain principles for which it stands, principles which are concerned with just two words—human rights. . . . They are principles by which we live and in which we believe. . . . Are dollars and our own welfare to take the place of a God given stand for human rights?" AJCongress's Isaac Toubin insisted, "We must be concerned with safeguarding the democratic process as the best way to preserve our integrity and our identity as Jews."[59]

With greater membership in the North, every policy decision put to the vote ultimately went the way the activists hoped, from resolutions on antidiscrimination to the filing of briefs in support of desegregation. Nevertheless, southern Jews' attempts to quiet the activism of their

58. Shad Polier, "The Law and Social Action," [*AJ*] *Congress Weekly* 17 (November 27, 1950): 3.

59. Klinger: AJCong 1956 convention, "Integration," 82. Goldman: ADL National Commission meeting, October 24–25, 1952, transcript, pp. 121, 123, ADL warehouse, box 176. Toubin: "Reply to Ben David," cited in Will Maslow, memorandum to CRCs and Group Relations Agencies, October 22, 1953, NAACP Papers, II A 360. There are dozens of such pronouncements and resolutions from the ADL, AJC, AJCong, JLC, and NCJW in these years.

national agencies were in the short run occasionally effective. By exploiting hesitations among the national leadership and by exercising their rights as voting members of those agencies, southern Jews managed not to derail Jewish civil rights efforts but certainly to slow them and to limit their impact.

IV. Conclusion

The Jews of the South proved ambivalent actors in the struggle for civil rights. While racism on the one hand and morality on the other exerted their own pressures, the primary self-interest of southern Jews lay in minimizing the dangers of anti-Semitism in a region that appeared inhospitable to religious as well as racial minorities. However, the self-interest argument was double-edged: it suggested both a fight for civil rights, in order to protect minority rights, and resistance to civil rights advances, since breaking down racial barriers might raise religious ones. This fear seemed particularly real since Jews were already viewed as outside agitators who could well be blamed for any changes in social structure the Civil Rights Movement imposed. While national Jewish agencies generally argued that civil rights victories would protect Jews, most southern Jews endorsed the second, more pessimistic conclusion that supporting civil rights efforts would jeopardize their precarious security.

One cannot account for these divergent conclusions on the basis of the social and demographic differences between Jews who settled in the North and those who settled in the South, real though they were. The greater conservatism of the latter seems to have been shaped more by external forces of southern conservatism, anti-Semitism, and legal racial segregation than by any internal differences between northern and southern Jews. As part of their struggle to avoid marginalization and discrimination, southern Jews adopted as much as possible their region's social mores. It was easy for northern Jewish leaders to proclaim, as did the ADL, "Human freedom is indivisible; it must apply to Negroes if it is to be effective for whites. . . . If the Negro is not safe, the Jew is not safe . . . there is no security for one unless there is security for all."[60] It was far more difficult for a southern community committed to blending in to make such bold and sweeping claims, not necessarily because they disagreed with the sentiments, but rather because they believed the consequences of the backlash against desegregation would land squarely on their shoulders. The impact of this resistance was to slow the civil rights

60. ADL, "Anti-Defamation League Vitally Interested in Welfare of the Negro Community," report (press release?) [1943], ADL "Y 1943 NRP."

efforts of Jewish national organizations not only through direct pressure but also by augmenting and aggravating internal divisions within the agencies.

There were, of course, notable exceptions to the pattern of southern Jewish resistance to active civil rights efforts. Individual southern Jews, from rabbis to community members, a substantial proportion of them female, embraced the civil rights cause. Their stories, what made them rise above the concerns of their neighbors and friends, still need to be fully explored. For that matter, those deeply racist southern Jews who defied the universalist teachings of their faith and whose views conflicted with those of the majority of their coreligionists, North or South, must be accounted for as well.

Nevertheless, while the story of Jews in the South contains examples of both heroism and racism, the central narrative primarily reveals hesitation born of fear. Much to the frustration of their northern coreligionists, southern Jews consistently hung back in the struggle for racial equality, rarely standing in active opposition, but also rarely willing to challenge openly the racist structures of their society.

Against the Grain

Black Conservatives and Jewish Neoconservatives

Nancy Haggard-Gilson

I N THE LAST twenty years, criticism of poverty programs and civil rights policies has become not only common but for many politically expedient. Conservatives and neoliberals of all varieties—Republicans and Democrats, northeastern ethnics and the California establishment right—have made opposition to welfare programs and affirmative action a central issue on their political agendas. But the debate is about far more than public spending and sensible budgeting. The coding of the policy lexicon, begun in the first Reagan administration with the criticism of "welfare queens," urban crime, and admissions quotas, has clearly turned the public discourse about social programs into an argument about "race."

In the growing coalition of conservatives, the small but vocal groups of African Americans and Jews have received a disproportionate amount of attention.[1] Their alliance with other critics of government policy is often taken to substantiate the claim that the debate is not biased or, even, about race at all. Indeed, the conservatives argue that their central point concerns the inherent limitations on the government's capacity to solve what are principally social problems. In fact, some Black conservatives have lashed out against the use of their racial background to bolster the position of White conservatives. Their anger, however, has fallen mostly on deaf ears.

I would like to thank Michael Rogin, Cheryl Greenberg, V. P. Franklin, and the participants of the conference for offering comments that strengthened both the details and the argument of this essay.

1. The political scientist Ronald Walters reacted to this attention in a July 15, 1991, editorial in the *Washington Post* criticizing the news media for seeing to it "that a sliver of a conservative opinion should equal in weight the dominant liberal values of the majority."

But the attractiveness of these African American and Jewish critics to the conservative cause goes beyond color and religion to their style of argument. Much of their writing, no matter how formal, is a mixture of personal anecdote and social scientific analysis. Their willingness to cast criticism in the terms of personal experience, appearing to suggest racial/ethnic complicity, lends them authority. These are supposed to be the "truth tellers," speaking apparently against their immediate self-interest because their criticisms leave them ostracized. This is almost as true for Jews as for Blacks; in retelling stories about their own immigrant poverty and subsequent success, Jewish neoconservatives make simultaneous claims to both kinship and insight, to what Irving Kristol has described as their "rabbinic" association with the world. Thus, when either insists that the real poverty problem is, as Glenn Loury puts it, the "enemy within" (a lack of community values), not the "enemy without" (racism), personal experience is automatically accepted as proof of a commonsense truth. This, unfortunately, is the beginning of considerable oversimplification for some and of undisguised political ill will for others.

The minority conservative policy critics are, in fact, quite diverse ideologically. The failure in the past to recognize this has had several consequences. First, it ignores the substantial differences between African Americans and Jews in their assessments of poverty and government capabilities. Indeed, the heart of the Black conservatives' criticism of poverty and civil rights policy is an argument about racial identity and community, whereas the Jewish neoconservatives focus primarily on the limitations of state intervention and 1960s New Left influences on liberal welfare policies. More important, lumping the conservative critics together also obscures the extent to which many African American critics *are* talking about race and racial identity, but from substantially different perspectives. In addition, overgeneralizing gives credence to the conservatives' contention that their work is driven by a normative, race-neutral theoretical interest in individuality and moral responsibility. They use autobiography as a sort of "everyman" evidence and suggest that they are proposing a kind of "color-blind" methodological individualism. Nonetheless, their criticism of "individuals" or "communities" is driven by their interest in seeing race and racial identity defined in very particular ways. The issue of race is, in fact, central to Black conservatives' thinking on government action, but they have different levels of commitment to the goal of "integration."[2]

2. Many Black conservatives are aware that they provide ammunition to White critics not only because of the cultural arguments but also because of their often barbed

This essay begins with a discussion of the origins and evolution of neo-conservatism, starting with its founding in the 1960s and concluding with a discussion of whether or not the politics of the new generation of so-called mini-conservatives follows the neoconservative model or is more traditionally conservative. It will then move to a consideration of the differences between African American and Jewish conservatives on social policy. The discussion will focus on two topics: affirmative action and welfare. Although both African American and Jewish critics believe that the contemporary social crisis has been enveloped by a "cultural" crisis, their understandings of cause, effect, and location are quite different. I will argue that, for the Jewish neoconservatives, the locus of fault is the disaffected White liberals whose insistence on unworkable social programs overloaded the "state," causing policy failure and a collapse of government authority. For them, the crisis is both political and societal, with important legislative implications. The African American conservatives agree that the state is incapable of ridding the country of poverty, but for them the problems originated not in the disaffection of policy makers but with the paternalism of government policy. The belief that Blacks cannot, as Shelby Steele has put it, "run fast once they get to the 'starting line'" led to programs that created and maintained dependence.[3] As a result, many in the Black community lost their cultural values and sense of identity. In this formulation, the crisis is moral and cultural.

Following the discussion of policy differences, the essay will then move to a discussion of "race" as it appears in the work of four Black conservatives, Glenn Loury, Stanley Crouch, Clarence Thomas, and Shelby Steele. I will suggest that their views about the value of integration and maintaining racially distinct communities are highly diverse, making it impossible to generalize about their ideas on race and Black identity. Their positions run the gamut from a traditional conservative race consciousness—in which race is a central component of identity, but neither nationalism nor integration is accepted for its own sake—to "liberal integrationism." Yet all of them insist that Black identity contains much that is distinctive and original.

---

comments about the current civil rights leadership. It should be noted, though, that Black conservatives are far from agreement about the value of past civil rights policies. Generally, the differences fall along the academic/politician cleavage with the latter more critical of all assistance and training programs.

3. The quotation from Shelby Steele is a reference to Lyndon Johnson's famous Howard University speech.

A word should be added here about the choices I made about whom to include and exclude in my discussions of both neoconservatives and conservatives. Thomas Sowell, for example, is obvious in his absence, although many of the general points I make about Black conservatives can be extended to the ideological positions taken by Sowell. Likewise, Norman Podhoretz, who served as editor in chief of *Commentary* from February 1960 to May 1995, is discussed only briefly. Although Podhoretz has written on social policy, his views vary little from those of Irving Kristol, who is discussed at length. Writers have been chosen who are both distinctive within their ideological camp and, at the same time, representative of conservative or neoconservative thinking.

Neoconservatism and Social Policy

"Neoconservativism" first appeared as a distinctive politics in the late 1960s. Almost from the moment that the socialist Michael Harrington gave them their name, neoconservatives became influential in the area of social policy. As Podhoretz has explained in an essay proclaiming "the death of neoconservatism," most members of the group "tended to reject the label. . . . So far as they were concerned, they were indeed still liberals, fighting to reclaim the traditional principles of liberalism from the leftists who had hijacked and corrupted it."[4]

This attachment to liberalism is, indeed, one of the characteristics that makes neoconservatism distinct from the traditional "conservatism" of American politics. Unlike the conservatives, the neoconservatives supported many of the governmental institutions and liberal social reform policies associated with the New Deal. They supported the creation of a limited welfare state, remained friendly to the labor movement, and agreed with much that was accomplished by Martin Luther King's nonviolent direct action protest campaigns, especially the passage of the civil rights laws in 1964 and 1965. Although staunchly anticommunist, the neoconservatives thought the domestic McCarthyite politics of conservatives verged on "political thuggery." To neoconservatives, the threat from communism was largely external. It was this position on communism that worked to sever ties between neoconservatives and conservatives on foreign policy issues.

On the domestic scene, it was the neoconservatives' cultural politics that made them distinctive. The heart of the Jewish neoconservative argument is a critique of the New Left "counterculture" of the 1960s, and

4. Norman Podhoretz, "Neoconservatism: A Eulogy," *Commentary* 101 (March 1996): 20.

Irving Kristol is, perhaps, its best-known proponent. In three volumes of essays, *On the Democratic Idea in America* (1972), *Two Cheers for Capitalism* (1978), and *Neoconservatism: The Autobiography of an Idea* (1995), Kristol voices a traditional conservative complaint: when the demand is made for the state to guarantee absolute equality among its citizens without also attempting to shape manners and morals, "a bizarre inversion of priorities" takes place. Too much "formalized democracy" destroys the "original, animating principles" of society, precipitating "grave crises in the moral and political order."[5] Kristol is quite clear that liberal democratic capitalism is "not . . . the best of all imaginable worlds" but can only be "the best, under the circumstances," if "the market," rather than the state, is its principal regulating mechanism. When the state assumes responsibility for what are essentially economic problems, both the fabric of society and the integrity of government are at risk.

Kristol's argument is straightforward. The United States was founded as a democratic capitalist state; the ideal of political equality and the market economy were, thus, intended to be mutually reinforcing. However, the drafters of the Constitution retained their skepticism about government, believing that it could easily be turned against personal liberty if limits were not strictly established; these were to be constitutional prohibitions against intervention in the economy and private economic relations. Kristol argues that the founding fathers "were sober and worldly men, and they were not about to hand out blank checks to anyone, even if he was a common man." Between the market and the Constitution, justice and fairness are guaranteed, but *only* by first securing stability. Kristol notes, "Under capitalism, whatever is, is just . . . all the inequalities of liberal-bourgeois society must be necessary or else the free market would not have created them, and therefore they must be justified."[6] Thus, from the conservative perspective, the first thing to be understood about American society is that inequality is inescapable. Liberal bourgeois society requires economic growth, and growth comes from free and open competition.

As Kristol understands the liberal policy makers of the 1960s, they decided that the original principles and design of American liberal capitalism were inherently inequitable. It is in his critique of this idea that

5. Irving Kristol, "Confessions of a True, Self-Confessed—Perhaps the Only—'Neo-Conservative,' " *Public Opinion,* October/November 1979, American Enterprise Institute for Public Policy Research, Washington, D.C.; *On the Democratic Idea in America* (New York: Harper and Row, 1972), vii.

6. Kristol, *On the Democratic Idea,* 53, and *Two Cheers for Capitalism* (New York: Basic Books, 1978), 65.

Kristol's discussion of democratic capitalism moves from the realm of traditional conservatism to that of neoconservatism. As Kristol understands it, liberals believed that the persistence of poverty in the United States after the passage of the 1964 Civil Rights Act demonstrated the need for more radical reform; hence, the advent of new welfare and affirmative action programs. But this was, according to Kristol, the beginning of an even greater crisis because the government was attempting to do something that it could not. That failure brought governmental interventionism into widespread disrepute. Not only did the problem of poverty remain, but the overall society was made to suffer the consequences of a general breakdown of respect for both the authority of government and the responsibilities of fundamental social institutions.

In 1979 Kristol argued that the reforms of the 1960s were "grafted onto liberalism." Neoconservatism intends to "reach beyond" contemporary liberalism through a "return to the original sources of the liberal vision and liberal energy."[7] It does not appear that, in saying this, Kristol or the other neoconservatives had definite or principled notions about where the expansion of the welfare state should end. Rather, they were governed by more "practical," though perhaps fuzzy, considerations, such as "the precise point at which the incentive to work was undermined by the availability of welfare benefits, or the point at which the redistribution of income began to erode economic growth, or . . . egalitarianism came into serious conflict with liberty."[8]

A consequence was a deterioration in social norms, not simply due to the failure of government resolve but because of the structural weakening of certain social institutions. National politics at that point became "interest group politics," thus causing Congress and the president to lose sight of the *national* interest. Furthermore, the scope and complexity of social programs forced Congress to turn discretionary and interpretative power over to various governmental agencies. As a result, the weakened congressional and executive branches have been upstaged by what neoconservative sociologist Nathan Glazer has called an "imperial judiciary" and the "permanent officials" of the federal and state bureaucracy.[9] As the neoconservatives understand it, the now legitimate complaint that government does not work is what underlies the clearly perceptible unraveling of the American social fabric.

    7. Kristol, "Confessions."
    8. Podhoretz, "Neoconservatism," 21.
    9. Nathan Glazer, *Affirmative Discrimination: Ethnic Inequality and Public Policy* (New York: Basic Books, 1975), xiv–xv. Also see Aaron Wildavsky, "Government and the People," *Commentary* 56 (August 1973): 25–32.

Glazer is at the center of the neoconservative attack on another controversial social policy issue—affirmative action. He does not deny that racism persists or that it has substantial consequences. Rather, his concern is that government has chosen to use race to solve the problem of racism and that the rights of groups have inappropriately supplanted the rights of individuals. In *Affirmative Discrimination: Ethnic Inequality and Public Policy* (1978), Glazer declares that in governmental actions "a person's color, race, and ethnic background are as decisive for his or her fate today as they were in 1964, when, with the passage of the Civil Rights Act, we thought we had taken a giant step in eliminating color, race, and ethnic origin from public and private decision making."[10]

Glazer and other neoconservatives disputed the commonly held liberal belief that the civil rights legislation of 1964 and 1965 was insufficient in the face of the economic consequences of racial discrimination. Kristol and Glazer have suggested that the new laws were not given enough time to be proved effective. Their focus on the limited impact that social legislation had on public institutions was meant to show that government has no, and *can* have no, role in solving the social problems associated with inequalities in income or economic opportunities.

In the early 1990s there was much talk about the death of neoconservatism. Many conservative critics, as well as the founding neoconservatives themselves, have described it as a transitional ideology that was important in moving right-wing politics from the nativist, "paleoconservatism" of the first half of the century to the "anti-statist conservatism" now associated with the mainstream of the Republican Party. There are several reasons this might be true. First, the generation and individuals most likely to carry the mantle of neoconservatism choose to call themselves, simply, conservatives. William Kristol (son of Irving), John Podhoretz (son of Norman), and Adam Bellow (son of Saul) have aligned themselves more squarely with the Republican Party than their elders did and thus have tended to cast the domestic issues in a much different light. The older generation, while inclined to the new language of "family values," is much less likely to be comfortable with the stridency of the anti-abortion or "right to life" movement. They are also in disagreement with the positions taken by the Republican Party on the issue of immigration. Second, earlier neoconservatives were not, as noted above, anti-statist, as the new generation most surely is. Finally, the circumstances that brought neoconservatism into being—the cold war and the 1960s counterculture movement—are no longer in existence. However, since

10. Glazer *Affirmative Discrimination*, xi.

the neoconservatives see their movement as largely victorious, it is perhaps most accurate to say that there has been substantial ideological convergence between conservatives and neoconservatives.

The African American Reaction to Neoconservatism

When the Jewish neoconservatives entered the public debate against welfare and affirmative action, there was a palpable sense of betrayal among
African Americans. Many Jews and African Americans were dismayed
by what they saw as the breakup of a decades-old alliance built upon a
common set of group experiences. Perhaps unpredictably, one of the
more interesting assessments of the Black-Jewish split comes from the
Black conservative Glenn Loury. In a 1986 essay, "Behind the Black-
Jewish Split," Loury shrewdly captured one of the critical differences between the Jewish and the African American conservatives. In noting that
the "absence of a shared public vision" is recent, Loury argues that "the
policy of racial preferences forces Blacks and Jews publicly to confront
their very different understanding of the American experience."[11] As
similar as the material circumstances of Jewish and Black exclusion may
have been, Loury insists, the difference between race and ethnicity renders them incommensurable. With a few exceptions, most of the Black
conservatives agree that the omnibus legislation of 1964 and 1965 did not
solve all the problems associated with racial discrimination in American
society.

   Loury does not dispute that Jews have been victimized but rather argues that the "standard melting pot story" that accounts for their success
does not apply to African Americans. In a speech from the early 1980s,
Loury dismisses the immigrant paradigm as "woefully simplistic" when
it comes to race. He makes several telling points. "First," he argues, "the
fact of skin color is a basis for separation qualitatively different from
those traits which distinguished the earlier ethnics." The "racial ideology
within which Blacks have had to function" is one that questioned, in
every instance, their claim to "equal humanity." This not only foreclosed
the possibility of assimilation but also made any failings by Blacks particularly damaging. Loury's second point is historical. The migration of
Blacks out of the South was ill timed. They arrived in the cities after the
boom in industrialization that gave Irish, Italian, and Jewish immigrants
an economic foothold. Loury concludes:

   11. Glenn Loury, "Behind the Black-Jewish Split," *Commentary* 81, no. 1 (January
1986): 24.

For all these reasons I believe the straightforward application of the melting pot model to the current Black underclass is inappropriate. The answer to the question, "Why don't they pull themselves up the way our parents did when they first came?" might well be: "Because they don't face the same structure of economic opportunities, and are burdened with social and psychological encumbrances which your parents did not face."[12]

Thus, Loury insists in "The Saliency of Race" that the problem of the underclass is one of "racial justice . . . the racial problem of our time."[13]

Loury is not alone among Black conservatives in believing that African Americans are "unique among minority claimants." Most of them would agree that the persistent accommodation of racism within American liberal democracy gives African Americans particular reason to be wary of anyone claiming or advocating "color-blindness." However, while this point leads Black liberals to believe that discrimination is a constant, Black conservatives argue that government can effectively manage its public aspects—in employment, education, and social welfare services. What remains to be restrained are cultural and private expressions of prejudice, expressions that are less susceptible to control by force of law.

Thus, when Loury claims that poverty is a racial problem, the point is more descriptive than explanatory. The problem is not racism per se but the failure of a racial community to protect its "social capital, . . . those social institutions within a community that generate economic dividends by shaping the values and attitudes of individuals, in effect making them more effective competitors in this society." Loury lists family, church, and peer-group associations as examples of important institutions that generate social capital. Like the sociologist James Coleman, Loury recognizes that the approach to social capital development cannot be entirely instrumental. Such institutions, because they are normative, stem from a community's character; they are maintained by values and traditions and cannot be manufactured at will. Thus poverty is, at root, an identity problem. Loury is adamant that African Americans are not at fault in causing poverty, but its perpetuation is a result of their being reactive instead of active. Loury speaks for conservatives Shelby Steele and Stanley Crouch in saying, "Our work today is not to change the minds of White people,

12. Glenn Loury, "Responsibility and Race: Ethnic America: Melting Pot or Mosaic," *Vital Speeches of the Day* 49 (April 15, 1983): 398–99.

13. Glenn Loury, "The Saliency of Race" in *Second Thoughts About Race in America*, ed. Peter Collier and David Horowitz (Lanham, Md.: Madison Books, 1991), 76.

but to involve ourselves in the lives of Black people."[14] An examination of these conservatives' arguments about affirmative action will make this idea clear.

The Affirmative Action Argument

Black conservatives are not unanimously opposed to governmental programs and policies to protect African Americans from racial discrimination and the denial of equal opportunities. Loury, for example, argues for the continuation of educational programs, job training, and "minimal subsistence to the impoverished" and suggests that financial and other government support could be used to help encourage "internally directed action" within the Black community. Stanley Crouch supports welfare, though with disincentives for "irresponsible sexual behavior."[15] And nearly all of the Black conservatives praise the civil rights legislation of the 1960s, though Clarence Thomas, the most conservative of this group, reserves his approval for the extension of protection to Blacks of long-established civil liberties and rights.

Affirmative action is the particular target of Black conservatives. They raise four general objections. First, instead of pointing to the New Left and the counterculture of the 1960s, as the Jewish neoconservatives do, Black conservatives fault the government for being too paternalistic. Paternalism, which for them is at bottom racist, fosters dependence. Shelby Steele, for example, discusses Lyndon Johnson's speech at Howard University in 1965, taking particular issue with the line, "You do not take a person who, for years, has been hobbled by chains and liberate him, bring him up to the starting line of a race and say, 'You're free to compete with others,' and justly believe that you have been fair":

> On its surface this seems to be the most reasonable of statements, but on closer examination one can clearly see how it deflects emphasis away from black responsibility toward white responsibility. The actors in this statement—"you (whites) do not *take* a person (Blacks)"— are whites; Blacks are the passive recipients of white action. The former victimizers are to be patrons, but where is the black chal-

14. Glenn Loury, "New Dividends through 'Social Capital,' " *Black Enterprise* 15 (July 1985): 36; see James Coleman, "Social Capital in the Creation of Human Capital," *American Journal of Sociology* 94 (1988 supplement): S95–120; Glenn Loury, "A Prescription for Black Progress," *Christian Century* 103 (April 30, 1986): 438.

15. Glenn Loury, "The Moral Quandary of the Black Community," *Public Interest* 79 (spring 1985): 9–22, and "Prescription for Black Progress"; Stanley Crouch, "Role Models," in *Second Thoughts,* ed. Collier and Horowitz, 61.

> lenge? . . . Nowhere in this utterance does President Johnson show respect for black resilience or faith in the capacity of Blacks to run fast once they get to the "starting line." This statement which launched Johnson's Great Society, had the two ever-present signposts of white guilt–white preoccupation and black invisibility.[16]

Steele's argument about White guilt and Black "race-holding" is complex and will be taken up later, but his criticism of affirmative action is straightforward: it discourages Black competitiveness.

In a recent work, Loury makes a similar argument using formal modeling to test whether affirmative action discourages the development of work skills. He argues that the "analysis shows how affirmative action can lead employers to patronize minority workers, that is, hold them to a different standard. This . . . can have the effect of making skill acquisition less beneficial."[17]

Loury's concerns about government behavior or "fickleness" have a second component. As Loury explains it, those in the Black community are confused about the nature of their responsibilities to themselves. Many assume, he argues, that because government ignored the consequences of racism for so long it has the responsibility to bear the entire burden of correcting the damage. Loury's insistence on personal responsibility is well known, but the point goes further. Unlike some of his fellow conservatives, Loury believes that public policy can play some role in encouraging the growth of a new community. In 1995 he wrote:

> I am convinced that direct and large-scale intervention aimed at breaking the cycle of deprivation and the limited development of human potential among the black poor is the only serious method of addressing the racial inequality problem in the long run. And while such intervention—to promote education, housing and jobs—may occasionally depart from purely colorblind practice, it is not what minority advocates mean when they call for "affirmative action."[18]

Like most conservatives, however, Loury distrusts public institutions. For him, the problem is not state capacity, as it was for the Jewish neoconservatives, but the likelihood that the politicians will pursue policies only as long as it serves their immediate, electoral interests to do so. In other words, dependence on government initiatives, even when they are worthwhile, is bound to end in disappointment when political winds

16. Shelby Steele, "White Guilt," *American Scholar* 58, no. 3 (autumn 1990): 504.
17. Glenn Loury, "Incentive Effects of Affirmative Action," *Annals* 523 (September 1992): 19.
18. Glenn Loury, "The Social Capital Deficit," *New Democrat* (May/June 1995): n.p.

shift.[19] This is why Loury favors the use of government to foster social capital, which is independent of political expediency.

The third criticism found in conservative writing about affirmative action is jurisprudential and, perhaps, best exemplified in the work of Clarence Thomas. Since offering its decision in the *Bakke* case in 1978, the Supreme Court has been skeptical of using race to solve the problems of racism. Since that time, it has nullified any program that gives even the appearance of using "quotas" for hiring, promotions, or college admissions. Thomas's complaint is that to do otherwise turns civil rights advocacy into "pork-barrel" politics with racial groups, instead of individuals, vying for government benefits. Such a politics not only contradicts basic constitutional principles, he argues, it also threatens the separation of powers by making the court "more concerned with meeting the demands of groups than with protecting the rights of individuals. . . . The dignity of the judiciary is not enhanced by its politicization."[20]

Finally, all of the Black conservatives argue that affirmative action policies have done nothing to alleviate poverty. They suggest that the real beneficiaries are middle-class Blacks who would have been able to gain access to schools and employment under the simple guarantees of the civil rights laws passed in the 1960s. Under such circumstances, they argue, the continuation of affirmative action has two important consequences. First, it allows the government to claim it has a poverty program when it does not, resulting in a de facto doctrine of "benign neglect." Of equal import to conservatives is the diversion of energy and interest that affirmative action creates within the civil rights leadership. One of the problems, as conservatives see it, is the failure to press the Black community for the development of an independent, group economy. Black conservatives accuse the civil rights leadership of being interested only in its own position and status. The political leadership has increasingly been drawn from the professional class, attracting people who have used affirmative action for advancement. Although it is simple interest-group politics, Thomas argues that the leadership defends its position by false appeals to integration. Affirmative action stresses integration; its emphasis is on outward mobility. But for Thomas and Loury, it is inevitable that this assimilationist orientation sacrifices Black institutions through inattention and lack of support.

Black conservatives have many other complaints about affirmative

19. Loury, "Prescription for Black Progress," 434.
20. Clarence Thomas, "Civil Rights as a Principle Versus Civil Rights as Interest," in *Assessing the Reagan Years*, ed. David Boaz (Washington, D.C.: Cato Institute Press, 1988).

action, but all ultimately rest on their perceptions about what is at stake for African Americans as a group. As serious as their charges are about ineffective policy and breaches of institutional integrity, they are more concerned that racial identity not be sacrificed to poverty or failed attempts to eradicate it. Although this part of their work is often dismissed as perpetuating "culture of poverty" arguments, the claim captures only a part of the conservative argument about race and community and suggests a unanimity among them that in reality does not exist. The following discussion will attempt to highlight the similarities and differences among Black conservatives on the topics of race, racial identity, and relations between Blacks and Whites in American society.

Black Conservatives and Race

In many ways it is difficult to summarize and assess Thomas's ideas on "race" because they appear so fraught with internal inconsistencies. On the one hand, Thomas criticizes affirmative action as placing the interests of groups before those of individuals and thus allowing remedies to some who may not be victims of discrimination. On the other hand, he has claimed in interviews and writings that he is attracted to the ideas of Louis Farrakhan and Malcolm X, Black nationalist leaders whose appeal to most African Americans rests precisely on their call for collective power and identity. The apparent contradiction leads many of Thomas's critics to dismiss his ideas out of hand, suggesting either that they are a psychological defense mechanism, protecting his underlying identification with the White status quo, or that they represent some type of utopian libertarian fantasy about the individual's ability to "make it on his own."[21] In either instance, there has been little attempt to make sense of what he says.[22] There is another perspective, however, which provides

21. Both of these explanations can be found in a roundtable held by *Tikkun Magazine* just after Thomas's nomination to the Supreme Court that included Kimberle Crenshaw, Harold Cruse, Peter Gabel, Catherine MacKinnon, Gary Peller, and Cornel West. See "Roundtable: Doubting Thomas," *Tikkun* 6:5, pp. 23–30.

22. Since Thomas's nomination to the Supreme Court there have been articles taking up pieces of his argument and attempting to treat them seriously. See Ronald Dworkin, "Justice for Clarence Thomas," *New York Review of Books*, November 7, 1991, 41–45, and Stephen Macedo, "Douglass to Thomas: The Roots of Black Conservatism," *New Republic*, September 30, 1991, 23–25. Dworkin is interested in Thomas's natural law jurisprudence; while he considers Thomas's claim that natural law is the best foundation for civil rights arguments, he does not address Thomas's ideas on race. Macedo, on the other hand, has written a piece of intellectual history, tracing Thomas's ideas back to Frederick Douglass. It is an excellent piece, but it overstates the legacy. Douglass was an integrationist and criticized what he called "complexional institutions," both ideas about which Thomas is ambivalent.

more coherence to Thomas's ideas and places him squarely within one strand of American intellectual thought.

As a member of the administrations of both Ronald Reagan and George Bush, Thomas made it clear that he supported their social policy agendas. He opposed affirmative action, busing, social welfare programs, and forced school integration. But he has also spoken out against the notion of a "color-blind society," the idea that was the cornerstone of the racial politics of both presidents. He argued that such a society would be impossible to achieve in the United States because Blacks will "never be seen as equal to Whites." But, more important, Thomas believes that the commitment to "color-blindness" sends a message to African Americans that Black cultural forms and institutions are unworthy because they are the products of a race- and color-conscious society.

Thomas is a staunch opponent of integration for its own sake. He has publicly criticized the philosophical rationale of *Brown v. Board of Education,* arguing that it is based on the assumption that anything that is all-Black is necessarily inferior. And he is on record as opposing the government's policy pressing southern states to merge their dual college systems. White liberals who insist on integration, he says, should "leave Black people alone." Thomas recognizes that both all-Black public schools and the historically Black colleges need financial help and reorganization, but he insists that with assistance and a strengthening of their curricula, their students will be more than competitive. "Black children gain nothing from simply sitting next to Whites and can do quite well in their own schools."[23]

Thomas draws his intellectual influences from a number of sources, but his ideas about a group economy are often credited to Booker T. Washington. In the following passage, Thomas could be paraphrasing from any number of passages in *Up from Slavery,* Washington's most famous autobiographical work.

> The American black man should be focusing his every effort toward building his own businesses and decent homes for himself . . . let the black people, whenever possible, however possible, patronize their own kind, hire their own kind, and start in those ways to build up the black race's ability to do for itself. That's the only way the American black man is ever going to get respect.

23. The quotations are from Juan Williams, "A Question of Fairness," *Atlantic Monthly,* February 1987, 72–73. Also see Thomas, "Civil Rights as a Principle" and "The Higher Law Background of the Privileges and Immunities Clause of the Fourteenth Amendment," *Harvard Journal of Law and Public Policy* 12, no. 1 (winter 1989).

According to Thomas, the issue "is economics—not who likes you."[24]

But Thomas is a more traditional American conservative than was Booker T. Washington. Thomas's writings suggest an inextricable interdependence between the community and the development of individuals. Communal cultural integrity is a prerequisite to individual success. Although the government must take the initiative in protecting personal rights, it must also remain at arm's length from communities, allowing them the freedom to determine their own norms and practices. Thus affirmative action offends Thomas because the claim that his community is in some way deficient threatens to make "weakness" an identity trait of its members. This, finally, may explain the contradiction that many see in Thomas's discussions of race. His nationalism is less cultural than it is genealogical; families (and, by extension, communities) are the root source of identity. They provide the substantive material for constructing a subjective identity, though not always in ways of their own choosing. Families cannot escape being conduits for social recognition and misrecognition. If the Black community has absorbed the message of affirmative action as Thomas understands it, then his personal identity may be compromised. Thus, from his perspective, affirmative action renders individuals both dependent on government largesse and racially oppressed.[25]

Whereas Thomas's ideas fall squarely within the tradition of American conservatism that has always attempted to find some way to accommodate both community-based values and individualism, and to reconcile national identity and distinct cultural value systems, Loury recognizes that "ordinary black people feel a genuine ambivalence about their American nationali[ty]."[26] The dual emphasis on collectivity and the individual that marks Thomas's work is absent from Loury's. Loury's perspective is more straightforwardly collective in emphasis, and his personal anecdotes and stories are less likely to be about individual successes, as Thomas's are, than about returning to the original values of the Black community.

---

24. Quoted in Williams, "Question of Fairness," 73.

25. For discussions of how social recognition and misrecognition affect identity, see Charles Taylor, "The Politics of Recognition," in *Multiculturalism*, ed. Amy Gutmann (Princeton: Princeton University Press, 1994). In the same collection see Kwame Anthony Appiah's "Identity, Authenticity, Survival: Multicultural Societies and Social Reproduction."

26. Glenn Loury, "A New American Dilemma," *New Republic*, December 31, 1984, 17.

Loury also understands that "racial" identity is different from either "ethnic" or "regional" identity, ideas that Thomas often conflates. And it is Loury's recognition of this significant difference that leads him to make a strong case for a racially drawn community as the only possible means of managing the effects of racism. Indeed, Loury argues that the recognition of an individual's racial identity cannot be "legislated or litigated out of existence," and it should be turned to a benefit. For this reason Loury, like Thomas, criticizes integration "for its own sake" because it both devalues race and weakens it as the connective tissue necessary for community building. Loury approvingly quotes civil rights leader Floyd McKissick, who observed that the push for integration seemed to suggest that "when you put Negro with Negro, you get stupidity." Loury concluded, "When the civil rights struggle moved from ending de facto segregation to forcing racial mixing, Blacks often seemed to be rejecting the very possibility of beneficial association with themselves."[27]

Loury's thinking about racial identity is more subtle and complex than that of most conservatives. He rejects the notion that race itself can be defined either "from the perceptual view of the oppressor" or from "the socially imputed definition" of being "black enough." In both cases, the individual would be led to see himself or herself "primarily through a racial lens."[28] For Loury, race is neither a relational idea—it is more than "not White"—nor one constructed completely in reaction to something else, for example racism. "Not being White" and victim status are insufficient material for the construction of a racial identity. To explain identity construction Loury says, "to shift the metaphor slightly, the socially contingent features of my situation—my racial heritage and family background, the prevailing attitudes about race and class of those with whom I share this society—these are the building blocks, the raw materials, out of which I must construct the edifice of my life."[29] Thus, Loury makes "race" a critical, distinctive component of his identity formation, but one that interacts with other influences.

Loury's criticism of affirmative action stems from his belief that it is fundamentally reductionist, defining African Americans first and only in terms of race. Its intention is to secure a racial balance rather than to convey respect for talent. If it is not a display of regard, then it must be an insult. Reliance on affirmative action is evidence that the emancipation of

27. Loury, "Prescription for Black Progress," 436.
28. Glenn Loury, "A Personal Perspective on Race and Identity in America," in *Lure and Loathing: Essays on Race, Identity, and the Ambivalence of Assimilation,* ed. Gerald Early (New York: Penguin, 1993), 7, 9.
29. Ibid., 9.

African Americans was not complete. Relying on Orlando Patterson's
Slavery and Social Death, Loury declares:

> Patterson rejects the "property in people" definition of slavery, argu-
> ing that relations of respect and standing among persons are also cru-
> cial. But if this is so, it follows that emancipation—the ending of the
> master's property claim—is not of itself sufficient to convert a slave
> (or his descendant) into a genuinely equal citizen. There remains the
> intractable problem of overcoming the historically generated "lack of
> honor" of the freedman.[30]

Affirmative action, because it is fixed to race (and gender), impedes the
ability freely to convey respect. This then sets up the cycle, as Loury sees
it, of pity breeding both anger in Whites and feelings of victimization in
Blacks that paralyze them.

Loury is not arguing that African Americans face only a psychological
barrier to mobility and points out that discrimination and limited past
opportunities for accumulation have left the community with little investment capital.[31] But when he states that poverty is a racial problem, he
is suggesting that its solutions are dependent on leadership within the
Black community. Feelings of victimization are an impediment to change
because they focus energy toward external solutions and, by neglect,
allow the disintegration of Black social capital. This is the critical point
for Loury.

Loury derived the idea of social capital from development economics.
The concept implies not only the building of institutions, such as businesses, markets, and schools, but also the reorientation of values and attitudes toward competition and individual change. Loury assumes that
traditional social values, such as responsibility, initiative, and mutual respect, have an inherent logic that, when aggressively maintained, cannot
be escaped. They necessarily lead to the pursuit of mobility and economic independence. In this vein, for example, we find Loury drawing a
causal connection from the "refusal" of familial responsibility by young
fathers to their "lack of initiative" in education and employment.[32]

Loury's argument is profoundly conservative. His idea of social capital is interesting, but the complaints from his critics that he is blaming
African Americans for the chronic character of their poverty are hard to
dismiss. Loury defends himself by arguing that he has separated fault
and responsibility; White racism is at fault in the creation of Black

30. Glenn Loury, "Beyond Civil Rights," *New Republic*, October 7, 1985, 25.
31. Loury, "New Dividends through 'Social Capital.' "
32. Glenn Loury, "The Family, the Nation and Senator Moynihan," *Commentary* 81
(June 1986): 26.

poverty, but African Americans are responsible for finding the way
out. Loury allows that government does have some limited role in the
process. But the distinction between fault and responsibility does not
make sense in the absence of an assurance that the factors that caused the
crisis in the Black community have been checked. Loury's belief that
there are sufficient legal procedures of redress for discrimination under-
estimates their difficulty for a community with few resources. Just as important, it minimizes the persuasive power of images and ideas that are
outside the reach of procedural protection. With some irony, it seems that
one who makes much of culture gives it too little weight as an adversary.

The Politics of Culture and Identity

The cultural critic Stanley Crouch takes up precisely that problem. In an
article titled "Who Are We? Where Did We Come From? Where Are
We Going?" he discusses the notion of Black identity by evaluating
W. E. B. Du Bois's famous metaphor of "double consciousness." Du Bois
described African Americans as being afflicted with a split personality,
by "a twoness," a sense of being both "an American, and a Negro."
Du Bois suggested that these two identities need to merge into "a better
and truer self." Crouch, however, calls Du Bois's discussion a "muddle of
ideas" that simplifies the nature and origins of Black identity in the
United States.[33]

Crouch argues, "Negroes, as Americans, are caught in the middle of
the national struggle between high and low, refined and rough, industrious and lazy, articulate and ignorant, moral and criminal, sincere and
hypocritical." It is important to see that he understands the struggle to be
national in scale, but not nationalist. Who Blacks are is a "human tale,"
thus these dichotomies are inherent to all human activity. At bottom,
what bothers Crouch about the notion of "twoness" is that Du Bois believed "race to have the upper hand" in the struggle for identity. This
necessarily implies nationalism and with it a potentially undemocratic
narrowness. Crouch argues:

> [T]he problem of a race consciousness of whatever stripe negates the
> question of the individual and imposes some sort of "authenticity"
> that can trap the single human life inside a set of limited expectations.
> [Ralph] Ellison was more interested in the incredible variety possible
> if any nation or any group truly grasps the idea of democracy and
> frees itself from all ideas that negate the broad human heritage avail-

33. Stanley Crouch, "Who Are We? Where Did We Come From? Where Are We
Going?" in *Lure and Loathing,* ed. Early, 83.

able to enriching interpretation by individuals, no matter what their ethnic origin.[34]

Crouch argues that the very character of the civil rights struggle was one of inclusion; thus, he describes any politics that emphasizes race as "balkanization" and a sign of intellectual backwardness. He is particularly pointed in his discussion of Afro-centrism and Pan-Africanism. Crouch finds two problems with these concepts. First, they perpetuate the image of Blacks as "a victimized but essentially royal 'we' " instead of celebrating their diversity and triumphs. More important, Crouch criticizes these belief systems for "feeding people myths" about their heritage. He argues that Afro-centrism has tried to make American Blacks "feel good about themselves" by insisting that the contributions of Egypt and Ethiopia be duly recognized as African. But the ancestors of most Black Americans are from West Africa, an environment more humble than and distant from the intellectual "bustle" that was found in ancient Egypt and Ethiopia.

Crouch also bristles at "irresponsible intellectuals" who perpetuate "visions of victimization," using them to justify "reductive ideas" about Black opportunity and potential. He claims that such intellectuals are "bootlegging liberal arts rhetoric to defend Afro-fascist rap groups like Public Enemy on the one hand, while paternalistically defining 'gangster rap' of doggerel chanters such as Ice Cube as expressive of the 'real' black community."[35]

Crouch's criticism of all of these intellectual trends is the same. He believes that they are at bottom anti-integrationist and, therefore, undemocratic. The "experiment that is American democracy," Crouch says, is an "astonishing gathering of information from the entire world."[36] Knowledge of the world, he suggests, is the only hedge against "sinking down," but it can be gained only when one's particularistic identity is checked.

Being an integrationist is not in itself enough reason to be labeled a conservative. Crouch is not an assimilationist, and he does not suggest that Blacks lose sight of their history or their unique and original contributions to American culture. His emphasis is always on the complexities in order to recognize the variations in race caused by family, region, gender, and intellectual inclination. But variation is an American characteristic, and African Americans are quintessentially American.

What makes Crouch a conservative is his insistence that the racial

34. Ibid., 85.
35. Crouch, "Role Models," 61.
36. Ibid., 57.

"simplification" of society is a leading cause of the decline in Black achievement. From one angle, the history of exclusion would seem to justify his point, and race has been used to credit "the values of civilized behavior" as the products of "white middle-class standards." Crouch argues that African Americans must no longer be "allowed to believe that excellence, mastery of our national language, tasteful dress, reliability, or any virtues that bring vitality to a society are the sole province of the white population."[37] From another angle, that of Thomas and Loury, the emphasis on race is intended as a foundation for reestablishing the "values of civilized behavior." But Crouch does not agree. One must be part of the "intellectual bustle" in order to influence it.

In comparison to the conservatism of Loury and Thomas, then, Crouch's conservatism is marked by his commitment to a particular type of integration. The solution to "sinking" is not the strengthening of racial identity, but moving out physically and intellectually into a broader context where differences are finer. One must gather more information, as Crouch puts it, and in the end race is not abandoned but is reduced to a second tier of influence. It should never be the lens through which other things are filtered. This was his grievance against Du Bois.

The Psychology of the Oppressed

While Crouch's conservative critique focuses on culture, Shelby Steele uses psychology to attack the "politics of difference" and racial nationalism. Steele has constructed an elaborate psychological theory to explain the persistence of Black isolation and immobility. Unlike the other conservatives who are also interested in poverty, Steele's focus is almost exclusively on affirmative action and the Black middle class. He speaks of campus politics, suburban living, and the behavior of Black professionals. When Steele speaks of isolation and immobility, the reference is to the failure of both social integration and individual initiative in the face of sufficient opportunity.

Steele argues that, in the aftermath of the Civil Rights Movement, there was ample reason to believe that an important historical lesson had been learned: the "marriage of race and power" must be avoided at all costs. But this was not to be. The Black Power Movement resuscitated the marriage and, therefore, the "suffering, misery and inequity" that were its consequence.[38]

Steele is not very clear on the origins of the demands for Black power.

37. Ibid., 61.
38. Shelby Steele, "The New Segregation," *Imprimis* 21, no. 8 (August 1992): 1.

In a few places, he speaks of Black power as a response to pent-up anger, but more often he credits it to what he calls "racial anxiety."[39] This anxiety comes from the internalization of stereotypes about inferiority and, paradoxically, was triggered by the offer of equality. With the ending of legal discrimination and segregation, the possibility of entrance into the mainstream caused "Black self-indictment." When the individual discovers that the new situation will not allow race as an excuse for shortcomings, he or she fears the exposure of personal vulnerabilities. The very recognition of this fear, what Steele calls "integration shock," causes the individual to fall back on the familiar anxiety about race. This behavior only reinforces the racist beliefs of "White bigots," providing them with further evidence of the inferiority of Blacks.[40]

The recognition of fear simultaneously creates a "defense mechanism" that allows the individual to deny both the fear and the evidence of inferiority. Steele calls this "race-holding" and describes it as the use of race as psychological camouflage. The point for Steele is that racial anxiety causes Blacks to adopt a racial identity that can then be used to explain failure—"the problem is race, not me." Therefore, racism is set up as the obstacle to entering the mainstream, instead of personal choices or competencies.[41]

Race-holding, however, is not the end of this psychological chain of events. If the ultimate point is to escape blame, and if the accusation of racism is to have any merit, Blacks must be able to absolve themselves of any fault. Steele calls this "seeing for innocence" and believes it to be the essence of White racism. He defines it as seeing in the interest of one's innocence rather than looking for the objective truth about oneself.[42] If seeing for innocence works, it easily becomes the grounds for power and demands for entitlement. Thus, in the end, fear of the exposure of personal vulnerabilities results in demands for collective racial compensations. As Steele puts it, some Black individuals demand compensations on the basis of the perceived victimization of Blacks as a group.

Steele suggests that the focus on race in a post-1964 world almost necessarily signals the eclipse of personal achievement for many. Race-holding makes race the locus of power, dissipates latent energies, and

39. See, for example, "The Recoloring of Campus Life," *Harper's*, February 1989, 47–55; "Being Black and Feeling Blue," *American Scholar* 58, no. 4 (autumn 1989): 497–508; and *The Content of Our Character* (New York: HarperCollins, 1990).
40. Shelby Steele, "Thinking beyond Race," *Wilson Quarterly* (summer 1990): 63.
41. Ibid., 64.
42. Shelby Steele, "I'm Black, You're White, Who's Innocent?" *Harper's*, June 1988, 48.

thus negates the need for individual effort. But that is the heart of the problem for Steele; in the contemporary world a collective identity is a hindrance to achievement. First, affirmative action confirms for Whites that Blacks are inferior; thus Whites "see for innocence" as well and believe themselves justified in abandoning the Black poor. Second, collective identity enhances the reliance on societal explanations for the worsening quality of Black life and legitimizes passivity within the sphere of personal activity. For Steele, it is precisely the power of personal ambition that is the key to dispelling the myths of inferiority.

It should be noted that there are serious problems with Steele's formulations. First, though Steele discusses only African Americans, the language he uses suggests his theory should apply to any racial or ethnic group with a history of exclusion. The problem is that no other community can be made to fit his description. The argument, in other words, is entirely conceptual without any empirical evidence—beyond his personal experience—to back it up. Second, he assumes that racism is all in the past; by implication, he suggests that no significant racist impediments exist in the present. Again, by ignoring empirical data, Steele is not forced to confront recent evidence on increases in residential segregation, employment and promotion discrimination, and the incidence of hate crimes. In many places he argues that racial anxiety is called into existence not by true inequality but by the memory of it.[43] Finally, Steele's complete rejection of racial identity is simply too extreme. It assumes that individuals act in a vacuum, that they can, on their own, will away the external context of their lives. He may be correct in arguing that African Americans must accept the individualistic imperative, but that need not rule out racial identity.

Conclusion

By way of conclusion, I would like to make a few generalizations and offer some criticisms. First, while Black conservatives and Jewish neoconservatives are often placed in close intellectual company, they share only the fact that they are critics of current social policy. Beyond that, they are quite different. The Jewish neoconservatives are closer to traditional philosophical conservatism; they fret about the consequences of too much democracy and an overlarge state. These are concerns not found in the writings of Black conservatives. If the Black critics restricted themselves to arguments about values, it would be possible to make the

43. See, for example, "The Memory of Enemies," *Dissent* 37 (summer 1990): 326–32, and "The Recoloring of Campus Life."

case that they are within the conservative mainstream, but their focus on race makes this difficult or at least, given the differences among them, makes the generalization false.

The only thing that the Black conservatives seem to agree on is that "race" should not be used as a legal device to solve the problem of "racism." Beyond that, their views are quite distinctive. The four discussed here—Thomas, Loury, Crouch, and Steele—fall in different places along the continuum from nationalist to assimilationist. They also disagree about whether the government has any role to play in solving the problems that now plague the Black community. Finally, there is only a slight overlap in what they credit as the mechanism of social dislocation: for Steele, it is deeply psychological; for Crouch, it is largely cultural; and for Loury and Thomas, it is a loss of values.

Despite these differences, their writings share many of the same weaknesses. First, at the most general level, none of them attempts to provide an answer to the hard question: how can the social or economic changes they recommend be implemented? For example, given Loury's admission that there is little accumulated capital in the Black community, how is the group economy to get off the ground? Would this require government funding? Aid to small business ventures? Tax incentives for new businesses? And, of course, answering these questions would also require answering the political question: would such programs be likely to be passed given the current political and economic climate? This criticism applies to Steele's work just as well, albeit with a different emphasis. If the psychological process works as he describes, how is the cycle interrupted?

A second problem with the Black conservatives' arguments is their narrow conception of the problems for Blacks in poverty. Their emphasis on values implies that moral disarray is the biggest problem facing the Black underclass, but surely that cannot be correct. The majority of the poor Black work, try to maintain their families, avoid the criminal justice system, and aspire to economic mobility.[44] What the Black conservatives fail to consider is that there are liabilities of class—poor education, bad neighborhoods, lack of access to employment, poor demeanor, lack of information—that are important variables in explaining chronic poverty. And many of these problems may best be solved through government assistance. The conservative argument about Blacks in poverty *is*

44. See William Julius Wilson, *The Declining Significance of Race* (Chicago: University of Chicago Press, 1978) and *The Truly Disadvantaged: The Inner City, the Underclass, and Public Policy* (Chicago: University of Chicago Press, 1987). Wilson shows that many of the images of poor Blacks are empirically false.

reductionist; everything is explained as a consequence of irresponsible personal behavior.

Another closely related issue is the failure of Black conservatives to engage the issue of the structural decline of American cities, the economic context for most Black poverty. It is clear that one of the consequences of Reagan-era politics has been the slow withdrawal of resources from the urban areas. Reagan's "New Federalism" reduced federal government grants to the states, forcing them, in turn, to decrease their spending in cities. State legislatures felt compelled to leave tax revenues in the suburbs, thus making it virtually impossible for big-city mayors to finance social services and educational improvements. The decline in revenues, combined with the movement of manufacturing businesses out of urban areas, resulted in fewer jobs, inadequate public education, poor service provision, and decaying housing. These results not only demoralize, they also inhibit the development of human capital.

Fourth, Black conservatives often premise their argument on the belief that enforcement of civil rights legislation has ended legal discrimination. Recent research suggests they are wrong. In a study of the impact of Reagan policies on Atlanta, Gary Orfield and Carole Ashkinaze show that systematic discrimination is still a factor in the lives of all Blacks, regardless of class, even in a city with a Black administration and a substantial Black elite. With budget cuts and the political shift to the right, federal agencies responsible for investigating and litigating discrimination complaints have become less aggressive, and some have even been closed. Incidences of redlining, neighborhood steering, and employment discrimination have increased in the last fifteen years.[45] While it is true that the laws are there to be used, there must be a fair and dependable process for advocates to help those with insufficient knowledge or economic means. Orfield and Ashkinaze show clearly that a consequence of conservative policies has been the abandonment of programs and resources that assist the poor and the victimized in the grievance process.

It should also be noted that in the work of Loury and Thomas, who have much to say about the implications of the supposed decline of the Black family, there are also subtle messages about gender. If the point was that female-headed families face gender-related economic disabilities, their arguments would be less objectionable. Instead, they suggest that women cannot raise strong, responsible boys or morally minded girls. When they direct the focus to family structure per se, rather than

45. Gary Orfield and Carole Ashkinaze, *The Closing Door* (Chicago: University of Chicago Press, 1989).

variables of the social structure, as the first cause of community disarray, women become the weak point. Cornel West, in a discussion of Clarence Thomas, has put it this way:

> Like all conservatisms rooted in a quest for order, the pervasive disorder in white and, especially, black America fans and fuels the channeling of rage toward the most vulnerable and degraded members of the community. For white America this means primarily scapegoating black people, women, gays and lesbians. For black America the targets are principally black women and black gays and lesbians. In this way black-nationalist and black-male-centered claims to black authenticity reinforce black cultural conservatism.[46]

If the conservatives are hard on women, they are equally guilty of fueling the negative stereotypes about Black men. The picture they paint of the Black community is one in which men are more likely than not to be disinclined toward work and personal obligations, easily enticed by the images of power and manliness in "gangsta rap" music, and smug about the decline of the community around them. Their arguments give solace to those who believe that the best social policies are those that include "third-strike" laws for hardened criminals, censorship of music and movies, the creation of public orphanages, and two-year caps on welfare even for families with children. If Black conservatives oppose these policies, they must learn to be more vocal in their dissent.

None of these criticisms means that the discussion about social capital should not be engaged. The fact that Jesse Jackson of People United to Save Humanity (PUSH) and Hugh Price of the National Urban League have recently begun to talk about "values" suggests that Black conservative ideas may be moving out of isolation.[47] The difficulty with the argument as the conservatives pose it, however, is that it is left to stand on its own, with few policy recommendations.

It is important to return to the issue of the conservatives' methodology and style of argument. Arguing from personal experience has been an enormously successful strategy for Black conservatives precisely because it makes criticism difficult. But the substantial flaws and weaknesses in their arguments cannot be dismissed. In the work of several of these critics, personal experience is used as evidence of "truth," suggesting that the causes of and solutions for poverty and inequality are neither complex nor honestly debatable. According to these social analysts, all we

46. Cornel West, "Black Leadership and the Pitfalls of Racial Reasoning," in *Race-ing Justice, En-gendering Power*, ed. Toni Morrison (New York: Pantheon, 1992), 396.
47. Although Jackson has been criticized by Black activists and intellectuals for "blaming the victim."

need to do is adopt a rational, methodological individualism and ask: How did it happen for *this* person? How was it experienced by *this* person? How did *he* succeed?

Autobiography has always been a significant part of Black intellectual history, and anyone knowledgeable of the field can point to the classic works by Frederick Douglass, Alexander Crummell, W. E. B. Du Bois, Malcolm X, Richard Wright, James Baldwin, and Maya Angelou. But these texts differ in one significant way from the work of the conservatives—they were intended to expose from a personal perspective the ravages of American slavery and racial oppression to those who denied or defended their existence. These are brilliantly conceived social documents that bring to life the statistical analysis found in social scientific investigations, but they made no claims to being "social science."[48] The Black conservatives, on the other hand, claim to be engaged in social science and social policy analysis, but for empirical evidence they rely upon their own personal experiences. Autobiography and social scientific research are two very different enterprises and utilize very different methodologies for getting at the "truth" about the human experience. As a literary form, autobiography can be enormously evocative and informative, but it is not held to the same rules of evidence as is social science. Oftentimes, the literary license and devices used and generally accepted as appropriate for autobiography would be considered completely unacceptable in social science.

Finally, the Black conservatives are inconsistent and contradictory on the idea of "racial identity." While most Black conservatives decry essentialist notions of race as limiting, unidimensional, and exclusionary, they are clearly equally dissatisfied with a racial identity based solely on physical identifiability, the idea that you are what you appear to be to others. This, their work suggests, is too "thin," lacking in cultural substance and historical specificity. Yet none offers a satisfying alternative that allows race to be something "thicker." Their failure to engage the historical experiences of African Americans, particularly those who have perennially suffered from poverty and powerlessness, allows their critics to claim that in moving against the grain, the Black conservatives have virtually severed their roots to the African American community.

48. See V. P. Franklin, *Living Our Stories, Telling Our Truths: Autobiography and the Making of the African-American Intellectual Tradition* (New York: Oxford University Press, 1996), 11–20.

II. Conflict, Competition, and Matters of Principle

African Americans, Jews, and the City

Perspectives from the Industrial Era, 1900–1950

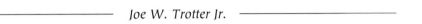

Joe W. Trotter Jr.

S CHOLARLY AND popular interest in African American–Jewish relations has increased considerably during the past two decades. Much
of this interest has focused on the civil rights and post–civil rights eras,
when the earlier Black-Jewish political coalition broke down and new
forms of ethnic and racial conflict emerged. Prevailing studies emphasize
the shifting attitudes and behavior of African American and Jewish elites;
the controversies involving Black anti-Semitism and Jewish racism;
and the role of Jews in African American civil rights and political organizations. Despite expanding knowledge of these issues, few studies offer
systematic historical analyses of African American–Jewish relations during the industrial phase of Black urban history.[1]

The dearth of historical scholarship on the subject during this period is
closely intertwined with the impact of race relations, ghettoization, and,
recently, proletarian approaches to research on Black urban life. These
various conceptualizations have enriched our understanding of race,
class, and spatial relationships in the city, but they neglect the very complicated history of African American relations with Jews and other European and non-European ethnic groups.[2] Examining scholarship on the
relationship between Jews and Blacks during the period from 1900
to 1950, this essay suggests that we need not only to subject African

1. Lenwood G. Davis, *Black-Jewish Relations in the United States, 1752–1984: A Selected Bibliography* (Westport, Conn.: Greenwood Press, 1984); Hasia R. Diner, *In the
Almost Promised Land: American Jews and Blacks, 1915–1935* (1977; rpt. Baltimore: Johns
Hopkins University Press, 1995); John Bracey and August Meier, "Towards a Research Agenda on Blacks and Jews in United States History," *Journal of American Ethnic History* 12, no. 3 (spring 1993): 60–67.
2. For a recent review of this scholarship see Joe W. Trotter, "African Americans in
the City: The Industrial Era, 1900–1950," *Journal of Urban History* 21, no. 4 (May 1995):
438–57.

American–Jewish relations to systematic historical analyses but also to bring them within the framework of Black urban community studies. A brief examination of the existing scholarship reveals the significance of this agenda.

As I have written elsewhere, Black urban history is deeply rooted in the discipline of sociology. Its sociological genesis is tied to the 1899 publication of W. E. B. Du Bois's *The Philadelphia Negro: A Social Study*. Like White social reformers in the United States and Europe during the late nineteenth century, Du Bois adopted the tenets of the expanding social "sciences" to address contemporary social problems, especially the constraints of racism and prejudice that hampered the lives of urban Blacks.[3] Partly because Du Bois hoped to reform patterns of Black-White relations in the City of Brotherly Love, he paid little attention to the precise relationships that emerged between Blacks and Jews.

The Philadelphia Negro treated the problems of "racism" and "prejudice" as forces that diminished the distances between White groups. Thus, in Du Bois's view, Jews and other European immigrants shared a status with American-born Whites. While Jews and their immigrant counterparts faced certain barriers to full participation in American society, none faced the constraints that confronted Blacks. As he put it: "There are other unassimilated groups: Jews, Italians, even Americans; and yet in the case of the Negroes the segregation is more conspicuous, more patent to the eye, and so intertwined with a long historical evolution, with peculiarly pressing social problems of poverty, ignorance, crime and labor, that the Negro problem far surpasses in scientific interest and social gravity most of the other race or class questions."[4]

Du Bois did specify the role of Italian and German workers in undermining the economic status of Blacks. In the barbering trade, for example, he notes that these two groups had nearly eliminated African Americans from their historic position by the late nineteenth century. However, such analyses were not extended to Jews and did not represent a systematic component of his study.[5]

Black urban life was the subject of only a few studies before World War I but gained increasing scholarly attention with the onset of the Great Migration. Reinforcing Du Bois's emphasis on race relations was a

---

3. Ibid.
4. W. E. B. Du Bois, *The Philadelphia Negro: A Social Study* (1899; rpt. New York: Schocken Books, 1967), 5.
5. Ibid.

growing number of studies that focused on the magnitude, causes, and consequences of Black urban migration. Coming in the wake of the bloody race riots of the war and immediate postwar years, these studies emphasized patterns of White hostility that greeted African Americans as they arrived in the city in growing numbers. They helped to link scholarship on Black urban life even more closely to the race relations paradigm. As such—like *The Philadelphia Negro*—the most important of these studies, Charles S. Johnson's *The Negro in Chicago: A Study of Race Relations and a Race Riot,* offered little insight into African American–Jewish relations.[6]

In the meantime, sociologists at the University of Chicago elaborated upon the race relations model and set the stage for a new decade of scholarship. The Great Migration, they argued, diminished the distances between Blacks and Whites at the different class levels and set in motion the transformation of Black Americans from a "caste to that of a racial minority." Such scholars—E. Franklin Frazier, Robert Park, and others— focused on Black life in New York City and Chicago, emphasizing the barriers of race prejudice and giving little attention to the precise nature of such prejudice among specific White ethnic groups, including Jews.[7]

As members of the Chicago school forged the race relations cycle theory of Black urban life, others adopted the caste-class model of social anthropologist W. Lloyd Warner. For Warner and others, the barriers facing Blacks offered compelling evidence that they could not be construed as another minority group. Again, the notion of specifying the nature of Black-Jewish relations gave way to the larger imperative of studying Black-White relations.[8]

Unlike the research on a race relations cycle, the caste-class model soon generated studies that illuminated important aspects of Black-Jewish relations. Working collaboratively with W. Lloyd Warner, St. Clair Drake and Horace R. Cayton brought the disciplines of sociology and social anthropology together in a single study, *Black Metropolis: A Study of Negro Life in a Northern City.* Unlike other sociological studies of the period, *Black Metropolis* documented a distinct pattern of Black-Jewish relations in depression-era Chicago. Noting that Jews made up about 75 percent of all merchants within the Black community, they

6. Joe W. Trotter, ed., *The Great Migration in Historical Perspective: New Dimensions of Class, Race, and Gender* (Bloomington: Indiana University Press, 1991), 1–21.

7. Trotter, "Afro-American Urban History," in *Black Milwaukee: The Making of an Industrial Proletariat, 1915–45* (Urbana: University of Illinois Press, 1985), 266–68.

8. Ibid.

stressed the conflict between middle-class Black leaders and Jewish merchants.[9]

Based upon extensive oral interviews within the Black community, Drake and Cayton analyzed Black resentment against Jewish merchants. Although considered apocryphal, the experience of one Black merchant circulated widely among Black businesspeople: "A Negro came in here with five dollars worth of Jew stuff in his arms and bought ten cent's worth of salt pork from me. He said: 'Every Sunday morning the Reverend wants all who bought groceries from a colored grocer to raise their hands. Now I can hold *mine* up with a clear conscience.' " Struck by widespread references to Jews in complaints against White merchants, Drake and Cayton concluded that "all complaints [against White businessmen] tend to assume an anti-Semitic tinge. It is hard to convince most merchants in Bronzeville that they are not victims of a 'Jewish conspiracy.' "[10]

Drake and Cayton also suggested that working-class Blacks developed their own stand on the Jewish merchant question. In Chicago during the 1930s, Black workers sometimes expressed dissatisfaction with Black businesspeople. As one Black customer related, "Some of these colored people make you hate them. When you go into a store and try to be choicy they get mad." Thus, some working-class Blacks patronized Jewish establishments in order to avoid mistreatment in Black businesses. Working-class Black customers also contrasted the range of stock and prices at African American and Jewish stores: "I try to spend as much as I can with Negro stores but most of them don't have what you want, or they are too high. That may be our fault for not trading with them more, but we are too poor and have to count pennies." Adding to the attractiveness of Jewish establishments was the credit that they provided to Black customers. "You see, I can get credit from him [a Jew] and I can't from the A&P or a colored store."[11]

Black Metropolis also anticipated more recent concerns with the intersections of class, race, and gender. Although Drake and Cayton did not use the term *gender*, they illuminated the exploitative class and sex dimensions of Black-Jewish relations. In *Black Metropolis*, Black working people, women no less than men, had their own complaints against Jewish employers. They directed some of their most pointed complaints at Jewish women who hired domestic help. As one Black woman stated: "The Jewish woman that I work for tries to get a colored woman to do all

9. St. Clair Drake and Horace R. Cayton, *Black Metropolis: A Study of Negro Life in a Northern City*, rev. and enlg. ed. (New York: Harcourt Brace and World, 1962), 432.
    10. Ibid., 432, 448.
    11. Ibid., 443–44.

of her work for as little as $2 a day and pay her own carfare. She is expected to do all the washing, including the linen and towels as well as all the clothes for the five members of the family. She is supposed to finish the work—that is iron the entire wash—and then clean the house thoroughly—all for $2. Because there are some women who will do all of the work for that amount, this Jewish woman feels that a colored woman who demands more is silly to think that she can get it." Moreover, the same woman expressed the belief that Jewish women held destructive stereotypes about Black women, partly because unemployment forced some to work under such conditions. "I know one woman who does all this work. This woman is an 'Uncle Tom' type of person who says, 'Yes, ma-a-am!' and grins broadly whenever the woman speaks to her. The woman prefers this type of servant to the more intelligent type."[12]

Drake and Cayton not only offered the closest analysis of Black-Jewish relations during the period but also played a key role in adapting the image of the Jewish "ghetto" to research on urban Blacks. The image of the ghetto as a theoretical construct had gained widespread attention following the publication of Lewis Wirth's *The Ghetto* in 1928. Emphasizing the experiences of Jews in Chicago, Wirth argued that the Jewish ghetto offered a useful model for research on other urban areas, including the expanding Black urban community. Drake and Cayton used the term *ghetto* as the strongest visual evidence of the "color line" in *Black Metropolis*. In the early aftermath of World War II, Robert Weaver employed the ghetto framework in his discussion of Black housing patterns. Although Weaver did not adopt Drake and Cayton's interest in Black-Jewish relations, he helped to establish the ghetto framework in historical research on urban Blacks.[13]

Between 1900 and 1950, a variety of studies advanced knowledge of Black life in cities and established the foundation for the emergence of Black urban history as a field. Yet, with the exception of Drake and Cayton, Black urban sociology offered little guidance on how the Black urban experience entailed relations with specific White ethnic groups, how these relations changed over time, and how they set the stage for subsequent interactions. Moreover, Black urban sociology made its contributions on the basis of a few major cities of the North and Midwest, giving little attention to Black life in the urban South, West, and even smaller cities of the urban North. Nonetheless, in the postwar years, historians

12. Ibid., 249.
13. Lewis Wirth, *The Ghetto* (Chicago: University of Chicago Press, 1928); Robert Weaver, *The Negro Ghetto* (New York: Russell and Russell, 1948).

would build upon this sociological heritage, emphasize dimensions of change over time, and carve out a place for Black urban life in the discipline of history. Perspectives on Black-Jewish relations would also undergo significant change.

Responding to the rapid growth of nearly all Black communities in the urban North, Black urban history fully emerged during the 1960s and 1970s. The first generation of Black urban historians focused almost exclusively on African American life in northern cities and used the "ghetto" as the primary conceptual and theoretical framework for understanding the Black urban experience. The Jewish population received treatment as part of the changing urban social geography, and their socioeconomic status—in terms of housing, jobs, and access to urban services—was compared to that of African Americans. Unlike the work of Drake and Cayton, however, these studies avoided labeling Black protests against Jewish businesses and politicians as evidence of Black anti-Semitism. They endorsed the position of middle-class Black leaders. In his study of Harlem, Gilbert Osofsky approvingly quotes the Black politician Fred Moore on the issue of representation: "There is an overwhelming sentiment among members of my group that one of their number should be the leader and another a member of the assembly of the 19th District. . . . All racial groups throughout the city advance a similar argument—the Italian, the Jew, etc. It is the only way by which [minority] groups get elective representation." Similarly, Alan Spear approved the political rhetoric of the *Chicago Defender:* "We must have a colored alderman . . . not because others are not friendly, but because we should be represented just the same as the Irish, Jews and Italians." Another Black political leader exclaimed, "The Poles, the Jews and all other nationalities are insisting on adequate representation in public affairs. . . . The colored Republicans comprise fully one half of the Republican voters of the 2nd ward and are entitled to one alderman."[14]

Despite significant attention to the Jewish dimension in the African American urban experience, the ghetto studies emphasized the relative assimilation of Jews into the mainstream of the urban political economy. They were less interested in charting the complicated nature of Black-Jewish relations than in documenting the ways in which Jews had succeeded, along with other White ethnic groups, and left Blacks behind as

14. Gilbert Osofsky, *Harlem: The Making of a Ghetto, Negro New York, 1890–1930* (New York: Harper and Row, 1963), 175–76; Alan Spear, *Black Chicago: The Making of a Negro Ghetto* (Chicago: University of Chicago Press, 1967), 123–24.

the least integrated element of the urban social structure. As Spear put it, "While the city's Irish, Polish, Jewish, and Italian sections had broken down or developed new forms in the suburbs, the Negro ghetto remained much as it had been—cohesive, restrictive, and largely impoverished." For his part, in discussing the rise of Harlem as a "slum," Osofsky emphasized the contrast between Black and all White residents: "Practically all the older white residents had moved away; the Russian-Jewish and Italian sections of Harlem, founded a short generation earlier, were rapidly being depopulated."[15]

During the 1980s and early 1990s, historians expressed growing dissatisfaction with certain features of African American urban history. Studies by James Grossman, Earl Lewis, Peter Gottlieb, and Dennis Dickerson, among others, emphasized the importance of class no less than ghetto formation. Yet, despite an increasing emphasis on class relations, few of the new studies treated in detail patterns of African American–Jewish relations. Like their ghetto predecessors, such studies emphasized the ways in which Blacks entered areas that Jews had occupied among other immigrant groups such as the Poles and Italians. According to Grossman, Black Chicago ignored cleavages among White ethnic groups and perceived the city in racial terms as "white Chicago."[16]

Among these writers, Lewis offers the most explicit analysis of African American–Jewish relations. Focusing on Norfolk, Virginia, during the early twentieth century, he provides a revealing portrait of Jewish businesses within the Black community. Jewish merchants apparently outnumbered other White businesses that served Black Norfolk. According to Lewis such enterprises thwarted the dream of Black economic independence in the city and "served as the agency for race-conscious mobilization." Antagonistic Black-Jewish relations gained expression not only in the economic sphere but in the social and political life of the community as well. Although Jews also faced ethnic discrimination in the New South city, African Americans found their behavior indistinguishable from that of other Whites. When the Jewish merchant Israel Banks shot

---

15. Spear, *Black Chicago,* 224; Osofsky, *Harlem,* 128–29.

16. Trotter, "Afro-American Urban History," 269–70, 272–73. James R. Grossman, *Land of Hope: Chicago, Black Southerners, and the Great Migration* (Chicago: University of Chicago Press, 1989), 164. Other studies transcended the ghetto model without adopting class analysis. See V. P. Franklin, *The Education of Black Philadelphia: The Social and Educational History of a Minority Community, 1900–1950* (Philadelphia: University of Pennsylvania Press, 1979), 79, 87, 108, 157, 16; and Douglas Henry Daniels, *Pioneer Urbanites: A Social and Cultural History of Black San Francisco* (Philadelphia: Temple University Press, 1980).

and killed an eleven-year-old Black youth in 1926, an all-White jury delivered a verdict of involuntary manslaughter. The incident enraged the
Black community, which emphasized Jewish participation in a larger
pattern of racial hostility directed against African Americans. According
to the local NAACP, the death of Le Roy Strother was part of an ongoing
pattern of Jewish assaults on African American men and boys: "This is
not the first time that colored men and boys have been shot down in this
city without just cause and to my knowledge this is the third child under
thirteen years of age that has been killed by [J]ews within the last ten
months."[17]

The Norfolk experience indicated that Black-Jewish relations reflected
the dynamics of class, race, and region in American society. Such relations also changed over time. Under the impact of the Great Depression
during the 1930s, for example, Jews played an important role in the
activities of the Communist Party in cities such as Birmingham and
Montgomery, Alabama. As in Norfolk, however, the issues of White anti-
Semitism and Jewish racism limited their effectiveness among Blacks.
Partly because they faced White anti-Semitism, violence, and boycotts of
their establishments, Alabama Jews reaffirmed the segregationist order.
As historian Robin D. G. Kelley concludes, Jews' "well-being and continued upward mobility often depended on their willingness to distance
themselves from blacks."[18] Thus, southern Jews accented their whiteness
in the larger community life of the Jim Crow South.

The complicated relationship between Blacks and Jews is also prominent in recent scholarship on New York City and the Communist Party.
In her study of Harlem during the depression years, historian Cheryl L.
Greenberg emphasizes the conflict between African Americans and Jews
during the "Don't Buy Where You Can't Work" campaigns. She documents the hostile encounter between African American nationalist leaders such as Sufi Hamid, who described Jewish merchants as "exploiters"
and the "worst enemies" of Black people, and the Jews of the Harlem
Merchants Association, who described Hamid in even more hostile terms

17. Earl Lewis, In Their Own Interests: Race, Class, and Power in Twentieth Century
Norfolk, Virginia (Berkeley: University of California Press, 1991), 79. See also Lewis,
"The Need to Remember: Three phases in Black and Jewish Educational Relations,"
in Who's Driving Miss Daisy's Car, ed. Jack Salzman and Cornel West (New York: Oxford University Press, forthcoming).

18. Robin D. G. Kelley, Hammer and Hoe: Alabama Communists during the Great De-
pression (Chapel Hill: University of North Carolina Press, 1990), 27–28, 48, 61–62, 88.
Cf. Philip S. Foner, "Black-Jewish Relations in the Opening Years of the Twentieth
Century," Phylon 36 (winter 1975): 359–67; Eugene Levy, "Is the Jew a White Man?
Press Reaction to the Leo Frank Case, 1913–1915," Phylon 35 (June 1974): 212–22.

as a "Black Hitler."[19] Until the onset of the Nazi regime, however, New York Jews usually downplayed their ethnicity.

In his book on Communists in Harlem, historian Mark Naison concludes that the majority of Whites in the Harlem section of the Communist Party were Jews. Although they were joined by small numbers of Finns, Italians, Hungarians, Germans, and Latinos, Jews were the most conspicuous ethnic group among Harlem Blacks. During the early 1930s, according to Naison, Jewish Communists adopted anglicized names, accented "their class backgrounds or political beliefs," and downplayed their ethnic identity, "as the major motivation of their actions." Thus, Blacks reacted to these Jewish radicals as "Whites" rather than as members of a specific ethnic group. At the neighborhood level, however, Blacks identified exploitative Jewish merchants in ethnic terms.[20]

As White anti-Semitism increased during the late 1930s and Hitler's destructive regime expanded in Germany, Jewish radicals found common cause with other Jews, promoted Jewish consciousness, and sought to make explicit an "ethnic alliance" between Blacks and Jews. At the same time, as a result of New Deal activism, Jewish Communists increased their influence in the social service and educational bureaucracies of the city. As this process unfolded, African Americans gradually revamped their perspective on Jewish radicals, who now exercised increasing influence in social welfare and educational networks and often determined the fate of Black applicants for jobs and social services. In November 1930, for example, one Black woman criticized Jewish Communists for discrimination on the Federal Theater Project. "The entire labor set," she complained, "is controlled by Jews who are for the most part communistic" and "keeps Negroes out of white collar jobs."[21]

Additional evidence suggests that the historical study of Black-Jewish relations is about to change for the better. One outstanding example of the emerging scholarship is Marshall Stevenson's manuscript "Points of Departure, Acts of Resolve: Black-Jewish Relations in Detroit, 1930–1967." Placing the question of Black-Jewish relations within the broader contexts of the origins and development of both communities, Stevenson concludes that the notion of a Black-Jewish alliance in practice was more

19. Cheryl Lynn Greenberg, *"Or Does It Explode?" Black Harlem in the Great Depression* (New York: Oxford University Press, 1991), 126. For a different perspective on Sufi Abdul Hamid's impact on the jobs campaign in Harlem see Winston C. McDowell, "Keeping Them 'In the Same Boat Together'?" in this volume.

20. Mark Naison, *Communists in Harlem during the Depression* (Urbana: University of Illinois Press, 1983), 322.

21. Ibid.

complex than either proponents or opponents of the notion would have us believe.[22] Specifically, "Points of Departure" documents the development of Black-Jewish relations within the diverse contexts of the Labor Movement, radical political parties, and the modern Civil Rights Movement. In each instance, Stevenson shows that Black-Jewish relations in Detroit were quite complex. Unlike most studies of African American urban life, for example, he shows that the Race Riot of 1943 was not merely a confrontation of Blacks and Whites but a confrontation of Blacks and Jews, with Jewish store owners as major targets of African American anger.

Stevenson offers a telling analysis of the efforts to build a Black-Jewish civil rights alliance in the aftermath of World War II. He shows how this interethnic movement faced a variety of challenges, including the growing cold war fear of communism and communists, the rise of the southern Civil Rights Movement, and the increasing militancy of Black Detroit itself by the mid-1960s. As such, Stevenson's study is not only a compelling work of historical scholarship but also one with substantial significance for understanding contemporary patterns of urban class, race, and ethnic relations.[23]

Studies of Jewish urban life offer another significant body of scholarship on the subject.[24] The focus on Black-Jewish relations in this scholarship is by no means uniform. Indeed, like African American historiography, some studies of Jewish urban life offer limited perspectives on Black-Jewish relations. For example, Irving Howe in his magisterial *World of Our Fathers* discusses Jewish-Irish and Jewish–"Native" White interactions in some detail but largely ignores Jewish-Black relations. Deborah Dash Moore provides extraordinary insight into the transitions from the first to the second generation of Jews in New York City during the interwar years, but this thick portrait of intra-ethnic change affords few opportunities to illuminate Black-Jewish relations.[25] Other studies

22. Marshall Stevenson, "Points of Departure, Acts of Resolve: Black-Jewish Relations in Detroit, 1930–1967" (manuscript).

23. Ibid. For Stevenson's assessment of Black-Jewish relations in the Detroit labor movement in the 1920s, 1930s, and 1940s see his essay "African Americans and Jews in Organized Labor" in this volume.

24. See Wirth, *The Ghetto;* Irving Howe, *World of Our Fathers: The Journey of the East European Jews to America and the Life They Found and Made* (New York: Harcourt Brace Jovanovich, 1976); Moses Rischin, *The Promised City: New York's Jews, 1870–1914* (Cambridge: Harvard University Press, 1962); Jeffrey S. Gurock, *When Harlem Was Jewish, 1870–1930* (New York: Columbia University Press, 1979); John Higham, *Send These to Me: Jews and Other Immigrants in Urban America* (New York: Athenaeum, 1975); Deborah Dash Moore, *At Home in America: Second Generation New York Jews* (New York: Columbia University Press, 1981).

25. Howe, *World of Our Fathers,* 374–77, 398–99; Moore, *At Home in America.*

provide more helpful analyses but emphasize either the hostile or the cooperative side of Black-Jewish interactions.

In his study of the Jewish ghetto, Wirth not only influenced later conceptualizations of scholarship on urban Blacks but also offered significant insights into Black-Jewish relations. According to Wirth, the Jewish ghetto offered the least resistance to the arrival of southern Blacks: "Many of the immigrants in the ghetto have as yet not heard of the color line. The prevailing opinion of the merchants on the near West Side is that the Negro spends his money freely, and usually has some to spend, and therefore is a desirable neighbor." Wirth also quotes one property owner as saying, "The Jews ought to be the last ones to hold a prejudice against another race, after all that we have been through." In his groundbreaking study of Jews in New York, Moses Rischin emphasizes the positive side of Black-Jewish relations, examining how the Jewish community expressed outrage at the mistreatment of Blacks and how Jewish labor organizations worked for social tolerance and attracted the support of Black and Italian women in strikes against the garment industry. Similarly, in *When Harlem was Jewish, 1870–1930* Jeffrey Gurock epitomizes much of this scholarship when he concludes that class and not racial factors dictated the depopulation of Jewish Harlem. "Jews did not leave this particular community specifically because of their feeling any special aversion to, or fear of, living among Blacks."[26]

At the same time that Rischin, Gurock, and others emphasized the antiracist attitudes and behavior of urban Jews, others gradually advanced a different portrait. In the collection *Send These to Me*, historian John Higham acknowledges the antagonistic side of Black-Jewish relations. Focusing on the work of Horace Kallen, the Jewish pioneer of pluralist theory, Higham stresses blind spots in Jewish conceptions of ethnicity and race. According to Higham, Kallen's notion of pluralism "from the outset was encapsulated in white ethnocentrism." His "ensemble" of the American peoples made room for Jews and other European immigrants but none for Blacks.[27]

If the historiography of urban Jews helps to deepen our knowledge of Black-Jewish relations, Black cultural and literary studies, which

---

26. Wirth, *The Ghetto*, 231; Rischin, *The Promised City*, 167, 213, 249; Gurock, *When Harlem Was Jewish*, 50, 145–50, 166–68.

27. Higham, *Send These to Me*, 208–9. Higham also compares Kallen's ideas with those of W. E. B. Du Bois, concluding that Du Bois had already enunciated the notion that race pride and solidarity were compatible with full participation in American society nearly two decades before Kallen advanced his theory of pluralism during World War I (209).

emerged alongside sociological and historical research, suggest even more fruitful avenues of analysis.[28] For the early twentieth century, for example, studies by Wallace Thurman, Claude McKay, and Roi Ottley illuminate the interaction of Blacks and Jews in the cabarets and theaters of Harlem, the "Don't Buy Where You Can't Work" campaigns, and the Communist Party.[29] In his *Negro Life in Harlem,* Thurman decries not only the Jewish merchants' exploitative retail practices but also their domination of Black dancehalls and theaters. According to Thurman, "Despite the thousands of dollars Negroes spend, in order to dance, the only monetary returns in their own community are the salaries paid to the Negro musicians, ushers, janitors and door-men. The rest of the profits are spent and exploited outside of Harlem." Thurman further states, "Saturdays, Sundays and holidays are harvest times, and the Jewish representatives of the chain to which a theater belongs walk around excitedly and are exceedingly gracious, thinking no doubt of the quarters that are being deposited at the box office."[30]

While early-twentieth-century Black writers such as Thurman decried the exploitative practices of Jewish businesspeople, they also urged Blacks to take note of the Jewish entrepreneurial model and build the Black business infrastructure. Their treatment of the "Don't Buy Where You Can't Work" campaigns underscores this point. Despite the charges of anti-Semitism leveled against Sufi Hamid, for example, Claude McKay defended the Black activist: "No one was more astonished than the Sufi himself when he was accused of organizing an anti-Semitic movement. . . . There was never any anti-Semitism in Harlem and there still is none, in spite of the stupid and vicious propaganda which endeavored to create an anti-Semitic issue out of the legitimate movement of Negroes to improve their social condition. . . . In fact, it is that reactionary attitude that is increasing anti-Jewish feeling."[31]

In the postwar years, Black intellectuals, artists, and cultural critics

28. I am indebted to cultural historian Gerald Early for pinpointing the importance of this literature for understanding Black-Jewish relations. See Early, "Response to Papers Presented at the Blacks and Jews Conference," Washington University, St. Louis, December 2–5, 1993.

29. Wallace Thurman, *Negro Life in New York's Harlem: A Lively Picture of a Popular and Interesting Section* (1900; rpt. Girard, Kans.: Haldeman-Julius Publications, 1927); Claude McKay, *Harlem: Negro Metropolis* (New York: E. P. Dutton and Co., 1940); Roi Ottley, *New World A-Comin': Inside Black America* (1943; rpt. New York: Arno Press, 1968). Cf. James Weldon Johnson, *Black Manhattan* (1930; rpt. New York: De Capo Press, 1991).

30. Thurman, *Negro Life,* 33, 37.

31. McKay, *Harlem,* quoted in Greenberg, *"Or Does It Explode?"* 127. Cf. Naison, *Communists in Harlem,* 323.

offered additional perspectives on Black-Jewish relations.[32] In 1948, James Baldwin addressed the growing tension between African Americans and Jews that had emerged during the depression and World War II. According to Baldwin, relations between Blacks and Jews were even more problematic than those between Blacks and Whites:

> When the Negro hates the Jew as a Jew he does so partly because the nation does. . . . At the same time, there is a subterranean assumption that the Jew should "know better," that he has suffered enough himself to know what suffering means. An understanding is expected of the Jew such as none but the most naive and visionary Negro has ever expected of the American Gentile. The Jew, by the nature of his own precarious position, has failed to vindicate this faith. Jews, like Negroes, must use every possible weapon in order to be accepted, and must try to cover their vulnerability by a frenzied adoption of the customs of the country; and the nation's treatment of Negroes is unquestionably a custom. The Jew has been taught—and, too often, accepts—the legend of Negro inferiority; and the Negro, on the other hand, has found nothing in his experience with Jews to counteract the legend of Semitic greed.

Against the backdrop of the depression and World War II, Baldwin doubted that "any real and systematic cooperation" between Blacks and Jews could be achieved. He believed that the "structure of the American commonwealth" had "trapped these minorities into attitudes of perpetual hostility."[33]

Nearly twenty years later, in his significant and controversial *Crisis of the Negro Intellectual*, cultural and political critic Harold Cruse echoed Baldwin's point, accenting the role of the Jewish left:

> The radical Left . . . was not a movement of Anglo-Saxons or their ideology. It was an ethnic movement dominated by Negroes and Jews, and it was the Jews who ideologically influenced the Negroes. Thus the radical Left in America had developed in such a way that the Jewish ethnic group, one of the smallest in the country, had more political prestige, wielded more theoretical and organizational power, than the Negro who in fact represented the largest ethnic minority. Consequently, all political and cultural standards on the radical Left were in the main established and enforced by Jews for, and

---

32. See James Baldwin, "The Harlem Ghetto: Winter 1948—The Vicious Circle of Frustration and Prejudice," *Commentary* 5 (February 1948): 165–70; Harold Cruse, *The Crisis of the Negro Intellectual: From Its Origins to the Present* (New York: William Morrow, 1967) and *Plural but Equal: Blacks and Minorities in America's Plural Society* (New York: William Morrow, 1987). Cf. Bettye Collier-Thomas and Bettye Gardner, "The Cultural Impact of the Howard Theater on the Washington Black Community," *Journal of Negro History* 60 (October 1970): 253–65.

33. Baldwin, "The Harlem Ghetto," 169–70.

on, Negroes. This Negro-Jewish state of affairs was paralleled outside the radical Left as well, in the civil rights organizations. One can explain this development, rationalize it, excuse it, condemn it or uphold it, call it negative or positive, but the fact remains that it was ethnically undemocratic.[34]

In his *Plural but Equal*, published precisely twenty years after *Crisis*, Cruse reiterates the same point but assigns greater responsibility to Black leadership for its dearth of cultural and political influence in the Black-Jewish alliance: "The less than favorable and amicable outcome of the Black-Jewish alliance was not the fault of Jewish leadership, nor that of Black leadership singly. The fault lay in the philosophy of liberalism itself, in its application to the emergent twentieth century problems of blacks as the largest nonwhite minority in the United States. All three leaderships—WASP, Jewish, and Black—retroactively share a portion of the blame for the failures of black leadership under the circumstances that prevailed."[35] As Gerald Early suggests, cultural interactions represented key indicators of the promise and limits of Black-Jewish relationships. Specifically, Early urges us to probe the significance of Jews in the "coming out" or promotion of Black popular culture. As he puts it,

> In popular culture, we find [that] a Jewish popular songwriting team of Eastern European ancestry, George and Ira Gershwin, was responsible for the further "coming out" [after the 1927 staging of Dubose Heyward's *Porgy* in 1927] of the Negro on stage, with the 1935 premiere of their folk-opera, *Porgy and Bess;* we find [that] Mike Jacobs, a Jewish promoter of Eastern European ancestry, was responsible for the "coming out," so to speak of heavyweight champion Joe Louis, coming to New York in 1935 and winning the championship in 1937; that Benny Goodman, a Jewish jazz musician of Eastern European ancestry, was responsible for the "coming out" of Lionel Hampton and Teddy Wilson, in a publicly integrated jazz band in 1937.[36]

The subject of Black-Jewish relations is replete with opportunities for future historical research. Such scholarship will no doubt expand as we enter the twenty-first century. Future studies will also no doubt adopt a variety of theoretical approaches and cover diverse time periods. Yet, we must also analyze such relations more systematically within the framework of Black urban community studies. Given the tremendous development of Black urban history over the past three decades, we are in an excellent position to accomplish this task. The field has not only

34. Cruse, *Crisis of the Negro Intellectual*, 516–17.
35. Cruse, *Plural but Equal*, 138.
36. Early, "Response to Papers Presented at the Blacks and Jews Conference."

accommodated a broader range of regions and cities of various types than before but has also deepened our understanding of African American workers, the middle class, women, education, family, and culture. In short, African American urban history has proved resilient enough to accommodate myriad new dimensions of Black life in cities. We may hope that it is also capable of expanding its framework to incorporate a more dynamic approach to African American–Jewish relations.

Keeping Them "In the Same Boat Together"?

Sufi Abdul Hamid, African Americans, Jews, and the Harlem Jobs Boycotts

Winston C. McDowell

O N ANY GIVEN day in New York City's predominantly African American community of Harlem during the early 1930s, pedestrians might have easily witnessed, at sidewalk locations near major intersections, such as 135th Street and Lenox Avenue, an individual haranguing passersby from atop a stepladder or some improvised platform. A persuasive speaker, wrote the writer and chronicler of Harlem life Jervis Anderson, could transform an urban street corner into a "small-town square, with people sauntering and lingering to hear what was going on."[1] Curious onlookers quickly discovered that some of these "stepladder orators" or "soapboxers" were simply barefoot prophets or self-proclaimed faith healers in search of an audience for their messages of salvation.

Over time, however, spectators discovered that many of the soapboxers had more pressing concerns than promoting pathways to redemption. Renowned early Harlem soapbox orators, such as the socialist labor leader Asa Philip Randolph, his colleague Owen Chandler, and an emerging West Indian–born Pan-Africanist named Marcus Garvey, had turned popular sidewalk locations into a forum for unfiltered expression.

I would like to thank Dwayne E. Williams, Walter B. Weare, Nancy Dunlap Bercaw, and Adrianne A. Andrews for their friendship, encouragement, and comments and the departments of Afro-American and African studies and history, University of Minnesota, Twin Cities, for providing research support. And a very special "thank-you" goes to V. P. Franklin and Genna Rae McNeil for their patience and suggestions.
1. Jervis Anderson, *This Was Harlem: A Cultural Portrait, 1900–1950* (New York: Noonday Press, 1981), 106; for the upcoming discussion about stepladder politics see 106–7; Irma Watkins-Owens, *Blood Relations: Caribbean Immigrants and the Harlem Community, 1900–1930* (Bloomington and Indianapolis: Indiana University Press, 1996), 92–113.

Each bypassed the narrow confines of the Tammany-controlled political arena to expound upon myriad radical political ideologies and numerous neglected issues. Sidewalk speakers also utilized street-corner meetings as an alternative to established and potentially constraining outlets for expression, such as the pulpit, the press, and the meeting hall. Granted, many of Harlem's greatest orators did obfuscate distinctions between the street corner and the traditional outlets. Hubert H. Harrison, the Virgin Island native known as the "Black Socrates" who reputedly established locally the soapbox technique popularized in the West by the syndicalist Industrial Workers of the World, had also used his publication, *The Voice*, to excoriate African American participation in World War I. Furthermore, the young, charismatic, and ambitious associate pastor of Harlem's most prominent African American church, the Reverend Adam Clayton Powell Jr. of Abyssinian Baptist Church, would bring the rhythms of the street to the confines of the church by the mid-1930s. Nevertheless, most speakers relished the uncensored freedom of the "open-air arenas," where they castigated those deemed as status quo collaborators, including merchants, landlords, and "respectable" African American leaders.[2] As nationalists, socialists, communists, West Indian immigrants, and southern Black migrants jockeyed for attention in an ideologically contentious environment, only those who could overcome ineffective elocution, inclement weather, and the sometimes hostile Harlem police were assured of a receptive audience.[3]

The combative, unrestrained world of sidewalk politics was well suited for a community struggling to come to grips with the Great Depression. During the 1930s, soapboxers would target White-owned establishments, whose alleged discriminatory hiring practices were seen as contributing to the economic woes faced by Black Harlemites. One newcomer to the Harlem stepladder scene, a man who referred to himself as Bishop Amiru Al-Minin Sufi Abdul Hamid and who would distinguish himself from his competitors, appeared around 1932. The six-foot-three-

2. Watkins-Owen, *Blood Relations*, 92.

3. Black Socrates quoted in ibid., 95. For additional soapbox militants and the soapbox tradition, see Franklin W. Knight, "The Caribbean Background of Richard B. Moore," in *Richard B. Moore, Caribbean Militant in Harlem: Collected Writings, 1920–1972*, ed. W. Burghardt Turner and Joyce Moore Turner (Bloomington and Indianapolis: Indiana University Press, 1988): 1–15; Judith Stein, *The World of Marcus Garvey: Race and Class in Modern Society* (Baton Rouge: Louisiana State University Press, 1986), 41–60; Donald E. Winters Jr., *The Soul of the Wobblies: The I.W.W., Religion and American Culture in the Progressive Era, 1905–1917* (Westport, Conn.: Greenwood Press, 1985), 52–53; Melvyn Dubofsky, *We Shall Be All: A History of the Industrial Workers of the World* (Chicago: Quadrangle Books, 1969), 173–97.

inch, 225-pound Hamid was usually seen atop a stepladder platform on 125th Street, the heart of Harlem's commercial district. Resplendent in his black, crimson-lined cape, green velvet blouse, black riding boots, and wearing a white turban, Hamid urged inquisitive Black bystanders to stop spending their money at White establishments that did not hire African Americans. Continuing to decry the injustices of job discrimination, he would then point to the doorways of stores along 125th Street and in a deep, rumbling voice shout, "Share the jobs!"[4]

Sufi Hamid's presence on 125th Street was a major salvo in the initial direct action phase of the Harlem jobs boycott. The Harlem jobs boycott was one of several "Don't Buy Where You Can't Work" campaigns that would occur in thirty-five mainly midwestern and northern cities by 1941, with Chicago as the site of the first boycott in 1929. Although the boycotts generally met with indifference at first, their gradual popularity in Harlem and in other African American communities mirrored the rise of direct action in depression-era Black protest. Nurtured in the economic upheaval of the 1930s, spurred by the efforts of Communist activists, and, to a lesser extent, encouraged by the pro-picketing provisions in the Norris–La Guardia Anti-Injunction Act of 1932, direct action flourished as a protest weapon. As the most significant and sustained form of Black direct action, the jobs campaigns reflected long-held Black resentment toward the hiring practices of White-owned retail establishments in African American communities that were starved for employment during the depression. Many African Americans viewed jobs boycotts as a viable way to redress local economic inequities.[5]

By tapping into Black Harlem's discontent as well as its demand for action, Sufi Hamid became a pivotal figure in the jobs boycotts in Harlem. Although his involvement with the jobs campaign was relatively brief, Hamid was nevertheless influential. He served as a lightning rod during

4. David Levering Lewis, *When Harlem Was in Vogue* (New York: Oxford University Press, 1989, 1981), 300–301; Claude McKay, *Harlem: Negro Metropolis* (New York: E. P. Dutton and Co., 1940), 140, 185–88; August Meier and Elliott Rudwick, "The Origins of Nonviolent Direct Action in Afro-American Protest: A Note on Historical Discontinuities," in *Along the Color Line: Explorations in the Black Experience,* ed. August Meier and Elliott Rudwick (Urbana: University of Illinois Press, 1976), 318–19; Roi Ottley, *New World A-Comin': Inside Black America* (1943; rpt. New York: Arno Press, 1968), 117; *New York Times,* October 9, 1934.

5. Meier and Rudwick, "Origins of Nonviolent Direct Action," 314–16; V. P. Franklin, *The Education of Black Philadelphia: The Social and Educational History of a Minority Community, 1900–1950* (Philadelphia: University of Pennsylvania Press, 1979), 118–21. For the Norris–La Guardia Act see Irving Bernstein, *The Turbulent Years: A History of the American Worker, 1933–1941* (Boston: Houghton Mifflin, 1971), 176, 648, 674.

the first phase of the Harlem boycott, as his tactics led prominent members of the community's Black middle class to reassess their views of direct action demonstrations. Furthermore, in a community with a rich Jewish past, Hamid's actions highlighted ethnic tensions that were rooted as much in the historical race betterment strategies as in the current jobs campaigns. Thus, the looming presence of Sufi Hamid and the quest for racial empowerment in Harlem provide the backdrop for this essay as it addresses the first stage of the Harlem jobs campaign and the role Sufi Abdul Hamid played in the relationship between African Americans and Jews in Harlem from 1932 to 1935. Because the jobs campaign and the relationship between Harlem's African American and Jewish communities also had their roots in the development of Black Harlem, this essay will examine the emergence of Black Harlem from its beginnings as a Jewish enclave during the late nineteenth century.

Although Sufi Hamid was an important figure in depression-era Harlem, he has been relegated to narrow historical parameters. In an otherwise superb public television documentary on Adam Clayton Powell Jr., Powell was given credit for being both the initiator of and the driving force behind the Harlem jobs boycott; Hamid's role was ignored. Political scientist Charles V. Hamilton and journalist Will Haywood took a more complicated view of the late congressman and Baptist minister's involvement with the jobs campaign in their respective biographies of Powell; when discussing Hamid, however, each presented him as somewhat of a gadfly with anti-Semitic leanings. To the neoconservative historian and Jewish activist Murray Friedman, Hamid was more than simply one of several boycotters in Harlem, as historian Ralph L. Crowder argued in his often disjointed narrative about the links between the 1930s jobs campaigns and post–World War II civil rights strategies. Instead, Hamid was one of the "most radical" among "a series of anti-Semitic orators" present in Harlem during the 1930s, proclaimed Friedman in his study of the historical relationship between African Americans and Jews. It was the racial demagoguery spewed by people such as Hamid and the social conditions in Harlem that led to the 1935 riot, continued Friedman; the "anti-Semitic aspects of the rioting," however, according to Friedman, have only been recently acknowledged during an era of "heightened ethnic identification" and "greater public candor."[6]

6. Murray Friedman, *What Went Wrong? The Creation and Collapse of the Black-Jewish Alliance* (New York: Free Press, 1995), 93–94. See Richard Kilberg, director, *Adam Clayton Powell, Jr.* (Public Broadcasting System, *The American Experience*, 1989); Charles V. Hamilton, *Adam Clayton Powell, Jr.: The Political Biographical of an American*

Historian Cheryl Lynn Greenberg presented a more balanced and complex view of Sufi Hamid in the course of discussing the Harlem jobs campaign. In the first book-length study to focus on Harlem after 1930, Greenberg addressed the jobs campaigns in her analysis of Black Harlem during the Great Depression. To Greenberg, Hamid was indeed one of several anti-Semitic taunters in the community who were aware that Harlem's Jewish past made Jews an easy target. Yet anti-Semitism was part of the "broader anti-white rhetoric" that occurred as Black nationalist boycotters such as Hamid struggled with those whom Greenberg classified as race "moderates" for leadership of the boycotts. This fluid, contentious struggle, she continued, resulted from the realization that the disparate constituencies in Harlem could agree on only one point: the need to end racial discrimination in white-collar jobs in the community.[7]

Sufi Hamid was nevertheless shortchanged in Greenberg's complex narrative. Her primary focus was to trace the organizational strategies and competing interest groups that emerged during the Harlem jobs campaigns. She presented Harlem as a "movement center," a conceptualization articulated by sociologist Aldon D. Morris in which preexisting groups provide leaders with an organizational network through which to work for a common goal.[8] Consequently, she correctly noted that the disparate constituencies affected the ebb and flow of the campaigns. Yet Greenberg overstated the role the jobs campaign coalition, known as the Citizens' League for Fair Play, played in the initial direct action boycotts in Harlem. Although the Citizens' League sought to create a community-wide "Don't Buy" coalition, African American elites still dominated the organization created in response to Sufi Hamid. Moreover, it is questionable that the Citizens' League would have gotten involved if Hamid and his controversial presence had not breathed life into what had been a morbidly ineffective jobs campaign. Also, for Greenberg to view the ethnic tensions in Harlem partially as the result of struggles among competing "moderates" and "nationalists" diminishes the fact that ideological distinctions were often overshadowed in the quest to extol the virtues of

Dilemma (New York: Atheneum, 1991), 89–107; Will Haygood, *King of the Cats: The Life and Times of Adam Clayton Powell, Jr.* (New York: Houghton Mifflin, 1993), 42–45, 79; Ralph L. Crowder, " 'Don't Buy Where You Can't Work': An Investigation of the Political Forces and Social Conflict within the Harlem Boycott of 1934," *Afro-Americans in New York Life and History* 15 (July 1991): 7–44.

7. Cheryl Lynn Greenberg, *"Or Does it Explode?" Black Harlem in the Great Depression* (New York: Oxford University Press, 1991), 114–31.

8. Ibid., 114; Aldon D. Morris, *The Origins of the Civil Rights Movement: Black Communities Organizing for Change* (New York: Free Press, 1984), 40, 73–76, ix–xiv.

"Buy Black" and other race betterment strategies. As this essay shows, it is more likely that these tensions were the historical liabilities inherent in all race-based strategies advocated and employed in a community such as Harlem with strong Jewish origins. While he was neither the sole boycott agitator in Harlem nor the most effective, the stepladder orator known as Sufi Abdul Hamid was among the first to reveal these significant liabilities even as he exploited them.

The Emergence of Black Harlem

The community of Harlem during the latter half of the nineteenth century would seem alien to anyone today who mistakenly perceives the area as nothing more than a long succession of innumerable impoverished African American neighborhoods. Annexed to New York City in 1873, Harlem was an amalgam of different class and ethnic groups.[9] Following annexation, Harlem became the site of fashionable homes built by several city officials connected with the Republican political machine, led by the notorious William "Boss" Tweed. This trend toward exclusiveness continued as improvements in public transportation during the 1880s made Harlem more accessible to those who could afford to move away from overpopulated downtown areas. On the periphery of these upper-class enclaves, however, impoverished Italian immigrants huddled in vile tenements located from 110th to 125th Streets, east of Third Avenue to the Harlem River. To the north of Harlem's Italian community and to the west of Eighth Avenue, Irish toughs roamed an unfilled marshlands area referred to by locals as "Canary Island." These gangs of Irish youths zealously guarded what they considered their territory when Blacks began to move into the Canary Island neighborhood at the turn of the twentieth century.

Among Harlem's early ethnic groups, Jews were by far the community's largest. At its peak during World War I, Harlem's Jewish community numbered approximately 178,000.[10] Jewish migration to Harlem had begun after the Civil War. German Jewish merchants, seeking new economic opportunities and fleeing overpopulated regions, trekked northward from the Lower East Side to Harlem's Third Avenue commercial

9. Here, and in the section immediately following, I am drawing upon Gilbert Osofsky, *Harlem: The Making of a Ghetto, Negro New York, 1890–1930* (New York: Harper and Row, 1963), 71, 81–82; Jeffrey S. Gurock, *When Harlem Was Jewish, 1870–1930* (New York: Columbia University Press, 1979), 50.

10. For the origins of Jewish Harlem see Gurock, *When Harlem Was Jewish*, 145, 6–7, 30, 40–41; Osofsky, *Harlem*, 88; Moses Rischin, *The Promised City: New York's Jews, 1870–1914* (Cambridge: Harvard University Press, 1962), 10, 52–61, 76–94.

district. These early German Jewish migrants were joined by a massive influx of Russian Jews, attracted to Harlem by several booms in housing construction around 1900, which provided dwellings at rents comparable to or better than those found on the Lower East Side. By 1910, Harlem had become home to the second largest concentration of immigrant Eastern European Jews—approximately 100,000—in the United States. The poorer segment of this population resided in an area east of Third Avenue and south of the Italian community, while the more affluent Eastern European Jews lived north of 110th Street and east of Morningside Avenue.

Blacks were also a part of Harlem's demographic mixture, as scattered African American communities during the 1880s and 1890s could be found along streets such as West 130th Street and West 146th Street, derogatorily referred to by Whites as "Darktown" and "Nigger Row," respectively. This native Black migration to Harlem, similar to the Jewish migration, was part of a continuous intracity movement northward by African Americans. Blacks had left unsavory areas in lower Manhattan, such as the Five Points district (presently encompassing City Hall and the surrounding neighborhoods) and the infamous Tenderloin district, which extended from the West 20s to the West 50s. Preparing the way for the Black migration to Harlem were the community's African American Realtors, most notably Philip A. Payton Jr., John E. Nail, and Henry C. Parker. Payton became a legendary figure in Harlem, as his incorporated stock enterprise, the Afro-American Realty Company, owned and operated apartment houses and brownstones scattered in sections previously closed to Blacks. When Payton's four-year-old enterprise collapsed in 1908, John Nail and Henry Parker became the new standard-bearers among African American Realtors when they formed Nail and Parker, Incorporated, in 1907. Among its many noteworthy undertakings, the Black-owned real estate firm handled the transactions stemming from the Harlem relocation of one of New York City's oldest and reputedly most exclusive African American churches, St. Philip's Protestant Episcopal Church, and the church's purchase of an entire Harlem block of apartment buildings in a previously all-White area. Due largely to the efforts of African American Realtors, middle-class Black families were residing in previously off-limits areas like West 131th Street by as early as 1914, as reported in the city's premier Black newspaper, the *New York Age.*[11]

11. *New York Age,* November 11, 1914. For the emergence of Black Harlem see Osofsky, *Harlem,* 9, 88, 92–104; Seth M. Scheiner, *Negro Mecca: A History of the Negro in*

The gradual appearance of Black Harlem was not solely attributable to intracity migration by native Blacks. Immigrants from the West Indies would make Harlem their home during the 1920s. Often referred to by Black and White Americans simply as "West Indians," the new arrivals were not ethnically monolithic. Instead, Harlem's new inhabitants came from numerous Caribbean islands, including Jamaica, Trinidad, Barbados, St. Kitts, Montserrat, the Bahamas, Martinique, and Antigua. While the majority arrived in New York from British possessions in the Caribbean and spoke English, some considered Spanish or French their first language, thus adding to the community's ethnic and cultural mixture. Estimates of the actual number of West Indians residing in Harlem by 1930 varied wildly. Federal census reports for Manhattan (an adequate approximation for Harlem, given the overwhelming concentration of the borough's Black population in the community) listed approximately 7,000 "West Indies" residents in the borough, while the scholar James Weldon Johnson, the first Black executive secretary of the NAACP, estimated that there were 50,000 West Indian immigrants in Harlem.[12]

Despite their growing presences in Harlem, the respective Black communities generally avoided the violent confrontations with Whites that had occurred in other urban areas, such as Chicago, during the early twentieth century. The absence of White resistance reflected the failure of any organization to unite all of the White property owners in the

New York City, 1865–1920 (New York: New York University Press, 1965), 15–18; Roi Ottley and William J. Weatherby, eds., *The Negro in New York: An Informal Social History, 1926–1940* (New York: Praeger, 1967), 183–85; Welfare Council of New York City, Research Bureau, *Population in Health Areas, New York City, 1930: Color, Nativity, Parentage, Sex, and Age,* 1931; Anderson, *This Was Harlem,* 5–67. For Harlem's Black Realtors see *New York Amsterdam News,* July 7, 1927, April 24, 1929; Osofsky, *Harlem,* 94–104; *[N.Y.] Interstate Tattler,* March 29, 1929, in "Harlem: Clipping File," Schomburg Center for Research in Black Culture, New York Public Library (hereafter cited as Schomburg Center); Olivia Frost, "Some Sociological Aspects of the Realty Investment Market in New York's Harlem" (Master's thesis, Columbia University, 1951), 9; Writer's Program, New York City, "Economic History of the Negroes of New York," n.d., 3, Schomburg Center; James Weldon Johnson, *Black Manhattan* (1930; rpt. New York: De Capo Press, 1991), 149; Wilson Jeremiah Moses, *Alexander Crummell: A Study of Civilization and Discontent* (New York: Oxford University Press, 1989), 18.

12. Osofsky, *Harlem,* 131–35; Johnson, *Black Manhattan,* 153; Ottley, *New World A-Comin',* 44–48; U.S. Department of Commerce, Bureau of the Census, *Fifteenth Census of the United States: 1930, Population: Volume III, Part 2;* Watkins-Owens, *Blood Relations,* 1–10, 39–55; Ira DeAugustine Reid, *The Negro Immigrant: His Background, Characteristics and Social Adjustment, 1899–1937* (1939; rpt. New York: Arno Press, 1969). For tabulating Harlem's West Indian population see Winston C. McDowell, "The Ideology of Black Entrepreneurship and Its Impact on the Development of Black Harlem, 1930–1955" (Ph.D. diss., University of Minnesota–Twin Cities, 1996), 123, n. 12.

community, as landlords eagerly succumbed either to "panic selling" or
to the opportunity to evade foreclosure following the end of the real estate boom in 1904 by renting to Blacks at high rates. White resistance was
also limited by the fact that the massive influx of Blacks into Harlem occurred at almost the same time that Jews and other ethnic groups were
leaving their ethnic enclaves behind. Jews, for example, no longer
thought of Harlem as a residential haven. Construction bans, a result of
shortages brought on by World War I, had led to overcrowding and rent
gouging by unscrupulous landlords. As construction restrictions were
lifted following the end of the war, Harlem's Jewish population poured
into the thousands of newly built, more expensive housing units in
the Morrisania and Hunts Points sections of the Bronx. These second-
generation Jews were not fleeing to new regions simply to avoid Blacks;
migration allowed them to affirm their newly improved economic
status—evidenced by their rise in New York City's professional, trade,
and clerical occupations—in a manner in which many of their parents
had done by moving to Harlem. As a result, by 1930 only 5,000 Jews remained in the geographical region defined as "Harlem": from approximately west of Fifth Avenue, north of West 110th Street and running up
to the Harlem River to approximately the Polo Grounds (155th Street),
and then west to the Hudson River. Approximately 172,000 Blacks of
American and West Indian descent were now calling the same area their
home.[13]

   Although Blacks and Jews avoided the violent conflicts that frequently
occurred in other cities whenever African Americans moved into pre-
dominately White communities, the turnover of Jewish Harlem was not
totally harmonious. In fact, Jews were often prominent in the movement
to resist Black advancement into Harlem. Adolph B. Rosenfield of the
Property Owner's Improvement Association was somewhat successful in
leading a drive to keep Blacks out of the area bounded by 90th Street,
110th Street, Riverside Drive, and Central Park West during the 1910s. In
the 1920s, Jews also participated in attempts to check Black advancement,
as evidenced in the efforts by Harry Goodstein and the West Side Property Owner's Association to limit the Black advancement to 127th Street.
Furthermore, Jewish resistance in other sections of the city could be quite
violent, as an incident recounted in the *Age* reveals. In July 1926, the
streets of a Brooklyn neighborhood erupted in a pitched battle between

13. See Gurock, *When Harlem Was Jewish*, 139–45; Osofsky, *Harlem*, 130; Welfare
Council, *Population in Health Areas*. For details about the population tabulations see
McDowell, "Ideology of Black Entrepreneurship," app. B.

Russian Jews and Blacks, the culmination of Jewish hostility toward what was perceived as Black encroachment.[14] Although the event occurred outside Harlem, it suggests that the intracity migration of Harlem Jews to the Bronx not only functioned as an affirmation of economic mobility but also helped to offset tensions between Jews and African Americans in the community.

The Coming of the Great Depression

The relative ease of the transition from Jewish Harlem to Black Harlem seduced those who envisioned a special relationship between Jews and Blacks. This view reflected the long-held belief articulated by, yet not exclusive to, African American and Jewish elites that Blacks and Jews shared the indignities of second-class citizenship in the United States. In the 1860 appeal of New York Negroes for Equal Suffrage, the authors emphatically declared that "with the exception of Jews . . . there is not to be found a people pursued with a more relentless prejudice and persecution, than are the free colored people of the United States."[15] Jews echoed a similar theme. During the Black migration into Harlem, several Yiddish and Anglo-Jewish newspapers chided those Harlem Jews involved in the resistance movement, reminding them of the hostility Jews often faced from other ethnic groups during their move uptown. Booker Taliaferro Washington, a champion of African American self-help as well as an unabashed promoter of Black entrepreneurship, extended the "joint sufferers" theme across the ocean in 1904. Commenting on the Russian pogroms in a statement for a Jewish relief organization, Washington averred that "as a member of a race which has, itself, been the victim of much wrong and oppression, my heart goes out to our Hebrew fellow-sufferers across the sea."[16] The African American press during the 1930s also transcended geographical space to connect the plights of African Americans and Jews. The *New York Amsterdam News,* by now the *Age*'s chief rival for New York City's Black readership, published an editorial cartoon titled "Another Klansman," with a caricature of Adolf Hitler

14. Steven Bloom, "Interactions between Blacks and Jews in New York City, 1900–1930, as Reflected in the Black Press" (Ph.D. diss., New York University, 1973), 171–72; *New York Age,* July 3, 1926.

15. Quoted in Philip S. Foner, "Black-Jewish Relations in the Opening Years of the Twentieth-Century," *Phylon* 36 (winter 1975): 360.

16. Quoted in Louis R. Harlan, "Booker T. Washington's Discovery of Jews," in *Race, Region, and Reconstruction: Essays in Honor of C. Vann Woodward,* ed. J. Morgan Kousser and James M. McPherson (New York: Oxford University Press, 1982), 267.

holding a swastika that cast the shadow of a Klansman clutching a burning cross.[17]

The theme of "joint sufferers" articulated by African Americans and
Jews, however, was irrelevant to Blacks in Harlem seemingly suffering
alone during the depression. To recount the legendary success stories
of former African American Harlemites, such as millionairess Madame
C. J. Walker, the cosmetologist and the richest self-made woman in the
United States by 1919, would be a cruel jab at the approximately 43 percent
of Harlem's Black families on relief in 1934 or the hundreds of working
Black families during the Great Depression who were barely able to sustain themselves with their meager, declining incomes.[18] For the thousands
of aspiring native and foreign-born Blacks who had moved to Harlem,
their dreams for a better life were quickly turning into nightmares.

While myriad explanations existed for the poverty confronted by
Harlem's Blacks, including exclusion from trade unions and limited opportunities in the higher-paying positions in manufacturing, many
African Americans in Harlem also pointed to their virtual exclusion from
either business ownership or employment within their own communities
as a reason for their economic misery. In one Harlem community, Whites
owned approximately 83 percent of the 2,308 business establishments
recorded in a 1931 survey reported in *Crisis*. Of these 1,927 White-owned
establishments, only approximately 29 percent employed Blacks, and
then in overwhelmingly menial, low-paying positions; the remaining establishments had no African American employees. Given their near absence as workers in White establishments, African Americans in this
particular Harlem locale, as well as throughout the community, had
to rely on the few job opportunities generated from those businesses that
either would or could take on Black employees.[19]

17. *New York Amsterdam News,* March 29, 1933. Comments among Jewish elites re-
garding Black migration to Harlem found in Gurock, *When Harlem Was Jewish,* 147.
See also David Levering Lewis, "Parallels and Divergences: Assimilationist Strategies
of Afro-American and Jewish Elites from 1910 to the Early 1930s," *Journal of American
History* 71 (December 1984): 543–64; Hasia R. Diner, *In the Almost Promised Land:
American Jews and Blacks, 1915–1935* (1977; rpt. Baltimore: Johns Hopkins University
Press, 1995).

18. Lewis, *When Harlem Was in Vogue,* 110; Ottley and Weatherby, eds., *The Negro in
New York,* 237–38, 187–88; *The Complete Report of Mayor LaGuardia's Commission on the
Harlem Riot of March 19, 1935* (New York: Arno Press, 1969), 45 (cited hereafter as *Riot
Commission Report*); *New York Age,* July 9, 1927. For the depression's overall effects on
Black Harlem see *Opportunity,* June 1935, 172; *New York Amsterdam News,* February 1,
1933; Greenberg, *"Or Does It Explode?"* 45–92, 140–97.

19. *Crisis,* May 1931, 161, 176. On African Americans in the industrial workforce
through the Great Depression see U.S. Department of Commerce, Bureau of the

Efforts to confront White economic domination of African American communities such as Harlem were rooted in the larger issue of race empowerment in the United States. Despite the various forums that had emerged during the second half of the nineteenth century and their respective strategies and intellectual arguments, the consensus was that African Americans must start their own businesses within their communities and that Black residents must patronize those enterprises in order for all to benefit. Yet in Harlem and in other African American communities, the onus for maintaining this symbiotic relationship was placed on the African American consumer. The Harlem Economic Association (HEA), an organization begun in 1924 and led by the West Indian businessman A. I. Hart, used its promotional literature to tell Black Harlemites unequivocally that patronage of African American businesses was a "Racial Duty" and that to patronize other businesses in the community was to "disgrace your own" and to "discard the principle of self-preservation."[20] The necessity of race consumerism also reverberated throughout several African American publications, regardless of their ideological leanings. Marcus Garvey's nationalist *Negro World* suggested to its readers: "the next time a little struggling Negro business in your neighborhood closes its doors, ask yourself how much you have contributed to that failure."[21] Less direct yet equally supportive of Black businesses, the often sensational and ideologically fluid *Amsterdam News* extensively covered the reopening of Hart's five-and-ten store, which had moved to occupy the entire ground floor of the Renaissance Theater at Seventh Avenue and 138th Street. Thinly disguising its pitch for race patronage, the paper exclaimed, "At last, Harlem has a real store owned, controlled and managed by colored people that commands respect and admiration."[22]

Census, *Negroes in the United States, 1920–35* (Washington, D.C.: GPO, 1935), table 7, and *Negro Population, 1790–1915* (Washington, D.C.: GPO, 1918), table 20; Osofsky, *Harlem*, 136–37, 193–95; William H. Harris, *The Harder We Run: Black Workers since the Civil War* (New York: Oxford University Press, 1982), 7–122; Joe W. Trotter Jr., *Black Milwaukee: The Making of an Industrial Proletariat, 1915–45* (Urbana: University of Illinois Press, 1985), 3–195; Dennis C. Dickerson, *Out of the Crucible: Black Steelworkers in Western Pennsylvania, 1875–1980* (Albany: State University of New York Press, 1986), 7–149; John Bodnar, Michael Weber, and Roger Simon, "Migration, Kinship, and Urban Adjustment: Blacks and Poles in Pittsburgh, 1900–1930," *Journal of American History* 66 (December 1979): 548–65.

20. Quoted in McDowell, "Ideology of Black Entrepreneurship," 103.

21. Quoted in Watkins-Owens, *Blood Relations*, 126.

22. *New York Amsterdam News*, December 20, 1922; Watkins-Owens, *Blood Relations*, 132, 134.

As the depression tightened its grip on Black America, appeals to promote Black entrepreneurship took on greater urgency. Advocates of Black business development mixed racial obligation, symbiotic uplift, and race patronage as the recipe for African American salvation in the midst of economic calamity. Several Black Harlem merchants offered "Race Loyalty" buttons at ten cents each, with each button portraying the head of a "Sphynx" [sic]. Whenever they wore the button, African Americans would be proudly proclaiming their "Negro ancestry" (a celebration of the Egyptian Sphinx as African), trustworthiness, and vision and would be showing others that they pledged "to buy from Race Enterprises whenever and wherever practicable (or from stores employing Negro help) thereby helping to create MORE and BETTER jobs right here in Harlem."[23] No doubt these pledges pleased the vicar of Harlem's St. Martin's Protestant Episcopal Church, the Reverend John H. Johnson, who emphatically believed that if African Americans wished to improve their lot, "we must spend our money among our own people."[24]

Several substantial obstacles to Black business growth, however, reduced both race appeals and the promises inherent in them to simply enticing rhetoric. Harlem's business landscape echoed the findings revealed in Black entrepreneurship surveys nationwide: the predominance of numerous functional, small-scale retail businesses, such as food establishments and clothing stores, along with equally small-scale personal enterprises, such as barbershops, beauty parlors, mortuaries, and cleaning and pressing businesses. Despite the benefits these low-capital investment ventures provided, they could not generate substantial job opportunities for any community desperate for work. Moreover, lending discrimination by financial institutions and unsuccessful efforts by Black entrepreneurship proponents to raise capital through numerous cooperative ventures fueled capital liabilities, which in turn limited the growth of race businesses. In addition, the onslaught of retail chain stores presented race businesses and their advocates with a host of new problems. Although all independent entrepreneurs faced a threat from chains, financially precarious Black-owned businesses in direct competition with a chain establishment were especially susceptible. Furthermore, employment discrimination by chain stores could potentially exacerbate Black unemployment, since displaced Whites had a far greater chance of find-

23. *Harlem Business Men's Bulletin* (March 1931), Albion L. Holsey Collection, box 43, Tuskegee University Library, Tuskegee, Ala.
24. Quoted in Greenberg, *"Or Does It Explode?"* 118.

ing work somewhere within the chains than did their African American counterparts. With the viability of Black entrepreneurship inextricably linked with the larger economy, advocates of race businesses were left issuing "Buy Black" appeals in order to maintain the survival of Black businesses.[25]

No amount of racial appeals could offset the fact that African American businesses in Harlem also lost much needed race patronage to Jewish-owned establishments that remained in the community. These enterprises often displayed a greater variety of goods and at prices lower than those found at African American businesses. As a further incentive for Black consumers, older Jewish establishments, with greater cash reserves than those possessed by more recently established Black enterprises, were able to offer credit, a practice welcomed by African American families struggling throughout the lean days of the depression. This sensible business practice in turn translated into immediate and long-term patronage from Blacks, at the expense of the race enterprises. As one Harlem woman recollected, her mother always admonished her to continue to buy from Jews because "they let us have anything we need even when we don't have any money."[26]

Strategies to Gain Black Employment

In light of the numerous problems that affected the growth of Black business, it was clear to all but their most self-interested proponents that race enterprises could not resolve Harlem's unemployment woes. Given the entrepreneurial landscape in Harlem, finding meaningful employment, especially white-collar positions, for African Americans throughout the community's White-owned establishments was a necessity. Beginning in the 1920s, the New York Urban League (NYUL) and the NAACP were among the organizations quietly negotiating with local White businesses to hire African Americans. In addition, Harlem's prominent Black publications periodically promoted Black hiring in White economic Harlem—at least, indirectly—when they inveighed against the local business climate. Job discrimination and unappreciated Black patronage,

---

25. McDowell, "Ideology of Black Entrepreneurship," 30–33, 65–74, 99, 101, 135–90, 226–28.

26. Quoted in Isabel Boiko Price, "Black Response to Anti-Semitism: Negroes and Jews in New York, 1880 to World War II" (Ph.D. diss., University of New Mexico, 1973), 219. Limitations to Black business growth in Harlem found in McDowell, "Ideology of Black Entrepreneurship," 94–105; Price, "Black Response to Anti-Semitism," 217–18; *Riot Commission Report,* 31.

proclaimed the *Amsterdam News* in a 1925 editorial that captured the
African American mainstream press's indignation, had created a "new
Negro slavery in Harlem" in a community that was now "the Mecca" for
"white businessmen interested in keeping the Negro in economic slavery," as well as for myriad unscrupulous entrepreneurs.[27] During the
early years of the depression, Black women from the recently created
Harlem Housewives League (HHL) confronted local businesses in an effort to rectify the community's dismal job situation. League members visited managers of area chain stores, including A&P and Woolworth's, and
requested that African American employment reflect the amount of
Black patronage at each establishment.[28]

The responses of African American elites failed to capture the attention
and imagination of Black Harlemites. Initial community ambivalence to
the jobs issue was partially to blame, even though African American unemployment in Harlem reached 25 percent as compared to approximately 17 percent citywide during 1930, the first full year of the
depression. Perhaps calls for African American white-collar employment
in White-owned retail establishments were inconsequential to a community where racial discrimination had consistently saddled many of its best
and brightest with underemployment, and where the depression's unre-
lenting economic effects exacerbated family deterioration, health crises,
crime, and homelessness in addition to unemployment. Yet Harlem's
leaders themselves undoubtedly abetted community ambivalence. Like
the Black elites who led efforts against segregated public transportation
in southern communities during the first decade of the twentieth century,
those who initially tackled the jobs issue in Harlem were political moderates or conservatives and not the community's firebrands. Although separated by time and space from the virulent racism and accommodationist
politics that constrained the actions of anti–Jim Crow streetcar strategists,
the African American editors, clubwomen, and leaders of advocacy organizations who constituted Harlem's inchoate jobs campaign nevertheless cautiously pursued strategies that were long on respectability and
short on creativity and substantive results.[29]

27. "New Negro slavery" quoted in editorial "Break the Bond," *New York Amsterdam News*, June 3, 1925.
28. Greenberg, *"Or Does It Explode?"* 117. See ibid. for Urban League and NAACP
efforts.
29. See ibid., 18–64, for a social and economic portrait of Harlem through 1933. For
Black elite composition and motivations see ibid., 116; August Meier and Elliott Rudwick, "The Boycott Movement against Jim Crow Streetcars in the South, 1900–1906,"
Journal of American History 55 (March 1969): 756–75; Darlene Clark Hine, "Lifting the

Therefore, what they offered could barely inspire the hopes of Harlem's besieged residents. Despite the fiery editorial rhetoric, African American newspapers presented tepid solutions revolving around familiar themes: the need for race-supported Black businesses and racially conscious consumerism.[30] Also providing little inspiration were the local efforts directed at White-owned businesses. Neither the quiet negotiations undertaken by the NYUL and the NAACP nor the personal visits employed by the HHL were successful in persuading local White business owners to hire African Americans. In fact, the HHL, bowing more to desperation than to limited resources, sidestepped the essential issue of placing African Americans in white-collar positions. The HHL instead asked local merchants to hire Blacks for any vacancy and celebrated any hiring as a victory for the organization and the community. Thus, upon learning that the proprietor of L. M. Blumstein, a local department store, had hired an African American doorman and elevator operator, HHL members proudly and graciously thanked him "for this recognition of the purchasing power of Negroes." HHL members certainly had reason to celebrate, for any job opportunity in employment-starved Black Harlem was important, regardless of classification; yet, as a result of its strategy, the HHL unwittingly reinforced and ultimately acquiesced to the prevailing views regarding limitations to African American occupational mobility.[31]

The Jobs-for-Negroes Campaigns

Approximately two years before Sufi Hamid's arrival in Harlem, several race organizations interested in the jobs issue appeared poised to move Harlem's early jobs campaign in a different direction. In April 1930, approximately two hundred Harlemites gathered at a local junior high school to hear Joseph Bibb, the editor of the *Chicago Whip* and a leader of Chicago's increasingly successful jobs campaign, which had begun the previous year. Bibb described what he referred to as the "non-violent"

Veil, Shattering the Silence: Black Women's History in Slavery and Freedom," in *The State of Afro-American History: Past, Present, and Future,* ed. Hine (Baton Rouge: Louisiana State University Press, 1986), 234–37; Evelyn Brooks Higginbotham, "African-American Women's History and the Metalanguage of Race," *Signs* 17 (winter 1992): 258–66.

30. For example, see sentiments expressed in *New York Amsterdam News,* June 3, 1925, December 11, 1929; Bloom, "Interactions between Blacks and Jews," 361.

31. Greenberg, *"Or Does It Explode?"* 117.

boycott and picketing tactics used in Chicago to an audience that consistently greeted his presentation with "burst[s] of applause and approval."[32] Yet the audience's enthusiasm was not shared by the gathering's sponsors, the NYUL, the HHL, and the National Negro Business League (NNBL). None of the organizations was inclined either to utilize direct action tactics in Harlem or to press more vigorously for jobs in the community. Both the NYUL and the HHL stuck with their preferred tactics, regardless of their limitations. The conservative, business-oriented NNBL was incapable of providing direction to a campaign that needed inspirational rhetoric and confrontational aggressiveness. In addition, the organization was preoccupied with what would prove to be an ill-fated effort to create a national African American grocer cooperative. Those in attendance as well as in the community were again pointed in a familiar direction by Lemuel L. Foster, the New York branch manager of the Victory Life Insurance Company. Although Foster told the audience that Blacks needed to wage "an active campaign" among local businesses in order to tackle joblessness, clearly the African American businessman was more comfortable with proposing that Blacks had to start their own businesses if they wished to address unemployment locally.[33]

In light of Harlem's soapbox tradition and the contributions both foreign-born and native African American radicals made to its development and evolution, the community's political radicals might have prodded jobs campaign leaders toward more decisive action. Yet Harlem's leftist radicals chose primarily to stand apart from the jobs campaign. While Garveyites and several local Black communists, led by the eloquent Barbadian Richard B. Moore, vociferously empathized with the racial overtones of the jobs campaign, most radical activists believed that race economic nationalism encouraged racial rather than interracial attacks against capitalism and government indifference. Furthermore, according to the West Indian–born socialist and Harlem labor organizer Frank R. Crosswaith, any tactic that placed "undue emphasis" on "color and community" confined Black employment to segregated communities and obfuscated the true weapon needed to improve African American living standards in Harlem and throughout the city: the unionization

32. Bibb quoted and Harlem meeting described in *New York Amsterdam News,* April 30, 1930. See also Meier and Rudwick, "Origins of Nonviolent Direct Action," 317–18.
33. *New York Amsterdam News,* April 30, 1930.

of Black workers.[34] As for Harlem's communists, demands for Black economic justice would exacerbate racial hostilities if White workers were
fired to make room for Blacks, proclaimed the Communist Party USA's
most prominent Black leader, James Ford. Even though fears of White
workers being displaced in favor of Blacks were unfounded, it was still
unlikely that party members during the pre–Popular Front period would
sacrifice the appeal of working-class unity in order to cooperate with a
movement that sought change within the capitalist system and from
which Black entrepreneurs could conceivably benefit. Thus, despite organizing a short-lived, quixotic jobs campaign in 1933 and flirting with
local boycotters two years later, Harlem's communists would remain on
the periphery of the jobs campaign.[35]

Devoid of both intellectual provocation from the left and creativity
from its middle-class leaders, the early jobs campaign in Harlem was in a
bind. In order for the campaign to survive, it needed to incorporate the
direct action tactics that had been used with varying success in midwestern cities such as Toledo and Chicago. And one person keenly aware of
these tactics was Sufi Abdul Hamid. Hamid was neither a savior nor a vi-
sionary. Instead, he was an individual with a penchant for drama—a
quality well suited for a community such as Harlem where the soapbox
tradition elevated the dramatic—and an opportunist who clearly understood the impact a jobs campaign could have in a community. Hamid arrived in Harlem around 1932, following his active involvement in the
Chicago jobs campaign sponsored by Bibb's *Chicago Whip* and the Reverend J. C. Austin of the Pilgrim Baptist Church. While in Chicago,
Hamid had referred to himself as Bishop Conshankin, mystic and Oriental philosopher. Advised by local neo-nationalist Black Muslims that his
predilection for mysticism would hinder Chicago's jobs campaign effort,
Bishop Conshankin became Bishop Amiru Al-Minin Sufi Abdul Hamid.
Yet Hamid never totally dissociated himself from his fascination with
mysticism, as evidenced by his inaccurate yet apparently intentional ap-
propriation of the Islamic term *sufi* (a "sufi" is an adherent of a popular
form of eleventh-century Islamic mysticism known as "sufism," taken
from the Arabic *suf*, wool, to indicate the wearing of a woolen robe). Sufi

34. Quoted in McDowell, "Ideology of Black Entrepreneurship," 207.

35. Mark Naison, *Communists in Harlem during the Depression* (Urbana: University of
Illinois Press, 1983), 50, 101–2, 170–77; Greenberg, *"Or Does It Explode?"* 118–19;
Knight, "Caribbean Background," 5; McDowell, "Ideology of Black Entrepreneur-
ship," 199–203, 205, 207–8; Meier and Rudwick, "Origins of Nonviolent Direct
Action," 320–21.

Hamid would also display his fondness for mysticism in 1938 when he became founder and high priest of the Universal Holy Temple of Tranquillity in Harlem.[36]

Hamid and members of his nationalist organization, the Negro Clerical and Industrial Alliance (NCIA), began picketing businesses along 125th Street early in 1932. Despite his outrageous appearance and confrontational rhetoric, Hamid's first jobs campaign success occurred indirectly and slightly more than two years after his initial arrival. In June 1934, Morris Weinstein, the new lessee of Koch's Department Store, announced both the reopening of the West 125th Street establishment and that African Americans would constitute one-third of the new clerical staff. Previously, Koch's had been Harlem's largest department store, founded by the German Jew H. C. F. Koch in 1890. As the Black population of Harlem increased, Koch, whose racist attitudes were known throughout the community, chose to close the store in 1930 rather than to serve African Americans. As the new owner, Weinstein recognized that success in Black Harlem would depend upon improving the store's image in the community. Yet Hamid's daily harangues along Harlem's major commercial thoroughfare threatened this effort. By employing African Americans in clerical positions, Weinstein avoided a confrontation with Hamid and his growing number of picketers, including Abyssinian's flamboyant Adam Clayton Powell Jr.[37]

Black-Jewish Conflict and the Jobs Campaign

Hamid's role in the hiring of Black clerical workers at Koch's Department Store went unrecognized by Harlem's African American elite. Instead, both the *Age* and the *Amsterdam News* chose to cite Weinstein for his fairness and business acumen.[38] By slighting Hamid in favor of Weinstein, the newspapers reflected the increasing disdain felt by segments of Harlem's socially conservative African American middle class toward Hamid's flamboyant appearance, bombastic rhetoric, and sometimes

36. For Hamid's Chicago background and subsequent journeys see McKay, *Harlem*, 185; *New York Amsterdam News*, April 16, 1938; *New York Times*, August 1, 1938. For Islamic connections see M. El Fasi, ed., *General History of Africa*, vol. 3, *Africa from the Seventh Century to the Eleventh Century* (London: Heinemann Educational Books; Berkeley: University of California Press; Paris: UNESCO, 1988), 42–43.

37. Meier and Rudwick, "Origins of Nonviolent Direct Action," 318; Osofsky, *Harlem*, 121; *New York Age*, June 9, 1934; *New York Amsterdam News*, June 16, 1934. Powell's presence on the picket lines reported in *New York Amsterdam News*, May 26, 1934.

38. *New York Age*, June 9, 1934; *New York Amsterdam News*, June 16, 1934; see also column by Theophilus Lewis in *New York Amsterdam News*, June 23, 1934.

crude picketing tactics. In fact, as early as 1932, the *Age,* without addressing Hamid by name, characterized his tactics as having too much
"ballyhoo [and] too much disturbance."[39] Furthermore, to some African
Americans in Harlem, Hamid was a crass opportunist, for his jobs campaign organization, the NCIA, charged membership fees in return for job
promises. The African American reporter Roi Ottley summed up the assessment of many Black elites when he declared that Hamid was nothing
more than a "crude, racketeering giant . . . posing as an evangelist of
Black labor."[40]

Just as Hamid's presence influenced Weinstein's decision to hire
Blacks, it also influenced the response of Harlem's Black elite to the jobs
campaign. Feeling the need to restore respectability to the jobs campaign,
along with recognizing the effort's growing popularity in the Black community, Effa Manly of the HHL began the Black bourgeoisie's counter-
part to Hamid's alliance in late May 1934, known as the Citizens' League
for Fair Play. Members of this broad-based yet elite-dominated and elite-
led coalition included such Harlem notables as Arthur Schomburg, curator of the Negro Division of the New York Public Library; Adam Powell;
Fred R. Moore, editor and publisher of the *New York Age;* and St. Martin
Church's John Johnson, the leader of the new organization. The Citizens'
League selected as its first target Blumstein's, which despite its earlier
hirings still adamantly refused to employ African Americans in any positions other than as janitors and elevator operators. After several weeks
of picketing, however, the Citizens' League reached an agreement with
the Blumstein management that called for the hiring of thirty-five Blacks
by September 1934.[41]

Yet the Citizens' League's victory in the boycott campaign against
Blumstein's was overshadowed by allegations of anti-Semitism. And
once again, Hamid was the vortex of the controversy. In October 1934
Hamid was taken to court on a disorderly conduct charge, based upon
statements he had allegedly made during the previous month. According
to the plaintiff, Edgar H. Burman, an insurance broker and the self-
described commander-in-chief of the Jewish Minutemen of America,
Hamid had referred to himself at a jobs rally as the "Black Hitler" and

39. *New York Age,* June 25, 1932. See also McKay, *Harlem,* 192.
40. Ottley, *New World A-Comin',* 116–17. See also McKay, *Harlem,* 194–95.
41. On emergence of the Citizens' League in the Harlem jobs campaign see Gary
Jerome Hunter, " 'Don't Buy from Where You Can't Work': Black Urban Boycott
Movements during the Depression, 1929–1941" (Ph.D. diss., University of Michigan,
1977), 182, 184; *New York Age,* May 26, June 23, August 25, 1934; *New York Amsterdam
News,* August 11, 1934; Osofsky, *Harlem,* 121.

had declared that he was the "only one fit to carry on the war against the Jews."[42] Other Jewish observers leveled similar accusations against Hamid. The author of an article in the *Jewish Day*, a conservative Jewish newspaper, declared that Hamid had not only urged the boycott of Jewish businesses but had also called for "an open bloody war against the Jews who are much worse than all other whites." Ironically, in concluding his account of Hamid's anti-Semitic remarks, the author revealed that Hamid was not the only one who could be accused of expressing unsavory sentiments. The Jewish writer declared that Harlem's Jews worried that Hamid's propaganda might provoke the African American community because although Blacks "are very good natured people with a sense of humor, . . . colored people are [also] so emotional."[43]

Hamid repeatedly denied charges that he was a dangerous anti-Semite. In a November 1934 interview with the Jamaican American writer Claude McKay, Hamid declared that he was vehemently opposed to anti-Semitism. His familiarity with anti-Semitic literature such as Hitler's *Mein Kampf*, he argued, made him aware of the evils of anti-Semitism. In fact, he revealed to McKay during another interview session that he had turned down an invitation to cooperate with the American Nazi Party. "I could not imagine cooperating with the Nazis," he stated, "any more than with the Ku Klux Klan." The merchants of Harlem fabricated the allegations, Hamid charged during the 1934 interview, because they "did not want to face the issue of giving them [Blacks] a square deal."[44]

Hamid's culpability was stronger than he admitted. There were indeed powerful business interests pushing for Hamid's conviction on the disorderly conduct charge; included among these was Bernard S. Deutsch, president of the city's Board of Aldermen, who had been implored by the all-White Harlem Merchants Association to intervene on its behalf. Consequently, the charges against Hamid were dismissed for lack of impartial witnesses at the proceedings. Nonetheless, Hamid was in a fierce battle for control of the jobs campaign with the Citizens' League. He was also known to spew ethnic slurs quite freely: Italian and Greek

42. Quoted in *New York Times*, October 9, 1934. See also *New York Age*, September 29, 1934.

43. The translation of the *Jewish Day* article appeared in the *New York Age* on September 29, 1934.

44. Hamid interview in *Nation*, April 3, 1935, 383; Hamid's additional comments quoted in McKay, *Harlem*, 203.

businessmen were referred to as "spaghetti slingers" and "swine herds," respectively.[45] Hamid was probably not shy about utilizing anti-Semitic remarks in order to attract followers, particularly those frustrated by the inability of African Americans to establish an economic foothold in areas dominated by Jewish businesses.

If Hamid entertained the notion that Harlem's African American elite would speak out on his behalf during his trial, he was sadly mistaken. The *Age* had signaled the official response of Harlem's African American elite back in August 1934 by describing the actions of Hamid's NCIA as "misguided and stupid." In subsequent editorials, Fred Moore would raise concerns that Hamid's continuing presence in the jobs campaign might result in reprisals from Jewish employers and their sympathizers. Angered by Hamid's histrionics, surmised Moore, they might summarily dismiss Blacks from jobs outside Black Harlem.[46] Added to Moore's concerns were views appearing in numerous African American publications reiterating jobs campaign assessments by radical critics. White workers would probably have to be fired to make room for newly hired Blacks, surmised boycott dissenters, such as the African American columnist and novelist George S. Schuyler, apparently believing that Harlem's depression-era economy was incapable of absorbing any new workers. Fired White workers might then retaliate by demanding the summary dismissal of Blacks employed in White establishments outside Harlem, thus negating attempts at establishing working-class unity. And if Blacks were indeed fired from their jobs downtown, any gains made during the Harlem jobs campaigns would be offset.[47]

More criticism was forthcoming. The *Amsterdam News*, which rarely missed an opportunity to fire volleys at the jobs campaign supported by its rival, the *Age*, chose instead to express dismay about Hamid and the anti-Semitism controversy. Although believing that the anti-Semitism charges were embellished by "zealous Yiddish newspaper reporters whose race consciousness exceeds their journalistic yen," the paper declared nevertheless that "hotheads" such as Hamid were indeed troublemakers. The *Amsterdam News* concluded by urging its Black

45. *New York Amsterdam News*, September 29, October 13, 1934; *New York Times*, October 9, October 12, 1934. Hamid's slurs quoted in Hunter, "Don't Buy," 189.

46. *New York Age*, August 25, September 29, 1934.

47. *Crisis*, September 1934; *New York Amsterdam News*, June 30, July 21, 1934. See also Abram L. Harris, *The Negro as Capitalist: A Study of Bank and Business among American Negroes* (Philadelphia: American Academy of Political and Social Sciences, 1936), 181.

readers to ignore "harbingers of hatred" such as Hamid, for "race prejudice has no place in Harlem."[48]

To the depression-era critics of the jobs campaign movement—including political scientist and future Nobel laureate Ralph J. Bunche and economist Abram L. Harris—Black middle-class leaders also bore responsibility for the tensions in the jobs campaign. As advocates of interracial working-class unity, and disdainful of either race-based economic strategies or White capitalist paternalism, these young African American intellectuals charged that race-based strategies were both ineffective and fueled anti-Semitism. Frustrated African Americans, claimed the critics, targeted Jewish merchants, whom they perceived as an obstacle to their attempt to establish what Harris described as a "miniature capitalism" within their own segregated communities.[49] This perception was unfair, continued Harris; for example, most Jewish businesses, with the exception of the large stores along 125th Street, did not hire African Americans because they relied primarily on family labor. Nonetheless, the perception remained, "deliberately nurtured by the self-seeking, sensitive Negro middle class," in its effort to establish an "economic base for [its] middle class aspirations," declared Bunche during one of his scathing attacks on African American middle-class leadership.[50]

It is inaccurate to assert that the anti-Semitic charges arose primarily from the racially oriented strategies of Harlem's African American petite bourgeoisie and nonmerchants. Granted, many frustrated Blacks caught up in the jobs campaigns probably did vent their anger at Jewish merchants. Yet, despite the involvement of Harlem's African American elite with the jobs campaign, it was Hamid who resuscitated what had been a virtually lifeless effort in Harlem, a fact overlooked by the intellectual outsiders Bunche and Harris. Furthermore, most of the anti-Semitic allegations revolved around Hamid, with no evidence that African American elites "deliberately nurtured" perceptions that Jews were obstacles to Black economic empowerment. Rather, the majority of African American

48. *New York Amsterdam News,* October 6, 1934.
49. Harris, *Negro as Capitalist,* 183.
50. Ralph J. Bunche, "The Programs, Ideologies, Tactics, and Achievement of Negro Betterment and Interracial Organizations," book 4 in Carnegie-Myrdal Study, "The Negro in America": Research Memoranda for Use in the Preparation of Gunnar Myrdal's *An American Dilemma,* 1940, 769, 551, 773–93 (cited hereafter as Carnegie-Myrdal Study). See also Harris, *Negro as Capitalist,* 179–81; William A. Darity Jr., "Abram Harris: An Odyssey from Howard to Chicago," *Review of Black Political Economy* 15 (winter 1987): 16–24; James O. Young, *Black Writers of the Thirties* (Baton Rouge: Louisiana State University Press, 1973), xi, 40; P. H. Norgen, "Negro Labor and Its Problems," book 4, Carnegie-Myrdal Study, 396–430.

elites rushed to denounce Hamid whenever possible. The responsibility of the Black elite instead lay more with its failure to realize that in an urban environment such as Harlem, with a strong Jewish past, a race strategy for economic betterment would place African Americans in conflict with the very same group they had been exhorted to emulate.

As one component of the "joint-sufferers" theme, African American leaders as well as proponents of Black entrepreneurship have long implored Black Americans to better themselves by copying the "business savvy" of Jews. African American writers celebrated as they held up any success by Jewish entrepreneurs as an example to the Black community. This celebration could intoxicate even normally levelheaded African Americans such as the editor of the African Methodist Episcopal (AME) Church's *Christian Recorder* and later the AME *Church Review,* Benjamin Tucker Tanner. It had been the successful pursuits of entrepreneurial strategies by persecuted individuals helping themselves, Tanner proclaimed to his African American readers during the 1880s, that led to the Jewish people becoming "masters of Europe." Never at a loss for intoxicating hyperbole himself, Booker T. Washington articulated a similar theme. Washington declared that the solution to the race problem for Blacks was to emulate the activities of Jews, for the Jew "has entwined himself about America in a business or industrial way."[51]

While images of the industrious Jew were intended to inspire African Americans by linking them with another historically downtrodden people, they simultaneously often contained stereotypical anti-Semitic references that no doubt reflected the American public's perception of Jews. The "savvy Jew" could easily become the "cheap Jew," as occurred in the 1920s when the Black-owned *Atlanta Independent* pondered why Jews "desecrate our Sabbath and insult our religion by conducting places of amusement that interfere with the sanctity of our Sabbath."[52] The juxtaposition of images in ways that blurred intent and consequences was also evident as the Black press demonstrated resentment toward Jews while concurrently championing their cause. In 1933, the *Amsterdam News,* while sympathizing with the plight of Jews in Nazi Germany, also chastised the U.S. government for being more concerned with the

51. Tanner quoted in August Meier, *Negro Thought in America, 1880–1915: Racial Ideologies in the Age of Booker T. Washington* (Ann Arbor: University of Michigan Press, 1966), 45; Washington quoted in Harlan, "Booker T. Washington's Discovery," 269.
52. Quoted in Arnold Shankman, " 'Friend or Foe?' Southern Black View of the Jew, 1880–1935," in *Turn to the South: Essays on Southern Jewry,* ed. Nathan M. Kaganoff and Melvin I. Urofsky (Charlottesville: University Press of Virginia, 1979), 113.

problems of Jews abroad than with those faced by African Americans at home. Although the newspaper's chastisement was unwarranted, for neither the U.S. government nor the American people would prove amenable to relaxing immigration laws to aid German Jews fleeing Nazi Germany, the African American publication was not only implicitly questioning the United States' commitment to civil rights but also pondering what made Jews so special as to warrant extra consideration.[53]

African American elites as well as their Jewish counterparts ignored any evaluations of the effects their respective actions were having on the tensions in Harlem and continued their efforts, separately and collectively, to lower the flames of discord between African Americans and Jews. The *Amsterdam News,* for example, proposed a cooperative strategy, with the controversial Sufi Hamid once again serving as bait. The newspaper reported that Magistrate Overton Harris, who had dismissed Hamid's disorderly conduct charge in October 1934, had downplayed one of Hamid's alleged street pronouncements, that Jews were "syphilitic consumptives spreading their filth through Harlem." Since Magistrate Harris had also been known to condone police brutality against Blacks, the *Amsterdam News* urged African Americans and Jews to unite against Harris in order to prevent his reelection to the bench in July 1939.[54] Among Jewish elites, Samuel S. Leibowitz, respected throughout Black Harlem for his work defending the nine Black youths falsely accused of rape in the infamous Scottsboro, Alabama, incident, took his crusade for ethnic and racial cooperation to the convention of the Negro Benevolent Protection Order of Elks, held at St. Marks Methodist Episcopal Church in 1939. In a speech drawing on the theme of "joint sufferers" that he had articulated five years earlier, Leibowitz pleaded with his Black listeners that neither they nor the Jews should ever succumb to the politics of hatred, for "both of us—you and I—are in the same boat together."[55]

Morris Weinstein of Koch's also tried his hand at fostering race relations. In November 1934 Weinstein sponsored a three-day rally in Harlem to raise money for the Scottsboro boys' defense. His fund-raising effort, along with his status as the first Jewish merchant to hire African Americans substantially in clerical positions, left an indelible impression

53. *New York Amsterdam News,* March 29, 1933; a similar sentiment was presented on April 2, 1938. For American attitudes about Jewish immigration see Leonard Dinnerstein, *America and the Survivors of the Holocaust* (New York: Columbia University Press, 1982), 1–8.
54. *New York Amsterdam News,* October 20, 1934.
55. *New York Times,* August 22, 1939; *New York Amsterdam News,* October 13, 1934.

on Black Harlemites. In March 1935 Harlem went up in flames as hundreds of Blacks, angered by rumors subsequently proved false that a White store owner had beaten and murdered a Hispanic youth caught shoplifting, destroyed White-owned establishments in the community. Yet Weinstein's 125th Street store was untouched by looters. Weinstein later described the occurrence as "one of the finest tributes paid to the store."[56]

Sufi Hamid would not be the recipient of any tributes, as the Black elite's attack against him intensified in 1935. In January 1935, Hamid was again hauled to court, and eventually convicted of selling inflammatory literature without a license and preaching atheism. While some, including Claude McKay, would question whether the pamphlet titled *The Black Challenge to White Supremacy* contained anything that could be construed as anti-Semitic or atheistic, the Citizens' League certainly approved of Magistrate Thomas Aurelio's decision to give Hamid two concurrent ten-day terms at a local workhouse. The organization had filed a letter with the court during the trial stating that Hamid was "a menace to the best interests of Harlem."[57] The league clearly wanted to distance itself from the anti-Semitic allegations as well as to remove Hamid from the jobs campaign scene. The organization feared that Hamid's continued presence would lead to more injunctions similar to the November 1934 court order prohibiting picketing at the A. S. Beck shoe store.[58] Although aimed primarily at the NCIA and other protest organizations operating at the time, the injunction and the threat of injunctions were crippling the Citizens' League's attempt at selecting stores along 125th Street for picketing. Hamid was thus the "sacrificial lamb" in the league's quest to continue its version of an orderly and respectable jobs campaign.

By the end of 1935, however, the Citizens' League would not have to worry about either removing Hamid or sustaining the jobs campaign movement. In July, the *New York Times* had reported that an injunction was granted prohibiting Hamid and his organization from picketing a women's apparel shop on 125th Street. The injunction was not a surprise. Nor was the fact that Fred Moore of the Citizens' League testified in its support. Just four months earlier, Moore, while echoing the popular

56. *New York Age*, March 30, 1935. Weinstein's Harlem rally reported in *New York Amsterdam News*, November 11, 1934. For the Harlem riot see *Riot Commission Report*, 7–12; Ottley and Weatherby, eds., *The Negro in New York*, 275–77; Greenberg, "*Or Does It Explode?*" 3–6.
57. *New York Times*, January 16, January 20, 1935; McKay, *Harlem*, 205.
58. See *New York Amsterdam News*, November 3, 1934.

sentiment that the Harlem riot was a reaction against the community's glaring economic and social ills, also bitterly suggested that the riot was due to the tensions stirred up the previous summer by "soapbox agitators" like Hamid.[59] African American elites again believed that by removing the controversial Hamid and individuals like him from the scene, a respectable jobs campaign could continue. Yet in the aftermath of the riot, New York City's White establishment made no distinctions between the jobs campaigns, respectable or otherwise, in its quest to restore order. Thus as 1935 came to a close, injunctions had effectively ended the "Don't Buy" jobs movement in Harlem.

Conclusion

The first phase of the Harlem jobs movement was over. The demographic change that contributed to the jobs movement, the shift from Jewish Harlem to Black Harlem, was free of the racial and ethnic violence that had marred so much of this nation's urban experience. This tranquillity undoubtedly pleased both African American and Jewish leaders, who consistently stressed ethnic and racial cooperation as essential between peoples who suffered from the iniquities of racism. Beneath this layer of tranquillity, however, lay tensions that were exposed not only during the attempt of Black Harlemites to gain control of their community from their Jewish cosufferers but also in the distorted perceptions that African Americans and Jews held of each other.

The stresses and turmoil that resurfaced during the Harlem jobs campaign between African Americans and Jews, however, never translated into violent conflict between the two groups. Ironically, this relative peace can be credited to the arrival of the inimitable and at times insufferable Sufi Abdul Hamid. His controversial yet vital presence during the first phase of the Harlem jobs boycott has been consistently overlooked, downplayed, or maligned. Unlike the African American elites who initially shied away from confrontational demonstrations, Hamid understood the impact direct action tactics could have in an African American urban community with a strong tradition of soapbox politics. His presence opened up what had been a closed, unimaginative jobs campaign and reinforced the cultural importance of soapbox oratory as political expression. At the same time, his involvement furnished African American and Jewish leaders with the ideal target for voicing their collective oppo-

59. *New York Times*, July 6, 1935; *New York Age*, March 30, 1935. See *Riot Commission Report*, 122–28; *New York Age*, March 30, 1935, for riot causes.

sition to anti-Semitism in order to lower the flames of discord before they engulfed both communities.

Yet in this frenzied rush to "bond," ethnic and racial cooperation had its price. By focusing on Hamid, African American elites and Jews blinded themselves to several salient issues that each needed to address. All African Americans who either aspired to become or were leaders in Harlem needed to recognize the liabilities inherent in race-based strategies for Black economic empowerment, even as those strategies suggestively offered Blacks the chance to achieve what historian V. P. Franklin refers to as the "cultural goal of Black self-determination."[60] Removing Hamid and other controversial individuals from the campaigns simply allowed African American strategists to convince themselves that they had indeed undertaken the daunting task of developing approaches that had mass appeal and simultaneously celebrated rather than denigrated African American cultural traditions. For Jews, the issue was less weighty, though nevertheless important. Jews needed to understand the importance of the jobs campaigns, despite their flaws, as one step in the quest of Black Harlemites for self-determination as they rid themselves of artificial economic, social, and political constraints.

Near the end of the decade, however, celebration rather than introspection was on the minds of most Harlemites. In August 1938, New York's Black weeklies reported the signing of an agreement between Adam Powell's Greater New York Coordinating Committee for Employment (GNYCCE) and the Uptown Chamber of Commerce, which called for Blacks to receive at least one-third of all white-collar jobs in White-owned establishments in Harlem. The agreement came as a result of renewed picketing in Harlem following the April 1938 decision by the Supreme Court upholding the right of groups to picket against establishments practicing racial discrimination. Both the jobs agreement and future GNYCCE-led efforts against public utilities, public transportation companies, and World's Fair organizers would engender criticism from some on the left about the repercussions of these efforts. Nevertheless, it was clear, unlike earlier in the decade, that direct action tactics to achieve economic justice had become a permanent part of the local scene.[61]

60. V. P. Franklin, *Black Self-Determination: A Cultural History of African-American Resistance* (Brooklyn: Lawrence Hill Books, 1992), 202.

61. *New York Age*, August 6, August 20, 1938; *New York Amsterdam News*, August 13, 1938 (which printed the full text of the agreement). For the court decision see *New York Amsterdam News*, April 9, 1938. See also Meier and Rudwick, "Origins of Nonviolent Direct Action," 326; McDowell, "Ideology of Black Entrepreneurship," 195–99.

Missing from the celebrations following the jobs agreements was an individual who would have undoubtedly thought he had every right to join the festivities. On July 31, 1938, Bishop Al-Minin Sufi Abdul Hamid died in a plane crash on Long Island. When rescuers arrived at the site, they found the lifeless body of the man vilified by his detractors as the era's "Black Hitler" in an open field at the intersection of Southern State Highway and an avenue called Jerusalem.[62]

62. *New York Times*, August 1, 1938.

African Americans and Jews in Organized Labor

A Case Study of Detroit, 1920–1950

— Marshall F. Stevenson Jr. —

C OMPARATIVELY little of the scholarship devoted to African American–Jewish relations in the twentieth century has considered the involvement of and interactions between the two groups within the American labor movement. What has been written on this important topic has focused primarily on the garment unions in New York City. While we know from the historical literature on Jewish trade unionism that the garment industry in general, and in New York City in particular, is a logical place to begin an examination of Black-Jewish relations within the American labor movement, there is a need to go further.[1] More than forty years ago, labor historian Henry David pointed out that students of Jewish unionism, such as Selig Perlman, never fully explored what they meant by the term *Jewish unionism* and thus overlooked a great deal. David rightly noted that if "Jewish unionism" is defined in terms of those labor organizations in which Jews were numerically dominant, a substantial number of unions in other fields will be ignored. Even more important for this discussion, neither Perlman nor historians writing since the early 1950s have paid much attention to the contributions of Jewish unionists in organizations where they were always a numerical minority.[2]

1. On Black-Jewish relations in the garment unions see Hasia R. Diner, *In the Almost Promised Land: American Jews and Blacks, 1915–1935* (1977; rpt. Baltimore: Johns Hopkins University Press, 1995); the standard work on Jewish unionism in the United States is Melech Epstein, *Jewish Labor in U.S.A.: An Industrial, Political, and Cultural History of the Jewish Labor Movement,* vol. 1, *1882–1914;* vol. 2, *1914–1952* (New York: Ktav Publishing House, 1969).

2. Henry David, "The Jewish Unions and Their Influence upon the American Labor Movement," *American Jewish History* 41, no. 4 (June 1952): 339–45. David's comments were in response to Selig Perlman, "Jewish-American Unionism: Its Birth Pangs and Contribution to the General American Labor Movement," in the same issue, pp. 297–307.

The historical research on African American unionism and the role and contribution of Black workers to the American labor movement is more extensive, and no less important, than that on Jewish workers. Yet here too, there has been an overwhelming focus upon the racially exclusionary practices of organized labor. The issue of racial exclusion has been cast in general Black-White terms, and little has been written about racial-ethnic relations within unions. A great deal of what we know about African American workers and interracial unionism is related to the activities of the Congress of Industrial Organizations (CIO) and the mass-production industries it organized.[3]

At the same time, any discussion of race and ethnicity in the CIO has to take into account the role of the Communist Party (CP), and in turn the CP's disproportionate recruiting efforts among African Americans and Jews. To be sure, the vast majority of Jewish and African American CIO members were not CP members.[4] Nonetheless, the most active and vocal proponents of Black-Jewish unity, those members who saw the need to vigorously confront racism and anti-Semitism within major CIO affiliates, such as the United Automobile Workers (UAW), could be found among African Americans and Jews connected with or influenced in some way by the CP during the 1930s. An examination of Black-Jewish relations in the UAW in Detroit allows us to survey the role and influence of Communists and their sympathizers in the affairs of the union from the 1930s through the early 1950s.

Detroit provides an ideal setting in which to examine Black-Jewish relations in industries primarily outside the garment trades and in unions dominated by native-born Whites and European ethnics who exhibited racist and anti-Semitic attitudes and behaviors. From a demographic standpoint, the number of Blacks and Jews who lived and worked in Detroit during the period under discussion is significant. By 1940 Detroit's Jewish population was nearly 90,000, making it the city with the sixth largest Jewish population. African Americans numbered close to 150,000, giving the Motor City the fourth largest number of northern Black urban residents, after New York City, Chicago, and Philadelphia.

No historical study of employment in Detroit can overlook the auto-

3. Two recent works outlining this historiography are Herbert Hill, "The Problem of Race in American Labor History," *Reviews in American History* 24, no. 2 (June 1996): 189–208, and Joe William Trotter Jr., "African-American Workers: New Directions in U.S. Labor Historiography," *Labor History* 35 (1994): 495–523.
4. Harvey Klehr, *Communist Cadre: The Social Background of the Communist Party Elite* (Stanford: Hoover Institute Press, 1978); Robert Zieger, *The CIO, 1935–1955* (Chapel Hill: University of North Carolina Press, 1995), 253–61.

mobile industry, the rise of auto unionism, and the UAW. Although August Meier and Elliott Rudwick have adequately described the impact of unionism on Detroit's Black community and, in turn, the influence of African Americans in the shaping of the UAW, they failed to describe racial-ethnic interactions, a complex and crucial aspect of Black-White relations in the automobile workforce and union. In 1930 nearly 60 percent of Detroit's autoworkers were foreign-born White ethnics and African Americans.[5]

The major controversy that developed during the period from 1920 to 1950 was over the issue of support by Jewish unionists for African Americans' demands for access to union offices in proportion to their presence and distribution within the membership. The earliest debates over "affirmative action," one of the more controversial issues dividing African Americans and Jews after 1975, originated within the ranks of organized labor and involved Black and Jewish members of the UAW.

African Americans, Jews, and Organized Labor in Detroit

Detroit's African American and Jewish workers were in no way strangers to labor unions and union organizing before 1935, but their historical experiences with organized labor contrasted sharply. During the 1880s when the Knights of Labor experienced considerable growth and promoted a general policy of racial nondiscrimination, African Americans were divided over whether or not to join because of past racial exclusion by trade unions and the fact that the Knights had both racially mixed and separate assemblies around the country.[6] Once the AFL replaced the Knights as Detroit's main labor organization in the late nineteenth and early twentieth century, Blacks were either excluded or admitted into racially segregated locals. Moreover, African Americans had been so relegated to unskilled occupations, few held jobs that were unionized.[7] Although Detroit's first prominent Jewish labor leader, Samuel Goldwater, who founded the Michigan Federation of Labor in 1889, did not make

5. August Meier and Elliott Rudwick, *Black Detroit and the Rise of the UAW* (New York: Oxford University Press, 1979); Joyce Shaw Patterson, *American Automobile Workers, 1900–1930* (Albany: State University of New York Press, 1987), 15.

6. On the early history of the Detroit labor movement see Richard Oestreicher, *Solidarity and Fragmentation: Working People and Class Consciousness in Detroit, 1875–1900* (Urbana: University of Illinois Press, 1986); David Katzman, *Before the Ghetto: Black Detroit in the Nineteenth Century* (Urbana: University of Illinois Press, 1973), 124; Philip Foner, *Organized Labor and the Black Worker, 1619–1973* (New York: Praeger, 1974), 51.

7. Katzman, *Before the Ghetto,* 125; Robert Rockaway, *The Jews of Detroit* (Detroit: Wayne State University Press, 1986), 69.

distinctions based upon race, his racial beliefs and personal influence failed to change the discriminatory policies and practices of Detroit's local unions.[8]

European ethnic and immigrant workers were generally segregated because they tended to specialize in particular crafts. During the early twentieth century, the Italians, for example, dominated the tile-working industry; the Germans, the brewery industry; and Scotsmen, the tool-making craft. In 1902 Detroit's Amalgamated Society of Carpenters had a "German Branch #2," while Local 4 of the United Cloth, Hat and Cap-makers of North America, Local 1191 of the Carpenters and Joiners Union, and Local 78 of the Bakers and Confectioners Union had only Jewish members.[9]

Between 1904 and 1915, when the revolutionary Industrial Workers of the World (IWW) challenged the authority of the AFL as the sole representative of workers in Detroit, Jewish IWW leaders distinguished themselves in several organizing struggles. The first episode was in late 1904 and early 1905 when the all-Jewish Local 4 of the United Cloth, Hat and Capmakers struck against the Detroit Cap Company. The local cutters union and the local IWW, led by Lazarus Goldberg, refused to cooperate with Local 4 in negotiations and signed separate contracts with the company. Within several months the cap company did away with these agreements and declared itself an open shop, destroying Local 4 in the process and severely discrediting the local IWW, which had been competing with the local AFL for worker support.[10]

Although African American workers remained on the periphery of unionization in the mid-1920s, there were some two thousand Black union members in several local unions, including three hundred female members of the Laundry Workers Union who worked in the overwhelmingly Jewish-owned laundry firms in Detroit. According to one of the city's main labor leaders, there remained "more or less ill feeling" against Blacks, presumably not because of their race, but because they would not join unions and were used as strikebreakers. Indeed, the Detroit Urban League (DUL) received significant financial support from the anti-union

8. David A. Boyd, "The Labor Movement of Detroit," n.d., David A. Boyd Papers, Labadie Collection, University of Michigan Graduate Library, Ann Arbor. Boyd was chairman of the organizing committee of the Michigan Federation of Labor. Robert A. Rockaway, "Samuel Goldwater in Detroit," *Michigan Jewish History*, May 1969, 89.
9. Steve Babson, *Working Detroit: The Making of a Union Town* (Detroit: Wayne State University Press, 1986), 26–27.
10. Rockaway, *Jews of Detroit*, 69; Epstein, *Jewish Labor in U.S.A.*, discusses the overall effect of the IWW intrusion into Jewish labor unions.

Employers Association of Detroit, which in turn relied on the DUL to find suitable replacements for White strikers, as was the case in 1921 when White metalworkers went on strike at the "Timken" Axle Company.[11]

From the mid-1920s until the onset of the Great Depression, there were approximately the same number of African American and Jewish unionists (between two and three thousand in each group) in Detroit, dispersed throughout various low-skill occupations. The depression, however, signaled the beginning of widespread discontent among industrial workers, particularly in automobile factories. The story of the formation of the CIO and the rise of its most important affiliate in Detroit, the UAW, has been recounted by numerous historians, as well as the struggle to incorporate African American autoworkers into the UAW.[12] From a numerical standpoint, the inclusion and organization of African American autoworkers was far more important to union growth than any special appeal to the small minority of Jewish autoworkers, and the CIO and UAW were distinguished from the AFL by their active and aggressive policy of nondiscrimination against racial and religious minorities.

Another distinguishing characteristic of the CIO and UAW in Detroit was their close ties to the CP and the role of Communist unionists and sympathizers in the locals. The Communists were the staunchest promoters of racial equality in the CIO, and it was their activities, both prior to the formation of the UAW in 1935 and afterward, that attracted the small number of Black autoworkers who supported the union in its early years. These Black unionists, including Walter Hardin, Joseph Billups, James Anderson, William Nowell, Lonnie Williams, Paul Kirk, and Samuel Fanroy, joined the UAW after positive experiences with CP-supported organizations earlier in the decade.[13]

The Communists went about the task of attracting African Americans and Jews in Detroit by creating racial and ethnic neighborhood groups, such as the Nat Turner Club (an extension of the larger League of Struggle for Negro Rights), the Jewish Borough of the CP, the Jewish Women's Council, and the Jewish Workers Club. Blacks and Jews also interacted

11. Glen Carlson, "The Negro in the Industries of Detroit" (Ph.D. diss., University of Michigan, 1929), 188–89; Babson, Working Detroit, 43–44.
12. See for example Zieger, The CIO; Walter Galenson, The CIO Challenge to the AFL: A History of the American Labor Movement (Cambridge: Harvard University Press, 1960); Meier and Rudwick, Black Detroit.
13. On Communists in the auto industry see Roger Keeran, The Communist Party and the Auto Workers Unions (Bloomington: Indiana University Press, 1980); Meier and Rudwick, Black Detroit, 45–60.

in the CP-sponsored Unemployment Councils, participating in public demonstrations for government relief programs and blocking tenant evictions. While class and racial unity were key issues promoted by these Communist organizations, there was also an underlying emphasis on Black-Jewish unity in classes conducted at the local CP Workers School in the early 1930s. Most of the students and teachers who attended (six to twenty-four people per class) were African Americans and Jews. It was during this period that these Blacks rubbed shoulders with Jewish party members and sympathizers, such as labor attorney Maurice Sugar, who actively worked against racial discrimination toward Detroit's Black community. During the early days of the UAW, Black unionists also respected the positions taken on racial issues by other Jewish leftists in Detroit, including William Weinstone, Nat Ganley, and Henry Krause.[14]

Perhaps these Jews drew upon personal experiences of anti-Semitism and compared them with the African American struggle against racism in Detroit in order to convince Black workers to join the unions. However, given the racially polarized and anti-Semitic climate of Detroit in the 1930s and early 1940s, these leftists very likely saw racism and anti-Semitism as products of the same flawed and corrupt capitalist system. Saul Wellman, a Jewish Communist appointed as the CP's national auto coordinator and sent to Detroit in 1946, was of the opinion that his and most Jewish Communists' activities on behalf of African Americans in the 1930s, 1940s, and early 1950s did not take on any special meaning derived from a common heritage of persecution. Rather, Jewish Communists generally followed the party line on racial matters, just as Gentile party members were expected to do. Wellman suppressed his Jewishness; only after traveling to Israel some years later was he able to begin to deal with his ethnic identity in a way that acknowledged his earlier denial of the problem of anti-Semitism.[15]

The Impact of World War II on Workers in Detroit

Although fewer than 4,000 of Detroit's Jews worked in automobile factories at any one time during the period (there were 2,347 in 1935 and 3,500

14. *Michigan Worker*, November 5, 1932, and miscellaneous materials in Henry Krause Papers, box 16, Walter P. Reuther Archives of Labor and Urban Affairs, Detroit (hereafter cited as ALUA); on Nowell see "UAW Appoints Negro Red," *Detroit Saturday Night*, October 23, 1937; Christopher H. Johnson, *Maurice Sugar, Law, Labor, and the Left in Detroit, 1912–1950* (Detroit: Wayne State University Press, 1988), 37, 158–61.
15. Interview with Saul Wellman, Baltimore, Md., April 1992.

in 1950), there were more Jewish autoworkers during the war years. Defense employment was one of the more significant ways in which Jews could express their patriotism as well as aid their persecuted coreligionists in Europe. Whether they were the 350 Jewish members of UAW Local 600, a local whose history suggested it would have the most Jewish autoworkers, or the employees of a small UAW-organized shop where fewer than a dozen Black and Jewish workers toiled, Jews had few confrontations with Blacks because, as one Black union leader saw it, there were too few Jews to be a problem.[16]

During the war years, the number of unionized working-class Jews in Detroit declined. Those who can be labeled as blue-collar workers were the last generational vestige of earlier Jewish skilled and unskilled workers who labored in Detroit factories or made their living at various skilled crafts. The other group of Jewish workers was only temporarily employed in defense industries during the war.

According to officials within the Jewish community, more Jews entered factory work in Detroit during a six-month stretch of 1942 than in the previous ten years. Many of these newcomers were said to have been attracted to the city by employment opportunities. While it is difficult to speculate on exactly how many were employed or whether they were all unionized, we can assume by the growth of industrial unionism throughout the city that most eventually joined.

Unfortunately, it was reported that they were subjected to organized rumormongering, barbed jokes, and satiric verses that denigrated them because they were Jews. One of the most popular attacks alleged that Jews were either Communists or on the side of war-profiteering international bankers. It was not uncommon for anti-Semitic flyers to be passed out during the noon hour in war plants around the city, several of which were said to have anti-Semitic employment practices that sometimes led them to dismiss their Jewish employees.[17]

Many of these Jewish workers, who held occupations ranging from superintendents to watchmen, blamed their inability to advance on anti-Semitism. One maintenance man in a large unionized plant believed that

16. Henry J. Meyer, "The Economic Structure of the Jewish Community in Detroit," *Jewish Social Studies*, April 1940, 3–24; interview with Shelton Tappes, January 30, 1987, Detroit; Joseph Billups, oral history, 1967, p. 10, ALUA; Negro Union Leader-Special Informant, "Detroit People in Perspective," p. 125, U.S. Department of Agriculture for Office of War Information, October 28, 1943, Rensis Likert Collection, box 9, Michigan Historical Collections, Ann Arbor (hereafter cited as MHC).
17. "Detroit People in Perspective, The Ethnic Axis: Jews," pp. 2–3, 6–7, MHC.

since Hitler had started persecuting the Jews, prejudice against Jews had "spread like wildfire," and he felt he had to work twice as hard because he was Jewish. Many Jews employed in various factories were said to have quit after only a few weeks because of the intense prejudice or to have been fired as a result of false reports and accusations made against them.

Unlike their Jewish counterparts, African Americans increased their numbers among the city's working class, particularly within the automobile factories and the UAW, during the 1940s. In 1941 Ford Local 600 had nearly twelve thousand African American members, three times the number of Jewish workers ever employed in the entire auto industry in Detroit. Peaking at some twenty thousand during the heyday of wartime defense production, the number still remained fairly high at fifteen thousand in 1950.[18] As one group evolved into a politically potent proletariat, the other became even more white collar and middle class. Despite such economic and occupational disparities, they were both informal and formal allies in an expanding New Deal order that espoused liberal and progressive racial policies inside and outside the Motor City. Detroit's wartime industrial economy especially provided the opportunity for informal alliances and cooperation between African Americans and Jews who applied for defense employment and confronted the problems of increasing racism and anti-Semitism.

Even though African Americans and Jews had relatively limited contact in Detroit's wartime industries, they were both mindful that they faced some of the same problems of employment discrimination. Such realization did not always suppress the anxiety that some Jewish workers felt as an increasing number of African American workers penetrated their workplaces and neighborhoods during the war years. While most Jewish wartime workers felt that African Americans deserved as much of a chance to work as everyone else, and few objected to working on the job with Blacks, their attitude often depended on whether new Black workers posed a threat to their own job security. The same maintenance worker who felt he had to work twice as hard because he was Jewish "flinched at the thought" of having to work directly with African Americans and viewed them as a threat to his job and social status. Although he admitted that "they are people too," he felt that since unionization (in this case by the UAW), Blacks had become "too bossy and sassy." More-

18. William D. Andrew, "Factionalism and Anti-Communism in Ford Local 600," *Labor History* 20 (spring 1979): 227–55.

over, he felt that Blacks should have been confined to the Hastings Street district (the center of Detroit's African American community) because they were "spoiling other neighborhoods." African Americans had begun to move into his neighborhood, but he doubted that they would penetrate his block.[19] A Jewish chemist who felt he had been denied a promotion because he was Jewish gained some measure of satisfaction when he learned that the company would be hiring Black chemists who had passed their entrance examinations. He readily identified with African Americans as fellow sufferers and reveled in the fact that the company managers had to hire members of a group he assumed they disliked more than Jews.[20]

The responses of African American workers toward Jews also were mixed. While some saw Jews as a possible cause of the war, others barely thought twice about them in the workplace because their numbers were so few. African Americans held the greatest animosity toward the southern White migrants because they brought their racial attitudes with them and were hired over Blacks by most industrial firms. Most of Detroit's Black workers felt a great deal of patriotism about producing war materials and about the need for unity among all of the city's citizens, whether Jew, southern White, native White, or European immigrant. Yet some held distinct reservations about the nature of the war and felt that African Americans and European Jews had the most to lose. When asked in 1942 what the war was about, and the effect an Axis victory might produce, one Black worker replied: "Damned if I know. For freedom, that's what they [Whites] say, but they aren't so much interested in the colored people being free. They just don't want Hitler and Japan to come over here and make slaves out of them. They might enslave the colored people too, but Hitler killed up all the Jews and they [Jews] are afraid they are going to come over here and do the same."[21]

This was the context in which Black and Jewish unionized factory workers associated with one another in Detroit's war industries, which revolved around large automobile factories and the UAW. Several Detroit UAW locals, most notably Ford Local 600 and Plymouth Local 51, but also Locals 155, 280, and 742, dealt with the disruptive influences of racism and anti-Semitism within their locals throughout the late 1930s and 1940s. An important ingredient in the political and ethnic/racial composition of these locals was the role of those influential Jewish and

19. "Detroit People in Perspective, The Ethnic Axis: Jews," pp. 11–13, MHC.
20. Ibid., 11.
21. "Detroit People in Perspective, The Ethnic Axis: Negroes," MHC.

African American members of the CP and fellow travelers who became leaders within the locals.

The Jewish Presence in Detroit's Unions during World War II

According to leftist sources, the percentage of Jews in leadership positions in Detroit's CIO locals, including the UAW, during the war years was far in excess of the percentage of Jews in the unions as a whole. While few Jews held elective office in the UAW for the obvious reason that there were so few in the industry, their number in the administrative offices of the international and local unions in Detroit was said to be "fairly high." Although sources close to the union movement and the Jewish community felt that Jewish leadership in the CIO, and in other Detroit labor organizations, was disproportionately high in relation to Jewish numerical strength in the unions, this provided Jewish union members with the opportunity to play an especially important role in mediating ethnic and racial conflict within the city's working class.

Prominent labor activists in the UAW, such as attorney Maurice Sugar, the UAW's legal counsel, and CP leader Nat Ganley, did not openly publicize their Jewishness for fear anti-Semites and anticommunist extremists would attack them because of their heritage. It became standard communist policy to convince Jewish labor organizers to change their names, but even those who did, like Ganley (Kaplan), were still said to be "handicapped" by their "Semitic appearance."[22]

Once the war began, local Communists, including Ganley and other Jewish unionists in Detroit, made no reservations about publicizing their "Jewishness" in leftist publications. Twenty Jewish American trade union officials issued appeals to the Jewish community to give wholehearted support to President Franklin Delano Roosevelt's policy of aid to American allies. In August 1942 more than two hundred Jewish unionists nationwide signed a call for the production of tanks and planes for the Red Army and the opening of a second front in Europe to save Russian Jews. Among the signatories were Ganley; Robert Lieberman of Ford Local 600; Daniel Avrunin, the educational director of Packard Local 190; Jack Ellstein of the Amalgamated Clothing Workers; Jack Kaller, the busi-

22. "Survey of Racial and Religious Conflict Forces in Detroit," vii–viii, study conducted by the Civil Rights Federation of Michigan, September 10–30, 1943, copy in Metropolitan Detroit Jewish Community Council Papers, Detroit. On Communist name changing see Harvey Levenstein, *Communism, Anti-Communism, and the CIO* (Westport, Conn.: Greenwood Press, 1981), 44; on Ganley's Semitic appearance see Bert Cochran, *Labor and Communism* (Princeton: Princeton University Press, 1977), 111.

ness agent of AFL Carpenters Local 1513; Robert Wolper and Isaac Litwak of the Detroit Teamsters union; Leo Polk of the Laundry Workers Union; Henry Sazer, the president of AFL Local 59 United Hat and Capmakers; Norman Siegel of CIO Local 79, State, City, and Municipal Workers; and Jerome Shore, the regional director of the CIO's United Office and Professional Workers.[23]

Observers sympathetic to the left at this time concluded that because of their Marxist ideological orientation, Jewish labor activists, such as Sugar, Ganley, and Sam Sweet of Plymouth Local 51, had a keen insight into the class and racial conflicts that beset the Motor City's employer-employee relationships. Finding a solution to racial and ethnic conflicts within organized labor in Detroit posed an important opportunity for Jewish leadership, "more so than leaders in other minority groups including [N]egroes."[24] The core Black and Jewish unionists in Ford Local 600 and Plymouth Local 51 were aggressive in challenging the racial discrimination and anti-Semitism that plagued their locals and permeated organized labor in Detroit in the 1930s and 1940s.

Communist Influence on Detroit's Unions

Ford Local 600 became the largest local union in the world after the successful UAW-CIO organizing drive of 1941. During the war years the membership grew to nearly eighty-four thousand, almost 20 percent of whom were African Americans, employed mostly in the foundry. An unofficial racial, ethnic, and religious survey conducted by the UAW claimed that approximately 350 Jewish workers were members of the local between 1942 and 1945. The mixed ethnic and racial character of Local 600's workforce, and the work of the Communist-supported Auto Workers Union (AWU) in the late 1920s and early 1930s, created a greater sense of racial, ethnic, and class solidarity than was common for most UAW locals during the war years. Yet racism, anti-Semitism, and anti-communism plagued Local 600 as well.[25]

The CP and AWU played key roles in developing the political and ideological philosophy of Local 600 prior to the formation of the UAW in 1935. Thereafter, the CP continued to wield decisive influence within the local, especially among African American, Polish, Italian, and Jewish

23. *Jewish Survey*, October 1941; "212 Jewish Labor Leaders Call: Tanks and Bombers for the Red Army," *Jewish Survey*, August 1942, 6–7, 29.
24. "Survey of Racial and Religious Conflict Forces," viii.
25. Billups, oral history, 5–20; Joe Pagano, oral history, 1960, ALUA; Keeran, *Communist Party and Auto Workers Unions*, 40–56; Andrew, "Factionalism and Anti-Communism," 228–55.

workers. The CP emphasized the necessity of ethnic and racial unity among the workers and sought to create a sense of "indigenous trade union awareness" by focusing on shop issues, labor-management relations, and progressive domestic policies and attacking racism and red-baiting.[26]

The Communist faction consistently supported the election of African Americans to union offices, and its overall racial philosophy served to attract a number of Blacks to the left-wing fold. Some, such as Nelson Davis, joined the CP and remained devoted throughout their lives. Davis, who lacked any formal education beyond the third grade, owed much of his knowledge about trade union issues to CP schools operating within the factory. As one student of the local has shown, "membership in the Party and work in Party schools were for the black worker a means for the furtherance of union goals and a means for personal and racial advancement." Black Communist Arthur McPhaul openly sold party literature and was elected district committeeman in 1943 when the left gained control of leadership positions within the local. The district committeeman held a key position and one the party worked vigorously to secure because this individual had a greater opportunity to mobilize workers and usually had a close relationship with the education and publication departments of the local.[27]

By the same token, Blacks who were not CP members, such as Shelton Tappes, were a part of the "progressive coalition" of Local 600, and they readily accepted party support and agreed to participate in party-sponsored functions in Detroit during the war. The heightened racial and ethnic tensions in the city at that time led Tappes to bring up at party-sponsored union gatherings his concern with the increasing anti-Semitism in the city's industries. He understood that anti-Semitism was as dangerous as were the pervasive anti-Black attitudes.[28]

Among the most active Black members of Local 600's left wing were Tappes, Davis, Dave Moore, Joseph Billups, and Arthur McPhaul. The most active Jewish members were Robert Lieberman, Max Chait, Morris Feldman, and Saul Galemba. While the left-wing faction extended beyond Blacks and Jews and included members of several ethnic groups,

26. Ibid.
27. Billups, oral history, 28; interview with Dave Moore, April 10, 1987, Detroit; Andrew, "Factionalism and Anti-Communism," 234–35; Frank Marquart, *An Auto Worker's Journal: The UAW from Crusade to One-Party System* (University Park: Pennsylvania State University Press, 1975).
28. "Testimony of Shelton Tappes," March 12, 1952, House Un-American Activities Hearings, Detroit, *Communism in the Detroit Area* (Washington, D.C.: GPO, 1952).

Local 600 also had perhaps an even stronger Catholic element that sought to attract ethnic workers but was decidedly anticommunist. Catholic workers in the UAW organized around the Association of Catholic Trade Unionists (ACTU), which was created in the late 1930s to combat Communist influence within organized labor. The members of the ACTU in Local 600 struggled with the Communist-backed left wing for political control within the local throughout the war years. The association's vice president, Paul St. Marie, was Local 600 president from 1941 to 1943. The left gained control of the local in 1943 and 1944, only to be defeated by the ACTU right-wing group in 1945. It was not uncommon for "Negro-baiting, Jew-baiting and red-baiting" to become intertwined with the political factionalism that became pervasive. Noncommunist African Americans who commented on the racial and political climate of Local 600 during the war agreed that "every man who labors for a living believes in some form of communism . . . and by travelling with such fellows the Negro has advanced in the Ford industrial set up today."[29]

Jewish CP member Robert Lieberman was in the forefront on racial issues affecting Black members of Local 600, as well as Black Detroiters in general. He was one of the first Whites to argue in favor of occupational upgrading for Black workers in Local 600, and he, as chairman of the local's War Policy Committee, and Shelton Tappes appeared before the Detroit Housing Commission at its first open meeting to discuss biracial housing in Detroit. According to Tappes, Lieberman was one of the most politically astute unionists he ever met and could "cut through any issue as soon as he heard it." Lieberman was one of three individuals responsible for educating Tappes in the main principles of trade unionism.[30]

Just prior to and immediately after the Detroit riot in June 1943, racial and ethnic tensions reached dangerous levels in Ford's River Rouge plant. Local 600's educational director warned the rank and file of the "noxious growth of factionalism" that used "Negro-baiting, Jew-baiting and red-baiting" as a tactic of dissension. He stressed that if the anti-Semites continued to freely distribute their printed "garbage" and were permitted to carry out their nefarious designs, it would not be long until Poles, Italians, and Negroes would also be attacked.[31]

29. Keeran, *Communist Party and Auto Workers Unions,* 254; Andrew, "Factionalism and Anti-Communism," 235; "I'd Rather Be Right," *Michigan Chronicle,* March 1943.

30. "Seek Showdown on Jim Crow Housing," *Michigan Chronicle,* May 1, 1943; "Letter to the Editor," *Michigan Chronicle,* May 29, 1943; Tappes interview, January 30, 1987; Moore interview, April 10, 1987; Keeran, *Communist Party and Auto Workers Unions,* 235.

31. Local 600, *Ford Facts,* August–October 1943.

Blacks and Jews in Local 600 also actively challenged discrimination outside the plant. Sometime during 1943, the local formed an integrated bowling team whose Black members were denied admittance to the Detroit Recreation Center. Jewish members of the local, led by Max Chait and Morris Goldstein, formed a picket line to protest against the recreation center's discrimination. The two leaders were attacked verbally by local Whites for being "Jew Nigger lovers" and were barred from the center. It was only after city officials promised to prosecute the center's administrators for violating the Diggs state civil rights law, which barred racial discrimination in public places, that they changed their policies.[32]

During the late summer and fall of 1943, anti-Semitic propaganda was deeply entrenched inside the plant. Mayoral candidate Edward Carey, a follower of the controversial radio priest Father Charles Coughlin, passed out leaflets attacking the city's withholding tax as "the 20% Jewish snatch racket." While admitting that few Jews worked in the auto plants, Carey claimed that those who did "wormed themselves into positions of influence and authority" and used "typical Jewish tactics" of attempting to turn Polish and native southern White workers against each other while telling Black workers that all the Whites were against them, except for the Jews. Carey's anti-Semitic campaign drew few supporters, even among Ford workers.[33]

During the union elections in 1945, Local 600 was one of several UAW locals in the Detroit area that reported widespread incidents of anti-Semitism and racial harassment. The incidents drew the attention of UAW officials and concerned unionists because they were flagrant violations of UAW policy. For union officials the paramount issue was how to separate anti-Semitism and racism as factors in the defeat of Black and Jewish candidates from charges of "communism, big-headedness, infidelity to official responsibilities, voting lethargy on the part of known supporters, loss of popularity, and just plain factionalism." While informal investigations indicated that anti-Semitism and race-baiting had cropped up in the elections of some dozen locals, they were most often associated with at least one of the other factors. Without formal complaints filed in accordance with procedures found in the union's constitution, the members of the union's Fair Practices Committee (FPC) had

32. Moore interview, April 10, 1987.
33. "Seek to Stop Anti-Semitic Literature," *Michigan Chronicle,* August 25, 1943; "Anti-Jewish Propaganda Turns Up in Rouge Plant," Local 600, *Ford Facts,* October 1943; comments of Edward Carey in "Survey of Racial and Religious Conflict Forces," 15–19.

strong reservations about interfering in the affairs of the locals. Yet, mindful that intolerance grew "by degrees and thrived on inaction," union officials searched for a way to maintain "due regard for local union autonomy on the one hand, and the danger of complete control of the UAW by fascist-minded anti–trade union elements on the other."[34]

One way in which the UAW attempted to confront the problems of racism and anti-Semitism in the aftermath of the union elections was by holding educational seminars for its leaders. The first of what was to become an annual affair was held in the summer of 1945 and involved officials not only from the UAW but also from the national CIO, the Detroit NAACP, and the DUL as well as members of the president's wartime Fair Employment Practices Committee (FEPC). The main theme of the initial conference was how organized labor could lead the way in overcoming racial and religious intolerance in the United States. Considerable attention was given to anti-Semitism and race-baiting in local union elections, discriminatory layoffs, and how antidiscrimination clauses and seniority provisions could be placed in union contracts for the benefit of all minority workers, especially African Americans. The thirteen Black members of the UAW's international staff participated regularly in these discussions and seminars, along with Jewish administrative officials, including attorney Ernest Goodaman, an associate of Maurice Sugar in the union's legal department.[35]

The Failed Campaigns for Black Representation in UAW Leadership

Racial discrimination against African Americans, and to a lesser extent anti-Semitism, continued to be a serious problem for the UAW throughout the late 1940s and 1950s. Yet the single most important issue that affected Blacks and Jews aligned with the left-wing faction in the UAW was the struggle to have an African American elected to the UAW's International Executive Board (IEB). This controversy developed as more and more African Americans began to join the union and was a reflection of their desire for a share in the union's political power. Throughout this period African American representation in leadership positions was an issue that plagued the national CIO and many of its affiliates with a substantial Black membership. The issue became highly divisive because it highlighted the problems of race, ethnicity, and political ideology within

34. George W. Crockett, "Labor Looks Ahead," *Michigan Chronicle*, May 26, 1945.
35. "National UAW-CIO Advisory Conference on Discrimination," July 27, 1945, Michigan AFL-CIO Collection, box 78, ALUA.

the unions. It became the topic of discussion in various UAW locals in Detroit in the late 1930s and gained unionwide attention at the annual convention in 1942.[36]

At the 1942 convention, Black unionists, including Hodges Mason and James Walker of Local 205, Shelton Tappes, Joe Billups, Nelson Davis, and Horace Sheffield from Local 600, along with William Lattimore of Dodge Local 3, John Conyers Sr. of Chrysler Local 7, and Walter Hardin, an international representative, had created a visible "Negro caucus" within the UAW and laid plans to see one of their own elected to the union's IEB. Yet the nearly one hundred Black delegates to the convention were not in complete agreement on how to achieve this goal. According to Mason, a central figure in the left-wing faction, their strategy was to run an African American for the IEB vice presidency, even though many left-wing unionists had serious objections. Undaunted, Mason nominated Oscar Noble from the floor of the convention, but to the shock of his colleagues, Noble declined the nomination, probably at the urging of CIO President Philip Murray.[37]

Over the next several months the Black caucus regrouped to reformulate its strategy for confronting the ongoing racial discrimination and race-baiting within UAW locals and many auto plants. In November 1942 the caucus members organized the Metropolitan Labor Council of Detroit for the express purpose of pressing specific cases of discrimination that the international union did not actively seek to resolve. The membership of the council expanded beyond the UAW to include Blacks in other CIO unions, as well as those in local AFL unions, such as the Hotel and Restaurant Employees Union, which had a growing Black membership. Moreover, the council was an integrated group in which

36. The earliest discussion of this controversy is in Irving Howe and B. J. Widick's *The UAW and Walter Reuther* (New York: Random House, 1949), 223–25, but it is biased because of the authors' overt anticommunism. For a more balanced assessment see Meier and Rudwick, *Black Detroit*, 208–12, and Martin Halpern, *UAW Politics in the Cold War Era* (Albany: State University of New York Press, 1988), 99–100, 212–14.

37. *Proceedings of the Seventh Convention of the United Automobile Workers of America* (Detroit, 1942), 301–3. This conflict was also exacerbated by members of the Black caucus themselves, as egos clashed over who the Black board member would be. Most of the evidence we have to draw from comes from the reminiscences of the leading Black participants, Tappes, Sheffield, and Mason, and from the Detroit Black press. Some Black unionists backed the idea of a board member at-large, while others supported the idea of nominating one of their own for a vice presidential position. Most leaned toward the board member at-large position because the Executive Board was thinking of creating another vice presidency, and past practice indicated it would be established based on industries under UAW jurisdiction. The next in line after automobiles and aircraft was farm implements, in which fewer Blacks worked.

sympathetic and progressive White—and most noticeably—Jewish unionists, took part.[38]

The formation of the Metropolitan Labor Council came at a time when leftist forces in various CIO unions in and around Detroit were consolidating their power in the Wayne County CIO Industrial Union Council. The Metropolitan Council in effect was a subgrouping of the progressive forces in the Wayne County CIO Council. As early as 1941, the Wayne County CIO Council established its Committee on Negro Work to deal with the problems of its African American members, and by 1943, when the committee was said to have come under Communist control, it was reestablished as the Race Relations Committee. The Wayne County CIO Council became one of the main venues in which Black, Jewish, and progressive White unionists could come together to plot their strategy for gaining more representation within the union. This was especially the case after Mason was elected vice president of the Wayne County CIO Council in 1943. While the Jewish Communists in Detroit's UAW, led by Ganley, Lieberman, and Sweet, were the most outspoken in their support for Black representation, others, including Jerome Shore of the local United Office and Professional Workers Association and Harold Shapiro of the International Fur and Leather Workers, were also important voices for Blacks' demands. Still others, such as Sugar (at the behest of the CP leadership), worked to persuade the leadership of the UAW to add a Black attorney to its staff.[39]

On the eve of the 1943 UAW convention, Black union members concluded that the majority of White delegates and officers would have to respond to the "need for official representation on the part of Negroes," in light of the increased racism in Detroit and the auto factories over the preceding year.[40] Although the debate over a Black board member or vice president has been discussed elsewhere, several aspects of this issue have been overlooked or glossed over. One concerns the "unity" of the Black caucus over the final form and content of the resolution to be presented to the convention. The other concerns the attitude of many White UAW members toward Jews as a minority in the union, and the position that Jews took on the resolutions.

---

38. *Michigan Chronicle*, November 4, 1943; Tappes interview, January 30, 1987.

39. Wayne County CIO "Minutes (1941)," box 30, Wayne County AFL-CIO Collection, ALUA; Shelton Tappes, oral history, 1967, p. 63, ALUA; interview with Harold Shapiro, January 31, 1987; Halpern, *UAW Politics*, 216; William Patterson to Maurice Sugar, July 17, 1942, Maurice Sugar Collection, box 5, ALUA.

40. "Hardin, Sheffield Urge New UAW Post," *Michigan Chronicle*, September 18, 1943.

The apparent absence of unity within the Black caucus can best be explained in terms of the political leanings and affiliations of its members. While no one individual could be considered the leader of the caucus, several individuals stood out and were considered by their peers and the local Black press as leaders. These were Shelton Tappes, Hodges Mason, Walter Hardin, and Horace Sheffield. All four had been among the earliest of Detroit's Black autoworkers to respond to unionization, and all had played crucial roles in the Ford organizing drive in 1941. Both Tappes and Mason came from leftist and communist-influenced locals, and both relied on leftist support for election to union office. Sheffield and Hardin, on the other hand, leaned more toward the right-wing faction of the UAW. Hardin was an international representative of the union and not affiliated with any particular local. Although Sheffield was a member of Local 600, he worked under Ford director Richard Leonard, who was a member of the Walter Reuther camp within the UAW leadership at this time.[41]

Throughout the late 1930s, Walter Reuther had positioned himself to become a part of the leadership of the UAW. In 1937, during the General Motors sit-down strike, he was the leader of UAW Local 174, which organized the workers of the Kelsey-Hayes Wheel Company. He also became a leader in the union's "unity" caucus, which at this time contained all the radical elements within the union. In the aftermath of the 1939 UAW convention, he was appointed director of the union's General Motor's Department and a vice president in the union. Over the next seven years he methodically built a coalition of "right-wing" supporters whose members ranged from Catholics to Trotskyite Socialists. While the UAW's "right wing" was decidedly left of center in general American political terminology, its main characteristic and attraction was its ardent anticommunism.[42]

Shortly before the 1943 convention, Hardin and Sheffield issued statements to the Black press about the need to create a new post in the UAW concerned with minority issues. They stated that much discussion had taken place as to how this was to be achieved, either by moving for a board member at-large or by creating a third vice president's position. Whatever the approach, it was necessary to nominate the best qualified person. Under the existing union organization, Black union members

41. Horace Sheffield, oral history, 1968, p. 7, ALUA; Meier and Rudwick, *Black Detroit,* 209–12; on Richard Leonard see Jack Stieber, *Governing the UAW* (New York: John Wiley and Sons, 1962), 8; and Babson *Working Detroit,* 142.
42. Nelson Lichtenstein, *The Most Dangerous Man in Detroit: Walter Reuther and the Fate of American Labor* (New York: Basic Books, 1995), 60–103, 123–31; Halpern, *UAW Politics,* 24–27, 95–131.

held little hope of one of their own rising up through the ranks and successfully securing a nomination and the votes needed to become a regional director or a vice president of the international union.[43]

It became clear during the weeks before the convention actually convened that the idea of nominating an African American for a newly created vice presidency held little chance of success. Although the leaders of both factions went on record in support of an African American board member, the arguments voiced by the Reuther-led faction once the final resolutions were presented to the convention foreshadowed defeat for the entire effort.[44]

As a member of the resolutions committee, Tappes presented a plan calling for the creation of a "minorities department" within the international union, headed by an African American who would also be a member of the union's IEB. Jewish Communist Nat Ganley, a member of the constitutional committee that decided what resolutions would be presented to the convention's delegates for approval or rejection, agreed to support the resolution. However, Ganley met opposition to the resolution from the other members of the nine-man constitutional committee. After some discussion, two proposals were put forth. The committee's "majority report" called for the UAW president to appoint the head of the minorities department, subject to the approval of the IEB. The "minority report," presented by Ganley, called for the convention to elect the department head, who would also serve as a member of the IEB. The first reading of the minority resolution by Ganley stated that an African American should head the minorities department.[45]

In an effort to rally support for the minority resolution, Mason emphasized to the convention delegates that Blacks were not asking for "special favors," because 27 percent of the union's membership was composed of "Negroes, Jews, Mexicans and so forth." The new union position was meant to be a safeguard against discrimination for all minorities. Nevertheless, Walter Reuther argued against the minority resolution as an extension of "Jim Crow" and special privilege, since the appointee would be chosen solely on the basis of his color, not his ability. His brother Victor Reuther continued by stressing that if there was "a special

43. "Hardin, Sheffield Urge New UAW Post," *Michigan Chronicle*, September 18, 1943.

44. "Addes-Frankensteen to Support Proposal for UAW Board Member," *Michigan Chronicle*, September 25, 1943; "Reuther for Negro on UAW Board," *Michigan Chronicle*, October 2, 1943.

45. *Proceedings of the Eighth Convention of the United Automobile Workers of America* (Detroit, 1943), 370.

post for Negroes then in all justice there should be a post for Catholics, women, Jews, and Poles." Union President R. J. Thomas further pointed out that Jews in the UAW were also discriminated against—he knew delegates at the convention who discriminated against them. Thomas asked the delegates if any of them thought that if an African American were elected, he would be able to solve the problems for Jewish members. His own opinion was resoundingly negative.[46]

With such opposition from the right-wing faction, and even from Thomas, who had been one of the staunchest supporters of Black rights in the union and in Detroit's Black community in the aftermath of the June 1943 riot, support among Black delegates also began to wane. Several Black delegates from locals in Detroit where African Americans had been in a minority, and who nonetheless were elected to office, spoke against the minority resolution. They felt that each local should be able to work out its own racial problems without any help from the international union. After a meeting of the Black caucus, it was decided to remove any racial designation for the minorities department head. Ganley stated before the convention that, "while the minority report does not make it mandatory that a Negro be a director of the Minority Department," he felt confident that "this great International convention would want to demonstrate to the entire nation our policy of racial solidarity by electing a Negro to this post." At this point, however, Sheffield spoke against the resolution's call for a Black board member, while still supporting the creation of a minorities department. This declaration so infuriated Mason that he came to blows with Sheffield's ally Walter Hardin on the floor of the convention.[47]

In a final attempt to convince convention delegates of the overwhelming obstacles Blacks faced in the union, Tappes emphasized that this was a racial question, not an ethnic or religious issue. Catholics, Poles, and Jews would have been able to enter the St. Louis hotels where the UAW had first considered holding the 1943 convention, but the hotels discriminated against African Americans, so the convention was moved. "We are just asking for a chance. If we [the union] don't like [the resolution], throw it out."[48]

46. Ibid., 373–78; Keeran, *Communist Party and Auto Workers Unions*, 233–34; Howe and Widdick, *The UAW and Walter Reuther*, 223–25.

47. *Proceedings of Eighth UAW Convention*, 380–86; Hodges Mason, oral history, 1967, pp. 29–30; "Delegates Battle over UAW Board Post," *Michigan Chronicle*, October 9, 1943; "Sheffield Explains Position on UAW Issue," *Michigan Chronicle*, October 23, 1943.

48. *Proceedings of Eighth UAW Convention*, 386–87; "What Local 600 Convention Delegates Said," *Ford Facts*, October 15, 1943.

Ultimately, the measures for a Black board member and a minorities department went down to defeat. This was the first significant confrontation over what some twenty years later would be labeled "affirmative action." The idea of so-called racial preferences split the various ethnic groups among the rank and file along both racial and political lines and even caused divisions within minority groups. Only a minority of the Jewish members, those closely aligned with the left, supported the minority resolution. Two of the Jewish members of the constitutional committee supported it, Tom De Lorenzo and Nat Ganley, the lone Communist on the committee (however, because of his fear of anti-Semitism, only De Lorenzo's closest associates even knew he was Jewish).[49]

As for African Americans in the UAW at this time, the majority of the 150 Black delegates to the convention supported the minority resolution, while Sheffield and Hardin, as well as delegates from Detroit Locals 50 and 157, opposed the measure. A Black member of Local 50 explained that there were five or six thousand Blacks in Local 50 out of a total membership of some thirty-five thousand. He felt that the two Black members of the local's executive board had been elected as "unionists not Negroes."[50]

The African Americans and Jews who joined together in support of the minority resolution always insisted that the person chosen *must* be qualified. Ganley later pointed out that there were "a large number of Negro UAW leaders who were as qualified, if not more so, than many of the people who were elected." Mason claimed that Walter Reuther told him face-to-face at the convention that there was not a Black qualified to be a member of the UAW's executive board. A delegate from Reuther's own Local 174 declared before the convention that he did not believe the UAW should go on record endorsing "black participation in social life. . . . I would never go to any union function and take my wife and daughter when they were supposed to mingle socially with the Negro race." In such a racially polarized setting, one in which autoworkers allegedly connected with a Ku Klux Klan offshoot known as the United Sons of America paraded around the convention floor, Black unionists experienced a bittersweet glimpse of "interracial unionism." It was

49. *Proceedings of Eighth UAW Convention*, 380–89; information on Tom De Lorenzo was obtained through correspondence from Al Nash of Cornell University, February 23, 1987; interview with B. J. Widdick, April 6, 1987, Ann Arbor, Mich. Nash, who is also Jewish, was a former autoworker in UAW Local 365 in New York City (1940–1945) and Chrysler Local 7 in Detroit (1949–1953). De Lorenzo was president of Local 365 during the 1940s.
50. *Proceedings of Eighth UAW Convention*, 377.

a kind of unionism that rhetorically deplored racism and anti-Semitism but made minimal effort to actively curb their presence inside the union.[51]

Union leaders, such as Thomas and the Reuthers, made a distinction between the type of discrimination found within the union that affected both Blacks and Jews and the need for the appointment of an African American to an important and influential position on the UAW's executive board. Moreover, while admitting to the entire convention that he personally knew anti-Semites in the union, Thomas offered no solution or action to stop them from persecuting Jewish union members. Instead, he argued that an African American could not help curb discrimination against Jews in the UAW and implicitly admitted he was not prepared to challenge the discrimination that existed against both groups through the proposed minority resolution.

The issue of black representation intensified over the next several years and became even more complex with the rise of overt anticommunism within the CIO and UAW. The issue was distorted over questions about the ability of the individual to be chosen and whether or not the entire idea was nothing more than "an extension of policy from the Soviet Union." Communist support of African American aspirations within the union created a complex dilemma for noncommunist Jews and other progressive Whites sympathetic to Black concerns. Black unionists as well faced a difficult time choosing the best approach to achieve their goal.

In the aftermath of the convention, members of the UAW's Black caucus were able to impress upon the union's leadership the idea that some kind of measure was needed to demonstrate genuine concern for African American aspirations. In November 1943, the IEB passed a resolution calling for every regional director and department head to have an African American on his staff. In the late spring of 1944 George W. Crockett, a recent graduate of the University of Michigan Law School who was working as a hearing commissioner for the FEPC, happened to travel from Detroit to Washington, D.C., in the company of UAW President Thomas. According to Crockett, Thomas expressed a concern over increasing racism and anti-Semitism in Detroit and feared that it would reach even more alarming levels in UAW plants and locals. By July,

51. Nat Ganley, oral history, 1960, p. 74, ALUA; Mason, oral history, 25; Keeran, *Communist Party and Auto Workers Unions,* 234; Civil Rights Congress of Michigan Collection, "Ku Klux Klan," box 16, ALUA.

Thomas had appointed Crockett as a consultant on minority affairs for the international union.[52]

Crockett was instrumental in promoting Black interests at the international level and became a central figure within the Black caucus. Although not a Communist, he felt the party and its sympathizers in the UAW were more militant about challenging racial discrimination and more attuned to minority concerns than was the Reuther faction. As he dealt with racial issues in the union, Crockett found that those union leaders who received Communist support, including George Addes, Richard Frankensteen, and Thomas, were the most responsive to issues affecting African Americans. Crockett and most Black unionists who sided with the left-wing faction, including Tappes and William Lattimore, realized they could never join the CP because party officials were devoted to promoting the interests of the Soviet Union. They chose instead to accept Communist support when it coincided with African American interests.

After the Black caucus again failed to elect an African American as UAW vice president at the 1944 convention, Crockett was able to convince Thomas and the IEB to create an internal fair practices committee to deal with cases of minority discrimination.[53] As director of the FPC, Crockett worked to resolve reported cases of racism and anti-Semitism inside the UAW. One of his major efforts was to convince the union to

52. George Crockett, oral history, 1967, ALUA; "Labor Record of George Crockett, Jr.," in Vertical File, ALUA; George W. Crockett, "Labor Looks Ahead," *Michigan Chronicle,* June 16, 1945.

53. With more than two hundred and fifty of the roughly two thousand delegates, Black unionists held a significant balance of power and were courted by both factions. Moreover, Black unionists and the local Black press felt that they had enough support to elect a Black vice president and defeat Walter Reuther in the process. Black unionist Leon Bates from Indianapolis was to be nominated for vice president. Bates, one of the earliest Black organizers in the UAW in Detroit, worked on the international staff of the union until he was assigned to work in Indianapolis in 1943. Meanwhile, Reuther ally Richard Leonard was convinced to turn against his friend by UAW President Thomas, who wanted to build a third faction within the union. When CIO President Murray was informed of Reuther's possible defeat, he began maneuvering to prevent such a development. According to Lattimore, the Black board member issue was pushed aside. While Frankensteen was able to defeat Reuther for the first vice presidency, Reuther emerged victorious over Leonard. Although members of the left in Local 600 led by President William G. Grant nominated Tappes for vice president, he declined. See Crockett, oral history; "Comments of William Lattimore, 26 January 1966," in Vertical File Biography of William Lattimore, ALUA. "Negroes Bid for Top UAW Post," *Pittsburgh Courier,* September 16, 1944; "Growing Negro Progress Shown at UAW-CIO Convention" and Horace Cayton, "UAW-CIO," *Pittsburgh Courier,* September 23, 1944.

actively enforce the November 1943 union resolution to employ more Blacks on the staffs of the international officers. This idea was opposed by Walter Reuther and several other UAW officers.[54]

Because of his success with the FPC, Crockett approached leading UAW officials about creating a permanent fair practices department. By the time of the 1946 convention, most UAW leaders, including Walter Reuther, were willing to support such a department. While Tappes and Mason still argued for an African American on the IEB, Crockett, although supportive of the idea, warned that if such a proposal came from the "ultra leftists," it would not only lose but also jeopardize the move for a permanent fair practices department.[55]

The 1946 UAW convention was significant for two reasons. Foremost was the election of Walter Reuther to the union's presidency, an event that marked the beginning of the end for the leftist faction within the UAW, led by Addes and Frankensteen. Underlying Reuther's victory was the African American board member issue. As in the past, both Blacks and Jews in the UAW played conspicuous roles in this debate. Since the 1943 convention, relations between Reuther and the Black caucus had been strained at best, and they took a further turn for the worse in 1946 when caucus members pointed to Reuther's moderate approach on racial issues in the union. The most recent example prior to the convention, according to Crockett, was Reuther's failure to see that an anti-discrimination clause was placed in the General Motors contract in 1945.[56]

In an effort to clarify further his position on the African American board member issue and to point out instances where he had worked to eliminate racial discrimination within the union, Reuther called a private meeting with the members of the Black caucus. Labeling the efforts of Black union members to see one of their own elected to the IEB board as "irresponsible politicking," Reuther again reduced the issue to one of race rather than representation. He argued that there was no short-cut solution to ending discrimination, especially if it involved "tricky maneuvering on top." Rather, "more aggressive action was needed in the local unions, and minds and hearts of the individual members." The key to

54. George Crockett to Jack Zeller, September 24, 1945, R. J. Thomas Collection, box 21, ALUA; "CIO Pledges $100,000 to Organize South," *Michigan Chronicle,* April 20, 1946.

55. "Labor Looks Ahead," *Michigan Chronicle,* March 30, 1946.

56. Crockett, oral history; George Crockett, "Labor Looks Ahead," *Michigan Chronicle,* March 23, 1946.

ending racial discrimination and anti-Semitism was creating full employment, full production, and increased consumption.[57]

Reuther's effort to convince Black caucus members of his commitment to equality changed few minds, even though he advocated a permanent dues-funded fair practices department within the union. On the floor of the convention, battle lines were drawn. The majority report called for the creation of a department with a director. The minority report called for the same, but the director would be a member of the IEB elected by the convention as a whole. Delegate Ben Garrison of Ford Local 400 attacked the majority report on the basis that it was promoted by the Communists within the union. As a Jew, Garrison did not ask for any special compensation for Jews in the UAW, implying that African Americans should not ask for any either. Another Jewish delegate related his experience of working in a town with "a lot of anti-Semitism and anti-Negroism" and went on record in support of the minority resolution. He emphasized, however, that he did not agree that the executive board member had to be an African American. Even though a number of Black, Jewish, and other White unionists were aware of the discrimination that minorities in the union faced, a core of leftist-oriented delegates (in addition to Communists) held the position that none had been as oppressed as African Americans, who deserved "real representation" in the form of an executive board member, if one was nominated under the terms of the minority resolution.[58]

Once votes were cast, the majority report was accepted and the former Fair Practices Committee headed by Crockett became the Fair Practices and Anti-Discrimination Department devoted to minority problems in the UAW. Although Reuther gained the presidency of the union that year, he lacked a majority on the executive board, and the next year and a half witnessed unprecedented factional infighting as the left tried to salvage its position of influence within the UAW. Reuther's victory also initiated a new era of UAW activism on racial issues within the union and the larger Detroit community.

The 1946 UAW convention thus marked the beginning of the end for the most controversial period in the union's history. Both African Americans and Jews had played crucial roles in the success of the union and had led the fight against the rampant racism and anti-Semitism among

57. Untitled and undated document in Walter P. Reuther Collection, box 89, ALUA.
58. *Proceedings of the Eleventh Convention of the United Automobile Workers of America* (Detroit, 1946), 103–17.

the rank and file. The most notable example of a Black-Jewish "alliance" within the union centered around the movement to see an African American elected to the union's executive board and involved Black and Jewish Communists and sympathizers. Over the course of the debate between 1943 and 1947, members of both groups disagreed over how an African American might win elected office. Some African Americans and Jews who had been able to win office in their local unions despite being in the minority saw no need for what appeared to be special preference for African Americans. Black Communist Art McPhaul of Local 600 concluded that even though "most of us clearly understand the necessity of making special provisions for Negroes when necessary, it is not logical to think we can get the average trade unionist to see this."[59] Indeed they did not.

Black and Jewish unionists aligned with the left spent the next several years regrouping within several UAW locals, most notably Ford Local 600 and Plymouth Local 51, and the Wayne County CIO Council. They actively promoted interracial cooperation and attacked racism and anti-Semitism inside organized labor in Detroit as well as in the surrounding community.[60]

Once Walter Reuther gained political control of the UAW executive council in 1947, however, he began a full-scale purge of his opposition. Regardless of whether one was an actual CP member or not, past association with the Communist faction in the union led to termination. Union pioneer Maurice Sugar, as well as prominent African American staff member George Crockett, felt the wrath of "the most dangerous man in Detroit."[61] A number of Jewish and African American members of the UAW and other left-leaning CIO unions, including Max Chait, Harold Shapiro, Dave Moore, and Detroit's future mayor, Coleman Young, all fell victim to the cold war hysteria that gripped the Motor City in the 1950s. The issue of seeing an African American elected to a leadership position never went away, however, even after Morehouse College graduate King Peterson was elected a UAW trustee in 1947 and Nelson Jack Edwards was actually elected to the executive council in 1962. By the early 1960s Reuther had backtracked from his position of some twenty

59. "Report on Negro Vice-President in UAW-CIO" (1947), Nat Ganley Collection, box 7, ALUA; "Drive to Elect Negro Vice President of UAW Started," *Michigan Chronicle,* October 25, 1947.
60. Halpern, *UAW Politics,* 212–22; Coleman Young and Lonnie Wheeler, *Hard Stuff: The Autobiography of Coleman Young* (New York: Viking Penguin, 1994), 91–105.
61. Lichtenstein, *Most Dangerous Man in Detroit,* 308–19; Johnson, *Maurice Sugar,* 296–98.

years earlier in light of the growing national Civil Rights Movement, in which he saw himself as a key player.[62]

Although Blacks and Jews on the left readily supported the earliest version of affirmative action to gain minority representation in the UAW leadership, the proposal also generated serious conflicts and disagreements among and between African American and Jewish trade unionists. CP-affiliated Jewish unionists supported the move to have an African American head the proposed minorities department, but they were in the minority among Jewish delegates. Basically, the Jewish unionists went along with the argument made by Thomas that discrimination against Jewish union members would not be addressed through the creation of a minorities department headed by an African American. While African American delegates were divided over the best strategy for obtaining Black representation in the union's national leadership, the vast majority supported the measure calling for the creation of a minorities department that would oversee the interests of all minority group members in the union. With the increasing attacks on Communists within the UAW at the outset of the cold war, the influence of Jewish leftists declined in Detroit's unions and African Americans lost important allies in their campaign to end discrimination and inequality in the organized labor movement in the Motor City.

62. Lichtenstein, *Most Dangerous Man*, 375–83; "King Peterson Elected to UAW Trustee Unit" and "An Ideal Leader," *Michigan Chronicle*, November 22, 1947.

Black-Jewish Conflict in the Labor Context

Race, Jobs, and Institutional Power

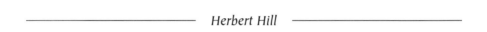

Herbert Hill

L ARGELY forgotten in the many discussions of Black-Jewish relations is the fact that the current conflict between the two groups was preceded by an older ongoing discord within the labor movement. Indeed, it may be argued that the antagonism that developed within labor unions is emblematic of the larger Black-Jewish conflict, one that has its roots in the profoundly different social conditions of Jewish Americans and African Americans.

Close scrutiny of the racial labor issues that developed soon after the merger in 1955 of the American Federation of Labor and the Congress of Industrial Organizations (AFL-CIO) reveals much about the characteristics of the subsequently strained relations between Blacks and Jews and the tensions between them. The years immediately following the merger were marked by widespread disappointment among African American workers as the AFL-CIO failed to implement the civil rights policy adopted with much fanfare at the time of the labor federation's formation. These were also the years of a great Black awakening, with the emergence of new militant Black protest movements in the North as well as in the South.

Soon after the merger, Black workers protested against the continuing pattern of discriminatory practices by many AFL-CIO-affiliated unions, both industrial and craft. The NAACP repeatedly documented discriminatory practices such as the inclusion of provisions in union contracts that limited Black workers to segregated job classifications, the widespread exclusion of Blacks from craft unions and union-controlled apprenticeship training programs, and the existence of segregated locals.

A shorter, earlier version of this essay appeared in *Race Traitor*, ed. Noel Ignatiev and John Garvey (New York and London: Routledge, 1996), and is reprinted by permission of the publisher.

Jewish Labor Committee

In April 1957, James B. Carey, president of the International Union of Electrical Workers, a former CIO affiliate, and a member of the federation's executive council, resigned as chairman of the AFL-CIO Civil Rights Committee because of its ineffectiveness, and he publicly criticized the federation. According to the *New York Times,* Carey believed that "the committee had not been given enough power or freedom to do an effective job of stamping out racial bias in unions" and felt that "he was being hamstrung in his anti-bias assignment." Carey was replaced as chairman by Charles S. Zimmerman, the vice president of the International Ladies Garment Workers Union (ILGWU) and a prominent leader of the Jewish Labor Committee (JLC). At the time of his appointment he was chairman of the National Trade Union Council of the JLC, and he later became president of the organization.[1]

The JLC was founded in 1934 in response to the rise of Nazism in Germany and provided assistance to European Jewish labor leaders. It performed valuable service in rescuing endangered antifascists and arranging for their resettlement in the United States and elsewhere.[2] With the end of World War II, the JLC had completed its task and, given its original purpose, no longer had a function to perform. In an effort to justify its continued existence, the JLC tried to become a civil rights organization within the labor movement.

By the late 1940s, with financial support mainly from the ILGWU, the JLC was revived and began referring to itself as "the civil rights arm of the labor movement." But although it presumed to represent the interests of minorities within organized labor, the committee had no contact with the great mass of African American workers in the industrial unions where they were concentrated, or with institutions of the Black community. The JLC was in a dubious position as it presumed to speak on behalf of those who had not authorized it to do so, since it had no membership and no constituency beyond a small group of Jewish labor leaders from the needle trades unions, mainly in New York City. Typical of its leadership was David Dubinsky, the president of the ILGWU, who was a founder of the JLC and served as its treasurer for many years.[3]

1. *New York Times,* April 12, 1957, 52; "Jewish Labor Body Elects Zimmerman," *AFL-CIO News,* Washington, D.C., May 11, 1968, 11.
2. For documentation on the activities of the Jewish Labor Committee during its early years see *The Papers of the Jewish Labor Committee: Robert F. Wagner Labor Archive, New York University,* ed. Arieh Liebowitz and Gail Malmgren, vol. 14, *Archive of the Holocaust* (New York: Garland Publishing, 1993).
3. "Jewish Labor Body Elects Zimmerman."

When Zimmerman became chairman of the AFL-CIO Civil Rights Committee, he remained a major figure in the leadership of the JLC, which intensified its efforts to expand its influence within organized labor. But Zimmerman's term in office was a stormy one and, as Black demands for effective action against racist labor union practices intensified, his impotence as a leader and his repeated attempts to defend or rationalize labor union discrimination increasingly placed him in direct conflict with Black workers and civil rights organizations.

A typical example—one of many—is the case of *Ross v. Ebert*, involving Local 8 of the Bricklayers Union in Milwaukee. This case began in 1946 when James Harris, who had settled in Milwaukee after serving three years in the South Pacific with the U.S. Air Force, was dismissed from his job at the insistence of the union because he was not a member, but subsequently the union refused his repeated requests for membership.[4] Harris had learned the trade while working with his uncles, who belonged to an all-Black local of the Bricklayers Union in his hometown of Opelika, Alabama, and in 1953 he and Randolph Ross, another skilled Black worker, applied for membership and were again rejected.[5] All efforts to obtain support from the international union and the AFL-CIO for Harris and other Black workers seeking membership in Local 8 were to no avail, as the international union defended its local affiliate, and George Meany, president of the AFL-CIO, urged the state government to refrain from legal enforcement of Wisconsin's antidiscrimination law.[6] This conflict, which came before the Supreme Court of Wisconsin, received national attention and resulted in the legislature amending the state Fair Employment Practices Law.

In 1955, the Wisconsin Fair Employment Practices Division, after long delay, found the union, whose membership had always been limited

4. *Ross v. Ebert*, 275 Wis. 223 (1957). "Personal Record of James Harris," Virginia Huebner, administrative assistant, Fair Employment Practices Division, Industrial Commission of Wisconsin, memorandum, September 25, 1946, Case Files 1945–1974, Series 1744, box 4, folder 16, Archives Division, State Historical Society of Wisconsin, Madison (hereafter FEPD).

5. Huebner memorandum, February 16, 1953, Huebner notes of meeting with Charles Ebert, March 13, 1953, and letter to Ebert, December 12, 1953, FEPD, series 1744, box 6, folder 16.

6. Herbert Hill, labor secretary, NAACP, memorandum to Boris Shishkin, director, Civil Rights Department, AFL-CIO, re *Ross v. Ebert*, January 21, 1957, AFL-CIO Department of Civil Rights, Discrimination Case Files [#36] box 3, folder 21, George Meany Memorial Archives, Silver Spring, Md. William R. Conners, 5th vice president, Bricklayers, Masons and Plasterers International Union, letter to Reuben G. Knutson, industrial commissioner, State of Wisconsin, January 25, 1954, and George Meany, letter to Huebner, April 26, 1957, FEPD, box 4, folder 16.

to Whites, guilty of racial discrimination in violation of state law and ordered the admission of two fully qualified Black men, but the union refused to comply and challenged the authority of the state agency.[7] On September 24, 1957, James Harris, Randolph Ross, and two other Black workers were finally admitted into the union, but only after the state legislature enacted a new judicially enforceable antidiscrimination law. After eleven years of efforts by public and private agencies, three rounds of litigation, and finally action by the legislature, Zimmerman defended the racist labor organization and stated in defiance of all the facts that "the denial of membership to them was not based on their race but was due to their failure to submit satisfactory evidence of their trade qualifications." The extensive litigation record in this case directly contradicts Zimmerman's statement, including the fact that former employers gave testimony verifying that both Harris and Ross were fully competent skilled masons.[8] Zimmerman repeatedly defended discriminatory labor unions in many other contexts, acting on behalf of a White labor bureaucracy committed to perpetuating the prevailing racial pattern.

The intransigence of the Milwaukee Bricklayers Union in refusing to admit African Americans was characteristic of many craft unions in the building trades. In New York City there were forty years of litigation involving the discriminatory practices of Local 28 of the Sheetmetal Workers Union;[9] in Philadelphia, many years of litigation against Local 542 of

7. Transcripts of hearing conducted by the Industrial Commission of Wisconsin, *Randolph Ross and James Harris v. Bricklayers, Masons and Plasterers International Union of America–Local 8,* January 19, 1955, FEPD, box 4, folder 14, and box 6, folder 12; also Virginia Huebner, letter to Boris Shishkin, director, Civil Rights Department AFL-CIO, April 15, 1957, AFL-CIO Department of Civil Rights, Discrimination Case Files [#35] box 3, folder 21, Meany Archives.

8. Charles S. Zimmerman, "Our Drive for Civil Rights," *American Federationist,* December 1957, p. 18. Jack Reynolds, assistant manager, Wisconsin State Fair Park, letter to Virginia Huebner, October 21, 1946, and Huebner, notes of discussion with R. E. Oberst, October 15, 1946; see also T. J. Novak, builder, letter to Huebner, August 27, 1953; "Report on Conference with Andrew Harenda, General Contractor," September 2, 1953, by Huebner; and Andrew G. Harenda, letter to Huebner, September 2, 1953, FEPD, box 4, folder 16.

9. *Local 28, Sheet Metal Workers International Association v. EEOC,* 478 U.S. 421 (1986). This union has been a defendant before a variety of administrative and judicial bodies since 1948. See *Lefkowitz v. Farrell,* C-9289–63, New York State Commission for Human Rights, 1948. For a discussion of the racial practices of other building trades unions in New York City see Herbert Hill, "The New York City Terminal Market Controversy: A Case Study of Race, Labor and Power," *Humanities in Society* 6 (fall 1984): 351–91. For information on the racial practices of construction unions nationally see Herbert Hill, "The AFL-CIO and the Black Worker: Twenty-Five Years after the Merger," *Journal of Intergroup Relations* 10, no. 1 (spring 1982): 5–78.

the Operating Engineers Union;[10] and in Chicago, extensive litigation against Local 597 of the Pipefitters Union,[11] to take but three examples.

At the 1959 annual convention of the NAACP, A. Philip Randolph, president of the Brotherhood of Sleeping Car Porters, called for the formation of the Negro American Labor Council (NALC), and at its founding convention he stressed that Black workers must speak for themselves within organized labor. He said that "[w]e ourselves must seek the cure" and that the establishment of the NALC would "make it possible for Negro workers to take a position completely independent of white unionists. . . . History has placed upon the Negro and the Negro alone this basic responsibility."[12] With the emergence of the NALC and the increasing involvement of the NAACP in the issue of labor union discrimination, the JLC found itself in conflict with Black unionists and civil rights groups. On December 12, 1959, there appeared the first of a series of articles on antagonism between Blacks and Jews within organized labor in the *Pittsburgh Courier*, a respected and widely circulated Black newspaper with editions in Chicago, Detroit, and New York. Under the front-page headline "Will Negro, Jewish Labor Leaders Split over Civil Rights?" an article by Managing Editor Harold F. Keith began, "Negro and Jewish labor leaders are on the 'brink' of outright war between themselves with the civil rights issue spread out before them as a prospective field of battle." In that issue and in those following, Keith reviewed the history of the conflicts between the AFL-CIO Civil Rights Committee and Black trade unionists. The *Courier* criticized the JLC and Zimmerman for presuming to speak for Blacks and reported that Jewish labor leaders had adopted a "paternalistic and missionary" attitude toward Blacks. The article in the *Courier* also reported that the AFL-CIO was "ignoring the mounting bitterness in Negro communities. . . . over scandalous racial discrimination" by both craft and industrial unions. According to Keith, the JLC "exerts more influence upon the AFL-CIO than any non-union group" and had "more say-so than the NAACP or the National Urban

10. *Commonwealth of Pennsylvania and Williams v. Local 542, International Union of Operating Engineers,* C. A. No. 71–2698, November 8, 1971, U.S. District Court, Eastern District of Pennsylvania, 18 FEP Cases 1560. In addition, on August 14, 1969, the Equal Employment Opportunity Commission initiated a commissioner's charge against the union. See EEOC, *In the Matter of Local 542, International Union of Operating Engineers,* Philadelphia, Pennsylvania, Case No. YCL 9–207.

11. *Daniels v. Pipefitters Local Union No. 597,* 53 FEP 1669 (N. D. ILL, 1990), aff'd., 945 F. 2d 906 (7th Cir. 1991), *cert. denied,* 503 U.S. 951 (1992), affirming on other grounds, 983 F. 2d 800, 60 FEP 942 (7th Cir. 1993). Injunctive relief and consent decree issued.

12. A. Philip Randolph, "The Civil Rights Revolution and Labor," address to the NAACP Annual Convention, New York, July 15, 1959.

League."[13] Keith also charged that pressure from the JLC was a factor in the failure of the federation to act against the racist practices of many affiliated unions.

Randolph and Roy Wilkins, the executive secretary of the NAACP, argued that the fundamental problem was discrimination and denied that the conflict with the AFL-CIO was an issue between Blacks and Jews. Zimmerman, who was trying to expand the role of the JLC within the AFL-CIO as well as advance his own career, was eventually forced to resign. However, the JLC, by defending discriminatory labor organizations, and by functioning as an apologist for racist unions, succeeded in transforming a Black-White conflict into a Black-Jewish conflict. Sadly enough, this was not the last time Jewish trade unionists would engage in such behavior.

In 1961 the NAACP issued a report documenting the continuing discriminatory racial practices of many AFL-CIO unions.[14] The NALC endorsed the NAACP's report, and Randolph in his address to the association's annual convention stated,

> We in the Negro American Labor Council consider the report timely, necessary, and valuable. . . . Moreover, the Negro American Labor Council can, without reservation, assert that the basic statements of the report are true and sound, and that delegates of the Brotherhood of Sleeping Car Porters have presented these facts to convention after convention of the American Federal of Labor for a quarter of a century.[15]

George Meany, at a conference of the JLC held at Unity House, the summer resort of the ILGWU, attacked the NAACP, the NALC, and the Black press for their criticism of the racial practices of organized labor.[16] That Meany chose a meeting of the JLC for his widely reported denunciation was not lost on Black workers and civil rights groups.

International Ladies Garment Workers Union

Events in the early 1960s involving the ILGWU in New York City were to have a major impact on Black-Jewish relations and also on the liberal

13. Harold F. Keith, "Will Negro, Jewish Labor Leaders Split over Civil Rights?" *Pittsburgh Courier*, December 12, 19, 26, 1959, and January 3, 10, 1960.

14. Herbert Hill, "Racism within Organized Labor: A Report of Five Years of the AFL-CIO, 1955–1960," NAACP, New York, 1961, reprinted in *Journal of Negro Education* 30 (spring 1961): 109–18.

15. Address by A. Philip Randolph to the 51st Annual Convention of the NAACP, St. Paul, Minn., June 24, 1961. Copy in author's files.

16. Joel Seldin, "Meany Hits Negro Groups for Attacking Union Bias," *New York Herald-Tribune*, May 28, 1961, 1.

coalition for years to come. On November 21, 1962, Roy Wilkins sent to all members of the Leadership Conference on Civil Rights and to other organizations a memorandum that said,

> Because of the current widespread discussion of the relationship between the NAACP, and organized labor, with particular but not exclusive reference to the International Ladies Garment Workers Union, and because a resolution of the Jewish Labor Committee on this subject has been distributed widely to labor groups and to persons in the intergroup relations field, we attach for your information, our letter of October 31, 1962.[17]

Wilkins was responding not only to recent attacks by the AFL-CIO against the NAACP but also to a resolution adopted by the JLC, widely distributed and reported in the press, which denounced the association and accused it of anti-Semitism. In his letter to Emanuel Muravchik, executive secretary of the JLC, Wilkins stated:

> When you declare in 1962 that the NAACP's continued attack upon discrimination against Negro workers by trade union bodies and leaders places "in jeopardy" continued progress towards civil rights goals or rends the "unity" among civil rights forces, or renders a "disservice" to the Negro worker or raises the question "whether it is any longer possible to work with the NAACP" you are, in fact, seeking by threats to force us to conform to what the Jewish Labor Committee is pleased to classify as proper behavior in the circumstances. Needless to say, we cannot bow to this threat. We reject the proposition that any segment of the labor movement is sacrosanct in the matter of practices and/or policies which restrict employment opportunities on racial or religious or nationality grounds. We reject the contention that bringing such charges constitutes a move to destroy "unity" among civil rights groups unless it be admitted that this unity is a precarious thing, perched upon unilateral definition of discrimination by each member group. In such a situation, the "unity" is of no basic value and its destruction may be regarded as not a calamity, but a blessed clearing of the air.

In reply to the charge of anti-Semitism Wilkins went on to say:

> This is a grave charge to make. . . . We do not deign to defend ourselves against such a baseless allegation. Its inclusion in the resolution, as well as in the statements to the press by Mr. Zimmerman, is unworthy of an organization like the Jewish Labor Committee which in the very nature of things, must be conversant with the seriousness

17. Roy Wilkins, executive secretary NAACP, memorandum to members of the Leadership Conference on Civil Rights, November 21, 1962, Reuther Collection, box 504, folder 1, Archives of Labor History and Urban Affairs, Wayne State University, Detroit.

of such a charge and with the evidence required to give it substance.
. . . Similarly, we do not feel that the general denials and outraged
protests which have been the response of the ILGWU to our charges
of discriminatory practices are in any way an adequate answer to
those charges.[18]

In taking its stand, the NAACP demonstrated that Black institutions
would no longer be junior partners in coalitions dominated by liberal
Whites whose institutional interests and priorities were often in conflict
with those of the Black community.[19]

A scholarly study published in 1953 of racial and ethnic conflict in the
ILGWU reported, "The strains and tensions in the shops are not without
their echo in the union, where they become problems of ideology, power,
and administration." Access to leadership was identified as "[t]he most
serious union problem in which the relation of ethnic groups enters. . . .
The leadership of the union is overwhelmingly in the hands of the old-
timers." The study concluded that "the crisis of leadership" in the
ILGWU was a consequence "of the cleavage between two membership
generations, differing very considerably in composition, background and
outlook."[20]

Although their numbers had greatly increased within the ILGWU, by
the 1960s Black workers were limited to the lowest paying, unskilled job
classifications in New York's garment manufacturing industry, as they
were largely excluded from the craft locals where much higher wages
prevailed. In the 1960s, Blacks in New York as elsewhere were increasingly struggling against the forces responsible for their subordinate and
depressed condition. This was the period in which rising Black expectations challenged the shoddy compromises of the past, in labor unions no
less than in other institutions.

The ILGWU, founded by European socialist immigrants in 1900, was
not immune to these developments, especially since its membership base
had become increasingly Black and Latino. Through a series of restrictive
procedures (of doubtful legality under the Labor-Management Reporting and Disclosure Act of 1959), the ILGWU excluded non-White

18. Roy Wilkins, letter to Emanuel Muravchik, executive secretary, Jewish Labor
Committee, October 31, 1962, Reuther Collection, box 504, folder 1.

19. For a detailed account of conflicts within the civil rights lobbying coalition during the 1960s see Herbert Hill, "Black Workers, Organized Labor, and Title VII of the
1964 Civil Rights Act: Legislative History and Litigation Record," in *Race in America:
The Struggle for Equality*, ed. Herbert Hill and James E. Jones Jr. (Madison: University
of Wisconsin Press, 1993), 263–341.

20. Will Herberg, "The Old-timers and the Newcomers: Ethnic Group Relations in
a Needle Trades Union," *Journal of Social Issues* 9, no. 1 (1953): 12–19.

workers from the leadership of the union. Not a single Black or Latino was an officer of the international union, served as a member of the General Executive Board, or functioned as the manager of a local union.[21] The social psychologist Kenneth B. Clark, in his study of the consequences of "ghetto life," stated, "A significant example of the powerlessness of the Negro worker in a major trade union with a 'liberal' reputation is found in the status of Negroes in the International Ladies Garment Workers Union in New York City." Clark recalled the discrimination his mother experienced as a member of the ILGWU. In a memoir he later wrote, "I was very pleased years later when the NAACP exposed the discriminatory pattern in New York's garment industry and attacked the racial practices of the ILGWU."[22]

The general suppression of membership rights within the ILGWU in conjunction with the extreme exploitation of workers in the garment industry resulted in an increasingly restive labor force. During this period the majority of Black and Puerto Rican garment workers in New York received less than $1.50 an hour in wages under ILGWU contracts. In 1960, according to the U.S. Bureau of Labor Statistics, only 11 percent of unionized garment workers in New York earned enough to maintain a "modest but adequate standard of living."[23] The union was rigidly controlled by a self-perpetuating bureaucracy of White males whose Jewish working-class base no longer existed and who were now increasingly in conflict with their non-White, largely female membership.

21. For a description of the restrictions on political activity within the ILGWU and the eligibility rules for union office during this period see Herbert Hill, "The ILGWU Today: The Decay of a Labor Union" and "The ILGWU: Fact and Fiction," in *Autocracy and Insurgency in Organized Labor,* ed. Burton H. Hall (New Brunswick, N.J.: Transaction Books, 1972), 47–160, 173–200.

22. Kenneth B. Clark, *Dark Ghetto: Dilemmas of Social Power* (New York: Harper and Row, 1965), 43, and "Racial Progress and Retreat: A Personal Memoir," in *Race in America,* ed. Hill and Jones, 7.

23. The wage rates of unskilled and semiskilled garment workers in New York, most of whom were non-White, were below subsistence levels as indicated by the 1960 Interim City Workers Family Budget for New York City ($5,048) established by the Bureau of Labor Statistics, "Employment, Earnings, and Wages in New York City, 1950–1960," Bureau of Labor Statistics, New York, Middle Atlantic Office, June 1962. The contract between Local 98 of the ILGWU and the Manufacturers Association in effect until August 14, 1963, was typical and provided the following minimum wages (p. 7, article 4[A]): floor girls, $1.15 per hour; operators, $1.20 per hour; shipping clerks, $1.20 per hour; cutters, $1.20 per hour. Describing the collective bargaining agreement in force in 1971 between Knitgoods Workers Local 155 of the ILGWU and the employers in New York City, New Jersey, and Long Island, the labor lawyer Burton H. Hall wrote that take-home pay was "between $57 and $59 for a full week. Sweatshops have not disappeared; they are hiding behind an ILGWU union label" ("The ILGWU and the Labor Department," in *Autocracy and Insurgency,* ed. Hall, 295).

The transformation of the ethnic and racial composition of the garment industry labor force that began in the 1930s caused serious problems for the ILGWU since its traditional Jewish leadership was unwilling to accept Blacks and Puerto Ricans as equal partners in an interracial union, to share control of the organization with them, and to permit them to share in the power that derived from such institutional authority. Instead of honestly confronting and resolving these issues, the union leadership, increasingly isolated from its membership, attempted to maintain the racist and sexist status quo by bureaucratic means. In response, rank-and-file workers protested in a variety of ways, including demonstrating at union headquarters and filing petitions with the National Labor Relations Board seeking the decertification of the ILGWU. Typical of this development was the action of Puerto Rican workers at the Q-T Knitwear Company in Brooklyn in 1958 who charged the union with negotiating a "sweetheart contract" with their employer. They marched around the factory with picket signs that read, "We're Tired of Industrial Peace. We Want Industrial Justice." A reporter noted after interviewing the workers that the wildcat strike was a protest against their boss and, "most important, against the workers' own union."[24] Conflict between the ILGWU and its membership intensified when Black and Puerto Rican organizations campaigned for a new $1.50 an hour city minimum wage, only to be opposed by the union.[25]

The increasing discontent of Black and Latino workers in the New York garment industry provided the context for actions that occurred in the 1960s on these issues. On April 4, 1961, Ernest Holmes, a Black worker who was an NAACP member, filed a complaint with the New York State Commission for Human Rights against Local 10, a craft unit of

24. Peter Braestrup, "Life among the Garment Workers, Puerto Ricans Rebel against Boss and Union," *New York Herald-Tribune*, October 8, 1958, 15. See also Braestrup, "Life among the Garment Workers," *New York Herald-Tribune*, October 6, 1958, 19, and October 10, 1958, 20. For the background to these developments see *Spanish Speaking Workers and the Labor Movement* (New York: Association of Catholic Trade Unionists, 1957) and the association's monthly publication, *Labor Leader*, which provided frequent reports of minority labor insurgency. A further source of information has been the author's interviews with Daniel J. Schulder, president of the Association of Catholic Trade Unionists, New York, November 18, 24, and December 2, 1958, together with examination of data in the association's files.

25. Murray Kempton, "The Wage Fight," *New York Post*, August 21, 1962, 17; Arnold Witte, *New York World Telegram and Sun*, October 5, 1962, 15; and Michael Myerson, "The ILGWU: Fighting for Lower Wages," *Ramparts*, October 1969, 51–55. See also Herbert Hill, "The Racial Practices of Organized Labor: The Contemporary Record," in *The Negro and the American Labor Movement*, ed. Julius Jacobson (Garden City, N.Y.: Anchor Books, 1968), 326–30.

the ILGWU, charging the union with discriminatory practices, including the refusal to admit him to membership on the basis of race, in violation of state law. The union's response was to engage in repeated evasion and distortion, as when Moe Falikman, the manager of Local 10, told the *New York Times* that there were "more than 500 Negroes and Puerto Ricans" in the cutters local. The ILGWU later said there were four hundred non-White members in this craft local but subsequently reduced the figure to three hundred and then to two hundred. The state commission challenged the ILGWU to produce names and addresses and places of employment of these alleged members, and the NAACP said it would withdraw the complaint if the union would comply, but such identification was never produced. When the NAACP asked the American Jewish Committee to provide such identification since it was circulating the union's claim under its own name, the committee also failed to respond.[26]

The *New York Herald-Tribune,* in a front-page report headlined "ILGWU Condemned for Racial Barriers," summarized the findings of the state commission with the comment that "the New York Cutters local of the International Ladies Garment Workers Union was judged guilty of racial discrimination in a report released yesterday by the State Commission for Human Rights." The newspaper noted that the cutters are "the most highly skilled and highly paid workers" and that wages for members of Local 10 "are roughly double that for other workers in the industry." According to the *New York Times,* the State Commission for Human Rights found Local 10 responsible for discriminatory acts, and "the union was told that the commission would maintain a continuing interest in its training and admission practices and that these would be reviewed

26. *Holmes v. Falikman,* C-7580-61, New York State Commission for Human Rights (1963). *New York Times,* May 18, 1961, 27. Herbert Hill, labor secretary, NAACP, to Harry Fleishman, director, National Labor Service, American Jewish Committee, October 23, 1962, NAACP Papers, Group III, box A 190, Manuscript Division, Library of Congress, Washington, D.C. Gus Tyler, assistant president of the ILGWU, wrote, "In Local 10, there are 199 known Negro and Spanish-speaking members" and explained that his figure included "Cubans, Panamanians, Colombians, Dominicans, Salvadorans, Mexicans, etc., as well as Puerto Ricans" ("The Truth about the ILGWU," *New Politics* 2 [fall 1962]: 7). But later he stated, "We had 275 black members in that local" (Gus Tyler, "The Intellectuals and the ILGWU," in *Creators and Disturbers, Reminiscences by Jewish Intellectuals of New York,* ed. Bernard Rosenberg and Ernest Goldstein [New York: Columbia University Press, 1982], 173). According to a tract published by the American Jewish Committee and distributed by the ILGWU, there were "250 Negro and Spanish-speaking cutters in Local 10"; see Harry Fleishman, "Is the ILGWU Biased?" National Labor Service of the American Jewish Committee, New York, November 1962. The evident disparity in these numbers and their obviously arbitrary nature requires no further comment.

periodically to assure that the terms of the decision would be fully and conscientiously carried out."[27]

The ILGWU initially failed to comply, but after additional hearings and protracted negotiations, on May 17, 1963, twenty-five months after the original complaint was filed in *Holmes v. Falikman,* the union entered into a stipulation agreement to comply with the law without admitting guilt.[28] The *Holmes* case received much public attention as it symbolized widespread Black and Latino discontent with the ILGWU, and it led to a congressional investigation of the ILGWU's racial practices.

The ILGWU was greatly embarrassed by the revelations of the investigation and often distorted the history of the congressional proceedings. Gus Tyler, assistant president of the union, wrote, for example, that Adam Clayton Powell, chairman of the House Committee on Education and Labor, was "riding a little wave of anti-Semitism" and that the union was exonerated. According to Tyler, "There was no case. There was nothing. . . . We won the round. We won the war." The official record directly contradicts Tyler's claim, for the union was not exonerated. Documentation in congressional files, together with extensive interviewing of congressional staff members by the author, revealed that the ILGWU used its considerable political influence at the highest levels of government to stop the hearings. An announcement was made at the last session, on September 21, that the hearings were "recessed, to reconvene subject to call." But they were never reconvened. After the union succeeded in making certain political arrangements, the congressional committee quietly abandoned the hearings, which were never formally concluded, and there was no final report.[29]

Mrs. Florence Rice, a Black member of ILGWU Local 155 in New York, had been warned by a union official that if she gave testimony before the congressional committee she would never again work in the garment industry. She told the committee in a sworn statement that "workers have

27. Joel Selden, "ILGWU Condemned for Racial Barriers," *New York Herald-Tribune,* July 2, 1962, 1; see also Fred Feretti, "Crusading Negro Finds Road Is Rough," *New York Herald-Tribune,* July 2, 1962, 8; "Union Told to Get Job for Negro," *New York Times,* July 2, 1962, 22.

28. *Stipulation and Order on the Complaint of Ernest Holmes v. Moe Falikman et al.,* Case No. C-7590-61, May 17, 1963 (*Holmes v. Falikman,* File 1963, New York State Commission for Human Rights). Copy in author's files.

29. Tyler, "Intellectuals and the ILGWU," 155–75; see *Hearings before the Ad Hoc Subcommittee on Investigation of the Garment Industry, Committee on Education and Labor, United States House of Representatives,* 87th Cong., 2d sess., August 17, 18, 23, 24, and September 21, 1962. For the author's testimony before the hearings see *Congressional Record-House,* January 31, 1963, 1496–99.

been intimidated by union officials with threats of losing their jobs if they so much as appear at the hearing." Soon after her appearance before the committee in open hearings, she was dismissed from her job and was not able to obtain employment thereafter as a garment worker.[30] She later became a leading community activist and director of the Harlem Consumer Education Council.

After the *Holmes* case, ILGWU officers, in an attempt to ward off further criticism, added a Black woman and a Puerto Rican man to the union's General Executive Board, moved some Black and Latino workers into better paying, more skilled jobs, and employed several in previously all-White positions within the union. Furthermore, anticipating exposure, the union canceled its financial support for the ILGWU wing of the Workmen's Circle Home in the Bronx, a home for retired workers built with union funds and annually subsidized by the union, but which did not admit Black and Puerto Rican members.[31]

Conflict between the ILGWU leadership and its minority group members continued as Black, Asian, and Latino garment workers filed a lawsuit against the East River Houses, known as the ILGWU Co-Operative Village, which refused to rent apartments to non-Whites. Federal Judge Robert L. Carter found that there was indeed a pattern of unlawful racial exclusion.[32] Documentation introduced into the court record revealed that the ILGWU had contributed more than $20 million of union funds to subsidize a housing project for middle-class Whites who were not ILGWU members, adjacent to a vast area of substandard housing inhabited mainly by members of racial minorities.

This became a major issue among ILGWU members in the New York area. Several thousand workers signed petitions demanding an end to the racist practices of the East River Houses, and union members

30. Testimony of Mrs. Florence Rice, *Hearing before the Ad Hoc Subcommittee on Investigation of the Garment Industry,* 167; interviews with Mrs. Rice, November 17, 1962, May 17, 1966, and April 9, 1972.

31. In 1959, the union had begun construction of the ILGWU wing, at a cost of $1.3 million; after it was dedicated on June 11, 1961, the union continued to make substantial annual contributions for its operation, though fully aware of protests by Latino and Black members against the use of union funds to build and maintain a facility closed to them. See *Report of the General Executive Board,* 32d convention, International Ladies Garment Workers Union, 1965, pp. 57–58, International Ladies Garment Workers Union Archives, Labor Management Documentation Center, Cornell University, Ithaca, N.Y.; also June 1961 issue of *Justice,* with front-page headline reading, "ILGWU Wing of Circle Home Opening June 11."

32. *Huertas et al. v. East River Housing Corp. et al.,* U.S. District Court (S.D.N.Y., 1977), 77 C. 4494 (RLC) 1977.

mounted a protest demonstration at the headquarters of the ILGWU.[33] One union member, Margarita Lopez, was quoted in a newspaper report of the demonstration as saying: "How could this happen? How could this happen in a union that is supposed to be so liberal? The blacks, Hispanics, the Chinese are the workers. The dues come from these people, but the housing is all white and middle class. These were union pension funds. They give union funds but union workers who are black and Hispanic and Chinese cannot live in those houses."[34]

Protests from workers against the racial practices of the ILGWU continued as Black, Latino, and Asian American workers began to organize dissident groups within local unions. This activity led to the filing of complaints with federal agencies and the initiation of litigation on a variety of issues relating to race and violations of internal union democracy. Among these was the intervention in 1971 by the U.S. Department of Labor in the election proceedings of the fifteen-thousand-member Knitgoods Local 155 of the ILGWU, in response to a formal complaint filed by a Black and Latino caucus known as the Rank and File Committee.[35]

The caucus charged that the union, in violation of federal law, had engaged in illegal practices to prevent the election of Black and Latino workers to leadership positions within the local. After investigation, the Department of Labor ordered a rerun of the election. At a press conference, the Rank and File Committee charged that ILGWU officials had signed contracts that forced them to work "under sweatshop conditions" and noted that Black and Spanish-speaking workers constituted 75 percent of the membership of Local 155 but were denied any voice in determining union policies.

In its press release, the Rank and File Committee protested racist characterizations of its members that had appeared in the *Jewish Daily Forward*, the leading Yiddish-language newspaper in New York. The

33. Interview with Frederic Seiden and Francis Golden of the Lower East Side Joint Planning Council, New York, March 24, 25, 1983. Sources that document the ILGWU's role in sponsoring and financing the $20 million ILGWU Co-Operative Village are Max D. Danish, *The World of David Dubinsky* (Cleveland: World Publishing Co., 1957), 305–7; David Dubinsky with A. H. Raskin, *David Dubinsky: A Life with Labor* (New York: Simon and Schuster, 1977), 216–18; and *Justice*, May 1, 1952, 1. See also *Report of the General Executive Board*, 32d convention, p. 8.

34. Quoted in Earl Caldwell, "When a House Can't Be Your Home," *New York Daily News*, June 1, 1983, 4.

35. *In the Matter of Edward J. Tucker, James Malloy and Raymond Tucker, Against Local 155, Knitgoods Workers' Union, International Ladies' Garment Workers' Union, AFL-CIO.* The complaint was filed pursuant to Section 482 of Title 29 of the United States Code (Landrum-Griffin Act).

committee cited articles in the *Forward* reporting on the conflict within Local 155, which contained "racist insults and slanderous lies . . . such as calling black and Spanish-speaking members of the Rank And File Committee a 'gang,' 'marijuana smokers,' 'drug addicts and pushers,' and 'bewildered children.' " According to the committee, such "slanders" were "a vicious and obvious attempt to whip up race hatred between the younger workers and our older, mostly Jewish co-workers in the shops. We are not anti-Semites. . . . We struggle with all workers, black, white and Spanish-speaking, of all religions, for a strong local."[36]

The *Jewish Daily Forward* reported that the "Communist Rank and File" was involved in a "Communist web of intrigues" and identified the Black and Latino caucus as the work of "Communist agents." The article concluded with the explanation that "the communists only really want to take over the locals and the Union and offer them up on a Red tray to the Stalin inheritors who, together with El-Fatah, want to eliminate Israel."[37]

To the great dismay of the union's leadership, after the effective date of Title VII, the employment section of the 1964 Civil Rights Act, union members filed complaints against the ILGWU with the U.S. Equal Employment Opportunity Commission. In many of these cases the EEOC sustained charges of race and sex discrimination against both the international union and its locals. In the *Putterman* case, a federal court in New York found "willful and intentional" violations of the legal prohibitions against discrimination by both the local and the international union. The many EEOC charges filed against the ILGWU included cases in Chicago, Philadelphia, Cleveland, Atlanta, and New York.[38]

To divert attention from the central issue of racial discrimination, the ILGWU conducted an intensive campaign characterized by prevarication and distortion in an effort to make anti-Semitism the issue. The ILGWU

36. Press release, Rank and File Committee of Local 155, ILGWU, February 24, 1971. Copy in author's files.

37. Y. Fogel, "Knitgoods Local 155 and the Elections," *Jewish Daily Forward*, February 17, 1971, 1. English translation by Abraham Friend. Copy in author's files.

38. *Violetta Putterman v. Knitgoods Workers Union Local 155 of ILGWU, International Ladies Garment Workers Union, Sol Greene and Sol C. Chaikin*, U.S. District Court, S.D.N.Y., Memorandum Opinion and Order, 78 Civ 6000 (MJL), August 20, 1983. The charges against the ILGWU filed with the EEOC include the following in New York: TNY9-0648; TNH1-1413, 9-0059, and 1754. In charge YNK3-063, the International Union itself was a respondent. The charges filed against the ILGWU outside New York included those in Chicago (TCH8–0277); Kansas City (TKC1-1101); Memphis (TME1-1091); San Francisco (TSF-0853); Baltimore (TBA3-0084); Philadelphia (TPA2-0651); Cleveland (TCT2-0468, 2-0043, 1-0002, 1-0004, 1-0006, 1-0010); and Birmingham (TB10-0954, 1-0357, 1-0195, 1-0873, 9-0098, 2-0975).

repeatedly claimed that criticism of its racial practices was a malicious anti-Semitic attack on the Jewish leadership of the union; many local and national Jewish organizations, including the American Jewish Committee, the American Jewish Congress, the Anti-Defamation League of B'nai B'rith (ADL), and the JLC, became actively involved, and each group distributed a torrent of resolutions, correspondence, newsletters, bulletins, press releases, and brochures defending the ILGWU.[39]

The reaction of the union leadership demonstrates how White immigrant groups, once they achieve integration into American society, defend their own privileges and power when confronted with demands from Blacks. The criticisms of the ILGWU raised in the course of the *Holmes v. Falikman* case, and in its aftermath, charged the union with perpetuating a pattern that limited non-Whites to the least desirable jobs and that violated the basic requirements of internal union democracy. To put it simply, an institution controlled by an established stratum of Jewish leaders who were anxious to preserve the privileges of their group within

39. The following is a small selection. The American Jewish Committee gave wide distribution to an eight-page tract, "Is the ILGWU Biased?" written by Harry Fleishman, a member of its staff, and through its newsletter, *Let's Be Human,* repeatedly praised the ILGWU and denounced its critics. A letter dated November 13, 1962, from John A. Morsell, assistant to the executive secretary of the NAACP, to Fleishman provides a thoughtful response to Fleishman's assertions, which contain many errors of fact; NAACP Papers, Group III, box A190. Data in ILGWU files indicate that Fleishman was actively involved in the union's campaign; ILGWU Zimmerman Collection, box 26, folder 8. Later, Fleishman tried to intervene with the State Commission for Human Rights on behalf of the ILGWU. See Harry Fleishman, director, National Labor Service, American Jewish Committee, letter to George H. Fowler, chairman, SCHR, December 19, 1962, NAACP Papers, Group III, box A184. The American Jewish Congress on December 6, 1962, sent a statement signed by Shad Polier, chairman of the organization's governing council, to all its members, defending the union and repeating Fleishman's distortions. The Anti-Defamation League of B'nai B'rith, the largest Jewish fraternal order in the United States, also came to the union's defense. Oscar Cohen, national program director of the league, reported its efforts on behalf of the union to Zimmerman in a letter dated December 3, 1962. He closed by promising to "do as much as I can." The JLC was extremely active on behalf of the union, as the ILGWU provided major financial support to the organization and many of its leaders were officials of the union. Among the many mailings sent by the JLC to individuals and groups throughout the country in defense of the ILGWU was that by Emanuel Muravchik to various organizations, September 5, 1962, and Muravchik's memorandum with enclosures, October 17, 1962, as well as many press releases and assorted statements and resolutions. Archival sources for documentation of this history are the NAACP Papers in the Library of Congress; Jewish Labor Committee Files, Robert F. Wagner Labor Archives, New York University, New York; Library of Jewish Information of the American Jewish Committee, New York; as well as the ILGWU archives cited above and the author's files.

the industry, and who by then had more in common with the employers than with the union's members, rejected the demands for advancement of a growing Black and Latino working class. With the rise of the labor bureaucracy and the racial conflicts of the ILGWU, the tradition of the Jewish left in organized labor came to an end.

The Response to Black Demands for Economic Advancement: A Case History

From the 1890s, the garment industry in New York City absorbed successive waves of European immigrants. Many became skilled workers within an industry that offered stable employment and increased earnings; some eventually became small entrepreneurs employing immigrant workers themselves, while others moved out of the industry entirely to take more desirable jobs in other sectors of the economy. Blacks were working in the New York garment industry as early as 1900.[40] The Census for 1930 reported that 35,400 Blacks were employed in the needle trades, and in that same year 20,000 Blacks were working in the garment industry in New York,[41] but for them such employment did not provide the means to escape from poverty and share in the economic and social progress enjoyed by White immigrant workers and their children. For them, the ILGWU was to become part of the problem.

Herman D. Bloch, in his study of Black workers in New York, concluded that in the 1930s

> both the International Ladies Garment Workers Union (ILGWU) and the Amalgamated Clothing Workers of America had Negro Americans in their New York locals; it was disputable as to whether these

40. See Sterling D. Spero and Abram L. Harris, *The Black Worker* (New York: Columbia University Press, 1931), 337. For information on Black workers in New York in the early 1900s see Mary White Ovington, *Half a Man: The Status of the Negro in New York* (New York: Longmans, 1911); Ovington, "The Negro in the Trade Unions of New York," *Annals of the American Academy of Political and Social Science* (May 1906): 64–75; George Edmund Haynes, "Effects of War Conditions on Negro Labor," *Proceedings of the Academy of Political Science* (February 1919): 299–312, and *The Negro at Work in New York City: A Study in Economic Progress* (New York: Columbia University Press, 1912); Charles L. Franklin, *The Negro Labor Unionist of New York: Problems and Conditions Among Negroes in the Labor Unions in Manhattan with Special Reference to the N.R.A. and Post N.R.A. Situations* (New York: Columbia University Press, 1936); Seth M. Scheiner, *Negro Mecca: A History of the Negro in New York City, 1865–1920* (New York: New York University Press, 1965), chap. 2, 45–64; and Herman D. Bloch, *The Circle of Discrimination* (New York: New York University Press, 1969).

41. U.S. Department of Commerce, Bureau of the Census, *Fifteenth Census of the United States: 1930, Population: Volume III, Part 2*; Lazare Teper, *The Women's Garment Industry* (New York: Education Department, International Ladies' Garment Workers' Union, 1937), 7.

unions practiced "egalitarianism." Both unions accepted the colored American primarily as a means of controlling the trade, but they restricted him to the least skilled trades (finishers, cleaners, and pressers). Control over these workers was essential to carry on effective collective bargaining in the industries. Secondly, the ILGWU accepted the bulk of its Negro American membership during organizing drives, taking the Negro American into the union in order to make a union shop. . . .

Unionization of the colored Americans neglected a crucial issue: What occupations were open to these black Americans? What chance of upward economic mobility was available through a seniority system? The cutters' locals of both unions had no Negro American behind a pair of shears.[42]

Thirty years later the same pattern prevailed in workshops organized by the ILGWU, the largest labor union in New York City.

The experience of African American workers was fundamentally different from that of European immigrants. For all their other problems, Jewish workers were White, and, together with other Whites, they benefited from racial exclusionary practices and from the limitations on job advancement imposed on Black workers because of their race. Attempting to explain the problems of Blacks in New York City as a consequence of their being the latest in a series of "newcomers" ignores history, ignores the fact that Blacks were not recent immigrants and had been in the New York area for many generations before the European immigration of the late nineteenth century, and ignores the factor of race that was decisive in determining their occupational status.[43]

Black organizations understood that what non-White workers were doing in attacking the union's practices was precisely what Jews and other immigrant groups had done in the past. Indeed, the history of immigrants in America is a continuum of efforts in which ethnic groups, as they rose, fought as a block within institutions to advance their interests, using the availability of particular occupations as a lever for achieving their goals. But in the 1960s, when the ILGWU was the focus of criticism, Jewish organizations viewed this tactic as an assault on the Jewish community. Thus they reacted as a community in defense of the ILGWU leadership and denounced advocates of Black advancement as anti-Semites.

42. Bloch, *Circle of Discrimination,* 107.
43. Among several studies see Scheiner, *Negro Mecca,* 1–12, and Bloch, *Circle of Discrimination,* 1–34. See also James Weldon Johnson, *Black Manhattan* (1930; rpt. New York: De Capo Press, 1991). Gilbert Osofsky, *Harlem: The Making of a Ghetto, Negro New York, 1890–1930* (New York: Harper and Row, 1963); and Roi Ottley and William J. Weatherby, eds., *The Negro in New York: An Informal Social History, 1626–1940* (New York: Praeger, 1967).

The response of Jewish institutions to the effort of Blacks to advance economically in New York's garment industry demonstrated the
profound changes that had occurred in the status of Jews in American
society. With the rising affluence of the Jewish population and its assimilation into American society, the foundations of Jewish radicalism disin-
tegrated. Many descendants of Jewish socialist immigrants now were
upwardly mobile professionals or corporate managers with a stake in the
perpetuation of existing social institutions. The intellectual skepticism
cultivated by previous generations of radicalized Jews gave way to an acceptance of the legitimacy, and indeed the virtue, of existing values and
institutions, including those relating to racial dominance and subordination. By the 1960s, Jews in America had become "White," that is, they had
become assimilated and affluent enough in a society sharply divided by
race to enjoy the privileges of "whiteness"; furthermore, they regarded
themselves as "White," and by and large they were accepted as such by
the majority of the population.

The unprecedented transformation of Jewish life in the United States
and its implications required analysis and explanations, especially
within the Jewish community, and this was the purpose of Nathan
Glazer's writing in *Commentary*, a publication of the American Jewish
Committee, as well as in other journals. In "Negroes and Jews: The New
Challenge to Pluralism," which appeared in the December 1964 issue of
Commentary, Glazer asserted that the crisis in the early 1960s between
Blacks and Jews occurred because these groups had "different capacities
to take advantage of the opportunities that are truly in large measure
open to all." The environment, Glazer said, is not prejudicial to one
group or the other. Jews, he asserted, are able to take advantage of the
"democracy of merit," which he believes characterizes American society.
In contrast to Jews, patterns of Negro personality and behavior, according to Glazer, are responsible for the African American's incapacity to
realize the opportunities available to all.[44]

In his version of cultural pluralism, Glazer argued that Jewish resistance to new Negro militancy was based "on a growing awareness of
the depths of Negro antagonism to the world that Jewish liberalism considers desirable." Jews, he wrote, lived a different kind of life in American society, with their own businesses, neighborhoods, schools, and

44. Nathan Glazer, "Negroes and Jews: The New Challenge to Pluralism," *Commentary* 38 (December 1964): 29–35. Reprinted in his *Ethnic Dilemmas* (Cambridge:
Harvard University Press, 1983), chap. 5. For a discussion of Jewish attitudes toward
African Americans, see Lawrence A. Kogan, "The Jewish Conception of Negroes in
the North: The Historical Approach," *Phylon* 28 (winter 1967): 376–85.

unions. Jews never attacked social discrimination per se, Glazer asserted, they never challenged "the right of a group to maintain distinctive institutions," but Black demands posed "a serious threat to the ability of other groups to maintain *their* communities." African Americans, Glazer complained, had no distinctive institutions of their own and wanted, therefore, to become integrated into all of American life. Glazer reprimanded Blacks for wanting to enter on an "equal footing" into "Jewish business . . . the Jewish union . . . or the Jewish (or largely Jewish) neighborhood and school." The "force of present-day Negro demands," said Glazer, "is that the sub-community, because it either protects privileges, or creates inequality, has no right to exist." The separatism that "other groups see as a value," Glazer wrote, "Negroes see as a strategy in the fight for equal rights." He also noted "the resistance of Jewish organizations and individual Jews to such demands as preferential union membership and preferential hiring."

Glazer's comment about "Jewish unions" and the irresponsibility of Blacks trying to enter them is an example of the application of his theory. What union did Glazer have in mind? The only union regarded as "Jewish" that came under attack from Blacks at the time because of discriminatory racial practices was the ILGWU. In what ways could the ILGWU be classified as Jewish? Jewish immigrants founded the ILGWU and constituted a majority of its membership until the late 1930s, and Jews remained in control of the organization long thereafter.

Two decades before Glazer wrote his article, Jewish membership in the union had fallen to 30 percent, and it continued to decline steadily.[45] The Blacks accused of forcing themselves upon this "Jewish union" constituted—together with Latinos—a far greater proportion of the union membership than did Jews. In the central ILGWU membership base of New York City, where the garment industry and the union were concentrated,

45. The percentage of Jewish membership in the ILGWU had been declining since the late 1930s. By 1960, Blacks together with Latinos constituted a majority of the union membership in New York City. See Ben Seligman, *Contemporary Jewish Record,* December 1944, 606–7; Herberg, "Old-Timers and Newcomers," 12–19; *Jewish Labor in the United States* (New York: American Jewish Committee, 1954); and Roy B. Helfgott, "Trade Unionism among the Jewish Garment Workers of Britain and the United States," *Labor History* 2 (spring 1961): 209; also, Irving R. Stuart, "Study of Factors Associated with Inter-Group Conflict in the Ladies Garment Industry in New York" (Ph.D. diss., New York University, 1951), and Robert Laurentz, "Racial/Ethnic Conflict in the New York City Garment Industry, 1930–1980" (Ph.D. diss., State University of New York at Binghamton, 1980). In 1995, as a result of dwindling membership and declining resources, the ILGWU merged with the Amalgamated Clothing and Textile Workers Union to form the Union of Needle Trades, Industrial and Textile Employees (UNITE).

Blacks and Latinos constituted a majority of the membership. In this context, the "privileges" of the ethnic "sub-community" described by Glazer in fact derived from the institutionalization of racial discrimination and the exploitation of subordinate groups. When the victims of that arrangement attempt to advance themselves by doing what other groups, including Jews, have succeeded in doing, they are, according to Glazer, "challenging the very system under which Jews have done so well."[46] What Blacks desired, according to Glazer, was structural integration as a group into American society, something Jews already had but that Blacks could not have because of their well-known defects; hence Glazer advised them to forgo that aim.

Glazer argued for an interpretation of the Black condition based upon the alleged inability of Blacks to take advantage of the "democracy of merit." He formulated a theory corresponding to the needs of an affluent Jewish population that, while highly assimilated, also sought to maintain an unusual degree of group distinctiveness. These divergent goals raise certain problems, however, notably an anxiety about the status of assimilated groups whose roots are in an immigrant past. Demands for substantive change in the racial status quo are understood to threaten established institutional arrangements that are conducive to Jewish advancement, but not to the advancement of Blacks.

Ocean Hill–Brownsville

If the 1962 conflict between Blacks and Jews regarding the racial practices of the ILGWU raised doubts about the future of a Black-Jewish alliance, the bitter conflict that developed in 1968 between Blacks and Jews in the Ocean Hill–Brownsville school controversy involving the United Federation of Teachers in New York City shattered whatever limited consensus may have still existed. According to Steven R. Weisman of the *New York Times*, "The 55-day teachers strike, an event so corrosive that, a generation later, people say it determined many of their views about race . . . [was] a war that lacerated the city and left wounds that have never fully healed."[47] The president of the union, Albert Shanker, who came from a Jewish socialist background, used the issue of anti-Semitism as a response to Black demands for decentralization and community control of public schools. Shanker widely circulated an anti-Semitic leaflet allegedly published by a Black community group that upon investigation

46. Glazer, "Negroes and Jews."
47. Steven R. Weisman, "A City at War: The Painful Legacy of a Teachers' Strike," *New York Times*, March 1, 1997, 18.

was found not to exist.[48] His purpose was to provoke Black-Jewish conflict, thereby stimulating support from the Jewish membership of the union and Jewish organizations during a strike initiated by the teachers' union. According to Dwight Macdonald, the United Federation of Teachers was actively seeking "to increase fear and hatred driving Negro against Jew in this city."[49] Ira Glasser, head of the New York Civil Liberties Union, reflecting on these events years later, stated, "I have always blamed Shanker for whipping up the anti-Semitism issue. I think the union manufactured much of it. It caused a rupture between blacks and Jews that hasn't healed and I think it's unforgivable."[50]

At the conclusion of the Ocean Hill–Brownsville teachers' strike, which Richard Parrish, a national vice president of the American Federation of Teachers, described as "a strike against black parents and teachers," the liberal coalition lay in ruins. The Ocean Hill–Brownsville confrontation symbolized the end of the liberal consensus on race in New York and throughout the North. Since Jews were such a significant part of that consensus, this development had of necessity much significance as a Jewish issue.

48. Earl Lewis, in an authoritative study, wrote, "Curiously, the patently anti-Semitic flyer attributed to Blacks identified a community group that did not exist. Certainly members of the Black community were capable of producing such statements. Nonetheless, in light of the scope of CONINTELPRO activities by the FBI and other law enforcement groups, one might also suspect agents provocateurs" ("The Need to Remember: Three Phases in Black and Jewish Educational Relations," in *Struggles in the Promised Land: Toward a History of Black-Jewish Relations in the United States,* ed. Jack Salzman and Cornel West [New York: Oxford University Press, 1997], 254–55). For information on Shanker's political involvement see Taylor Branch, *Pillar of Fire: America in the King Years, 1963–65* (New York: Simon and Schuster, 1998), 292.

49. Dwight MacDonald, "An Open Letter to Michael Harrington," *New York Review of Books,* December 5, 1968, 48. For a discussion of these issues see the exchange between Albert Shanker and Herbert Hill, "Black Protest, Union Democracy and the UFT," in *Autocracy and Insurgency,* ed. Hall, 218–35.

50. Quoted in John Kifner, "Ocean-Hill Brownsville, '68, Echoes of a New York Waterloo," *New York Times,* December 22, 1996, E5. The literature on this history is extensive; see esp. *Confrontation at Ocean Hill–Brownsville: The New York School Strikes of 1968,* ed. Maurice Berube and Marilyn Gittell (New York: Praeger, 1969), which contains some of the most important documents of these conflicts. See also Naomi Levine, *Schools in Crisis* (New York: Popular Library, 1969); Mario Fantini, Marilyn Gittell, and Richard Magat, *Community Control and the Urban School* (New York: Praeger, 1970); Henry Levin, ed., *Community Control of the Schools* (Washington, D.C.: Brookings Institution, 1970); Diane Ravitch, *The Great School Wars: New York City, 1805–1973* (New York: Basic Books, 1974), esp. 251–404; David Rogers, *110 Livingston Street Revisited: Decentralization in Action* (New York: Random House, 1983); and Jerald E. Podair, " 'White' Values, 'Black' Values: The Ocean Hill–Brownsville Controversy and New York City Culture, 1965–1975," *Radical History Review* (spring 1994): 36–59.

Buttressed by the emergence of a new body of constitutional law on race and the adoption of the 1964 Civil Rights Act, Blacks demanded not merely an abstraction called "equal opportunity," which usually resulted in little change, but rather substantive equality as a fact. Black institutions sought affirmative measures to narrow the great gap between the condition of Blacks and that of Whites in every aspect of the society. Such an approach demanded the recognition of racism, in the past and in the present, as a basic and pervasive fact of American life. Confronted by this challenge, the traditional appeals of liberalism fell before the imperative of race. It is in the context of affirmative action that the consequences of this development were most sharply demonstrated.

Affirmative Action and the Intensification of Conflict

An examination of briefs amici curiae filed in Supreme Court cases involving affirmative action reveals the very active role of Jewish organizations in attacking affirmative action. In 1974 in the *De Funis* case,[51] where the issue was access to higher education for minorities, briefs to the Supreme Court opposing affirmative action came from the ADL, the American Jewish Committee, the American Jewish Congress, and the Jewish Rights Council. On the other hand, the National Organization of Jewish Women filed a brief in support of affirmative action that was endorsed by the Commission on Social Action of the Union of American Hebrew Congregations. In 1978 in *Bakke*,[52] also an education case, among the groups that filed amici briefs against affirmative action were the American Jewish Committee, American Jewish Congress, ADL, JLC, and National Jewish Commission on Law and Public Affairs. The two Jewish groups that had supported affirmative action in the *De Funis* case did not file in *Bakke*.

In 1979 in *Weber*,[53] a case involving employment discrimination, the ADL and the National Jewish Commission on Law and Public Affairs urged the Supreme Court to decide against affirmative action. In 1980 in *Fullilove*,[54] a challenge to an act of Congress providing a contractual set-aside for minorities in federally subsidized construction, the ADL joined with employer groups and the reactionary Pacific League Foundation to argue against affirmative action. The ADL also filed briefs in opposition to affirmative action in several lower court cases and has been among the

51. *De Funis v. Odegaard*, 416 U.S. 312 (1974).
52. *Regents of the University of California v. Bakke*, 438 U.S. 265 (1978).
53. *United Steelworkers of America v. Weber*, 443 U.S. 193 (1979).
54. *Fullilove v. Klutznick*, 448 U.S. 448 (1980).

most active of all groups in attacking affirmative action in the courts. For example, the ADL filed a brief against minority interests in 1983 in *Boston Firefighters Union, Local 718 v. Boston Chapter, NAACP* and in 1984 in the Memphis case known as *Firefighters Local Union No. 1784 v. Stotts*,[55] and this pattern of opposition to affirmative action was to continue. In addition to filing briefs amici, ADL has also initiated its own litigation against affirmative action.[56] For more than two decades, Jewish organizations have led the attack against affirmative action, and prominent Jewish leaders, institutions, and publications have engaged in a campaign against affirmative action characterized by misrepresentation and the exploitation of racial fears.[57] They have succeeded in making the term *quota*, like *busing*, a code word for resistance to demands for the elimination of prevailing patterns of discrimination.

The pages of *Commentary* have been repeatedly filled with shrill denunciations of affirmative action. Jewish neoconservatives, including Irving Kristol, Nathan Glazer, Norman Podhoretz, Elliott Abrams, and Carl Gershman, have provided the ideological basis for the civil rights retreat of the Reagan and Bush administrations, the most reactionary administrations on civil rights in the twentieth century.

In defense of their attacks on affirmative action, Jewish leaders often cite the experiences of Jews as victims of discriminatory quota systems. But no justification can be found for the continuing attack on affirmative action by invoking the memory of discrimination against Jews in the czarist empire or by elite educational institutions in the United States. The issue is current racial discrimination, and the purpose of affirmative action is to include those groups that have long been excluded on the basis of race. Affirmative action developed as the most effective means of eliminating the present effects of past discrimination and of correcting the wrongs of many generations. Affirmative action is not directed

55. *Boston Firefighters Union, Local 718 v. Boston Chapter, NAACP*, U.S. Supreme Court 1983, remanded as moot, 31 FEP Cases 1167. *Firefighters Local Union No. 1784 v. Stotts*, 467 U.S. 561 (1984).

56. See for example, press release, Anti-Defamation League of B'nai B'rith, New York, January 14, 1975.

57. Two exceptions in later cases should be noted; *Local 28, Sheet Metal Workers International Association v. EEOC*, 478 U.S. 421 (1986), and *United States v. Paradise*, 480 U.S. 149 (1987), where the American Jewish Committee, American Jewish Congress, Union of American Hebrew Congregations and the Central Conference of American Rabbis joined in an *amicus brief* in support of affirmative action. These cases involved a challenge to court-ordered affirmative action plans for admitting Blacks to a construction labor union in New York and to jobs in a public agency in Alabama. There were extensive judicial findings of prior discrimination in both cases, and the Supreme Court sustained affirmative action plans.

against Jews, it is directed against White racism. One must also note the disingenuous argument of those Jewish spokesmen who state that they are not against affirmative action but only against "quotas." Affirmative action without numbers, whether in the form of quotas, goals, or time-tables, is meaningless; there must be some benchmark, some tangible measure of change. Statistical evidence to measure performance is essential; there cannot be effective affirmative action without numbers.

By now it should be clear that the opposition to affirmative action is based on narrowly perceived group self-interest rather than on abstract philosophical differences about "quotas," "reverse discrimination," "preferential treatment," and all the other catchphrases commonly raised in public debate. After all the pious rhetoric equating affirmative action with "reverse discrimination" is stripped away, it is evident that the opposition to affirmative action is rooted in the effort to perpetuate the privileged position of Whites in American society.

Race has been and remains the great division in American society, and as the civil rights gains of the 1960s are eroded, the nation becomes even more mean-spirited and self-deceiving on the issue of race. That Jews have played an all too prominent role in this retreat reveals much about the status of Jews in American society and about how the descendants of Jewish immigrants are playing out their role in the continuing anguish of American racism.

From History to Mythology

The current conflict between Blacks and Jews has stimulated racism among some Jews and anti-Semitism among some Blacks, and these destructive forces feed upon and reinforce each other. In such volatile circumstances, it is often a quick jump from history to mythology, hence the myth of the "grand old alliance" of Blacks and Jews or the countermyth of their innate antagonism accompanied by a growing mutual demonization. John Bracey and August Meier have pointed out, "There has been much speculation about the nature and extent of Jewish support for black causes, and involvement in black advancement organizations, but precious little careful empirical research exists . . . of an alliance which has been romanticized and considerably exaggerated."[58]

Sherman Labovitz, in his *Attitudes towards Blacks among Jews: Historical Antecedents and Current Concerns*, concludes that there is "a general

58. John Bracey and August Meier, "Towards a Research Agenda on Blacks and Jews in United States History," *Journal of American Ethnic History* 12, no. 3 (spring 1993): 65–66.

tendency to romanticize the relationships and overemphasize the extent
to which Jews and Blacks have worked harmoniously." Cornel West, for
example, celebrates an imagined past of interracial cooperation when he
calls the decades between 1910 and 1967 "the period of genuine empathy
and principled alliances between Jews and blacks [that] constitutes a
major pillar of American progressive politics in this century." But Kenneth Clark writing in *Commentary* in 1946 argued against the view that
Blacks and Jews perceived their struggles against White racism and anti-
Semitism as similar. According to Clark, such beliefs ignored "the very
wide difference between Jewish and Negro social, political, and economic status." While Jews who survived the horrors of World War II rejected racism, many were not sensitive to the differences between their
own experience and that of African Americans: "Many Negroes, rightly
or wrongly, see the struggle of Jews in American society as primarily a
conservative one, to consolidate gains already made; and secondarily to
expand those gains to a higher level of economic, political, educational
and social integration with the dominant group." Clark observed that,
for their part, "many Negroes are disinclined to view [American Jews']
struggles as fundamental or as critical as their own—the struggle of the
Jew is after all not one of life and death, to wring from society the bare ne-
cessities of life."[59]

Based on my own experience of more than three decades in the Civil
Rights Movement, I am forced to question the much exaggerated assumptions of a Black-Jewish alliance. What did emerge in the 1940s was
the participation of some Jewish organizations in the legal and legislative
civil rights efforts of that period, activities limited to leadership elites and
professional staffs, but there was no mass involvement of the Jewish people with African Americans in a joint struggle for racial justice. The National Council for a Permanent Fair Employment Practices Committee,
formed in 1943, was a typical example of this pattern, where relations between the respective organizations were entirely bureaucratic in nature
and did not in any way address the profound class and racial differences
between the participating groups.[60] Since that time two distortions have
emerged regarding the history of the Civil Rights Movement during the
late 1950s and 1960s: that Jews and other Whites dominated and diverted

59. Sherman Labovitz, *Attitudes toward Blacks among Jews: Historical Antecedents and Current Concerns* (Saratoga, Calif.: RPE Research Associates, 1975), 7; Cornel West, *Race Matters* (Boston: Beacon Press, 1993), 73; Kenneth B. Clark, "Candor About Negro-Jewish Relations," *Commentary* 1 (February 1946): 12–13.
60. Records of the National Council for a Permanent Fair Employment Practices Committee are to be found in the NAACP Papers, Group II, boxes A351, 353, and 186.

the struggle into safe, irrelevant, integrationist channels against the true interests of Blacks, or that the Jewish community, having deeply involved itself in the battle for racial justice, was displaced by ungrateful, racist Blacks and is therefore understandably resentful and hostile to Black demands. Both of these falsifications ignore the crucial fact that the leadership of the civil rights struggle was African American. No one could be involved in the movement during those years without recognizing that Black people were taking their destiny into their own hands and leading their own struggles. This was, of course, the most important characteristic of that history. The southern Civil Rights Movement, wrote George M. Fredrickson, "was in many ways an expression of black autonomy and self-determination. Led by blacks, premised on black solidarity, and drawing on the distinctive traditions of the black church, it was in its own way a manifestation of African-American ethnic identity and assertiveness."[61]

The always small group of civil rights workers and volunteers involved in direct action and mass protest during the 1960s has mythically grown into an army. But there were only about three hundred Freedom Riders in all, and the Mississippi voter registration campaign of 1964 brought no more than a thousand volunteers to the South for a few weeks, and often less than that. Clayborne Carson reported, "Even after an influx of Jewish volunteers during the Mississippi Summer Project of 1964, Jews working full time with SNCC were outnumbered by white Protestants and even more by blacks, northern and southern."[62]

The Civil Rights Movement of the 1960s was based on the mass involvement of local Black communities,[63] while the number of organizational staff and volunteers was very small and accordingly included an even smaller number of Jews. Although Jewish students were represented disproportionately in the voter registration campaigns, in not a single one of the movement groups—the Southern Christian Leadership Conference (SCLC), Congress of Racial Equality (CORE), Student Non-

61. George M. Fredrickson, "America's Caste System: Will It Change?" *New York Review of Books*, October 23, 1997, 70.

62. Clayborne Carson, "Blacks and Jews in the Civil Rights Movement: The Case of SNCC," in *Bridges and Boundaries: African Americans and American Jews*, ed. Jack Salzman, Adina Back, and Gretchen Sullivan Sorin (New York: George Braziller and the Jewish Museum, 1992), 37.

63. See John Dittmer, *Local People: The Struggle for Civil Rights in Mississippi* (Urbana: University of Illinois Press, 1994), and Charles M. Payne, *I've Got the Light of Freedom* (Berkeley: University of California Press, 1995). See also Aldon D. Morris, *The Origins of the Civil Rights Movement: Black Communities Organizing for Change* (New York: Free Press, 1984).

Violent Coordinating Committee (SNCC), NAACP, and in Mississippi the Council of Federated Organizations (COFO)—did Jews or other Whites play a decisive policy role, certainly not in the field, hardly ever among the headquarters staff. A very small number of Jews functioned as second-level staff at the national offices of CORE and the NAACP, and a few others sat on the largely honorific boards of directors of some organizations. (The NAACP Legal Defense and Educational Fund, Inc., was not part of the NAACP and did not engage in mass protest activities. Since 1957 it had been a separate organization of lawyers engaged solely in litigation.)[64]

Jews and other Whites who joined in civil rights activity out of a private passion for racial justice correctly perceived the historic significance of the movement as the struggle of African Americans for their own liberation. Involved Jews undoubtedly believed that social justice was not the concern only of the oppressed, but they were few in number, and at no time were Black and Jewish communities joined together in an alliance.

With the adoption of the Civil Rights Act of 1964, the attention of Black interest groups was drawn increasingly to the urgent problems of African Americans trapped in the decaying ghettos of the urban North. In large measure, emerging Black-Jewish conflict was a consequence of the shift of civil rights activity to the North. After substantive civil rights enforcement began, there was intense opposition by northern Whites to compliance with the law, in regard to affirmative action, school desegregation, housing, and job seniority. These and other issues now clearly affected the lives of urban Whites, including Jews. Earlier civil rights struggles were concentrated largely in the South, and advances required no change in the daily lives of White people living in the North. But after 1964, the Civil Rights Movement directly affected the lives of northern Whites, who sought to maintain their traditional race-connected privileges.

I have argued above that the charges of anti-Semitism made by the leadership of the ILGWU in 1962 not only had no justification but were a dishonest attempt to divert attention from the union's own discriminatory practices. Thirty-five years later, self-declared Black messiahs are resorting to anti-Semitism in their effort to control and manipulate Black anger, and there is a danger that in some instances the struggle against White racism may take the degraded form of anti-Semitism.

The epic legacy of the Black struggle for freedom must not be

64. See Jack Greenberg, *Crusaders in the Courts* (New York: Basic Books, 1994), chap. 35.

tarnished, must not be compromised, by anti-Semitism, which is not part of the Black heritage in America or in Africa. On the contrary, there is an old strain of folk philo-Semitism in African American life that continues to be expressed within the church community.[65] Anti-Semitism belongs to the history and culture of the White Christian world. It belongs to those who are responsible for the creation and perpetuation of a culture of racism based upon White supremacy.

While Black and Jewish leaders have a mutual responsibility to break the cycle of charge and countercharge, it may be argued that Jews have a special, unique obligation to initiate action on behalf of justice and reconciliation. Steven Schwarzschild, a professor of Philosophy and Judaic Studies at Washington University and a dear friend until his death in 1989, explained why:

> Jews are defined by neither doctrine nor credo. We are defined by *task.* That task is to redeem the world through *justice.* To accomplish that task, the Jewish people needs to stay alive, but survival is not an end in itself but rather a means to enable us to pursue our task. Indeed to make survival into an end in itself, to seek it for its own sake, is to belie the values of the Jewish tradition, of Jewish law. If the notion of "chosenness" means anything supportable, it is that our portion, our task, is unlike that of other peoples, being in fact the duty to refine, exemplify and apply human and social justice.[66]

65. For a valuable account that demonstrates this tradition see Hollis R. Lynch, "A Black Nineteenth-Century Response to Jews and Zionism: The Case of Edward Wilmot Blyden," in *Jews in Black Perspectives: A Dialogue,* ed. Joseph R. Washington Jr. (Lanham, Md.: University Press of America, 1989), 42–54. Blyden's essay "The Jewish Question" is his own statement on this subject. For an interesting discussion regarding the cultural implications of the diaspora experience of both Blacks and Jews see Paul Gilroy, *The Black Atlantic, Modernity and Double Consciousness* (Cambridge: Harvard University Press, 1993), 208–17.

66. Steven Schwarzschild, letter to Herbert Hill, February 22, 1988.

The Portrayal of Jews in
The Autobiography of Malcolm X

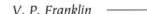

V. P. Franklin

I will bet that I have told five hundred such challengers that Jews as a group would never watch some other minority systematically siphoning out their community's resources without doing something about it. I have told them that if I tell the simple truth, it doesn't mean that I am anti-Semitic; it means merely that I am anti-exploitation.

THE AUTOBIOGRAPHY OF MALCOLM X

MALCOLM X HAS become one of the most influential African American leaders and intellectuals in the second half of the twentieth century. The controversial and charismatic spokesperson for the Nation of Islam and later the Organization for Afro-American Unity rose to prominence in the early 1960s and is generally considered the major ideological progenitor for the Black Power movement in the second half of that decade. Malcolm X preached "Black self-defense" in the face of the widespread attacks on nonviolent civil rights protesters in the South and the even more pervasive assaults by local police on law-abiding Black citizens in various parts of the country. While the nonviolent, direct-action protests led by Martin Luther King Jr., the Southern Christian Leadership Conference, and other civil rights groups were primarily responsible for the end of "American apartheid" through the passage of the Civil Rights Act of 1964 and the Voting Rights Act of 1965, many historians now believe that it was Malcolm X's militant Black nationalism that forced legislative leaders to respond positively to the civil rights demands. Those political leaders who initially opposed Dr. King's social and political objectives found Malcolm X and the Nation of Islam to be a much less palatable alternative.[1]

1. On the significance of the leadership provided by Malcolm X and Martin Luther King Jr. see James Cone, *Martin and Malcolm and America: A Dream or Nightmare?*

Although Malcolm delivered hundreds of speeches and gave numerous interviews throughout his public career, his major contribution to the
African American literary tradition is *The Autobiography of Malcolm X*,
written with journalist Alex Haley and published shortly after his death
in April 1965. Upon publication, *The Autobiography of Malcolm X* became
an immediate bestseller, and it has remained in print for more than thirty
years, attracting larger and larger audiences.[2] Literary critics and historians have suggested several reasons for the work's immense popularity and importance within the American autobiographical tradition.
G. Thomas Couser in *American Autobiography: The Prophetic Mode* found
that Malcolm X's writing exemplified a "prophetic" tradition that emphasized "the conflation of the personal and the communal, the conscious creation of exemplary patterns of behavior, and their didactic,
even hortatory, impulses." Couser found that Malcolm's "awareness of
his prophetic role in life is obvious in the narrative, and evidence in his
collaborator's epilogue suggests that he was aware that tact and delicacy
were required for the successful treatment of that role in autobiography.
He [Malcolm] strove to resist the temptation to attribute too much importance to himself and to write an exemplary and didactic narrative in
which his own experience of family instability, poverty, unemployment,
and discrimination would stand for the plight of American Blacks."[3]

During Malcolm's incarceration in a Massachusetts prison, he underwent a profoundly religious "conversion experience." While Couser understood the significance of the conversion experience for structuring
and organizing the autobiography, he did not recognize the "cultural"

(Maryknoll, N.Y.: Orbis Books, 1991). For biographical information on Malcolm X see
John Henrik Clarke, ed., *Malcolm X: The Man and His Times* (New York: Macmillan,
1969); Peter Goldman, *The Death and Life of Malcolm X* (New York: Harper and Row,
1973); Eugene V. Wolfenstein, *The Victims of Democracy: Malcolm X and the Black Revolution* (Berkeley: University of California Press, 1981); Bruce Perry, *Malcolm: The Life of
the Man Who Changed Black America* (New York: Station Hill Press, 1991); David Gallen
et al., *Malcolm X As They Knew Him* (New York: Carroll and Graf, 1992); Benjamin
Karim with Peter Skutches and David Gallen, *Remembering Malcolm* (New York: Carroll and Graf, 1992); Joe Wood, ed., *Malcolm X: In Our Own Image* (New York: St. Martin's Press, 1992); William Sales, *From Civil Rights to Black Liberation: Malcolm X and the
Organization of Afro-American Unity* (Boston: South End Press, 1994); and Michael Eric
Dyson, *Making Malcolm: The Myth and the Meaning of Malcolm X* (New York: Oxford
University Press, 1995).
   2. Malcolm X with Alex Haley, *The Autobiography of Malcolm X* (New York: Grove
Press, 1965); reprinted by permission of Random House, Inc. Parenthetical page references in the text are to this edition.
   3. G. Thomas Couser, *American Autobiography: The Prophetic Mode* (Amherst: University of Massachusetts Press, 1979), 1, 165.

and "spiritual" importance of this "miraculous" occurrence. Couser believed that Malcolm was "less successful at communicating a sense of this experience than he had been at re-creating his previous life" as a high school dropout, street hustler, pimp, and burglar. Malcolm's reticence about "the most liberating experience in his life" suggested to Couser that it was nothing more than "an intellectual and emotional commitment to an ideology which offered him a redeeming self-image and a useful mythology. Nor does Malcolm acknowledge at this point that his experience of liberation had made him, in a sense, a prisoner of racist ideology. Instead of indicating the provisional nature of the conversion, he lets it stand as a crucial, if imperfectly communicated experience."[4]

Other literary critics, biographers, and commentators on *The Autobiography of Malcolm X* have also speculated about what Malcolm and Haley may have felt based on this account of his life, and some have gone out of their way to try and discredit particular statements and descriptions of events. However, a careful examination of what Malcolm and Haley actually wrote reveals descriptions of events that Malcolm thought were "miraculous" and that served to strengthen his faith in Elijah Muhammad and the teachings of the Nation of Islam. In fact, the autobiography includes a detailed description of the miraculous experience that Malcolm underwent one night in his cell in the Massachusetts prison where he was serving a ten-year sentence for burglary.

Malcolm's brother Reginald had joined the Nation of Islam while Malcolm was incarcerated, and it was Reginald who actually introduced Malcolm to the religious teachings of the Honorable Elijah Muhammad, the Messenger of Allah. According to the Messenger, African Americans were members of the "Lost Tribe of Shabazz" who had spent four hundred years in captivity in America. The period of White world domination is coming to an end, however, and the Messenger of Allah has been sent to separate his Black children from the "white devils" who have ruled for six thousand years but will be destroyed on the coming Judgment Day.[5]

Malcolm's brother had been suspended from the Nation of Islam after being found guilty of charges of adultery. Malcolm recalled that one

---

4. Ibid., 168. For similar observations see Carol Ohmann, "*The Autobiography of Malcolm X*: A Revolutionary Use of the Franklin Tradition," *American Quarterly* 22 (summer 1970): 131–49, and Paul John Eakin, "Malcolm X and the Limits of Autobiography," in *Autobiography: Essays Theoretical and Critical*, ed. James Olney (Princeton: Princeton University Press, 1980), 181–93.

5. Elijah Muhammad, *Message to the Blackman in America* (Chicago: Nation of Islam, 1965), 4–19.

evening he was lying on his bed in the cell praying to Allah for Reginald's reinstatement.

> I suddenly, with a start, became aware of a man sitting beside me in
> my chair. He had on a dark suit. I remember. I could see him as
> plainly as I see anyone I look at. He wasn't black, and he wasn't
> white. He was light brown-skinned, an Asiatic cast of countenance,
> and he had oily black hair. I looked right in his face. I didn't get
> frightened. I knew I wasn't dreaming. I couldn't move. I didn't speak,
> and he didn't. I couldn't place him racially—other than that I knew
> he was non-European. I had no idea whatsoever who he was. He just
> sat there. Then, suddenly as he had come, he was gone. (186–87)

Malcolm later learned that the man he saw in his vision was Wallace D.
Farad (Muhammad), who claimed to be God and taught Elijah Muhammad the religious tenets of the Nation of Islam. At the time, this miraculous event served to convince Malcolm to learn more about the Nation of
Islam, which he would later join.[6]

The description of the religious conversion is at the center of *The Autobiography of Malcolm X*, reflecting a narrative strategy found in many
other "spiritual autobiographies." Within the Western autobiographical
tradition, from *The Confessions of Saint Augustine* in the fifth century to the
present, literary scholars have identified a type of conversion discourse
that is often not confined to the religious sphere. Peter A. Dorsey in *Sacred
Estrangement: The Rhetoric of Conversion in Modern American Autobiography*
finds that during the last three centuries "conversion became a model for
many kinds of psychological changes, yet the secular autobiographies of
the period continued to respond to the socializing function implicit in
conversion rhetoric: like the works in the Christian tradition, many of
these narratives are centered on the acceptance of vocation." Dorsey argues that nonreligious writers often "departed from Christian models by
using conversion rhetoric to affirm the dignity of their inner selves, but
they nevertheless were also engaged in a process of reform—whether social, philosophical, or cognitive. They may have distrusted the kind of
unquestioned submission associated with religious conversion, but they

6. For information on Wallace D. Farad (Muhammad), who instructed Elijah Poole,
later Muhammad, in the tenets of the Nation of Islam see C. Eric Lincoln, *The
Black Muslims in America*, 3d ed. (Trenton, N.Y.: Africa World Press, 1994), 12–19;
E. U. Essien-Udom, *Black Nationalism: A Search for an Identity in America* (Chicago: University of Chicago Press, 1962), 55–75; Louis Lomax, *When the Word Is Given: A Report
of Elijah Muhammad, Malcolm X, and the Black Muslim World* (Cleveland: World Publishing Co., 1963), 14–17; and Mattias Gardell, *In the Name of Elijah Muhammad: Louis
Farrakhan and the Nation of Islam* (Durham: Duke University Press, 1996), 50–59,
170–74.

continued to affirm the value of community—even if the communities they valued became quite elusive."[7]

Miracles of Faith

Within the African American autobiographical tradition, from the slave narratives of the early nineteenth century to *The Autobiography of Malcolm X*, this conversion rhetoric, preoccupation with reform, and search for community are readily apparent. In Ida Wells-Barnett's *Crusade for Justice*, W. E. B. Du Bois's *Dusk of Dawn* and *Soliloquy*, Richard Wright's *Black Boy* and *American Hunger*, Harry Haywood's *Black Bolshevik*, Gwendolyn Brooks's *Report from Part One*, Adam Clayton Powell Jr.'s *Adam by Adam*, and many other autobiographical works by African American artists and intellectuals, the central conversion experience marks a significant turning point in the personal narrative.[8]

The Autobiography of Malcolm X describes not only Malcolm's numerous conversion experiences during his brief lifetime but also the miraculous nature of those transformations, which reflected the Nation of Islam's basic religious tenets. The fifth tenet of the statement published in every issue of *Muhammad Speaks* describing "What the Muslims Believe" states, "We believe in the resurrection of the dead—not in physical resurrection—but in mental resurrection. We believe the so-called Negroes are most in need of mental resurrection; therefore they will be resurrected first." Unlike the conversion experiences described in most Christian spiritual autobiographies, Malcolm's conversion to Islam is described as "a resurrection from the dead." For example, when he is assessing his early life and the dangerous things he did as a burglar and hustler, he declares, "[S]ometimes, recalling all of this, I don't know, to tell the truth, how I am alive to tell it today. They say God takes care of fools and babies. I've so often thought that Allah was watching over me. Through all this time of my life, I really *was* dead—mentally dead. I just didn't know that I was" (125). At the end, after Malcolm has reluctantly come to the conclusion that Elijah Muhammad may be behind the recent attempts on his life, he declares that he must speak to his "spiritual father" about this because "he had virtually raised me from the dead. Everything I was that

7. Peter A. Dorsey, *Sacred Estrangement: The Rhetoric of Conversion in Modern American Autobiography* (University Park: Pennsylvania State University Press, 1993), 8–9.
8. For more on conversion experiences in autobiographical works by African Americans see V. P. Franklin, *Living Our Stories, Telling Our Truths: Autobiography and the Making of the African-American Intellectual Tradition* (New York: Oxford University Press, 1996).

was creditable, he had made me. I felt that no matter what, I could not let him down" (296).[9]

Ideological Continuities

While personal, ideological, and even miraculous changes are found at the core of the stories and events described in *The Autobiography of Malcolm X*, there is also much ideological continuity in a number of the topics and issues discussed. While it is clear by the end of the autobiography that Malcolm's views on White Americans have changed from hatred and total rejection to tolerance and acceptance of some as close friends, his beliefs about White liberals did not change. It becomes clear that Malcolm never really trusted White liberals because of their entrenched racist attitudes and behavior. In the third chapter, for example, where Malcolm describes the destruction of his family following his mother's mental breakdown and his stay as a foster child in the home of Mr. and Mrs. Swerlin, he recalls that "one of their favorite parlor topics was 'niggers,'" even when Malcolm was standing right there. "It just never dawned upon them that I could understand, that I wasn't a pet, but a human being. They didn't give me credit for having the same sensitivity, intellect, and understanding that they would have been ready and willing to recognize in a white in my position." What he disliked most was the "kindly condescension which I try to clarify today, to these integration-hungry Negroes, about their 'liberal' white friends, these so-called 'good white people'—most of them anyway" (27).

In the fifteenth chapter, in discussing the positions he took on various civil rights issues and campaigns, Malcolm explains why he felt the northern Freedom Riders in 1961 were hypocrites. Why should they be traveling by bus to integrate Mississippi, when "ultra liberal New York had more integration problems than Mississippi"? When Malcolm suggested that northern White liberals go into the Black ghettos, where there were "enough rats and roaches to kill to keep all the Freedom Riders busy," he was roundly denounced. "Snakes couldn't have turned on me faster than the liberal. Yes, I will pull off that liberal's halo he spends such efforts cultivating! The North's liberals have been for so long pointing accusing fingers at the South and getting away with it that they have fits when they are exposed as the world's worst hypocrites" (271).

In the final pages of the last chapter, Malcolm reiterates: "I never really trust the kind of white people who are always so anxious to hang around

9. See Franklin, "Malcolm X and the Resurrection of the Dead," in ibid., 319–45.

Negroes, or to hang around Negro communities. I don't trust the kind of whites who love having Negroes always hanging around them." He traces this belief to his experiences with Whites throughout his life, particularly in Boston and Harlem. He also opposed letting Whites into Black organizations.

> I know that every time that whites join a Black organization, you watch, pretty soon the Blacks will be leaning on the whites to support it, and before you know it the Black may be up front with a title, but the whites because of their money, are the real controllers. . . . Let sincere white individuals find all other white people they can who feel as they do—and let them form their own all-white groups, to work trying to convert other white people who are thinking and acting so racist. Let sincere whites go and teach non-violence to white people! (377)

Rhetoric and Reality in Black–Jewish Relations

Even more important were the ideological continuities found in Malcolm X's portrayal of Jewish Americans. Historians and other scholars have debated the idea that the anti-Jewish rhetoric associated with Malcolm X and other African American spokepersons represents a distinctive type of "Black anti-Semitism." Historian Leonard Dinnerstein in *Antisemitism in America* examines African American attitudes toward Jews from the 1830s to the 1990s and concludes that they represented a particularly virulent form of anti-Semitism. According to Dinnerstein, African Americans learned these anti-Semitic attitudes from the dominant White majority and imitated the behavior of White Christians. "One means of identifying with the majority, and therefore gaining greater self-confidence and esteem, has been to take on the prejudices of the majority group. To some extent, Black antisemitism has been a psychological, perhaps an unconscious one at that, response to their positions in American society. By adopting a majority prejudice, members of minorities can feel superior to the group that they too despise."[10]

Dinnerstein's conjectures about how African Americans may have absorbed anti-Semitic beliefs have not been corroborated by recent social scientific research. Dinnerstein argues that,

> like members of the dominant culture, a number of African Americans have been comfortable scapegoating Jews for their difficulties. Having the strong religious undergirding of Christian theology, it

---

10. Leonard Dinnerstein, *Antisemitism in America* (New York: Oxford University Press, 1994), 248–49.

can easily be seen how African Americans have personified the Jews as sources of their woes. And added to that underlying belief, since the 1930s there have been enough specific examples of negative interactions between African Americans and Jews for African Americans to assume that they are responding to realities in their lives rather than building on myths from the past.[11]

Recent social scientific surveys of African Americans, however, suggest that religious "myths from the past" encourage favorable attitudes toward Jews because the more religious African Americans are likely to identify with the Jews, particularly the Israelites in the Old Testament. The William O. Douglas Institute surveyed 189 Black Protestants in Seattle, St. Louis, and Buffalo in 1986. The overall issue addressed in the survey was: "What are the attitudes of Black Protestants toward Jewish people in contemporary American society." Also in 1986 the consulting firm of Tarrance, Hill, Newport, and Ryan was commissioned by the Anti-Defamation League to conduct a national survey by telephone of one thousand White Protestants to determine the attitudes of White Christians from the mainstream denominations (Episcopalians, Presbyterians, Congregationalists) as well as Evangelicals toward Jewish people. These were the findings:

> The essential conclusion of the Tarrance survey was that a majority of white Protestants showed no anti-semitism; and there were some indications that evangelical Christians were, on the whole, more positive to Jews than were Christians generally. From the findings reported here, the same can be said of Black Protestants. If anything they appear to be less anti-Jewish than their white counterparts. Certainly there are no indications here of significant anti-semitic sentiments, although some skepticism exists about Israel and its treatment of the Palestinian Arabs.
>
> Therefore, to the essential query posed for this study, namely "what are the attitudes of Black Protestants toward Jewish people in contemporary American society?" we can answer: generally tolerant and largely favorable. They are plainly not anti-semitic and, on the whole, quite like the white Protestants surveyed in the Tarrance project.[12]

One of the major reasons given for the "largely favorable" attitudes toward Jews among Black Christians in the United States was the historical reality that they identified closely with the slavery and deliverance of God's "Chosen People" as described in the Old Testament. Hubert Locke noted in the Douglas Institute report,

---

11. Ibid., 248.
12. Hubert G. Locke, *The Black Anti-Semitism Controversy: Protestant Views and Perspectives* (Selinsgrove, Pa.: Susquehanna University Press, 1994), 56.

Black Protestantism draws upon the Jewish Biblical tradition and experience for its frame of reference in providing a religious interpretation of the Black experience in America. In Black preaching, the
themes of slavery and deliverance and of oppression and freedom as
experienced by the people of Israel in Biblical times form a distinctive
core of the Sunday message. The heroic figures of Biblical Judaism—
Moses, David, Saul, and Elijah—are used as models for exhortation
and instruction, while the messages of the Hebrew prophets become
primary sources for the affirmation of principles regarding social justice and responsibility.[13]

In light of these historical and sociological data, what then accounts for
the numerous charges of Black anti-Semitism being leveled by Jewish
scholars and leaders? The authors of the Douglas Institute survey suggested that while there are some African Americans who express anti-
Jewish attitudes on the basis of interactions with Jewish Americans in the
political and economic sphere, "it is because Jewish citizens are so
acutely aware of and sensitive to the consequences of such attitudes that
many are inclined to respond immediately and vigorously to any negative expressions about Jews as signs of anti-semitism." But the authors
argued that the anti-Jewish attitudes of a small element within the
African American community "should not be confused with those of the
mass of Black America or projected onto the entire populace as the unfortunate use of the term 'Black anti-semitism' does. The term gives rise
to the unwarranted impression that hatred of the Jews is widespread
among Black Americans. It confuses those anti-semitic outbursts that
do occur with the range of other expressions and attitudes that can be
heard occasionally or even frequently in Black communities about Jewish
people."[14]

The authors of the Douglas Institute survey also suggested that where
anti-Jewish attitudes and behavior have been detected among African
Americans, they were understandable, though still unacceptable, given
Blacks' experience of oppression and discrimination in American society.
These anti-Jewish attitudes among African Americans could be accounted
for by "the availability of a palpable target of animosity, a Jewish
landlord or banker or employer, who functions as a kind of lightning rod
to focus anger on the perpetrators of injustice (who happen to be Jewish).

13. Ibid., 32. African Americans not only identified with God's Chosen People in
the Old Testament but also came to believe that they were among God's Chosen People in the United States. For a detailed examination of this topic see V. P. Franklin,
Black Self-Determination: A Cultural History of African-American Resistance (Brooklyn:
Lawrence Hill Books, 1992), 34–67.
14. Locke, *Black Anti-Semitism Controversy*, 94–95.

We do not typically ask of the victims that they engage in rational analysis about the relative numbers of Jewish oppressors or about a system of
which particular Jews are merely accidental representatives. Rather, we
understand the ugly delusion as a byproduct of oppression."[15]

Whereas recent research suggests that religious African Americans are
less likely to have anti-Semitic attitudes, Dinnerstein's analysis seems to
better explain the development of racist attitudes among European Jews
who immigrated to the United States. David Roediger in *The Wages of
Whiteness: Race and the Making of the American Working Class,* Noel Ignatiev in *How the Irish Became White,* and several other researchers who
have examined the social construction of "whiteness" have argued that
the European immigrants who arrived in the United States in the nineteenth and early twentieth centuries not only became acculturated to the
manners and mores of "Anglo-America" but also adopted a "white racial
identity" and used "whiteness" to advance their social, economic, and
political circumstances at the expense of native-born African Americans.
As "White" Americans, these newly arrived European immigrants were
granted certain "white skin privileges," and they used them to exclude
African Americans and other "non-Whites" from competition in employment, housing, education, and other areas of social and economic life.[16]
According to the researchers of the social significance of "whiteness" in
American history, Dinnerstein's observation that "by adopting a majority prejudice, members of minorities can feel superior to the group that
they too despise" more appropriately applied to European ethnic minorities in their interactions with African Americans and other non-
White groups in the United States. This argument is also relevant in
explaining racist behavior exhibited by American Jews and in answering the still unanswered question, "How Did the Jews Become White
Folks?"[17]

15. Ibid., 85.
16. David R. Roediger, *The Wages of Whiteness: Race and the Making of the American
Working Class* (New York: Verso, 1991); Theodore W. Allen, *The Invention of the White
Race,* vol. 1, *Racial Oppression and Social Control* (London: Verso, 1994); Noel Ignatiev,
How the Irish Became White (New York: Routledge, 1995); Ian F. Haney Lopez, *White by
Law: The Legal Construction of Race* (New York: New York University Press, 1996). See
also Mike Hill, ed. *Whiteness: A Critical Reader* (New York: New York University
Press, 1997).
17. For a too brief discussion of this topic see Karen Brodkin Sacks, "How Did the
Jews Become White Folks?" in *Critical White Studies: Looking Behind the Mirror,* ed.
Richard Delgado and Jean Stefancic (Philadelphia: Temple University Press, 1997),
395–401. See also Louis Harap, "Anti-Negroism among Jews" (1943), in *Bridges and
Boundaries: African Americans and American Jews,* ed. Jack Salzman, Adina Black, and
Gretchen Sullivan Sorin (New York: George Braziller and the Jewish Museum, 1992),

Novelist and social critic James Baldwin offered an assessment of the racist and discriminatory attitudes and practices of Jewish Americans in their dealings with African Americans and concluded, "Negroes Are Anti-Semitic Because They're Anti-White." In the essay by that title first published in the *New York Times Magazine* in April 1967, Baldwin observed that, "in the American context, the most ironical thing about Negro anti-Semitism is that the Negro is really condemning the Jew for having become an American white man—for having become, in effect, a Christian. The Jew profits from his status in America, and he must expect Negroes to distrust him for it. The Jew does not realize that the credential he offers, the fact that he has been despised and slaughtered, does not increase the Negro's understanding. It increases the Negro's rage."[18]

Malcolm X on Black-Jewish Relations

According to reporter Peter Goldman, Malcolm X made a similar observation in a speech given at a rally in New York City in 1965. In *The Death and Life of Malcolm X*, Goldman reports,

> Once, at a Harlem rally just after his break with Muhammad, someone in the question-and-answer period mentioned the six million Jews sent to the ovens in the Third Reich. "Everybody talks about the six million Jews," Malcolm said. "But I was reading a book the other day that showed that one hundred million of us were kidnapped and brought to this country—*one hundred million*. Now everybody's wet-eyed over a handful of Jews who brought it on themselves. What about our one hundred million?" The line got a good hand; the Jews Harlem sees tend to be landlords, storekeepers and welfare workers, and nobody gets wet-eyed about them.[19]

Dinnerstein's only reference to Malcolm X in his lengthy book on anti-Semitism in America is to quote part of this passage as evidence of anti-Semitic statements made by African American leaders.[20] However, there are numerous additional statements and references to Jews and their interactions with African Americans in *The Autobiography*, and Malcolm declares over and over in that work that his assessments of Black-Jewish

---

74–78; and David Roediger, "Whiteness and Ethnicity in the History of 'White Ethnics' in the United States," in *Towards the Abolition of Whiteness* (New York: Verso, 1994), 181–98.

18. James Baldwin, "Negroes Are Anti-Semitic Because They're Anti-White," in *The Price of the Ticket: Collected Nonfiction, 1948–1985* (New York: St. Martin's and Merek, 1985), 430.

19. Goldman, *The Death and Life of Malcolm X*, 14–15.

20. Dinnerstein, *Antisemitism in America*, 210.

relations in the United States were based, not on Christian or Islamic religious teachings, but on his own personal experiences in Boston, New
York, and other places. Indeed, Malcolm makes it clear that when he
studied their history during his incarceration and afterward, he developed a deep appreciation for the "rich Jewish ethnic and cultural roots."

The first personal reference to Jews in *The Autobiography* comes in the
seventh chapter, where Malcolm describes his life as a "hustler" in New
York City. Malcolm got a job with a Jewish merchant, Hymie, who
bought, refurbished, and resold at a profit bars and restaurants in
Harlem. The interactions between the Black street kid and the Jewish
merchant were quite positive, and Malcolm learned a great deal about
Jewish self-concept and received personal instruction in how the Jews
became White folks. "Hymie really liked me, and I liked him," Malcolm
recalled.

> He loved to talk. I loved to listen. Half his talk was about Jews and
> Negroes. Jews who anglicized their names were Hymie's favorite
> hate. Spitting and curling his mouth in scorn, he would reel off the
> names of people he said had done this. Some of them were famous
> names whom most people never thought of as Jews. "Red, I'm a Jew
> and you're Black," he would say. "These Gentiles don't like either
> one of us. If the Jew wasn't smarter than the Gentile, he'd get treated
> worse than your people." (123)

Malcolm's main job was transporting Hymie's bootleg liquor, which
had been funneled into brand-name bottles. "Many people claiming they
drank only such-and-such a brand couldn't tell their 'only' brand from
pure week-old Long Island bootleg. Most ordinary whiskey drinkers are
'brand' chumps like this." One day something happened involving
Hymie and the State Liquor Authority. Malcolm recalled sadly, "Hymie
didn't show up where he had told me to meet him. I never heard from
him again . . . but I did hear that he was put in the ocean and I knew he
couldn't swim" (124).

Chapter 15 is titled "Icarus," after the son of Daedalus in Greek
mythology who was given wax wings by his father so he could escape
imprisonment; when Icarus flew too close to the sun, the wax in his
wings melted and he plunged to his death in the sea. In this chapter, Malcolm describes how high he had flown ideologically as the spokesperson
for the Nation of Islam just before his tremendous fall. Much of the chapter is devoted to an unrelentingly negative assessment of his bête noire
throughout the autobiography, not White Americans but "the so-called
educated Negroes" who favor integration. "Only a few thousands of Negroes, relatively a very tiny number, are taking any part in 'integration.'

Here, again, it is those few bourgeois Negroes, rushing to throw away their little money in the white man's luxury hotels, his swanky night-clubs, and big, fine, exclusive restaurants." The bourgeois Negroes were going to these places just to prove they are "integrated." But the bottom line in this move toward integration was "intermarriage." "I'm right *with* the Southern white man who believes that you can't have so-called 'inte-gration,' at least not for long, without intermarriage increasing" (276).

Malcolm then presents a detailed condemnation of integration because it would lead to "assimilation." "What we arrive at is that 'integration,' socially, is no good for either side. 'Integration' ultimately would destroy the white race . . . and destroy the Black race" (276). For Malcolm the as-similation by Blacks into White society would bring certain death, and he uses the situation of the Jews in Germany to make his point. Some White ethnic groups resisted assimilation in order to preserve their culture and heritage. "Look at how the Irish threw the English out of Ireland. The Irish knew the English would engulf them. Look at the French-Canadians, fanatically fighting to keep their identity" (277). The German Jew, however, represents "history's most tragic result of a mixed, there-fore diluted and weakened, ethnic identity."

> He had made greater contributions to Germany than Germans them-selves had. Jews had won over half of Germany's Nobel Prizes. Every [cultural institution] was led by the Jew; he published the greatest newspaper. Jews were the greatest artists, the greatest poets, com-posers, stage directors. But those Jews made a fatal mistake—assimi-lating. From World War I to Hitler's rise the Jews in Germany had been increasingly intermarrying. Many changed their names and many took other religions. Their own religion, their own rich Jewish ethnic and cultural roots they anesthetized, and cut off . . . until they began to think of themselves as "Germans." (277)

Hitler rose to power using the Jews as scapegoats for the social and economic problems facing Germany.

> Most mysterious is how those Jews—with all of their power in every aspect of Germany's affairs—how did those Jews stand almost as if mesmerized, watching something which did not spring on them overnight, but which was gradually developed—a monstrous plan for their own *murder*. Their self-brainwashing had been so complete that not long after, in the gas chambers, a lot of them were still gasp-ing, "It can't be true." If Hitler *had* conquered the world, as he meant to—that is a shuddery thought for every Jew alive today. (278)

Malcolm also makes it clear that he now respected the Israeli Jews be-cause they "will never forget that lesson. Jewish intelligence eyes watch every neo-Nazi organization." Following the war "the Jews' Haganah mediating body stepped up longtime negotiations with the British. But this time the Stern gang was shooting the British. And this time the British acquiesced and helped them wrest Palestine away from the Arabs, the rightful owners, and then the Jews set up Israel, their own country—the one thing that every race of man in the world respects, and understands" (278).

While Malcolm understood and was sympathetic toward the plight of Jews in Nazi-dominated Europe and respected them for establishing the state of Israel as the Jewish homeland, he criticized Jewish Americans' racist attitudes and behavior toward African Americans. When he made statements in his speeches condemning the racist behavior of White Americans in general, he always found the Jews in the audience to be "the most subjective" and "hypersensitive." "I mean you can't even say 'Jew' without him accusing you of anti-Semitism. I don't care what a Jew is professionally, doctor, merchant, housewife, student, or whatever—first he, or she, thinks Jew." Malcolm believed that Jewish support of Black causes had a very practical side: "all of the bigotry and hatred focused upon the Black man keeps off the Jew a lot of the heat that would be on him otherwise." He sometimes mentions that Jewish merchants in Black communities siphoned out money, "which helped the ghetto stay poor. But I doubt that I have ever uttered this absolute truth before an audience without being hotly challenged, and accused by a Jew of anti-Semitism. Why? I will bet that I have told five hundred such challengers that Jews as a group would never watch some other minority systematically siphoning out their community's resources without doing something about it. I have told them that if I tell the simple truth, it doesn't mean that I am anti-Semitic; it means merely that I am anti-exploitation" (283).

In the final chapter, Malcolm complains about his "constant surveillance" by the government and the fact that the agent who had been assigned to watch him "was a particularly obvious and obnoxious one." Malcolm saw the man lurking around wherever he went, and so he decided to confront him. "I told him I knew he was following me, and if he wanted to know anything, why didn't he ask me. He started to give me one of those too-lofty-to-descend-to-you attitudes. I told him right to his face he was a fool, that he didn't know me, or what I stood for, so that made him one of those people who let somebody else do their thinking; and that no matter what job a man had, at least he ought to be able to think for himself. That stung him; he let me have it" (371).[21]

21. It is likely that this agent worked for the FBI. See Clayborne Carson, *Malcolm X: The FBI File* (New York: Carroll and Graf, 1991).

The agent accused Malcolm of being "anti-American, un-American, seditious, subversive, and probably Communist." Malcolm told the agent that it was clear from these statements that he understood nothing about him or his beliefs. But through these exchanges and the agent's "consistent subjectivity in just about everything he asked and said, I deduced something, and I told him, 'You know, I think you're a Jew with an Anglicized name.' His involuntary expression told me I'd hit the button." The agent asked how he knew this and Malcolm explained. "I told him I'd had so much experience with how Jews would attack me that I usually could identify them. I told him all I held against the Jew was that so many Jews actually were hypocrites in their claim to be friends of the American Black man, and it burned me up to be so often called 'anti-Semitic' when I spoke things I knew to be the absolute truth about Jews" (372).

Malcolm told the agent that he gave the Jews credit for supporting the Civil Rights Movement, but they did this to divert the prejudices of Gentiles away from them. Malcolm believed the Jews were insincere in this support for civil rights because "so often in the North the quickest segregationists were the Jews themselves. Look at practically everything the Black man is trying to 'integrate' into for instance, if the Jews are not the actual owners, or are not in controlling positions, then they have major stock holdings or they are otherwise in powerful leverage positions— and do they really sincerely exert these influences? No!" (372–73).

Malcolm believed that in Harlem and other cities American Jews demonstrated their true feelings when they fled streets and neighborhoods once African Americans began to move in. In chapter 5, he describes his early years in Harlem and briefly mentions that at the turn of the century the area was predominantly Jewish, "then in 1910, a Negro real estate man somehow got two or three Negro families into one Jewish Harlem apartment house. The Jews flew from that house, then from that block, and more Negroes came in to fill their apartments. Then whole blocks of Jews ran, and still more Negroes came uptown, until in a short time, Harlem was like it still is today—virtually all-Black" (82).[22]

In his discussions with the government agent, Malcolm made the same point. The Jews' true beliefs about Blacks were demonstrated, Malcolm believed, "whenever a Negro moved into a white residential neighborhood that was thickly Jewish. Who would always lead the whites'

22. See James Weldon Johnson, *Black Manhattan* (1930; rpt. New York: De Capo Press, 1991), 145–59; Gilbert Osofsky, *Harlem: The Making of a Ghetto, Negro New York, 1890–1930* (New York: Harper and Row, 1963), 88–89; Jeffrey S. Gurock, *When Harlem Was Jewish, 1870–1930* (New York: Columbia University Press, 1979).

exodus? The Jews! Generally in these situations, some whites stay put—you just notice who they are: they're Irish Catholics, they're Italians; they're rarely Jews. And, ironically, the Jews themselves often still have trouble being 'accepted.' Saying this, I know I'll hear 'anti-Semitic' from every direction again. Oh, yes! But truth is truth" (373).

Whether or not these statements in *The Autobiography of Malcolm X* should be considered examples of "Black anti-Semitism" will likely be a subject of debate for decades to come. But what we do know is that Malcolm did not consider himself an anti-Semite; he felt he merely spoke the truth about the nature of Black-Jewish relations in twentieth-century America. At the same time, however, if modern anti-Semitism is defined as "overt expressions of active prejudice, frequently exploited for political reasons," then certain other African American spokespersons could be considered "anti-Semitic" and their reprehensible statements examples of "Black anti-Semitism." These leaders and statements should be and have been condemned, but they should not be used to label the masses of African Americans in the United States as anti-Semitic. While it is likely that political and economic conflicts and differences between African Americans and Jewish Americans will continue to exist, any attempt to resolve these issues would be greatly hindered by blanket condemnations of Jews as racists and African Americans as anti-Semites.

The Increasing Significance of Class

Black-Jewish Conflict in the Postindustrial Global Era

Walda Katz-Fishman and Jerome Scott

If ever America undergoes great revolutions, they will be brought about by the presence of the black population on the soil of the United States; that is to say, they will owe their origin . . . to the inequality of condition.

ALEXIS DE TOCQUEVILLE

CONVERSATIONS about African American and Jewish American relations and even rigorous scholarship too often take place in a context devoid of economic, political, and cultural considerations. In this essay African Americans and Jews are located within the American class system, and the impact of the economic transformations of the late twentieth century on both of these communities, as well as on the growing tensions between them, is examined. The assertion that class is increasing in significance does not imply or suggest that race is decreasing. Indeed, institutional racism remains an enduring feature of American society seemingly impervious to political remedy, and its cultural expression, White supremacy, is, if anything, on the rise.

The understanding of class and race (and gender, though it is not the focus of this essay) is not an "either/or" formulation. Rather, the interrelationship between class and race is a dynamic process that has developed and changed throughout American history. Today's postindustrial global economy plays a critical role in the growing social inequality and the polarization of wealth and poverty in American society. These processes are giving rise to a disproportionate and permanent presence of Black workers—including many women and children—among the poor and very poor but are also creating a growing White majority of poor workers. At the same time, the upper class includes an overrepresentation of American Jews and an underrepresentation of African Americans, who are concentrated at the lower end of the upper class.

Issues of politics with regard to the welfare state reforms of the New Deal, civil rights, and Great Society eras, including affirmative action, are

understood within this larger context of economics and culture. Central
to this analysis is the fact that the high-technology, global market economy is driving today's political and cultural reaction and is exacerbating
tensions between African Americans and Jewish Americans. The essay
will conclude with considerations of new forms of political movements
and coalitions arising in civil society to address these new realities, to
bridge the economic and cultural divide between Blacks and Jews in contemporary American life, and to transform the society and world both
groups share.

Blacks in the American Class System: From Field to Factory to Joblessness

"Let's restate the problem of Black liberation in a White, conservative,
and capitalist society: to end racism, we must end inequality." Social
commentator Manning Marable was basically accurate when he declared, "Our goals cannot be simply the assimilation or integration of
black elites into the white cultural and corporate mainstream. Nor can we
combat inequality by going it alone, divorced from real and potential
allies. The problem of the twenty-first century is the challenge of multicultural democracy."[1]

Blacks and Jews occupy very different positions in the American social
class structure. African Americans are disproportionately in the lower
strata of the class system—the middle and working classes, including the
"underclass"—though some Blacks have moved into the upper class
in the post–civil rights era.[2] On the other hand, Jewish Americans are

---

1. Manning Marable, *Black Liberation in Conservative America* (Boston: South End
Press, 1997), 23.
2. The concept of the underclass is widely used to refer to the concentrated Black
urban ("ghetto") population in the last four decades of the twentieth century that is
overwhelmingly poor, permanently unemployed or underemployed, and engaged in
forms of "social pathology." We have critiqued the use of this concept (see Ralph
C. Gomes and Walda Katz-Fishman, "A Critique of *The Truly Disadvantaged:* A Historical Materialist Perspective," *Journal of Sociology and Social Welfare* 16, no. 4 [1989]:
77–98) for not fully reflecting the dynamics of capital and labor in the postindustrial
high technology global economy of the late twentieth century and for once again
"blaming the victims." We argued that what is called the "underclass" is really that
part of the working class that is at the cutting edge of permanent technological displacement from work and permanent deep poverty, that these realities are at the root
of any so-called social pathology, and that it is politically dangerous to separate this
lowest section of the working class from the larger class both theoretically and practically. We also suggested the need to view Black urban poverty within the larger context of the intensification of other forms of poverty in this period, for example,
poverty on Indian reservations, in Appalachia, and in rural America. For these
reasons, when we employ the term *underclass* here, we will use quotation marks to

disproportionately in the upper strata of the class system—the middle and upper classes.[3] Different paths to and experiences in the United States and different ethnic/racial and class positions have created a divergence of interests between these two highly visible groups on the American scene.

African American participation in American economic and social life has always been conditioned by the stage of technological development within the economy and the capitalists' need for Black labor, as well as by the corresponding legal and extralegal expressions of White supremacy. The inextricable linkage of Black workers to these technological and structural processes is evident in the agricultural economy of the late eighteenth, nineteenth, and early twentieth centuries, in the industrial economy of the midtwentieth century, and in the postindustrial global economy of the late twentieth century. In each instance, new technologies brought Black labor into the production sector and subsequent technological advances pushed them out. Thus low-skilled Black labor—which is most of Black labor—has gone from plantation to factory to permanent underemployment and unemployment.

Africans, forced into chains and ships, were brought to the shores of America beginning in 1619 and coerced into service—as indentured servants and as slaves by the mid-1600s—in the expanding plantation market economy of the colonial and antebellum periods. In 1790 the first national census reported 750,000 African Americans, most of whom were

indicate both our appreciation for what scholars generally mean by the term and our critique.

3. Works documenting the social and economic status of Blacks include Reynolds Farley, ed., *State of the Union: America in the 1990s,* vol. 1, *Economic Trends* (New York: Russell Sage Foundation, 1995); Gerald David Jaynes and Robin Williams Jr., *A Common Destiny: Blacks and American Society* (Washington, D.C.: National Academy Press, 1989); Walda Katz-Fishman and Jerome Scott, "Diversity and Equality: Race and Class in America," *Sociological Forum* 9, no. 4 (1994): 569–81; Manning Marable, *How Capitalism Underdeveloped Black America: Problems in Race, Political Economy, and Society* (Boston: South End Press, 1983); Melvin L. Oliver and Thomas M. Shapiro, *Black Wealth/White Wealth: A New Perspective on Racial Inequality* (New York: Routledge, 1995); William Julius Wilson, *The Truly Disadvantaged: The Inner City, the Underclass, and Public Policy* (Chicago: University of Chicago Press, 1987) and *When Work Disappears: The World of the New Urban Poor* (New York: Alfred A. Knopf, 1996); and U.S. Bureau of the Census, *Statistical Abstract of the United States: 1996,* 116th ed. (Washington, D.C.: GPO, 1996), selected tables. Those doing so for Jewish Americans include Seymour Martin Lipset and Earl Raab, *Jews and the New American Scene* (Cambridge: Harvard University Press, 1995); Richard L. Zweigenhaft and G. William Domhoff, *Jews in the Protestant Establishment* (New York: Praeger, 1982) and *Diversity in the Power Elite: Have Women and Minorities Reached the Top?* (New Haven: Yale University Press, 1998).

slaves residing in the South.[4] The 1793 invention of the cotton gin by Eli Whitney revolutionized cotton production, making the production of short-staple cotton extremely profitable. Cotton became king; production soared from 13,000 bales in 1792 to almost 5 million bales in 1860.[5] The invention of the cotton gin and the expansion of cotton production drove the need for an increasing supply of cheap slave labor. By 1860 the ranks of African Americans had swelled to 4.4 million—90 percent of whom were slaves residing in the South.[6] In the thirty years prior to the Civil War, the United States was the greatest slave power in the West, and most White citizens were opposed to the abolition of slavery.[7]

The Civil War, fought between the supporters of southern slave capital and those of northern industrial capital, abolished chattel slavery as a legal system but did not free the African American agricultural worker from the land and from slavelike conditions imposed through tenancy, sharecropping, debt peonage, and convict-leasing. The technological revolution that would mechanize cotton production and transform the position of the Black agricultural worker was more than seventy-five years away.[8]

Thus, after a brief period of progressive governmental policies with Black participation and leadership in the Reconstruction era, northern capital used the Hayes-Tilden Compromise of 1877 as an excuse to withdraw the remaining federal troops from the South and set in motion almost one hundred years of legalized, Jim Crow segregation. The continuation of the plentiful supply of cheap Black labor needed to work the reorganized plantation economy was insured by the reactionary legal and extralegal rule of this period. The government's refusal to carry out agrarian land reform—the unfulfilled promise of "forty acres and a mule"—kept most southern Blacks in economic bondage. African Americans began their American sojourn poor and propertyless, and they remained so more than two hundred and fifty years later. The disfranchisement of Blacks and poor Whites, lynchings, and the terror of the Ku Klux Klan and even of the legal authorities further embedded White

4. August Meier and Elliott Rudwick, *From Plantation to Ghetto* (New York: Hill and Wang, 1993), 41–43; Jay R. Mandle, *Not Slave, Not Free: The African American Economic Experience since the Civil War* (Durham: Duke University Press, 1992), 5.

5. Meier and Rudwick, *From Plantation to Ghetto*, 55, 57.

6. Mandle, *Not Slave, Not Free*, 5; Bureau of the Census, *Statistical Abstract*, 14.

7. Robert William Fogel and Stanley L. Engerman, *Time on the Cross: The Economics of American Negro Slavery* (Boston: Little, Brown and Co., 1974), 1:29.

8. Mandle, *Not Slave, Not Free*, 21–43, 50, 93.

supremacy within the economic, political, and social institutions of the United States.[9]

Blacks, who had entered the American class system as slave laborers, were allowed to practice and hone only their agricultural and domestic skills and, in some cases, to carry out unskilled tasks in the nascent industrial economy of the North and South. Black laborers in the slave and postbellum plantation economy had created enormous wealth for White capitalists but were unable to accumulate any wealth of their own. The absence of a material base for freedom among African Americans was compounded through the "sedimentation of racial inequality."[10] It had been illegal to educate African Americans during slavery and, though free public education was a priority during Reconstruction, its promise also faded with the imposition of Jim Crow legislation across the South. The culture of White supremacy and its codification in the legal, political, and social system of the American nation contributed to the institutionalization and resilience of racism in every sphere of life.[11]

Black workers sought escape from the oppressive conditions of the plantation economy in the emerging industrial and commercial economy of the cities both North and South. In 1910 more than 73 percent of Blacks lived in rural areas, while only 27 percent were urban; 90 percent remained in the South. In 1970, 81 percent of African Americans lived in urban areas, while 19 percent were rural, and only 2 percent of those lived on farms. The exodus of Blacks to the urban centers of North and South throughout this period was driven in part by Blacks' search for the illusive American dream, the pull of the wartime economies, and the use of Black workers as strikebreakers. Between 1910 and 1970, 6.5 million Blacks migrated from countryside to city; 5 million did so after 1940.[12]

This precipitous drop in Black rural and agricultural workers after 1940 was directly related to the mechanization of agriculture and the development of weed-killing chemicals in the 1940s. Only 6 percent of southern cotton was harvested with the mechanical picker in 1949. That

9. Meier and Rudwick, *From Plantation to Ghetto*, 152–231.

10. Oliver and Thomas, *Black Wealth/White Wealth*, 1–52.

11. See, for example, Marable, *How Capitalism Underdeveloped*; Derrick Bell, *Faces at the Bottom of the Well: The Permanence of Racism* (New York: Basic Books, 1992); and Cornel West, *Race Matters* (Boston: Beacon Press, 1993).

12. Meier and Rudwick, *From Plantation to Ghetto*, 232–34; Bureau of the Census, *The Social and Economic Status of the Black Population: An Historical View, 1790–1978* (Washington, D.C.: GPO, 1980), 14. Jeremy Rifkin, *The End of Work: The Decline of the Global Labor Force and the Dawn of the Post-Market Era* (New York: Jeremy P. Tarcher/Putnam, 1995), 72.

figure increased to 78 percent in 1964 and reached 100 percent by 1972. Blacks began their journey from field to factory, from southern plantations to northern ghettos. However, the cruel irony for Black workers was that just as they were making their way into the manufacturing jobs in the industrial heartland, the mass-production industrial system itself was on the verge of yet another technological revolution, this time based on the microcomputer chip and electronics.[13]

Thirty years before the mechanization of agriculture, changes were taking place in industry that revolutionized production and brought about the shift from craft production—where highly skilled workers used simple tools to produce custom items, one at a time—to mass production—where unskilled and semiskilled workers used standard expensive single-purpose machines to produce large quantities of uniform items. In 1915 in Detroit, Henry Ford and Alfred Sloan of General Motors initiated the historic shift from craft to mass production, made possible through the development of interchangeable parts—simple and easy to attach—and the moving assembly line. The new system of mass production, often called "fordism," was fully implemented by the 1920s and reached its zenith in the 1950s.[14]

Black unskilled agricultural workers, made obsolete by the mechanical cotton picker, entered the mass-production system of manufacturing in large numbers in the 1950s and 1960s. In 1940, 32 percent of Black workers fourteen and older were employed in agriculture, 28 percent in blue-collar work, 36 percent in service jobs, and 4 percent in professional, technical, and managerial (white-collar) jobs. By 1960 the percentages were 8, 38, 39, and 7, respectively (with 8 percent "occupation not reported"). In 1970, only 3 percent of Black workers were in agriculture, 37 percent were in blue-collar jobs, 39 percent were in service jobs, and 10 percent were in white-collar jobs (11 percent "occupation not reported").[15]

But even as Blacks were migrating by the millions into the industrial urban centers, the manufacturing system of mass production that they sought to enter was undergoing a profound restructuring with increasingly automated production. More than 1.5 million manufacturing jobs

13. Rifkin, *The End of Work*, 69–89; William Greider, *One World, Ready or Not: The Manic Logic of Global Capitalism* (New York: Simon and Schuster, 1997).

14. James P. Womack, Daniel T. Jones, and Daniel Roos, *The Machine That Changed the World: The Story of Lean Production* (New York: HarperCollins, 1990), 11–13, 43; Richard J. Barnet and John Cavanagh, *Global Dreams: Imperial Corporations and the New World Order* (New York: Touchstone, 1995), 259–68.

15. Bureau of the Census, *Social and Economic Status of the Black Population*, 74.

were eliminated between 1953 and 1962. In 1964 Tom Kahn wrote, "It is as if racism, having put the Negro in his economic place, stepped aside to watch technology destroy that place." In that year Black unemployment rose to a high of 12.4 percent, compared to 5.9 percent for Whites; and Black unemployment has remained at least twice that of Whites since the mid-1960s.[16]

The new production system was called "lean" because it used only half of what mass production used—half the workers, half the factory space, half the investment in tools, half the inventory—along with automated machines to produce huge volumes of products. More and better products were produced in a flexible system by fewer and more highly skilled workers using new automated technologies.[17] What drove lean automated production and the "deindustrialization" it brought in its wake in the 1950s, 1960s, and 1970s, and what is driving the entire restructuring of the global economy in the late twentieth century, was capital's imperative for maximum profits and the related need to minimize the amount and costs of labor. Capital's demand for ever greater competitiveness, productivity, and "lean and mean" production ruled the day.[18]

The technological innovation that made all this possible and revolutionized the entire system of economic production was the development of the silicon integrated circuit or chip in 1958 and 1959. Computers were transformed into very small, very quick, and very powerful tools in the new "high-tech" production process; and their microprocessing capacity changed forever the economic system of production, distribution, and communication. The computer revolution created "smart" or "intelligent" machines at the heart of the new lean, reengineered, and downsized system of computer-automated production that eliminated more and more labor in the new economic system. Job elimination disproportionately affected Black unskilled workers, substantiating the oft-heard phrase "last hired, first fired, and lowest paid."[19]

The transformation of the automotive industry in Detroit vividly illustrates this process. In the late 1940s and 1950s Detroit automakers began

16. Tom Kahn, "Problems of the Negro Movement," *Dissent* 10 (winter 1964): 115, 113; Wilson, *Truly Disadvantaged*, 30.

17. Womack, Jones, and Roos, *Machine That Changed the World*, 13–15.

18. Barry Bluestone and Bennett Harrison, *The Deindustrialization of America: Plant Closings, Community Abandonment, and the Dismantling of Basic Industry* (New York: Basic Books, 1982); David Gordon, *Fat and Mean: The Corporate Squeeze of Working Americans and the Myth of Managerial "Downsizing"* (New York: Free Press, 1996).

19. Greider, *One World*, 25–29; Rifkin, *End of Work*, 59–80.

implementing their new corporate strategy: the automation, decentral-ization, and suburbanization of their plants, particularly those with large and militant workforces. Ford's River Rouge complex employed 85,000 workers in 1945, and its United Auto Workers local 600 was more than 30 percent Black and very active. By 1960 employment at River Rouge had fallen to 30,000, and management was well on its way to achieving its goals of reducing wages and breaking union militancy.[20]

From 1945 through 1957 Ford spent more than $2.5 billion on its pro-gram of plant automation and suburbanization. Chrysler and General Motors joined Ford in 1947 and by 1958 had built twenty-five new sub-urban Detroit plants, adding 116,000 new automotive jobs in Michigan, 72,000 of which were suburban. Black migration from the South and the United Auto Workers' policy of Black inclusion helped fill the labor shortage for war production and increase the number of Black workers in the auto industry from 4 percent in 1940 to 15 percent in 1945. By 1960, 26 percent of Chrysler workers and 23 percent of GM workers were Black. Yet racial discrimination kept Black workers in unskilled jobs. In 1960 Blacks held only 24 of the 7,425 skilled jobs at Chrysler and 67 of the 11,125 at GM.[21]

Then came the new production system with the new smart machines that drove total manufacturing employment in Detroit from a high of 338,400 in 1947 to 200,600 in 1963.[22] Blacks, victims of a history of dis-crimination, were concentrated in the unskilled jobs—the very first to be eliminated as automation advanced—and were increasingly pushed out of the job market and into poverty.

Thus, even as Black workers migrated from field to factory in pursuit of a better life, the oppressive conditions and lack of economic opportu-nities they found in the waning days of the mass-production system en-ergized their historic struggles against the injustices and indignities of the American economic and political system. This ongoing movement of the African American people for freedom and economic justice and against Jim Crow, combined with the technological, economic, and de-mographic transformations of this period, culminated in the modern Civil Rights Movement. These struggles resulted in the Civil Rights Act

20. Thomas Sugrue, "Structures of Urban Poverty: The Reorganization of Space and Work in Three Periods of American History," in *Underclass Debate*, ed. Katz, 85–117 (100–103 for material in text).
21. Ibid., 103–7; for a discussion of the struggles for racial equality in the Detroit auto industry see Dan Georgakas and Marvin Surkin, *Detroit, I Do Mind Dying: A Study in Urban Revolution* (New York: St. Martin's Press, 1975).
22. Sugrue, "Structures of Urban Poverty," 105.

of 1964, ending legal segregation in public accommodations; the 1965 Affirmative Action Executive Order 11246, which went beyond anti-discrimination to seek remedy for historic disadvantage; and the Voting Rights Act of 1965, which eliminated literacy tests and other restrictions on the right to vote.[23]

African Americans remained at the lower end of their respective so-cioeconomic classes—upper, middle, and working.[24] The period from the 1960s to the 1990s saw the development of increased class stratification and polarization within the Black community, a deepening crisis of struc-tural joblessness and poverty among Black workers in the postindustrial high-tech global economy, and the continuing disadvantage of all African Americans with regard to wealth and power in American soci-ety. A growing sector of the Black community moved into the middle, upper-middle, and upper classes, while the ranks of the Black poor and very poor—the "underclass"—increased as well.[25]

The income share of Black families in the bottom fifth of the socioeco-nomic ladder declined from 4.7 percent in 1967 to 3.3 percent in 1995. For those in the middle three-fifths, it also declined, from 50.7 to 48 percent. In contrast, the income share of Black families in the top fifth increased

23. For an assessment of the impact of affirmative action on educational and employment gains and government contracts and the affirmative action debate on race and class see *The Affirmative Action Debate,* ed. George E. Curry (Reading, Mass.: Addison-Wesley Publishing Co., 1996) particularly Manning Marable, "Staying the Path to Racial Equality," 3–15; Cornel West, "Affirmative Action in Context," 31–38; Eleanor Holmes Norton, "Affirmative Action in the Workplace," 39–48; Heidi Hart-mann, "Who Has Benefited from Affirmative Action in Employment?" 77–98; Kweisi Mfume, "Why America Needs Set-Aside Programs," 121–29; Linda Faye Williams, "Tracing the Politics of Affirmative Action," 241–57; Mary Frances Berry, "Affirma-tive Action: Why We Need It, Why It Is Under Attack," 299–313; and Louis Harris, "The Future of Affirmative Action," 326–36; Carol M. Swain, ed., *Race Versus Class: The New Affirmative Action Debate* (Lanham, Md.: University Press of America, 1996); and Richard D. Kahlenberg, *The Remedy: Class, Race, and Affirmative Action* (New York: Basic Books, 1996); Stephen Steinberg, *Turning Back: The Retreat from Racial Justice in American Thought and Policy* (Boston: Beacon Press, 1995).

24. For a further discussion of this point see Katz-Fishman and Scott, "Diversity and Equality," 575–77; Walda Katz-Fishman, Ralph C. Gomes, Nelson Peery, and Jerome Scott, "African American Politics in the Era of Capitalist Contraction," in *From Inclusion to Exclusion: The Long Struggle for African American Political Power,* ed. Ralph C. Gomes and Linda Faye Williams (New York: Greenwood Press, 1992), 85–91; Walda Katz-Fishman, Jerome Scott, Ralph C. Gomes, and Robert Newby, "The Poli-tics of Race and Class in City Hall," in *Research in Urban Sociology: Race, Class, and Urban Change,* ed. Jerry Lembcke (Greenwich, Conn.: JAI Press, 1989), 1:135–73.

25. Marable, *How Capitalism Underdeveloped,* 23–69, 133–95; West, *Race Matters,* 1–13, 51–70, 91–100, 155–59; Wilson, *When Work Disappears* and *Truly Disadvantaged;* Oliver and Shapiro, *Black Wealth/White Wealth;* Zweigenhaft and Domhoff, *Women and Minorities in the Power Elite,* chap. 4.

from 44.6 to 48.7 percent between 1967 and 1995, and for those in the top 5 percent it increased from 17.3 to 20 percent.[26] From 1967 to 1995 the bottom 80 percent of Black families lost 4.1 percent of Black family income to the top 20 percent; and by 1995 the top 5 percent of Black families had more income than the bottom half of all Black families.

Average Black family income (in constant 1995 dollars) revealed similar patterns. The poorest fifth lost income, from $5,873 in 1967 to $5,524 in 1995. The top four-fifths of Black families gained income, with the amount of gain increasing with each fifth in the income scale. The second fifth of Black families gained just over $2,000 in income, from $12,792 to $14,859. Average Black family income went from $20,333 to $25,924, an increase of $5,591 for the middle fifth. The next fifth gained more than $11,000 in income, from $29,787 in 1967 to $41,015 in 1995. Family income for the top fifth increased by more than $27,000, from $55,397 to $82,733. But the most dramatic increase in average income was among the top 5 percent of Black families, whose income went from $85,860 to $135,811.[27]

Among Black families, as among all families, the rich were getting richer while the poor were getting poorer. The family income of the Black middle and upper classes increased, sometimes dramatically, but the Black working class remained mired in poverty. While the proportion of Black families with income under $15,000 was the same at 32.2 percent in 1970 and in 1994, the proportion with incomes of $50,000 and higher almost doubled, from 11.6 percent in 1970 to 21.2 percent in 1994. Black median family income was up only slightly from $22,531 in 1970 to $24,698 in 1994 (in constant 1994 dollars); but the proportion of Black families with incomes of $75,000 and higher almost quadrupled from 2.2 percent to 7.9 percent.[28]

The income gap between the richest (top 5 percent) and poorest (bottom 20 percent) Black families grew from almost $80,000 in 1967 to slightly more than $130,000 in 1995. At the same time, in 1995, Black poverty was 29.3 percent—the first time Black poverty fell below 30 percent since the Census Bureau began measuring it in 1966. But, among Blacks living at or below the poverty level, 45 percent were below 50 percent of the poverty level—an increase of almost 13 percent over the 32.1 percent in 1975.[29]

26. Jennifer Sturiale, *Poverty and Income Trends: 1995* (Washington, D.C.: Center on Budget and Policy Priorities, 1997), 55.
27. Ibid., 61; see also Wilson, *When Work Disappears*, 193–95.
28. Bureau of the Census, *Statistical Abstract*, 466.
29. Sturiale, *Poverty and Income Trends*, 12, 46. For a family of four in 1995 the poverty level was $15,569.

The Black middle and upper classes were prospering relative to the Black working class but remained disadvantaged and well short of parity when compared to their White counterparts. In 1970 Black median family income, $22,531, was 61.3 percent of White median family income, $36,731. By 1994 Black median family income, $24,698, was slightly less, 60.4 percent, of White family income, which was $40,884. In 1994, 39.4 percent of White families had incomes of $50,000 and higher compared to 21.2 percent for Blacks; and 18.5 percent of White families had incomes of $75,000 and higher, more than double the number of Black families, at 7.9 percent.[30]

More dramatic were the disparities between Black wealth and White wealth and the resulting precariousness of the Black middle class. In the late 1980s middle-class Blacks possessed only fifteen cents of wealth (all assets less all debts) for every dollar in wealth of middle-class Whites. The higher up the income ladder, the closer Black wealth came to White wealth. High-income Blacks had fifty-two cents of wealth for every dollar of high-income Whites. When net financial assets (wealth excluding equity in homes and vehicles) were examined, middle-class Blacks had none. But poverty-level Whites had higher mean net financial assets, $28,683, than high-income Blacks, with $28,310.[31]

Similarly, the number of Black-owned businesses increased 46 percent between 1987 and 1992, going from 424,165 to 620,912. But Blacks remained underrepresented among business owners and especially among large businesses. They were 12.4 percent of the population but owned only 3.6 percent of all U.S. firms in 1992; of the businesses they owned, 94 percent were sole proprietorships. Their firms had $32.2 million in sales receipts, an increase from $19.8 million in 1987, but still representing only 1 percent of all receipts.[32]

Richard L. Zweigenhaft and G. William Domhoff, in a systematic study of Blacks, other minorities, and women in the "power elite," found that, in the 1970s, middle- and upper-class Blacks began to enter the ranks of the power elite—the corporate officers, high federal officials, general officer ranks of the military, and Congress (though they remained underrepresented there as well).[33] In 1973 *Black Enterprise* identified seventy-two Black directors (sixty-seven men and five women)

30. Bureau of the Census, *Statistical Abstract*, 466.
31. Oliver and Shapiro, *Black Wealth/White Wealth*, 7, 97.
32. Bureau of the Census, *Statistical Abstract*, 14; Bureau of the Census, U.S. Department of Commerce, *1992 Black-Owned Businesses* (Washington, D.C.: GPO, 1995).
33. This discussion on Blacks in the power elite draws on Zweigenhaft and Domhoff, *Women and Minorities*, chap. 4, "Blacks in the Power Elite."

among the 14,000 directors of the *Fortune* 1,000 companies, thus making Black directors less than 1 percent of all directors. This number remained virtually unchanged as late as 1981 when *Business and Society* reported seventy-three Black directors.

By 1992, the effects of civil rights legislation, affirmative action, and the push for diversity in corporate boardrooms began to yield modest results for the inclusion of African Americans, including an increasing number of Black women among corporate directors of the *Fortune* 1,000 companies. In that year 118 directors, or 1.6 percent, were Black, of whom 92 were men and 26 were women. This number increased to 175 in 1995, or 2.5 percent of directors, of whom 137 were men and 38 were women. Many Black directors held multiple seats, and a small number sat on three or more boards. Thus, the number of seats held by Blacks increased from 223, or 2.3 percent, in 1992 to 353, or 3.6 percent, in 1995. Blacks in the middle and upper classes were now part of corporate America, but they remained grossly underrepresented there.

Beginning with the Johnson administration in 1966, through 1992, eight African Americans—six men and two women—served as Cabinet members, with all but one coming from a background of relative privilege. In the post-Reconstruction era, there have been only two Black U.S. senators—Edmund Brooke, a Republican from Massachusetts from an upper-middle-class family, and Carol Moseley-Braun, a Democrat from Illinois from a middle-class background. A total of 186 Blacks have served in the House of Representatives, twenty-five in 1990 and thirty-eight in 1994, two of whom were Republicans. It is possible that these numbers will decline with the Supreme Court decision undermining districts in which minorities are an electoral majority.

Finally, Black enlisted men were, by the 1950s, in the armed forces, especially the army, in numbers roughly equal to their numbers in the population, but they were absent from the ranks of general officers (one star or higher). In 1985, 36 such officers out of 1,067 in all branches of the armed services, or 3.4 percent, were Black. By 1995 the number was the same but represented 4 percent of such officers. In the army, the percentage of Blacks at the general-officer rank went from 6.3 in 1985 to 7.3 in 1995.

By the 1990s, 375 years after being forced as slaves to American shores, some African Americans had indeed entered the middle and upper classes, though at their lower ends. Some African Americans had become part of the power elite, though underrepresented relative to their numbers in the population. To be sure, even these highly educated, skilled, affluent, and elite Blacks had not yet reached parity with comparable

Whites in the middle and upper classes and in the power elite of American society.

But a crisis of unprecedented proportions became the daily reality for Black workers—employed, underemployed, and unemployed—and especially for the poorest of the poor, the "underclass." The civil rights reforms, affirmative action guidelines, and calls for diversity over the last three decades left untouched those unskilled and semiskilled African American workers at the very bottom of the socioeconomic ladder.[34] Legal reforms that guaranteed civil rights and called for equal employment opportunities were rendered useless in the face of the larger trends toward economic reengineering, restructuring, and downsizing, the sweeping globalization of the economy, and the devastating effects of this new stage of economic history on Black workingpeople and their families.

Millions of poor and very poor Black children, youths, women, and men were forced into a struggle for their very survival. In 1995, in the midst of the so-called new economic recovery, 9.9 million Black Americans, 29.3 percent of all Blacks, lived in poverty. Of these, 44.8 percent, or 4.4 million Blacks, were below 50 percent of the poverty level. The younger Blacks were, the worse off they were. The poverty rate for Black youths under eighteen was 41.9 percent, or 4.8 million youths; the rate increased to 48.9 percent for Black children six years and younger, representing 1.9 million children. The poverty rate for African Americans living in nonmetropolitan or rural areas was slightly higher than the rate for central-city Blacks—34.8 percent as compared to 33.3 percent. But, because so many Blacks had moved into the central cities during industrialization, in 1995 six out of ten poor Blacks lived in inner cities and only slightly less than two of ten lived in nonmetropolitan areas.[35]

Black workers and their families were systematically excluded from the new high-tech, global economy. Their communities, once supported by their participation in the economy, collapsed. The social infrastructure and safety net the government had constructed, however flimsy, was eroded.[36]

On the eve of the computer revolution, Norbert Weiner, the father of cybernetics, alerted the nation and the world to the likely negative effects of the new automated technologies, particularly the disastrous consequences for human labor. In 1950 he wrote: "Let us remember that the

34. Marable, "Staying the Path"; West, "Affirmative Action."

35. Sturiale, *Poverty and Income Trends*, 12, 46, 21, 26, 31.

36. Marable, *Black Liberation* and *How Capitalism Underdeveloped*; West, *Race Matters*; Wilson, *When Work Disappears* and *Truly Disadvantaged*.

automatic machine . . . is the precise economic equivalent of slave labor. Any labor that competes with slave labor must accept the economic consequences of slave labor."[37]

Less than fifteen years later, in 1964, the Ad Hoc Committee on the Triple Revolution, a group of renowned scientists, economists, and academicians headed by J. Robert Oppenheimer, director of the Institute for Advanced Study at Princeton University, issued a warning to President Johnson and the American people about the cataclysmic effects of automation on the economic future of the country. In an open letter in the *New York Times*, they wrote: "A new era of production has begun. Its principles of organization are as different as those of the industrial era were different from the agricultural. The cybernation revolution has been brought about by the combination of the computer and the automated self-regulating machine. This results in a system of almost unlimited productive capacity which requires progressively less human labor. . . . The Negroes are the hardest hit of the many groups being exiled from the economy by cybernation."[38]

The early warnings from scientists and scholars most directly connected to the technological revolution at the heart of the new automated production system were prophetic. But few were listening and even fewer could comprehend the profound impact of these new technologies not only on economic production but on all of social life. The effects of the new technological system of production were swift, dramatic, and particularly devastating for the large pool of Black unskilled and semiskilled workers. Unskilled jobs were increasingly eliminated and by the 1990s had virtually disappeared from the economy. The high-tech global economy created whole communities with little or no relationship to the market economy. The inner-city concentration of unemployed and underemployed, of poor and very poor Black workers and their families, stirred great debate among scholars and politicians about the causes, effects, and solutions for what came to be called the "underclass."[39]

---

37. Norbert Weiner, *The Human Use of Human Beings: Cybernetics and Human Beings* (Boston: Houghton Mifflin, 1950), 10.

38. "The Ad Hoc Committee on the Triple Revolution Memorandum," March 22, 1964, in Robert McBride, *The Automated State: Computer Systems as a New Force in Society* (Philadelphia: Chilton Book Co., 1967), 192–93.

39. *Underclass Debate*, ed. Katz, 3–26, and the following essays in this collection: Jacqueline Jones, "Southern Diaspora: Origins of the Northern 'Underclass,' " 27–54; Joe William Trotter Jr., "Blacks in the Urban North: The 'Underclass Question,' " 55–81; Sugrue, "Structures of Urban Poverty," 85–117. Christopher Jencks and Paul E. Peterson, eds., *The Urban Underclass* (Washington, D.C.: Brookings Institution, 1991); Wilson, *When Work Disappears*, xiii–xxii, 3–50, and *Truly Disadvantaged*.

In the 1970s and 1980s social scientists joined in the discussion as the social effects—initially for Black labor—began to express themselves in terms of persistent poverty, joblessness, and the resulting destruction of community. Black workers, no longer needed in economic production, were increasingly obsolete. Anticipating other social scientists, in 1970 Sidney Willhelm in *Who Needs the Negro?* described the bleak future for Black workers: "White America, by a more perfect application of mechanization and a vigorous reliance upon automation, disposes of the Negro; consequently, the Negro transforms from an exploited labor force into an outcast."[40]

The mid-1970s marked a turning point in the U.S. economy and in the condition not only of Black workers but of all workers.[41] The post–World War II economic expansion of the nation-based industrial system had reached its limits and was drawing to a close. Europe and Japan had been rebuilt following the destruction of the war and, in some instances, were leading the emerging global economy. The industrial system of capitalist production and markets now embraced the U.S. South and the developing countries of the world, under the rule of nationally based finance capital. The imperative of profit maximization demanded the thorough restructuring and downsizing of the industrial economy and its reorganization along the lines of lean automated production.

All aspects of production and commerce were increasingly integrated into a global economy—capital flows, equipment flows, labor markets, and commodity markets.[42] Robert Reich, former secretary of labor,

40. Sidney Willhelm, *Who Needs the Negro?* (Cambridge, Mass.: Schenkman, 1970), 156–57.
41. See, for example, Bluestone and Harrison, *Deindustrialization;* Sheldon Danziger and Peter Gottschalk, *America Unequal* (New York: Russell Sage Foundation, 1996); Gordon, *Fat and Mean;* Lawrence Mishel and Jared Bernstein, *The State of Working America, 1994–95* (New York: M. E. Sharpe, 1994); Michael Moore, *Downsize This! Random Threats from an Unarmed American* (New York: Crown, 1996); Thomas S. Moore, *The Disposable Work Force: Worker Displacement, and Employment Instability in America* (Hawthorne, N.Y.: Aldine de Gruyter, 1996); Robert B. Reich, "The Unfinished Agenda," Washington, D.C., U.S. Department of Labor, January 9, 1997; and Chris Tilly, *Half a Job: Bad and Good Part-Time Jobs in a Changing Labor Market* (Philadelphia: Temple University Press, 1996).
42. See, for example, Barnet and Cavanagh, *Global Dreams;* Jeremy Brecher and Tim Costello, *Global Village or Global Pillage: Economic Reconstruction from the Bottom Up* (Boston: South End Press, 1994); Kevin Danaher, ed., *Corporations Are Gonna Get Your Mama: Globalization and the Downsizing of the American Dream* (Monroe, Maine: Common Courage Press, 1996); Greider, *One World;* David Korten, *When Corporations Rule the World* (West Hartford, Conn.: Kumarian Press; San Francisco: Berrett-Koehler, 1995); Jerry Mander and Edward Goldsmith, eds., *The Case against the Global Economy: And for a Turn toward the Local* (San Francisco: Sierra Club Books, 1996);

described the new global economy: "As almost every factor of produc-tion—money, technology, factories, and equipment—moves effortlessly across borders, the very idea of an American economy is becoming meaningless, as are the notions of an American corporation, American capital, American products, and American technology. A similar trans-formation is affecting every other nation."[43]

What was already a crisis of growing joblessness and poverty for African American workers deepened and increasingly extended to in-clude all workers—workers of color and White workers, blue-collar and white-collar workers. The combined effects of the automation and subur-banization of the lean production system and the globalization of the economy propelled the downward spiral. Automated production and downsizing eliminated millions of jobs. It was not until 1981 that the Bu-reau of Labor Statistics began tracking permanent job loss, that is, work-ers displaced from their jobs because of plant closures, insufficient work, or elimination of positions. In 1981–1983, 9 percent of displaced workers suffered such permanent job losses. The percentage fell to 5.5 in 1987–1989, but in each two-year period from 1989 to 1995 it was 8 or higher. Despite the creation of new jobs—usually part-time, contingent, lower paying, and with low or no benefits—permanent job loss remains a huge problem for workers in the postindustrial high-tech economy.[44]

In the global context, American workers were thrown into competition with more than 2 billion workers worldwide—some of whom made as little as 28 cents an hour—including more than 800 million unemployed and underemployed workers. The huge supply of workers in search of jobs created great downward pressure on wages, benefits, and working conditions. Production was mobile—going from central city to the sub-urbs to the South and offshore in pursuit of the optimum conditions for profits.[45]

As late as 1970, more than 70 percent of Black workers in metropolitan areas held blue-collar jobs, and about half of these were in goods-

Robert B. Reich, *The Work of Nations: Preparing Ourselves for 21st Century Capitalism* (New York: Vintage Books, 1992); Gary Teeple, *Globalization and the Decline of Social Reform* (Toronto: Garamond Press, 1995); and Lester Thurow, *The Future of Capitalism: How Today's Economic Forces Shape Tomorrow's World* (New York: William Morrow, 1996).

43. Reich, *Work of Nations*, 8.

44. Reich, "The Unfinished Agenda," 12, 2, 6, 8–10.

45. National Labor Committee, *Mickey Mouse Goes to Haiti: Walt Disney and the Sci-ence of Exploitation* (New York: Crowing Rooster Arts, 1996); Rifkin, *End of Work*, xv–xvii.

producing industries. Industrial restructuring and automation eliminated millions of these jobs. In the Northeast and Midwest alone more
than one million manufacturing jobs were lost between 1967 and 1987. In
Philadelphia 64 percent of goods-producing jobs were destroyed, in
Chicago 60 percent, in New York City 58 percent, and in Detroit 51 percent. In numbers this represented 160,000 jobs in Philadelphia, 326,000 in
Chicago, 520,000 in New York City, and 108,000 in Detroit, for a total of
1.1 million jobs. A report issued by the Equal Employment Opportunity
Commission indicated that almost one-third of the 180,000 manufacturing jobs lost in 1990 and 1991 had been held by Black workers.[46]

With the destruction of blue-collar jobs, low-skilled men lost jobs and
wages and some dropped out of the labor force altogether. In the late
1980s the proportion of men who had "permanently" left the workforce
was more than double the proportion in the late 1960s. Those who remained experienced joblessness for an average of eight and a half weeks
longer in 1987–1989 than in 1967–1969. Among prime-age men, aged
twenty-two to fifty-eight, the proportion working full-time, year-round
in eight of the ten years of the decade fell from 79 percent in the 1970s to
71 percent in the 1980s. For prime-age Black men, the proportions were
70 percent in the 1970s and only 50 percent in the 1980s, a dramatic decrease. Among Black men in the inner city these proportions were even
lower. Finally, even when they worked, the wages of low-income male
workers plummeted. Men in the bottom fifth of the wage scale experienced a 30 percent drop in real wages between 1970 and 1989.[47]

For example, among employed Black men, ages twenty to twenty-
nine, in 1973 three in eight were in manufacturing jobs; the figure was
down to only one in five by 1987. When Black men were employed in the
1980s, it tended to be in retail trade and service jobs. By 1987, 27 percent
of young Black men were in retail trade jobs and 21 percent were in service jobs. Wages were 25 to 30 percent lower in these jobs than in manufacturing, and benefits were less, if there were any.[48]

Black women were always concentrated in the low-wage retail and
service jobs. They had higher unemployment rates than men in the 1960s
and 1970s and thus did not experience the extraordinary job loss of Black
men, but all ended up in the 1990s at roughly the same place. Black
women workers were hard hit by the erosion of the minimum wage,

46. John D. Kasarda, "Industrial Restructuring and the Changing Location of Jobs,"
in State of the Union, ed. Farley, 1:239; Wilson, When Work Disappears, 29–30; Rifkin,
End of Work, 78.
47. Wilson, When Work Disappears, 25–26.
48. Ibid., 31.

which, in 1995, was 26 percent below its average level in the 1970s. They were also hurt by the loss of Aid to Families with Dependent Children benefits for families with two children and working mothers whose incomes were less than 75 percent of the poverty level. In the 1970s AFDC payments were made in forty-nine states, but in the 1990s they were made in only three states.[49]

The official unemployment rate for Blacks went from a low of 9.4 percent in 1973 to a high of 15.1 percent in 1985 and decreased to 10.4 percent in 1995. Thus, despite the record economic growth of the mid-1990s, in 1995 Black unemployment remained 1 percent higher than in 1973 and twice the White unemployment rate of 4.9 percent. Almost twice as many Black workers were jobless—846,000 in 1973 versus 1.52 million in 1995.[50] Unemployment rates for Black youths were two and three times higher. In 1995 young Black women aged sixteen to nineteen had an unemployment rate of 34.3 percent, while Black men of the same age had a slightly higher rate of 37.1 percent. Black women aged twenty to twenty-four were unemployed at a rate of 17.8 percent, and Black men of the same age at a rate of 17.6 percent.[51]

These extraordinary rates of unemployment for Blacks, which were even greater in the inner city, led William Julius Wilson, in *When Work Disappears*, to observe: "For the first time in the twentieth century most adults in many inner-city ghetto neighborhoods are not working in a typical week. . . . Inner-city joblessness is a severe problem that is often overlooked or obscured when the focus is placed mainly on poverty and its consequences. Despite increases in the concentration of poverty since 1970, inner cities have always featured high levels of poverty, but the current levels of joblessness in some neighborhoods are unprecedented."[52]

Jeremy Rifkin, in *The End of Work*, summed up the situation of Black workers at the end of the twentieth century: "Today millions of African-Americans find themselves hopelessly trapped in a permanent underclass. Unskilled and unneeded, the commodity value of their labor has been rendered virtually useless by the automated technologies that have come to displace them in the new high-tech global economy."[53]

What was not initially understood was that structural job elimination

49. Center on Budget and Policy Priorities, "The Earned Income Tax Credit Reductions in the Senate Budget Resolution," Washington, D.C., June 5, 1995, p. 3.

50. Bureau of the Census, *Statistical Abstract*, 394.

51. U.S. Department of Labor, Bureau of Labor Statistics, *Employment and Earnings,* January 1997.

52. Wilson, *When Work Disappears*, xiii.

53. Rifkin, *End of Work*, 80.

and globalization and the wage and benefit squeeze would not stop with unskilled African American workers, and would not stop with blue-collar workers of all races, but revolutionize the service sector of the economy and encroach on white-collar professional and managerial workers. New jobs and new economic sectors to absorb the displaced surplus workers did not materialize, as had happened when industry absorbed displaced agricultural workers. Under the pressure of automation and global labor markets, average gross weekly earnings (in 1995 dollars) of all U.S. nonsupervisory production workers plummeted from a high of $470 in 1972 to a low of $395 in 1995. Workers lost 16 percent of their buying power. Earnings in 1995 were even lower than the 1963 earnings of $413. By 1995, 10.5 percent of all people living in poverty worked full-time and year-round.[54]

The service economy was also being automated and downsized. A highly skilled information economy—the knowledge industry—was developing; but, given that it too was automated and computer driven, it would never produce the number of jobs needed to absorb the millions of workers eliminated from the mass-production system, even if they did have the skills. The excess of workers in the labor market domestically and globally was driving down wages for low-skilled as well as high-skilled labor.[55]

Thus, even in white-collar and professional jobs Blacks found themselves the first and hardest hit. In the 1960s and the 1970s Black workers, including many middle-class professionals, sought and found jobs in the public sector. In 1960, 13.3 of all Black workers were on the public payrolls; a decade later that figure had increased to 21 percent. In 1970 the government employed 72 percent of college-educated Black women and 57 percent of college-educated Black men, often administering programs for the Black poor—creating what has been called "welfare colonialism." By 1982 roughly 25 percent of Black workers, 1.6 million, were employed in the public sector. When government began downsizing in the 1990s, Blacks in professional jobs were disproportionately affected. Similarly, when private-sector white-collar and service jobs were being eliminated in the 1990s, Black workers suffered disproportionately because they were in the most expendable jobs—office and clerical.[56]

Robert Heilbroner explained it this way: "As with manufacturing,

54. Bureau of Labor Statistics, *Employment and Earnings,* June 1996, Table B-2 and prior reports; Sturiale, *Poverty and Income Trends,* 77.

55. Rifkin, *End of Work,* 59–68, 165–80.

56. Ibid., 76–77; Steinberg, *Turning Back,* 167; Andrew Hacker, *Two Nations: Black and White, Separate, Hostile, Unequal* (New York: Ballantine, 1992), 121, 78.

Walda Katz-Fishman and Jerome Scott

technology in the service sector created with one hand and took away with the other. The sector grew on the back of the typewriter and the telephone, shrank under the impact of the Xerox machine and the mail order catalogue. But it was the computer, of course, that brings the drama to a close, threatening to allow the corporation to sit on its island, turning its crank while the automata go to work."[57]

Jews in the American Class System: A Privileged Minority

In *Jews and the New American Scene*, sociologists Seymour Martin Lipset and Earl Raab pointed out that "the scions of the German Jews who immigrated in the nineteenth century and the Eastern European Jews who came later have been able to become the best educated, the most middle-class, and, ultimately, the most affluent ethnoreligious group in the country. . . . Jews are often wary of drawing attention to their financial status, which has sometimes served as a provocation for anti-Semites. In America, however, the economic achievement of Jews paralleled their deep integration into the society."[58] At the same time, historically as well as in the contemporary era, the Jewish American experience stands in stark contrast to that of African Americans. Jews came to America as immigrants with commercial, craft, manufacturing, and intellectual skills shaped in the developing industrial and commercial context of Europe; some even came with capital assets. The rabbinic tradition of Talmudic study translated into a continuing cultural tradition of education and study, both sacred and secular. The commercial and financial occupations and craft background of Jewish immigrants equipped them with skills and expertise that would serve them well in the American context. These skills were precisely what the fledgling urban industrial nation needed; and Jews were allowed to use them all. Also significant was the fact that Jews, though of minority religious status, were of European origin and fit into the "White" category in the color scheme of America.[59]

Jewish immigrants came to America in three waves. The Sephardic Jews from Spain and Portugal came during the colonial period; the German Jews came in the mid-1800s; and the Eastern European Jews came between the 1880s and 1920s. Economic and social class data for American Jews are less systematic and comprehensive than comparable data for African Americans; but significant studies documenting Jewish

57. Robert Heilbroner, foreword to Rifkin, *End of Work*, xii–xiii.
58. Lipset and Raab, *Jews and the New American Scene*, 27–28.
59. Ibid., 1–28; Zweigenhaft and Domhoff, *Jews in the Protestant Establishment*, 9–16, and *Women and Minorities*, chap. 2.

representation and, indeed, overrepresentation in the American economic and political elite are persuasive.[60]

The hundreds of Sephardic Jewish families in the colonial period and early years of the republic settled primarily around the leading port cities of New York, Newport, Philadelphia, Charleston, and Savannah and in lesser numbers in ports such as New Orleans and Mobile. They were successful merchants in the growing import-export business and included among their ranks some who were slave owners.[61] A. Manners described these very early Jewish Americans: the "Sephardim were first among equals in the new democracy for which they had fought in the Revolutionary War. . . . They were the elite, among the founders of such Establishment institutions as the New York Stock Exchange, Columbia University, New York University, the American Medical Association, and the Boston Athenaeum."[62]

Because they arrived without rabbis and with few women, however, these early Sephardic Jews often intermarried and eventually assimilated into American society. In 1790 these commercially successful and elite Jewish Americans numbered 2,000.[63] They were at the top of the emerging American class structure—at the opposite end from the 750,000 African Americans, most of whom were slaves living in the South.

German Jews, fleeing a rising tide of anti-Semitism in Germany, immigrated in significant numbers to the United States beginning in the 1830s, this time bringing rabbis and families with them. The American Jewish population increased ninefold between 1820 and 1860 to 150,000. By 1880 Jewish communities existed in every state, though the Jews were not as yet a primarily urban people.[64]

Jews were not the first peddlers in America; however, on the eve of the Civil War the majority of the 20,000 itinerant traders were German Jews, and by 1870 peddling had become a largely Jewish occupation. Not all

60. Lipset and Raab, *Jews and the New American Scene*, 1–28; Zweigenhaft and Domhoff, *Jews in the Protestant Establishment*, 9–16.

61. Lipset and Raab, *Jews and the New American Scene*, 12–13; Zweigenhaft and Domhoff, *Jews in the Protestant Establishment*, 9; Bertram W. Korn, "Jews and Negro Slavery in the Old South, 1789–1865," in *Jews in the South*, ed. L. Dinnerstein and M. D. Palsson (Baton Rouge: Louisiana State University Press, 1973), 95; Bertram W. Korn, *The Early Jews of New Orleans* (Philadelphia: American Jewish Historical Society, 1969), 159; Walda Katz-Fishman and Richard L. Zweigenhaft, "Jews and the New Orleans Economic and Social Elites," *Jewish Social Studies* 44 (1982): 292.

62. A. Manners, *Poor Cousins* (New York: Coward, McCann and Geoghegan, 1972), 63.

63. Zweigenhaft and Domhoff, *Jews in the Protestant Establishment*, 9.

64. Lipset and Raab, *Jews and the New American Scene*, 14; Zweigenhaft and Domhoff, *Jews in the Protestant Establishment*, 10.

Jewish American peddlers rose to fortune and fame, but among those who did were Benjamin Bloomingdale, Adam Gimbel, Isidor Strauss, Joseph Seligman, Joseph and Emanuel Rosenwald, Simon and Meyer Guggenheim, Henry Lehman, and Anthony Zellerbach. They became department store magnates, bankers, investment brokers, and mining tycoons. Other wealthy and influential German Jewish Americans included Jacob H. Schiff, the Warburgs, the Brentanos, Adolph Gluck, the Michaelsons, the Speigelbergs, and the Seasongoods.[65]

In 1872, the *Philadelphia Evening Telegraph,* the country's most widely read newspaper, celebrated the accomplishments and contributions of American Jews in an editorial. "Wherever there is a chance for enterprise and energy, the Jew is to be found. . . . And Americans should be glad that such is the case, for the Jew as a citizen is to be highly esteemed. He brings into every community wealth and qualities which materially assist to strengthen and consolidate its polity. . . . He takes care of himself and his own. . . . He is sober and industrious."[66]

The Sephardic and German Jewish immigrants in the eighteenth and nineteenth centuries achieved great success and, until the last quarter of the nineteenth century, found great acceptance in American society. These Jews became part of the economic and social elite that was shaping the American nation. But in 1877 Jewish Americans began to experience systematic anti-Semitism for the first time on American soil—exclusion from posh resorts and elite social clubs and quotas limiting their numbers in institutions of higher education. It was probably not accidental that 1877 was also the year of the Hayes-Tilden Compromise that signaled the defeat of Reconstruction in the South and the unleashing of almost one hundred years of unbridled White supremacy and social and political reaction. Anti-Semitism was part of the racial and religious prejudice and discrimination of this dawning era that was to last until after World War II.[67]

Some suggested that the very success of American Jews in business and in higher education was also implicated in the rising tide of anti-Semitism. For example, Lipset and Raab observed, "Anti-Semitism in the late nineteenth century was directed against the growing affluence of the German Jews at a time when the Jews numbered about 250,000. . . . Some

65. Zweigenhaft and Domhoff, *Jews in the Protestant Establishment,* 10–11; Lipset and Raab, *Jews and the New American Scene,* 14, 16–18; Manners, *Poor Cousins,* 65.
66. *Philadelphia Evening Telegraph,* "In Praise of the Jews," in *A Documentary History of Jews in the United States, 1654–1875,* ed. Morris U. Schappes (New York: Schocken Books, 1971), 57–58.
67. Zweigenhaft and Domhoff, *Jews in the Protestant Establishment,* 11–13.

were among the founding members of the high-status social clubs formed in many cities immediately before and after the Civil War. But as the number of affluent Jews grew, wealthy non-Jews began to look for ways to deny them social access."[68] In the first two decades of the twentieth century Jews were disproportionately represented among the students at such prestigious universities as Harvard and Columbia, where they comprised 40 percent of the student body. Quotas specifically limiting Jews, as well as geographical quotas, were introduced at these schools and others to reduce Jewish overrepresentation.[69]

In addition, the 1880s marked the beginning of the greatest Jewish immigration to American shores. This time Jewish immigrants came from Eastern Europe pushed by the economic ruin of their small businesses within the collapse of the larger agricultural economy.[70] Unlike their Sephardic and German predecessors, Eastern European Jews were mostly working class in occupation, radical in politics, and urban in locale. Stephen Birmingham described these new and different Jewish immigrants as "ragged, dirt-poor, culturally energetic, toughened by years of torment, idealistic, and socialistic."[71]

By the time the more than 3 million Eastern European Jews arrived in America, the open expanse of the frontier entrepreneurial economy had ended and the corporate economy was in view. Establishing a business enterprise required far more capital than these Jews possessed and far more than had been needed by the Sephardic and German Jews who had come before, many of whom had begun as peddlers. Eastern European Jewish immigrants did, however, have craft skills, and many found employment in the growing garment industry, owned in large part by German Jews.[72]

More than 50 percent of American Jewish business owners were involved in the clothing industry in the 1880s. In New York City, the center of the industry, more than 95 percent of garment manufacturing was owned by German Jews.[73] The capital investment in the garment industry alone more than tripled between 1880 and 1900, increasing the wealth of upper-class German Jewish Americans.[74] Generally, the fortunes of

68. Lipset and Raab, *Jews and the New American Scene*, 82.
69. Zweigenhaft and Domhoff, *Jews in the Protestant Establishment*, 12.
70. Lipset and Raab, *Jews and the New American Scene*, 19.
71. Stephen Birmingham, *Our Crowd: The Great Jewish Families of New York* (New York: Harper and Row, 1967), 289.
72. Henry L. Feingold, *Zion in America* (New York: Twayne, 1974), 114.
73. Naomi W. Cohen, *Encounter with Emancipation* (Philadelphia: Jewish Publication Society of America, 1984), 29.
74. Lipset and Raab, *Jews and the New American Scene*, 20.

these upper-class Jews were constantly on the rise. Between 1860 and 1900 the number of Jewish-owned businesses receiving commercial ratings increased more than fivefold, from 374 to more than 2,000.[75] In 1889, 62 percent of Jewish Americans were in banking, investments, or commerce. An additional 17 percent were in the professions.[76] By 1900 the proportion of Jews among the nation's millionaires was two and a half times the proportion of Jews in the total population.[77]

Jewish American business owners were also able to hire hundreds of thousands of Eastern European Jews, particularly as garment workers. In 1897 roughly 60 percent of all New York City workers were employed in the garment industry, and of these 75 percent were Jewish.[78] The fact that in many instances both owners and workers were Jewish did little, if anything, to alleviate the sweatshop working conditions and desperate living conditions of Eastern European Jewish workers in New York's Lower East Side ghetto.[79]

The American industrial economy at the turn of the century did offer Jewish American workers a way out of the ghetto on the Lower East Side, unlike the labor intensive agricultural economy of the Jim Crow South that kept many African Americans locked in slavelike conditions for more than forty more years. In fact, one observer of Russian Jewish workers, the vast majority of all Eastern European workers, had this to say: "I have met very few wage-workers among Russian Jewish people who regard it as their permanent lot in life to remain in the condition of laborers for wage. Almost all are bending their energies to get into business or to acquire an education so that they may fit themselves for some other calling than that of the wage workers of the ordinary kind."[80]

Eastern European Jewish workers, including many women, were aggressive in their pursuit of the American dream and were an integral part of the "Great Revolt" against the garment industry owners beginning in 1909 and ending with the protocol of peace in 1910, an agreement negotiated with the help of Jewish lawyer Louis Brandeis and Jewish financier Jacob Schiff, who were brought in at least in part because upper-class

75. Moses Rischin, *The Promised City: New York's Jews, 1870–1914* (Cambridge: Harvard University Press, 1962), 52–54.

76. Lipset and Raab, *Jews and the New American Scene*, 82.

77. Isaac M. Rubinow, "New York," in *The Russian Jew in the United States*, ed. Charles S. Bernheimer (Philadelphia: John C. Winston Co., 1905), 103.

78. Gerald Sorin, *A Time for Building: The Third Migration, 1880–1920* (Baltimore: Johns Hopkins University Press, 1992), 74.

79. Howard M. Sachar, *A History of the Jews in America* (New York: Alfred A. Knopf, 1992), 141.

80. Abraham Bosnio, "Chicago," in *The Russian Jew*, ed. Bernheimer, 135.

American Jews were upset by the negative public image of Jewish workers and Jewish factory owners publicly fighting over conditions in the industry.[81]

In this same period upper-class German Jews, excluded from upper-class Gentile social clubs, established their own social clubs from which they, in turn, excluded Eastern European Jews. This remained policy through the 1930s. By the end of World War II, however, German Jewish Americans had dropped their restrictions against Eastern European Jewish Americans, as these restrictions were also beginning to ease in Gentile society.[82]

While a few Eastern European Jews did make the difficult transition from factory worker to factory owner, particularly in the garment industry, far more followed the more direct path to the middle class via education and professional and white-collar jobs as physicians, lawyers, dentists, pharmacists, and teachers, whose numbers increased thirteenfold between 1870 and 1940. A 1908 study of seventy-seven institutions of higher education revealed that, while only 2 percent of the population was Jewish, 8 percent of the students preparing for careers in law, teaching, dentistry, and pharmacy were Jews. In 1930 American Jews, who were 25 percent of the population of New York City, comprised 55 percent of the physicians, 64 percent of the dentists, and 65 percent of the lawyers. Some of these professionals, such as lawyer Morris Hillquit (formerly Hillkowitz), who had begun as a garment worker, maintained their ties to the working-class movement by representing labor in negotiations. But they were often criticized for their middle-class—evolutionary and gradualist—tendencies within the socialist movement and for abandoning a more radical view of class struggle.[83]

The American Jewish population in 1930 was 4 million, 80 percent of whom were of Eastern European origins.[84] Most American Jewish descendants of the Sephardic and German Jewish immigrants were securely within the upper class and, despite the Great Depression, even those of Eastern European Jewish origins were upwardly mobile into the middle and upper middle classes. As early as the 1920s, despite growing anti-Semitism in the United States, many Jewish Americans were among those listed in *Who's Who in America*.[85] Several decades before the mass

81. Lipset and Raab, *Jews and the New American Scene*, 23.
82. Zweigenhaft and Domhoff, *Jews in the Protestant Establishment*, 13.
83. Lipset and Raab, *Jews and the New American Scene*, 23–25.
84. Zweigenhaft and Domhoff, *Jews in the Protestant Establishment*, 11; Manners, *Poor Cousins*, 51; Birmingham, *Our Crowd*, 289.
85. Lipset and Raab, *Jews and the New American Scene*, 25, 26.

production industrial system came to a close in the 1950s, Jewish American workers had left that sector of the economy and were establishing themselves within professional, technical, and managerial occupations and the emerging knowledge industry—the only sectors of the economy that would grow in the second half of the twentieth century.

After World War II, the economic expansion and the removal of anti-Semitic barriers further solidified the position of Jewish Americans as the most successful and affluent ethnoreligious group in the country. Many American Jews joined in the larger political movement for civil rights, affirmative action, and the elimination of discrimination based on race, religion, gender, and nationality. These policies hastened the end of exclusionary policies directed toward Jews that had been established in the 1870s and the early decades of the twentieth century.

In the 1944–1945 *Who's Who in America*, 2 percent of the entries were for Jews. By the mid-1970s the figure was 8 percent, though Jews were roughly 3 percent of the population; they surpassed even Americans of English descent in terms of representation. From the 1960s to 1990 American Jews averaged 50 percent of the top two hundred intellectuals, 40 percent of American Nobel Prize recipients in economics and science, 20 percent of professors at top universities, 21 percent of high-level government workers, 40 percent of law partners in leading New York and Washington firms, 26 percent of top staff and management in major broadcast and print media, 59 percent of producers, directors, and writers of the fifty top-grossing movies between 1965 and 1982, and 58 percent of the writers, directors, and producers who worked in two or more prime-time television series.[86] In the 1992 *Who's Who in America*, American Jews were 2.76 times as likely to be listed as their religious membership figures would indicate.[87]

In 1982 *Forbes* magazine reported that sixteen of the forty wealthiest Americans were Jewish—40 percent of the very wealthiest versus about 2.5 percent of the population—and that 23 percent of the four hundred richest Americans were Jewish.[88] Steven M. Cohen, in a 1988 study conducted for the American Jewish Committee, found that the per capita income of Jews was almost double that of non-Jews. American Jews were also overrepresented among White Americans with incomes of more than $50,000—two and a half times more Jews than non-Jews were in this income category. Conversely, almost twice as many non-Jews as Jews

86. Ibid., 26–27.
87. Zweigenhaft and Domhoff, *Women and Minorities*, chap. 2.
88. Ibid., 26.

reported incomes of $20,000 or less.[89] In the early 1990s Jewish Americans remained overrepresented among college students. Of college-age Jews, 87 percent were enrolled in college, compared to 40 percent for all college-age youth, and 25 percent for Black college-age youth.[90]

For middle-class American Jews, the high-tech, postindustrial economy and the automation and globalization of even white-collar and professional jobs introduced a new reality of economic insecurity into their daily lives. These highly educated and highly skilled Jewish Americans were now in competition with middle-class Blacks and others for the shrinking number of white-collar, professional, and technical jobs in a restructured economy with shrinking public and private sectors. At the same time, the postindustrial global economy furthered the concentration of wealth and fortune for American Jews in the upper class. Jewish Americans finally broke the glass ceiling and truly entered the inner sanctum of elite economic power in 1973 when Irving Shapiro, the son of an immigrant pants-presser, was named to head Du Pont de Nemours and was subsequently elected chair of the Business Roundtable, the most elite group of corporate heads in the United States.[91] Zweigenhaft and Domhoff, who conducted a systematic study of women and minorities in the power elite, corroborated the overwhelming evidence that Jewish Americans have been the most overrepresented of any American minority group in the power elite throughout the twentieth century and that their presence has increased in recent decades.[92]

Jewish Americans had been in the corporate elite ever since there was one—as directors on boards of *Fortune* 500 companies or in comparable positions—and were overrepresented there. In 1900 Jewish Americans were 3.4 percent of the corporate elite. As their numbers in the population gradually declined, from 3.4 percent in 1925 to 2.3 percent in 1995, their representation in the corporate elite increased steadily, from 4.3 percent in 1925 to 7.7 percent in 1995. By 1995 American Jews were overrepresented by a factor of three in the corporate elite. This included an increasing number of directors on the boards of the top one hundred companies, from eleven in 1975 to seventeen in 1995. Jewish American

89. Steven M. Cohen, *The Dimensions of American Jewish Liberalism* (New York: American Jewish Committee, 1989), 28–29.

90. Lipset and Raab, *Jews and the New American Scene*, 27; Deborah J. Carter and Reginald Wilson, *Minorities in Higher Education, 1996–97: Fifteenth Annual Status Report* (Washington, D.C.: American Council on Education, 1997), 69.

91. Lipset and Raab, *Jews and the New American Scene*, 26; Zweigenhaft and Domhoff, *Women and Minorities,* chap. 2; "Jews in the Power Elite."

92. The discussion of Jews in the power elite is taken from Zweigenhaft and Domhoff, *Women and Minorities,* esp. chap. 2.

corporate directors have tended to be very well educated, very highly skilled, and very wealthy.

American Jews have had a presence in all cabinets from Eisenhower's (he appointed Lewis Strauss commerce secretary in 1958) to Clinton's (he appointed Robert Reich labor secretary in 1993 and Dan Glickman agriculture secretary in 1995), with the exceptions of Reagan's and Bush's. A total of twelve Jewish men have been among the 201 cabinet appointments of these presidents, representing 6 percent of all cabinet positions from 1956 to 1996. Jewish cabinet appointments were 12 percent of Democratic presidential appointments during this period, but only 2.3 percent of Republican presidential appointments. Jewish cabinet members have, like the corporate elite, come from the upper rungs of the class ladder.[93]

Six Jewish males served as U.S. senators between 1844 and 1913. Then no Jews were elected for thirty-six years, until Herbert Lehman won a special election as a Democrat from New York in 1949. Since then, sixteen Jews have been elected to the U.S. Senate, with a substantial increase after 1975. Of the seventeen, fourteen were Democrats and three were Republicans; and the first women—Barbara Boxer and Dianne Feinstein—were elected in 1993. The class background of these Jewish American senators ranged from middle class to millionaire.

The number of Jews elected to the U.S. House of Representatives also increased dramatically after 1975, when only ten Jews were in the House, most from heavily Jewish districts in New York. By 1993, thirty-three Jewish women and men were in the House from diverse districts, including some with less than 1 percent Jewish voters. Of these thirty-three, twenty-seven were Democrats, five were Republicans, and one was Independent, Bernie Sanders of Vermont. After the 1994 elections, the number of Jewish representatives fell to twenty-four, nineteen of whom were Democrats. Even so, Jews remained overrepresented in both Senate and House.

Jews had fought on both sides of the Civil War and, in the late twentieth century, they were also visible and prominent in the U.S. Armed Forces and military establishment. With Clinton's appointment in 1995 of John Deutch to head the CIA, Jews broke through the glass ceiling in the defense community.

Clearly, American Jews had a presence and, in most instances, were overrepresented in the power elite of American society—on top cor-

93. History will have to record whether Madeleine Albright will be counted as "Jewish" and thus the first Jewish woman to serve in the cabinet of any president.

porate boards, among the rich and the superrich, in the cabinet, in Congress, and in the military. They were also overrepresented among the most highly educated Americans, among the professional and managerial class, and among the cultural and media artists and moguls. With this fabulous success of the American Jews and their integration into society's power elite also came their embrace of the worldview and ideology of the ruling class, distancing them more than ever from their advocacy for the truly disadvantaged in the United States.

Politics in the Era of the Postindustrial Global Economy:
Canceling the Social Contact

In *One World, Ready or Not: The Manic Logic of Global Capitalism,* William Grieder observes that "the present [global] economic revolution, like revolutions of the past, is fueled by invention and human ingenuity and a universal aspiration to build and accumulate. But it is also driven by a palpable sense of insecurity. No one can be said to control the energies of unfettered capital, not important governments or financiers, not dictators or democrats. . . . The Robespierre of this revolution is finance capital. Its principles are transparent and pure: maximizing the return on capital without regard to national identity or political or social consequences."[94] Each stage of economic development has a definite political expression and a specific set of social policies. The defining political dimension of the industrial nation-state stage of economic development, especially following World War II, was the social contract—the social reforms and "social safety net" fashioned by the welfare state—and the politics of inclusion. In the United States unprecedented economic growth and expansion in the era of industrial capitalism and its machine-based economy gave rise to the social contract between labor and capital and to the growing inclusion of each section of labor—including African Americans and other minorities and women. This social contract between capital and labor began in the New Deal era and extended through the period of the Civil Rights Movement and the Great Society.[95]

Initially, it included only limited and particular reforms in response to the demands of workers, especially the trade union movement, regarding collective bargaining, wages, and working conditions and in response to the needs of corporations to socialize the costs of—that is, have the public sector pay for or subsidize—health care, education, housing,

94. Greider, *One World,* 12, 25.
95. Bluestone and Harrison, *Deindustrialization,* 111–39; Brecher and Costello, *Global Village,* 37–46; Teeple, *Globalization and the Decline,* 9–23.

nutrition, child rearing, and old age and to contain worker unrest and the destabilizing effects of unemployment. At the end of World War II, the United States was poised to take leadership in the global economic and political reconstruction. The United States, in 1946, had half of the world's usable productive capacity, sufficient finance capital to become banker and creditor to former allies and former enemies, and the only major functioning armed forces. But 1946 was also the year in which more American workers went on strike than in any previous year in U.S. history. Labor peace on the domestic front was essential for American capital to realize its global potential. To secure labor cooperation for the global tasks of the postwar period, U.S. capital, between 1946 and the early 1970s, enlarged the social contract and provided a rising standard of living to most American workers, especially organized labor and the middle class, with the enormous wealth generated from economic expansion.[96]

In this period the social wage—worker benefits and protections, legal rights, and social entitlements—was greatly expanded. As Black labor moved from agriculture into industrial production, the social contract was expanded to include Black workers. Civil rights legislation went beyond protections for Blacks, prohibiting discrimination based on race, color, nationality, gender, and religion in employment, education, and federal contracts. Affirmative action guidelines, mandated by executive order, called for goals and timetables to compensate for the historic effects of slavery and legal segregation.[97] The Great Society programs further expanded the social contract to include the antipoverty policies and programs of the late 1960s.

The welfare reforms from the New Deal through the early 1970s represented the prevailing ruling-class consensus that welfare state liberalism was the best strategy for governance at this stage of economic development. The masses always struggled, but only the leaders that the capitalist establishment was willing to recognize were allowed to sit at the table to affirm the terms of the contract with the political representatives of capital, most often from the Democratic Party. At different times throughout the social reform era leaders from organized labor, from racial and ethnic minorities—including African Americans and Jewish Americans—and women were part of these negotiations and the proposed economic solutions.

What these leaders, especially those from constituencies that were

96. Bluestone and Harrison, *Deindustrialization*, 12, 133.
97. *Affirmative Action Debate*, ed. Curry.

largely working class, did not fully appreciate was that capital was in control, that the social contract was not permanent, and that the very welfare state reforms they were negotiating would all too soon be dismantled. The terms of the social contract were such that so long as capital required large amounts of labor for industrial production, labor would be covered by the social contract. But when labor or sections of labor were no longer needed in production, their coverage could be canceled. This is exactly what happened in the last quarter of the twentieth century. The ascendancy of reactionary and conservative politicians and policies from the ranks of both Democrats and Republicans in the period from the mid-1970s to the 1990s occurred within the context of the new high-tech global economy.

Black workers—last hired, first fired, and disproportionately poor— were the first to experience the effects of the cancellation of the social contract and the unraveling of the social safety net. They were disproportionately among the permanently unemployed and underemployed and those living at or below the poverty line. The passage of welfare "reform" legislation in 1996 eliminating welfare as an entitlement confirmed what others had said as early as the 1950s, that Black labor had little or no value in the postindustrial global economy. But the politics of exclusion—the cancellation of the social contract between capital and labor— had profound negative consequences for all working people and all poor people, the majority of whom were White.

At the root of the assault on the social contract and its welfare reforms was the fact that the nation-state industrial stage of economic development was over. It had been replaced by a new stage of economic development, the postindustrial high-tech global economy, which required a new political realignment, the reversal of social reform agenda, and the exclusion of those working-class women, men, and children no longer needed in industrial production. Automation and computer-driven production greatly reduced the number of workers needed in the manufacturing and service sectors, even as more and more goods and services were being produced. At the same time, globalization placed American workers in all sectors in competition with workers worldwide. The lowest skilled and poorest workers, made obsolete by the high-tech global economy, were abandoned first. They were not needed and would not be needed at any future time for capitalist production. But by the 1990s it was increasingly clear to middle-class, white-collar, and professional workers in government and the private sector that the social contract was being canceled for them, too.

Capital, in its drive for maximum profits, refused to honor the social contract that kept wages, benefits, and working conditions at a level that allowed workers to work safely and live decently. Wealthy capitalists challenged the idea that the government should provide for the well-being of the young, the old, and the environment and offer a safety net for the poor, the disabled, and the dispossessed. The privatization of public functions, the downsizing of the government sector, and the dismantling of social programs moved rapidly. Education, health care, housing, nutrition, sanitation, prisons, the military, and even welfare itself were being privatized. Corporate capital was in pursuit of the best business climate, and that meant the very lowest costs of production. The cost of the social contract was more than corporate capital in this new stage of economic development was willing to pay.

For African American workers, the postindustrial global economy and the cancellation of the social contract and dismantling of social reforms were devastating and, in some instances, life threatening. For Jewish American corporate elites and the superrich, these new economic and political realities furthered their accumulation of capital. Black workers and upper-class Jews were thus on opposite sides of the growing economic and political divide. At this stage of economic and political development, affirmative action, a clause introduced into the social contract during the civil rights era, was not directly relevant either to low-skilled Black workers, for whom there were no jobs, or to upper-class Jews, who were already overrepresented among the power elite.

It was, in fact, middle-class and upper-middle-class African Americans and Jewish Americans, pursuing a shrinking number of good professional jobs and contracts and facing a new reality of economic insecurity, who often found themselves in competition, and for whom affirmative action was relevant and a point of contention. They too tended to be on opposite sides of the divide. Many Blacks, though not all, supported a continuation of affirmative action to remedy still remaining disadvantages of history for African Americans. Some also acknowledged that affirmative action was ineffective for the Black poor and "underclass" and offered a radical critique of capitalism and patriarchy, along with White supremacy.[98] Many Jews, though not all, argued that affirmative action as a race-based policy had outlived its usefulness, undermined the principle of people being judged on the basis of individual

98. See ibid., esp. Marable, "Staying the Path"; West, "Affirmative Action"; Norton, "Affirmative Action in the Workplace"; Mfume, "Why America Needs"; Williams, "Tracing the Politics"; Berry, "Affirmative Action."

ability and merit, and, in the worse instance, promoted quotas and "reverse discrimination."[99]

The affirmative action debate of the early 1990s took place within a radically new context. Just as nation-based industrial capitalism was replaced by postindustrial global capitalism, the ruling-class political strategy of welfare state liberalism was being replaced by a new set of policies appropriate for this new stage of economic history. A new ruling-class consensus had emerged—one that canceled the social contract and dismantled the social reforms of the welfare state. It brought austerity programs and structural adjustment programs home to U.S. cities, rural areas, and even suburbs from the developing countries where these policies were first implemented. Some called capital's new political program and strategy for rule in the postindustrial global era "neoliberalism."

Gary Teeple in *Globalization and the Decline of Social Reform* describes "the coming tyranny" this way:

> Neo-liberal policies mark the transition between two eras, from a world of national capitals and nation-states to a world of internationalized capital and supranational organizations, commissions, and agencies. They represent the coming transformation of long-established social and political institutions in the industrial nation-states. They embody a shift *from* the expansion of social reforms, rising national wealth, and limited political alternatives *to* the dismantling of reforms, the supersession of national economies, and political reaction. While they consolidate the triumph of capitalism over the world and increase the possibilities for expanded accumulation, they also accelerate its consequences. Capitalism must increasingly confront the world it has made, the results of its own expansion: seriously degraded nature, an increasingly impoverished working class, growing political autocracy and declining legitimacy, and new forms of resistance.[100]

New Political Movements and Coalitions: Building a New Society

Given our understanding of the three interrelated systems of domination in the United States today—capitalism, White supremacy, and patriarchy—it is essential to consider how the economic, political, and

99. Lipset and Raab, *Jews and the New American Scene*, 178–79; Paul Berman, ed., *Blacks and Jews: Alliances and Arguments* (New York: Delacorte Press, 1994), 17–18; Michael Lerner and Cornel West, *Jews and Blacks: A Dialogue on Race, Religion, and Culture in America* (New York: Plume/Penguin, 1996), 157–79; Kahlenberg, *The Remedy*, ix–xiii, 42–80; and Nathan Glazer, *Affirmative Discrimination: Ethnic Inequality and Public Policy* (New York: Basic Books, 1975).
100. Teeple, *Globalization and the Decline*, 150.

cultural developments of the late twentieth century have transformed these dynamic systems.[101] We are confronted immediately with the fact that the ruling class and media have promoted an ideological formulation and picture of the society that denies the historic realities of these three systems—class domination inherent in capitalist political economy, White supremacy imbedded in culture and law and reproduced in social institutions, and male privilege contained within patriarchal relations in the public and private spheres.

Our first task in resisting and mobilizing to transform the inequalities of these societal structures and to achieve genuine racial, economic, and social justice must be to gain clarity about this historic moment. We must struggle for an understanding of American society "as it is" and not accept the "myths" presented by those in power. There needs to be articulated a vision for a new society built on social and economic justice. We must educate ourselves and those around us about the new realities of the postindustrial global economy. Working people of all races are neither unemployed nor poor because they come from pathological cultures and deformed families, nor are they at fault. Working people are unemployed and they and their children are poor very simply because good jobs have disappeared from the economy, and many of the jobs workers are forced to take do not provide a living wage.

In arguing for the increasing significance of class, we have not argued for a decreasing significance of race or gender. What we have really argued for is the recognition of the profound, indeed revolutionary, changes that have permeated our communities as a result of the coming of the postindustrial global economy. Within this new technological and economic stage of development, inequalities and injustices of class, race, and gender have, in fact, been intensified. Wealth and poverty are more polarized in the United States and globally than ever before. Today's 447 world billionaires have combined wealth greater than the income of the poorest half—2.5 billion—of the world's people.[102] At the same time, racial and gender injustice and inequality are on the rise. Our grasp of our world and our strategies for change must reflect these new technological and global economic realities that provide the context for capitalism,

101. See, for example, Marable, *How Capitalism Underdeveloped* and *Black Liberation*; West, *Race Matters* and *Beyond Eurocentrism and Multiculturalism*, vol. 2, *Prophetic Reflections, Notes and Race and Power in America* (Monroe, Maine: Common Courage Press, 1993).

102. John Cavanagh, "Failures of Free Trade," *Washington Post*, January 23, 1997, A17.

White supremacy, and patriarchy in this society and throughout the world at the end of the twentieth century.

Socially and politically conscious actors cannot pretend that we are still living in an industrial system, that the social contract is in force, or that it is even under serious discussion by the power elite. Many capitalist societies are already being rapidly reorganized politically and socially in relation to the new high-tech systems of production, communication, and commerce. The political realignment of both Democrats and Republicans around the reactionary and exclusionary neoliberal policies of this postindustrial period indicates the urgent need for new political movements and coalitions that are truly independent of the ruling class and that give voice and shape to the interests and aspirations of working people of all races, religions, and nations, especially the truly disadvantaged.

The respective class positions of Blacks and Jews reflect their historical experiences before coming to this country, but especially their pre-twentieth-century and twentieth-century experiences in the United States. The restructuring of the late-twentieth-century postindustrial global economy intensifies the disadvantage and poverty of all working Americans but especially of low-skilled African American workers—employed and unemployed—and, indeed, threatens the very survival of those in the "underclass." It also introduces a new element of economic insecurity into the lives especially of middle-class Blacks but also of middle-class Jews. At the same time, it solidifies the privilege and wealth of upper-class Americans, including Jewish Americans, who are overrepresented in the upper class, and even upper-class Blacks, who are striving to maintain their position in the new economy. These differences of history and of contemporary class locations fuel the growing tension and conflict between African Americans and Jews. They cannot be resolved short of addressing the underlying realities of race and class in the United States, as well as the issue of the ownership and control of the productive forces and the distribution of the abundant social and economic products.

In this light the well-publicized affirmative action debate, even with the nuances of race versus class, still leaves out important structural considerations. As long as the capitalist market economy prevails, there will be only a limited number of good "slots" in the labor market and in prestigious institutions of higher education. Competition for these scarce slots will pit those with the least against each other, will pit middle-class Blacks and Jews against each other, and will pit the middle class against the working class and the poor. These divisions have been created and maintained throughout American history by a ruling class that sees divisions among workers in the middle and working classes as promoting the interests of the corporate capitalist elite because it diverts the attention away from those at the top.

Today Americans have the opportunity to shape the next chapter in their collective history. The movements and coalitions they build must be guided by an inclusive vision and strategy that ends poverty as we know it and resolves the problems of those most disadvantaged and adversely affected by the current economy. The demand must be for more than equal opportunity, even in class-based terms, since the possibility of any real opportunity has been virtually eliminated by the new productive system. Universal demands that pay special attention to historic and current structural constraints of class, race, and gender must also acknowledge the realities of the postindustrial global economy.

As early as 1964, before the major accomplishments of the Civil Rights Movement and the War on Poverty, Oppenheimer and the Committee on the Triple Revolution anticipated the scenario we are now living. They "urged the President and Congress to consider guaranteeing every citizen `an adequate income as a matter of right' as a way of distributing funds to the millions of people made redundant by the new labor-saving technologies."[103] The ruling class then and the ruling class now have not taken heed. But the millions of American workers—the permanently unemployed, underemployed, and soon to be unemployed, and those living at or near poverty—are beginning to stir. Black workers, women, and children were first; but White workers and the middle class are already feeling the adverse effects of the postindustrial global economy.

Our second task in building a truly just, humane, and egalitarian society is to join in, strengthen, and develop new leadership in the new political movements and coalitions that have been taking shape over the last decade.[104] Cornel West has cogently articulated the principles that pro-

103. Rifkin, *End of Work*, 82.
104. See, for example, M. Bahati Kuumba, Jerome Scott, Walda Katz-Fishman, "Liberation Research and Project South: Weapons in the Hands of the Oppressed," in *Selected Proceedings of the First National Conference on Urban Issues—Crossing Boundaries: Collaborative Solutions to Urban Problems*, ed. Douglas Koritz, P. Rudy Mattai, Stephen Phelps, Kevin Railey, and Janet Riley-Hunt (Buffalo: State University of New York College at Buffalo, 1995), 253–63; Jerome Scott and Walda Katz-Fishman, "Race, Class and Social Movements in the U.S. South: The Freedom Struggle Continues," *Project South Working Paper* (Atlanta: Project South, Institute for the Elimination of Poverty and Genocide, May 22, 1996), 1–25; Emily Kawano, "An ELAN Is Born: Economic Literacy Meeting, November 8–9, 1996" (paper, Philadelphia, American Friends Service Committee, February 11, 1997). In addition, we have been both participants and observers in aspects of these three movements—economic justice, third party, and

vide a starting point for developing new movements and setting new agendas:

> We live on the brink of a new wave of social activism in America. . . . Our regulative principles are fourfold—a more egalitarian redistribution of wealth and power that includes the elimination of poverty, a head-on assault against White supremacist ideas and practices which embraces moral accountability of police power in the inner cities, a monumental pushing back of patriarchal and homophobic structures and a cultural renaissance that give moral meaning and social hope for citizens in a more free, just and ecologically sound future.[105]

These are our tasks. We must reaffirm our human agency—our capacity to act collectively and cooperatively and to make our own history within the material and cultural context of our lives at the dawn of the new millennium.

---

popular education for more than ten years. Thus, much of this brief discussion comes from our personal observations.

105. West, *Beyond Eurocentrism*, ix.

About the Contributors

Hasia R. Diner is Paul S. and Sylvia Steinburg Professor of American Jewish History at New York University. She is the author of *In the Almost Promised Land: American Jews and Blacks, 1915–1935, Erin's Daughters in America: Irish Immigrant Women in the Nineteenth Century,* and *A Time for Gathering: The Second Migration, 1820–1880.*

V. P. Franklin is Professor of History and Director of African-American Studies at Drexel University in Philadelphia. He is the coeditor of *New Perspectives on Black Educational History* and the author of *The Education of Black Philadelphia: The Social and Educational History of a Minority Community, 1900–1950, Black Self-Determination: A Cultural History of African-American Resistance,* and *Living Our Stories, Telling Our Truths: Autobiography and the Making of the African-American Intellectual Tradition.*

Murray Friedman is Director of the Feinstein Center for American Jewish History at Temple University and the Middle Atlantic States Director of the American Jewish Committee. He is the author of numerous articles and *What Went Wrong? The Creation and Collapse of the Black-Jewish Alliance.*

Cheryl Greenberg is Associate Professor of History and Director of American Studies at Trinity College in Hartford, Connecticut. She is the editor of *A Circle of Trust: Remembering SNCC* and the author of *"Or Does It Explode?" Black Harlem in the Great Depression* and the forthcoming *"Troubling the Waters: Black-Jewish Relations in the American Century."*

Nancy Haggard-Gilson teaches in the departments of Political Science and Liberal Studies at California State University at San Marcos. She recently completed *Wounded in the House of Friends* and a study of Black conservatives.

Herbert Hill is Evjue-Bascom Professor of African-American Studies and Professor of Industrial Relations at the University of Wisconsin–Madison. He is the former National Labor Secretary for the NAACP and the author of numerous books and articles, including *Black Labor and the American Legal System.*

Robert A. Hill is Associate Professor of History and Director of the Marcus Garvey Papers Project at the University of California at Los Angeles. He served as editor of the volumes 1–10 of *The Marcus Garvey and Universal Negro Improvement Association Papers* and is the coauthor of *Marcus Garvey: Life and Lessons* and the author of the forthcoming "Lion Zion: Marcus Garvey and the Jews."

Walda Katz-Fishman is Professor of Sociology at Howard University in Washington, D.C., and Board Chair of Project South: Institute for the Elimination of Poverty and Genocide. She is the author of numerous articles on Black-Jewish relations and the coeditor of *Readings in Humanist Sociology: Social Criticism and Social Theory.*

Winston C. McDowell is Visiting Assistant Professor in the Department of Afro-American and African Studies at the University of Minnesota–Twin Cities. He is completing a book-length study on the ideology of Black entrepreneurship in Harlem, 1930–1955.

Genna Rae McNeil is Professor of History at the University of North Carolina at Chapel Hill. She is the author of *Groundwork: Charles Hamilton Houston and the Struggle for Civil Rights* and coeditor of *Historical Judgments Reconsidered* and *African Americans and the Living Constitution.*

Michael Rogin is Robson Professor of Political Science at the University of California at Berkeley. His books include *"Ronald Reagan," the Movie, and Other Episodes in Political Demonology* and *Blackface, White Noise: Jewish Immigrants in the Hollywood Melting Pot.*

Jerome Scott is Executive Director of Project South: Institute for the Elimination of Poverty and Genocide. He is the author or coauthor of numerous articles on race, class, and political economy.

Marshall F. Stevenson Jr. is Associate Professor of History at Dillard University in New Orleans. He is the author of the work in progress "Points of Departure, Acts of Resolve: Black-Jewish Relations in Detroit, 1930–1967" and, with David Schoem, "Teaching Ethnic Identity: The Case of the Black Jewish Dialogue."

Joe W. Trotter Jr. is Mellon Bank Professor of History at Carnegie-Mellon University in Pittsburgh. His books include *River Jordan: Blacks in the Urban Ohio Valley; Coal, Class, and Color: Blacks in Southern West Virginia;* and *Black Milwaukee: The Making of an Industrial Proletariat, 1915–45.*

Vernon J. Williams Jr. is Professor of History and American Studies at Purdue University in Lafayette, Indiana. He is the author of *From a Caste to a Minority: Changing Attitudes of American Sociologists toward Afro-Americans, 1896–1945, Rethinking Race: Franz Boas and His Contemporaries,* and several articles on Black-Jewish relations in the twentieth century.

Index

Abernathy, Ralph, 103, 116, 118
Abrams, Elliott, 287
ACTU. *See* Association of Catholic Trade
   Unionists
Adam by Adam (Powell), 297
Addes, George, 259, 260
ADL. *See* Anti-Defamation League
Adler, Felix, 69
Affirmative action, 11, 165, 171, 174–77,
   179–81, 186, 239, 257, 263, 286–88, 317,
   338, 340–41, 343
Affirmative Discrimination (Glazer), 171
AFL, 125, 239, 240, 241, 247, 252
AFL-CIO, 119, 264, 265, 266, 268, 269, 270
Africa: West Africa, 183; Blyden on, 43–44;
   and Garveyism, 40–41; German colonies
   in, 49; Pan-Africanism, 44, 47, 183;
   African Association, 4, 45–47; after
   World War I, 49. *See also* Black Zionism
African American–Jewish relations: anti-
   Semitism and African Americans, 9, 11,
   204, 211, 212, 227–32, 270–71, 284–85,
   288, 291–92, 299–308; in Detroit automotive unions, 9–10, 237–63; Baldwin on,
   205; split in, 172–74; Boas's contributions
   to, 54–86; caste-class model of race relations, 195–96; in Civil Rights Movement,
   27–29, 35, 90–91, 102–23, 163, 202,
   289–91, 306, 307; conflict between Blacks
   and Jewish merchants, 9, 195–96,
   199–202, 204, 230, 306; in early twentieth
   century, 3–4, 27–39, 87, 217; Garvey on,
   41–42, 52; Glazer on, 282–84; and
   Harlem jobs campaign, 226–36; in Hollywood movies, 5–6, 91–101; and Jewish
   blackface minstrelsy, 87–92; and labor
   movement conflicts, 10–11, 264–86; Mal-

colm X on, 303–8; in postindustrial
   global economy, 11–12, 337–45; racism
   of Jews, 127–33, 201, 277–78, 288, 302–3,
   306–8; southern Jews' resistance to civil
   rights efforts, 6–7, 123–64, 200; in turn-
   of-the-century United States, 58–59,
   239–40; University of Chicago scholarship on, 195; in urban areas, 193–207. *See
   also* African Americans; Anti-Semitism;
   Jews; Racism against African Americans
African Americans: and affirmative action,
   174–77, 179, 180–81, 186, 340; as agricultural workers, 313–14; and anti-Semitism,
   9, 11, 204, 211, 212, 227–32, 270–71,
   284–85, 288, 291–92, 299–308; Boas on,
   4–5, 54–56, 59–86; as boxers, 96–97; brain
   size and intellectual ability of, 61–64,
   66–67, 70, 76, 77, 81–84; as business owners, 219–21, 223, 224, 231, 319; and class
   structure, 75–76, 128, 230, 309–28, 343;
   and Communist Party, 9–10, 90, 241–42,
   248, 253, 258, 259; conflicts with Jewish
   merchants, 9, 195–96, 199–201, 202, 204,
   230, 306; as conservatives, 7–8, 165–68,
   172–90; in corporate elite, 319–20; economic history of, 12, 310–28, 339, 340;
   employment of, 196–97, 226, 227, 235,
   313–16, 324–28; families of, 181, 188–89;
   in federal government, 320; and ghetto,
   197, 199; in Hollywood movies, 93–101;
   housing discrimination against, 147, 150;
   identification with Jewish biblical tradition, 300–301; immigrant paradigm as
   inadequate for, 172–73; income of,
   317–19; intelligence of, 61–64, 66–73, 78,
   82–86; in intelligentsia, 5, 55, 76–80,
   85–86, 230–31; and Jewish blackface

Bowles, Chester, 119
Boxer, Barbara, 336
Boxing, 94–99, 206
Boycotts. *See* Bus boycotts; Jobs boycotts
Bracey, John, 288
Branch, Taylor, 104, 108, 110, 111n27, 120n52
Brandeis, Louis, 332
Bricklayers Union, 266–67
Briggs v. Elliott, 151
Brigham, Carl C., 84
Brinton, Daniel G., 62–63, 73
Broca, Paul, 61
Brooke, Edmund, 320
Brooks, Gwendolyn, 13, 297
Brotherhood of Sleeping Car Porters, 34, 141, 268
Brown, John, 30
Brown, Mayme Osby, 133
Brown v. Board of Education, 102, 111, 113, 129, 137, 141, 151, 152, 178
Bulkley, William Lewis, 66
Bunche, Ralph J., 230
Burman, Edgar H., 227
Burns, George, 89
Bus boycotts, 102–3, 112
Bush, George, 7, 178, 287, 336
Business and Society, 320
Business owners: African Americans as, 219–21, 223, 224, 231, 319; Jews as, 9, 128, 130, 132–33, 142, 195–96, 199–204, 221, 230, 231, 306, 330, 331–32
Busing, 156, 178

Cahan, Abraham, 31
Canady, Herman, 84
Cantor, Eddie, 89
Carey, Edward, 250
Carey, James B., 265
Carpenters and Joiners Union, 240
Carson, Clayborne, 103, 290
Carter, Asa, 125
Carter, Jimmy, 115
Carter, Robert L., 276
Catholics, 249, 254, 308
Cayton, Horace R., 8, 195–97, 198
Central Conference of American Rabbis, 145, 287n57
Chait, Max, 248, 250, 262
Chamberlain, Alexander, 79
Chandler, Owen, 208
Chanes, Jerome, 1–2
Charities, 66
Chicago, 8, 9, 195, 199, 210, 215, 223–24, 225, 268
Chicago Defender, 198

Chicago Seven, 113
CIA, 336
CIO, 9, 125, 238, 241, 246, 247, 251–53, 258, 262. *See also* AFL-CIO
Citizens' League for Fair Play, 212, 227, 228, 233
Civil disobedience. *See* Nonviolent civil disobedience
Civil liberties, 155–56
Civil rights legislation of 1964, 168, 170, 171, 174, 278, 286, 291, 293, 316–17
Civil rights legislation of 1965, 168, 171, 174
Civil Rights Congress, 133
Civil Rights Movement: accusation of communism against, 152–56; 112; 102–3; and Black-Jewish labor network in New York, 102–22; Blacks' leadership of, 102–3, 107, 117–18, 290; bus boycotts, 102–3, 106–8, 111, 112, 113, 116–17; Communist involvement in, 6, 103–13, 117, 119, 134; Freedom Riders, 290; Freedom Schools, 123; Grant's involvement in, 15; and Jews, 27–29, 35, 90–91, 102–64, 202, 289–91, 306, 307; March on Washington (1963), 114, 119; militancy of, 156; Mississippi Summer Project, 290; and national Jewish organizations, 134–64; and neoconservatives, 168; 1960s legislation, 168, 170, 171, 174, 278, 286, 291, 293, 316–17, 338; and nonviolence, 105, 107, 168, 293; Prayer Pilgrimage for Freedom, 113–14; and reemergence of the left, 6, 102–22; and Reuther, 263; southern Jews' resistance to active involvement in, 6–7, 123–64, 200; voter-registration campaign, 119, 290; Youth Marches for Integrated Schools, 115. *See also* King, Martin Luther, Jr.; specific organizations and leaders
Civil War, 312
Clark, Kenneth B., 129, 141, 272, 289
Clark, Mamie, 141
Class structure: and African Americans, 75–76, 128, 230, 309–28, 343; Black-Jewish relations in urban areas, 195–97; Du Bois on race versus, 75–76; and global economy, 11–12, 321–28, 335, 337–45; and Jews, 128, 309–11, 328–37, 343; and race generally, 75–76, 309–10; and southern Jews and African Americans, 128; "underclass," 310, 317, 321, 322, 326, 340, 343
Clinton, Bill, 336
CLSA. *See* Commission for Law and Social Action

Wofford, Harris, 108, 116
Wolper, Robert, 247
Wolters, Raymond, 19
Women: in Congress, 320, 336; in corpo-
rate elite, 320; employment and unem-
ployment of Black women, 325–26, 327;
in ILGWU, 10, 265, 269–84; Jewish
women's involvement in civil rights,
142, 150; relationship between Black and
Jewish women, 196–97
Woodson, Carter G., 55
Work, Monroe N., 55, 77
Workers' Defense League (WDL), 124, 136,
147
Works Progress Administration, 112
World of Our Fathers (Howe), 202
World War I, 47–50, 84, 209, 216
World War II, 9, 131, 242–47
Wright, R. R., Sr., 70
Wright, Richard, 190, 297

Yiddish newspapers, 3–4, 29–34, 36–37, 87,
217, 229, 277–78

Yiddishe Tageblatt (Jewish Daily News),
29–30, 31, 32–34, 36
Young, Andrew, 115, 116, 120, 121
Young, Coleman, 262
Young Communist League, 105, 119
Youngerman, Rabbi, 160
Young Negro Cooperative, 112
Youth Marches for Integrated Schools,
115

Zangwill, Israel, 90
Zellerbach, Anthony, 330
Zimmerman, Charles S., 265, 266, 267, 269,
279n39
Zionism: affinity with Black Zionism, 4, 29,
33, 34, 41–42, 47–50; and Balfour Declaration, 4, 48, 52; Blyden on, 42–44; competition with Black Zionism, 41–42,
52–53; foundation of, 52; goal of, 41; and
Herzl, 4, 34, 40, 42–47; and Society of
Jews, 45, 46; and World War I, 47–48. *See
also* Black Zionism
Zweigenhaft, Richard L., 319, 3351